D1639703

THE FAILURE
of the
EDEN
GOVERNMENT

By the same author

Montgomery in Europe: Success or Failure?
The Ghosts of Peace 1935–45

THE FAILURE
of the
EDEN
GOVERNMENT

Richard Lamb

962

SIDGWICK & JACKSON
LONDON

First published in Great Britain in 1987 by
Sidgwick & Jackson Limited
1 Tavistock Chambers, Bloomsbury Way
London WC1A 2SG

ISBN 0 283 99534 3

Photoset by Rowland Phototypesetting Limited
Bury St Edmunds, Suffolk
Printed in Great Britain by Butler and Tanner Limited
Frome, Somerset

Contents

Foreword

I ADMIRED Anthony Eden. He was a great patriot with an attractive platform manner and the gift of summing up situations in a way which made them clear to everyone. He had beautiful manners and was most charming, both privately and in public.

In my younger days he was greatly encouraging to me when I stood as a Conservative candidate in his native county of Durham. Towards the end of his life he bought a country estate near me in Wiltshire, and we had a mutual interest in breeding Hereford cattle. I will always remember his delight when I bought one of his best animals so that she remained in the valley, and how pleased he was when I was able to help him with his dispersal sale.

He must have been one of the hardest-working politicians of his day, with exceptional skill in diplomatic negotiations. Over the Far East in the dying days of the Churchill Government, and as Prime Minister, he almost certainly saved the world from the disaster of a third – nuclear – world war. He was moderate over home affairs, although it would have been better for the nation if he had been more decisive over the contemplated controls on West Indian immigration and secret ballots before strikes. His romantic attachment to the Commonwealth was responsible for his turning his back on the Common Market when the Messina powers would have welcomed Britain with open arms.

Eden's premiership foundered solely because of the Suez affair. Writing this book has filled me with a deep sympathy for Eden. Few now argue that the Cabinet decision to go to war with Egypt at the end of October 1956 was justifiable. At that time Eden's health was not good. His doctors prescribed him amphetamines to buck him up when he felt tired, and barbiturates to help him sleep. Thirty years ago top physicians prescribed these dangerous drugs in a way which would shock modern practitioners. I am convinced that these drugs flawed his judgment during the three months of strain after the Suez Canal was nationalized. However, going to war was the unanimous decision of the Cabinet; it was in no way a unilateral decision by the Prime Minister, and no other member of his

Cabinet had the excuse that they were being prescribed damaging drugs.

Yet Macmillan and Home became Prime Minister; Lloyd, Chancellor of the Exchequer and Speaker; Thorneycroft, Heathcote Amory and Macleod, Chancellor of the Exchequer; and Hailsham is Lord Chancellor at the time of writing. As far as history is concerned their reputations have become linked with their subsequent careers. Unlike theirs, Eden's political life ended with Suez, and in the eyes of historians and other commentators he has become the scapegoat for the affair. This is unfair.

There are no archives in the Public Record Office which shed fresh light on the disappearance of Commander Crabbe RN; the defection to Russia of the diplomats Burgess, Maclean and Philby; nor the alleged Anglo–American secret plot to assassinate Nasser in 1956. I have omitted these subjects from this book.

Richard Lamb
Broadchalke, June 1987

Acknowledgments

I AM MUCH indebted to my Research Assistant, Elizabeth Evans of Leeds University, for her invaluable help. I am also most grateful to the following people, who have been good enough to assist me:

Dr Martin Alexander
The Hon. David Astor
John Barnes
Sir Harold Beely
Robert Belgrave
Robert Blackledge
Russell Bretherton
Samuel Brittan
Professor McGeorge Bundy
The Rev. Arthur Burrell
Sir Michael Butler
Lord Caccia
The late Sir Hugh Carleton
    Greene
Sir John Colville
Wing Commander Jock
    Dalgleish
Sir William Deakin
Professor David Dilks
Gordon Etherington-Smith
Sir John Figges
General Lord Michael Fitzalan
    Howard
The Marquis de Folin
Lord Gladwyn
Field Marshal Lord Harding
The Rt Hon. Edward Heath
Peter Hennessy
The Rt Hon. Lord Home of the
    Hirsel

Richard Hornby
Marilyn Levine
Sir Donald Logan
The Rt Hon. the Earl of
    Longford
Brian MacDermot
Wendell R. Mauter
Sir William Rees-Mogg
Anthony Moncrieff
The Rt Hon. Sir Anthony
    Nutting
Alec Peterson
John Pinder
Lord Plowden
Professor Don K. Price
Air Marshal Sir Charles
    Pringle
Lord Sherfield
Sir Evelyn Shuckburgh
Sir Andrew Stark
The Rt Hon. Lord Stewart of
    Fulham
The Rt Hon. Lord
    Thorneycroft
The Rt Hon. Lord Wilson of
    Rievaulx
Sir Philip de Zulueta

I am much indebted to the staffs of the London Library and the Public Record Office for their unfailing courtesy and help.

I give warm thanks to Joan Moore and John Mark for their secretarial help, and to Robert Smith of Sidgwick and Jackson and Esther Jagger for their editing.

List of Illustrations

All photographs supplied by The Photo Source except the one marked with an asterisk, which was supplied by the Imperial War Museum.

The Eden Government, April 1955

List of Cabinet Members

Prime Minister	Sir Anthony Eden
Lord President of the Council	Lord Salisbury
Foreign Secretary	Mr Macmillan (replaced by Mr Selwyn Lloyd 23.12.55)
Chancellor of the Exchequer	Mr Butler (replaced by Mr Macmillan 23.12.55)
Lord Privy Seal and Leader of the House of Commons	Mr Crookshank (replaced by Mr Butler 23.12.55)
Lord Chancellor	Lord Kilmuir
Minister of Defence	Mr Selwyn Lloyd (replaced by Sir Walter Monckton 23.12.55, and by Mr Head 18.10.56)
Home Secretary	Mr Lloyd-George
Colonial Secretary	Mr Lennox-Boyd
Secretary for Commonwealth Relations	Lord Home
Secretary of State for Scotland	Mr Stuart
Minister of Labour	Sir Walter Monckton (replaced by Mr Macleod 23.12.55)
President of the Board of Trade	Mr Thorneycroft
Minister of Housing and Local Government	Mr Sandys
Chancellor of the Duchy of Lancaster	Lord Woolton
Minister of Education	Sir David Eccles
Minister of Agriculture	Mr Heathcoat Amory
Minister of Pensions	Mr Peake

(Sir Walter Monckton remained in the Cabinet as Paymaster-General after Mr Head took over from him as Minister of Defence on 18.10.56)

1

The Handover and General Election
1955

IN OCTOBER 1951, when Churchill's Conservative Government replaced Attlee's Labour Government, Anthony Eden became Foreign Secretary again, sixteen years after he had first held the post under Neville Chamberlain. He was fifty-four. Winston was seventy-seven. Eden was the obvious crown prince; his reputation was high, and it seemed he must soon move to 10 Downing Street.

The handover was far from smooth, and very prolonged. Eden became more and more impatient; he wanted to dominate the Cabinet over foreign policy, and would not brook interference by Churchill. The Prime Minister, who loved foreign policy, insisted on putting forward his own strong views. Although there were bonds of affection between the two, there were frequent policy clashes resulting in squabbles. In Opposition Churchill had blazed the trail for a United Europe with great speeches at Zurich and Strasbourg, but Eden wanted nothing to do with either the European army or the European Coal and Steel Community. This annoyed Churchill, prodded by his pro-European son-in-law, Duncan Sandys, but he let the Foreign Secretary have his own way over Europe rather than risk a major Cabinet row.

Over the Far East Eden had definite plans which were sharply different from US foreign policy, and acquitted himself well. Churchill tended to take the American side in the dispute, and deplored Eden's rows with Secretary of State Dulles, which were also strongly resented by President Eisenhower. Churchill loved meetings in Washington reminiscing with the President about their great days together during the war. This left Eden cold, and the worst row between Churchill and Eden came in July 1954 during the Geneva Conference on Vietnam. Churchill had arranged a trip to Washington against Eden's wishes. Eden, maddened by a Dulles speech, wanted to have a stand-up row in public with Dulles and to cancel the Washington meeting. Churchill curtly refused, and denied Eden his public quarrel with Dulles.

They clashed also over the Middle East. Churchill was pro-Zionist. At this stage Eden was anti-Zionist and pro-Arab, determined to withdraw British troops from the Canal base and give Egypt full independence under Nasser. Churchill wanted Britain to stand on her Treaty rights, and pandered to the Suez Group of Conservative MPs who took the same line.

This bickering did not produce happy relations, and they became more strained by Churchill's constantly postponing the date of his retirement. On 4 April 1953 Eden went into a nursing home for an operation on his gall bladder. By a cruel stroke of fortune the surgeon's knife slipped, and the operation was unsuccessful. An emergency second operation was necessary; afterwards Eden's life was in danger, and he made only a partial recovery. His bile duct became blocked from time to time, and further surgery was necessary if there was to be any chance of restoring him to perfect health. After an eight-hour operation in America in June the damage was put right, but at considerable cost to Eden's health. Thereafter he was subject to sudden short fevers, although he was to live to the age of eighty.

As a result of Eden's three operations and the need for a long convalescence, he was out of action from April to mid-October 1953. Churchill took on the Foreign Office gleefully. Then, on 23 June, the Prime Minister had a severe stroke; it seemed to his intimates and family that he must resign. If he had, with Eden out of action and his health suspect, Rab Butler, then Chancellor, would almost certainly have become Prime Minister. However, Churchill hung on and made a spectacular recovery, although his powers of concentration were affected. In August 1953 Churchill said he would carry on until spring 1954.

At the end of July Eden had returned temporarily to London, frail but in good spirits, and burning with the question: 'When do I take over?' Churchill told his private secretary, John Colville, 'The more I am hustled, the longer I shall be.' He chose to delay his decision until he saw how he performed at the Conservative Party Conference at Margate in October. His fifty-minute speech there was a great success and Colville recorded that at Margate Eden, who had himself been very well received, on the surface seemed resigned to Winston remaining in power.[1] Unfortunately for Eden, Stalin had died soon before, so Churchill had another motive for staying on; he believed that he, as the only survivor of the wartime Big Three, had a mission to unfreeze the cold war.

In January 1954 various Cabinet Ministers became restless at Churchill's continuing as Prime Minister when he was obviously failing, and they feared that this would spoil Conservative chances in the General Election. When Oliver Lyttelton (now Lord Chandos) resigned on 28 January Evelyn Shuckburgh, Eden's private secretary, wrote in his diary that there was 'more talk of resignation . . . unless the Old Man will go', and on 6 April Eden, the Chief Conservative Whip, Patrick Buchan-Hepburn, and the Secretary to the Cabinet, Sir Norman Brook, agreed that the Prime Minister must be made to resign at latest by Whitsun.[2]

In June Eden had 'a very depressing letter from Churchill looking well beyond July'. As everyone was expecting Churchill to retire in July 1954, this must have added greatly to Eden's frustration.[3] On 22 September Eden talked to Churchill about the succession, but got nowhere. Churchill told him paradoxically that he (Eden) could not leave the Foreign Office for the moment, but if he stayed there until a week or so before the General Election he 'wouldn't have [any] chance to make an impression on the home front'. On 22 December, at a meeting of Ministers, it was suggested that Winston should retire. He took it ill and said it was clear 'they wanted him out'. Nobody contradicted, according to Eden's diary.[4]

At the beginning of 1955 there was no indication of the retirement date. Churchill still had successes in carefully prepared speeches and at Question Time in the Commons. Eden told Harold Crookshank, the Lord Privy Seal, that Easter must be the deadline for Churchill to go. Meanwhile Churchill became cross at how keen Eden and other Ministers were for him to go, while Eden became more and more tense at the frustrating delay. In March there was a short, sharp quarrel between Eden and Churchill over a suggested visit to London by Eisenhower and the possibility of a May General Election. When Eden in despair raised the subject of the succession at a Cabinet meeting, Churchill stated coldly that this was not a matter for Cabinet discussion.

However, soon afterwards Churchill told Eden and Butler that he would resign at the beginning of the Easter recess. Then came another hiccup. On 29 March the Edens were due to dine at Downing Street. That morning the Prime Minister sent Eden a message that, with two serious national strikes pending, the Budget, and the date of the General Election undecided, he could not possibly resign. Eden got ready for a showdown that evening, but Colville, never one of

Eden's greatest admirers, tactfully sent a message that he must be 'amiable'. Eden took the hint and exerted his considerable charm on the Prime Minister. It worked. The next morning Churchill told Colville that he had been 'altered' and 'affected' by Anthony's manner, and called in Butler and Eden to say that he would definitely resign; this time he kept his word.[5]

On 6 April 1955, when Eden entered Downing Street, he faced two urgent major decisions. One was to fill the post of Foreign Secretary, which he had vacated, and the other was to decide the date of the General Election. Eden's inclination was to make his close friend Lord Salisbury Foreign Secretary, but he decided that the time had passed when a Foreign Secretary could be in the House of Lords; this was invalidated later by the appointment of Lord Home. Instead he appointed Harold Macmillan, who was delighted because he knew that his popularity and standing in the Conservative Party was so great that, once installed in a top office, he could only be dislodged with difficulty. The Prime Minister soon rued his decision and wanted foreign affairs more under his own control.

Parliament still had plenty of time to run, and Eden would not have bumped up against the five-year rule until October 1956. In 1951 Labour had won more votes than the Conservatives, although the Government had a majority of 17. By-elections and opinion polls showed no firm swing to the Conservatives, and it needed courage for the new Prime Minister to decide on a dissolution six weeks after taking office, because it could result in his becoming the holder of the shortest premiership in the nation's history.

Contrary to the impression given in his memoirs, Eden was in doubt whether to ask for an immediate dissolution or not. At first he favoured a six months' wait to give the nation the impression that his Government was working well. But he was seriously worried that the economic situation might deteriorate. The balance of payments situation and speculation over sterling gave grounds for concern. The Churchill Government had given a hostage to fortune by making overseas sterling convertible, and the strength of the £ was a major worry to the Government by the spring of 1955.

A strange handwritten note by Butler from 11 Downing Street, dated 1 April, shows that there had been discussion about the election date even before Churchill had formally retired.

Dear Anthony,

Nice to hear your voice. Here is the Lancs paper. Circumstances move me from time to time and by degrees towards the month of 'May ing' when merry lads are playing! If you see what I mean.

Yours ever,

Rab[6]

The reference to the 'Lancs paper' must have been to a press cutting about the habit of workers in the Lancashire cotton towns to go on holiday in May, which would mean that a considerable number of traditional Labour voters would be unable to vote in a May election.

In the event the Conservatives did well in the cotton towns in the election of May 1955. In his autobiography Eden wrote that 'early summer holidays would probably cost us a seat or two', because the Conservative Party had not in the past been fortunate in summer elections. Obviously Eden and Butler had been discussing the pros and cons of a summer or spring election.

The deciding factor was probably the following note by Robert Hall, economic adviser to the Government, dated 6 April:

I think that the general economic situation is much better than it was in 1952. Production has increased and we have absorbed the increased defence burden. The reserves are better and our overseas debts not so awkwardly held. Thus I think that the dangers of convertibility are much less now than they were then. But our policy of ending controls and rationing has made it much more desirable to have a floating rate as a means of adjustment, and I think that on economic grounds it is very desirable that we should take the remaining steps to convertibility very soon.

Our current position is worse than it was in mid 1954, when it was very strong. This is mainly because of rising imports; we are importing more and prices are higher. But import prices have fallen a little in recent weeks and exports are holding up rather better than we expected. I do not think there is anything seriously wrong and if we could rule out confidence factors I would expect us to be able to hold the present position for some time. On the other hand, a fairly firm economic policy is necessary to get us back into a comfortable surplus position.

Lord Cherwell [Churchill's wartime adviser] considers that there is danger of an adverse movement of confidence. I agree with him about this. Until an election has taken place, there is bound to be uncertainty both about Government policy and about the result of the election. It is now easier than it used to be to get out of sterling into dollars and it seems likely that those who can do this, will do so, as an insurance against our position getting worse. This would be a cheap way of avoiding risks.

No-one can predict the outcome of economic events which depend on so many unknowns. But it is my opinion that the combination of
   (a) the deterioration in our economic position,
   (b) the increased facilities for moving from sterling to dollars while the exchange rate is fixed,
   (c) political uncertainty,
make the economic outlook between now and the election very uncertain. It would be rash to rely on the continuance of the present international atmosphere, which is now quite favourable to sterling. A speculative movement against sterling is a distinct possibility, and we are not at present very well placed to defend ourselves.[7]

Here were compelling economic arguments for an early election, and Eden wrote on the memorandum: 'Lord President to see. A. E. April 7.' The Lord President was Lord Salisbury.

How the Prime Minister's decision about the election date was influenced by the economic situation is clear from minutes of internal Treasury meetings. On 17 March the Chancellor of the Exchequer told his top Treasury advisers that he had 'expressed the view in the Cabinet that the economic prospects were such as to favour an early Election. It seemed quite likely that the date chosen would be 26 May.' The next day Butler told them that the Foreign Secretary (Eden, the incoming Prime Minister) favoured 'an early appeal to the country', but wanted 'a real attack on the problem of earned income relief'. Butler said this would only be possible if the idea of a reduction in the standard rate of income tax were dropped. However, on 24 March Butler told his Treasury meeting that it might be some little time before a definite decision was taken for or against an early election, because Eden had told him he might well wish to consult the Cabinet before deciding, and it was still possible that the decision would go in favour of an election early the following year.[8]

The Chancellor's meeting on 4 April with Sir E. Bridges, Permanent Secretary to the Treasury, Sir B. Gilbert, Sir L. Rowan, Sir H. Brittain, Burke Trend and Louis Petch, all Treasury officials, recorded: 'It was the unanimous view that the economic situation was such that it would be wise to get the General Election over as soon as possible.' Butler told the meeting 'he had already made this clear to Eden',[9] and eleven days later Eden plumped for 26 May. In his autobiography Eden wrote: 'I wanted to feel that I had the country's support for the work I wished to do. Nothing but the verdict of the nation at the polls could really give me that.' He did not mention the expected deterioration in the economic situation, although the importance of this as a factor is revealed in a letter Eden wrote to Churchill on 8 April:

There is no doubt that other things being equal the autumn would suit us better. The 26th of May is uncomfortably near the Whitsun holiday. But unfortunately other things are not equal. It seems that we are now about 70% convertible, though I confess that I was not clear at the time that we had moved so far. However having done so it seems that the best course is probably to go completely convertible. If we are to do this there must be political confidence in our country's future. We cannot be sure that there will be such confidence in the fourth year of the Parliament with the advent of a Socialist Government as a possibility.

Therefore it seems to me the financial remedy which we have to use, should our exchange position deteriorate further, would probably be effective after a General Election but might not be so before. This as I see it is the disagreeable reality which pushes us towards a May Election. As you know I have been tempted to try to show that we can be a good Administration for at least six months before appealing to the Country but I am increasingly compelled to take account of these distasteful economic factors.

Over and above all this we are finding increasing difficulty in selecting any date early next year. These wretched valuations [Quin-quennial Rating Assessments], though they do not come into force until April, are likely to become known as early as December, or in any event in January. This seems to rule out a month by which you and I had both been much attracted.

I should be grateful if you would treat this letter as between ourselves alone because I am not showing a copy of it to anybody.

I fear that the decision cannot be taken on Tuesday but we are fixing a code word with you.

Clarissa joins me in love to you and Clemmie – we were so touched by your telegram.

Yours ever,
Anthony.[10]

Eden also wrote on 17 April to Oliver Lyttelton, who had left the Government voluntarily some months previously to go into business and had written to Eden suggesting a revaluation of the £ before the election: 'You will see that we have taken the leap. I am sure that we had to, though I should have preferred six months for international work.'[11]

On 15 April, nine days after becoming Prime Minister, Eden plumped for a General Election six weeks later, on 26 May. However, first a Budget was needed. It was introduced on 4 May, two days before the dissolution, and turned out to be the first of the electioneering Budgets which from then on bedevilled the British economy with 'stop-go'. In 1955 wage claims were escalating because Sir Walter Monckton, as Minister of Labour, was determined to avoid strikes even though they could only be averted by inflationary wage settlements. In February 1955 the Chancellor of the Exchequer had decided to support 'transferable sterling' in the market, which effectively meant that sterling was convertible into other currencies at the official rate by non-residents and international companies. This imposed on the Bank of England the task of supporting the £ in unofficial markets in Zurich and New York – hence Eden's remark to Churchill, quoted above, that we 'were 70% convertible'. When the decision to support transferable sterling was announced in the Commons on 24 February Hugh Gaitskell, the Shadow Chancellor, commented that 'it meant in effect convertibility of sterling by the back door'. The £ was at the mercy of scares about the British economy; it should therefore have been the moment for a cautious Budget.

The Prime Minister was determined on continued economic growth. During the election campaign he gave glowing prospects of economic progress and called for large doses of expansion. He egged Butler on to make the maximum tax reductions in the April Budget. Butler slashed income tax by 6d in the £ and abolished purchase tax on all cotton goods as part of a package of £135 million in tax reliefs (£155 million in a full year), relying on 'monetary' policy – for instance interest rates – to stop any resultant overheating. There was not only full, but over-full, employment, and these tax cuts were inflationary to the point of danger for the £. Surprisingly, Butler was advised by the Treasury knights that he could safely hand out these £135 million tax cuts in the middle of a raging boom when the reserves were under strain and the economy was suffering from both demand and wage push inflation.

Indeed, in February 1955 the Government had been forced to reduce demand because of the deteriorating balance of payments and speculation against the £. Hire purchase restrictions had been intro-duced, bank rate raised from 3 to 4½ per cent, and the banks asked to reduce lending to private individuals and businesses. A significant Treasury minute on 9 March reads: 'Sir Edward Bridges and Sir Bernard Gilbert would see the Deputy Governor [of the Bank of England] . . . and broach the idea of tightening credit still further.'[12] This was just what Eden did not want to do.

The Treasury advice to Butler in the spring of 1955 was at variance with the Treasury Economic Survey for 1954, which had spotlighted Britain's falling share of world trade and warned that, with a rise in internal costs (a rise in wages or a fall in the value of the £), we might take 'a short cut to national bankruptcy because our competitive power would be disastrously weakened and the consequent worsening of the balance of payments would destroy for the time being any chances of a further improvement in the standard of living'.[13] Striking evidence of this contradiction comes from a memorandum from Bridges to Butler dated 25 February: 'On the assumption that you have money for tax concessions this year, and that you decide to use this money in the income tax field, they [the Inland Revenue] put forward the following scheme for consideration: reducing the standard rate by 6d, and each of the reduced rates by 3d; and reductions in personal allowances.' He estimated that the cost of the proposals would be £160 to £170 million in a full year, and went on: '. . . this may be more than you can afford to give away in present circumstances. But the proposals . . . are a good balanced scheme. And if you could carry it out you could claim that you had satisfied the spirit, if not the letter, of the more worthwhile recommendations in the Second Report of the Royal Commission.'[14] This advice, following the February steps to curb spending, shows how completely Bridges had departed from the caution urged in the 1954 Economic Survey.

What had happened to explain this Treasury volte-face? According to Samuel Brittan, the Bank of England and the Treasury had suddenly rediscovered the doctrine of monetarism which thirty-five years later was to dominate the economic policy of the Thatcher Government. Like Conservative Chancellors of the Exchequer from 1979 onwards, in 1955 Butler overestimated the effect of high interest rates as a curb on consumer spending. Over the spring 1955 Budget Butler and Eden were misled by their Treasury advisers.

Significantly, in his Budget speech Butler referred to 'the resources of a flexible monetary policy. I judge that the claims which domestic demand is likely to make on our production will leave a margin for exports . . . in conditions of monetary discipline industry will have to scrutinise its plans with a shrewder and more flexible eye' – a warning perhaps that all might not go according to plan. The tools of the Treasury monetarists of 1955 were the same as those of the later Thatcher Government.

Eden knew the election was likely to be close run, but Labour was split. Attlee, the Labour leader, was ageing; Aneurin Bevan was strongly opposed to the manufacture of the H-bomb by the UK, contrary to Attlee's official line, and Attlee could not impose his will on Bevan. In the Conservatives' favour Macmillan, as Minister of Housing, had reached his target of 300,000 houses a year, and inflation had been checked. Since Labour had left office in 1951 all food rationing had ceased; the number of private cars had risen by one-third, and television licences were up from just over one million to four and a half million. Standards of living were vastly lower than in the 1980s, but improving fast, and with full employment job prospects for everyone were excellent, with wages rising faster than prices. Average real earnings rose by 20 per cent between 1951 and 1959.

Eden fought an intelligent election campaign. He was an excellent platform speaker and well briefed on all aspects of policy. Moderate and non-controversial over home policy, he sensibly did not attack Attlee or the other Labour leaders. Throughout the campaign Eden was unfailingly courteous, always referring to his opponents, for example, as 'our Socialist friends', in contrast to Churchill who in his post-war elections called them 'the Socialist Party'. This attitude undoubtedly won votes. Neither side had a good record over the cost of living, and a *Times* leader pointed out that 'differences over social security policy were not great', although Labour wanted to abolish all health charges.

Surprisingly, foreign policy almost dominated the campaign, whereas in 1950 and 1951 it had not been a controversial issue. Labour began by claiming that the Tories had 'dragged their feet' over negotiations with the Russians. This ran out of steam when, during the election campaign, agreement was reached for a summit conference between Britain, France, the USA and the Soviet Union. Eisenhower agreed to participate because he did not want to see Britain under Labour rule again. While Foreign Secretary, Eden had strongly resisted Churchill's desire for a summit meeting with Russia. Now that he was Prime Minister he was enthusiastic for one. Aneurin Bevan correctly stated that Eisenhower had only agreed to the summit becuse he wanted to help Eden to win the election.

Once the summit was arranged, Labour fell back on the line that Attlee would be better than Eden at talking to the Russians. Eden countered that he was asking for a mandate for East–West talks. He boasted of his successes over peace in Korea and Indo-China, and said 'one reason for the Election was that I felt those who represent us at international talks must have a mandate to do so. How can you give a mandate to a divided party?'[15] This was a smack at Attlee and Bevan's dispute over the H-bomb.

Labour did not make a strong issue out of the denationalization of steel, which was proceeding at this time, nor about the repeal of the development charge on building land. In Labour's 1947 Town and Country Planning Act a 100 per cent development charge had been imposed whenever planning permission was given on farmland. This had created a shortage of building sites, and the Conservatives abolished the tax. Development charge in effect ceased on 1 December 1952, and building sites became more freely available. Landowners could harvest bonanza profits by selling land with planning permission, but in 1955 Labour had no enthusiasm for the reintroduction of a tax on building land profits, although the Wilson Government returned to the attack and sought to tax 'betterment' in the mid-sixties.

Eden did not want Churchill to play an important role in the election, perhaps fearing that it would divert attention from himself. Churchill was not asked to take part in the party political broadcasts on radio or television, but his appearances at the hustings received great publicity, sometimes pushing Eden off the front pages of the national press. Winston emphasized the importance of the summit talks and said, with a curious use of double negatives: 'It was by no means certain there was not another new look on the faces of the Kremlin which might still be more helpful to the overwhelming masses of people.'[16] This was what the country felt, and with considerable skill Eden used the prospect of the summit to gain support.

The 1955 General Election was the first in which television played an important role. Eden, with his charisma and charm, used it extremely well; undoubtedly this was an important factor in the Conservative victory. On 18 May the Conservatives inaugurated a new era in electioneering when Eden, Macmillan, Butler and Iain Macleod (Minister of Health) appeared on television to be cross-questioned by editors. The result was a triumph for Eden. However, the questioner who came closest to the ball was Vinson of the *Western Morning News*, who quoted Hartley Shawcross, the former Attorney General, as saying that the election had been 'timed for now' because of economic uncertainty. This, as has been seen, was true. Eden, like any other political leader would have done, replied tendentiously but emphatically: 'It has never entered my mind.'[17] Attlee did a cosy fireside television chat with his wife and one journalist; it too was a considerable success.

Labour emphasized the need for price control legislation to ban private trade courts, price rings and all restrictive practices in an effort to keep down prices. This was embarrassing for the Conservatives because in January the Monopolies Commission, set up under Labour's 1948 Monopolies Act, had delivered to the Board of Trade their Report on Rubber Tyres, which condemned secret manufacturers' courts, imposed fines on any retailer who sold tyres below the list price, and accordingly concluded that rubber tyre manufacturers operated massive price rings against the public interest. Dunlop, who were influential within the Conservative Party, made strong representations to the Board of Trade and to Tory MPs and Ministers that the Report should not be published. The Cabinet had considered publication, but decided to put it into cold storage until after the election. Eden himself on one occasion was badly heckled about 'the secret courts of the motor trade', and for once was at a loss for a reply. Butler was outspoken about the evil of price rings, but Eden ducked the issue.[18] The Report was not published until six months later.

The Conservatives received two fillips during the campaign. The first was the signing of the Austrian Peace Treaty; the second was the success of Tory candidates in the borough elections on 12 May, when they gained 783 seats from Labour. The Austrian Treaty was unique: it represented the only time that Communist-occupied territory was voluntarily evacuated, and was a tribute to the patient efforts of Eden and Ernest Bevin, Labour post-war Foreign Secretary. On 15 May, with great publicity, Macmillan went to Vienna where he, Dulles, Molotov, the Russian Foreign Minister, and Pinay, the French Foreign Minister, signed a treaty with Austria by which occupation troops were removed in return for a pledge of permanent neutrality. It was luck for the Conservatives that this dramatic occasion coincided with the election campaign. Photographs of Macmillan in cahoots with Molotov, who had made war inevitable in 1939 by negotiating the pact with Ribbentrop, aroused cynical comments.

On the evening of 26 May the first result, from Salford, showed a decline in the Labour vote which heralded a Conservative victory. Overall the Conservatives won 49.7 per cent of the vote against Labour's 46.4 per cent. It was a vote of confidence for the Eden Government and a triumph for the Prime Minister.

However, Eden's popularity soon declined. By the end of the year, as happens to all Prime Ministers, his honeymoon period with the electorate was over. Still, few Prime Ministers have encountered such a barrage of hostile press criticism as assailed him in January 1956. It began with *The Times* writing in its top leader on 2 January that the Government had lost its grip, and that unless it showed more 'high purpose' the people would drive it from office. The next day the *Daily Mail* accused the Government of 'delay and indecisiveness' and said it had only itself to blame for 'scandal and crisis'. Then the *Daily Telegraph*, normally the good friend of Conservative Prime Ministers, asked 'Why are the men who triumphed at the polls last May now under a cloud of disapproval with their own supporters?' It accused the Prime Minister of relying too much in home affairs on the technique of 'smoothing and fixing', and leaning too much over the shoulder of the Foreign Secretary. The author was the much respected journalist Donald McLachan.

According to his intimates, Eden was most hurt by the following sentence in McLachan's article: 'There is a favourite gesture with the Prime Minister. To emphasise a point he will clash one fist to smash the open palm of the other hand but the smash is seldom heard.' Not surprisingly, the left-wing *Mirror* and *Herald* joined in, and the *Mirror* headline was 'Eden is a flop.' Eden's press officer, William Clark, tactfully wrote on the cutting from the *Mirror*: 'If Eden is a flop so is William Clark.' The *Observer* of 9 January proclaimed on its front page: 'Eden must go. Move grows', and the *Sunday Despatch* of that date, in a survey of the views of 500 voters in 50 towns, reported that 361 said the Government had lost popularity and 175 wanted Sir Anthony replaced. Eden could not stand this criticism and ill-advisedly issued a statement from Downing Street that rumours of his imminent resignation were 'false and without any foundation whatsoever'.[19] Butler, about to go on holiday in the south of France, issued a Freudian statement of loyalty which did no good.

It was not a press plot. The Beaverbrook papers took no part. What happened was that the *Daily Telegraph* had been receiving letters and reports indicating the growth of despair in Conservative constituency parties about the credit squeeze and the rising cost of living. The *New Statesman* alleged that this was swollen by widespread reports from MPs to their constituents of the Prime Minister's 'vanity' and 'indecision'.

In his memoirs Lord Kilmuir, then Chancellor of the Exchequer, wrote of the Prime Minister's chronic 'restlessness'; Butler of innumerable telephone calls received 'on every day of the week and at every hour of the day'. Both Lord Thorneycroft and Lord Home told the author that they received similar constant interference in their work from the Prime Minister, but Home commented that he 'was such a nice chap and so good-mannered and charming that I did not mind'.

Sir Anthony Nutting, Eden's Minister of State at the Foreign Office, told the author that he was frequently in charge of the Foreign Office during Macmillan's and Selwyn Lloyd's absence abroad. On many occasions when he had gone home in the evening, having approved telegrams to Ambassadors all over the world, he would return in the morning to find they had been cancelled during the night by the Prime Minister. He would then telephone No. 10 to find out the reason, and almost invariably Eden would say it was because he had not been consulted. When Nutting pointed out that he was the Minister responsible to Parliament, and that there was nothing in the telegrams contrary to Government policy, Eden would climb down and apologise.[20] Eden offended some Conservatives because he did not want to break up the harmony of the two front benches, and above all did not want to be the Prime Minister who broke the magic spell of full employment. But the root cause of the rebellion was the desire of Conservative supporters for a realistic policy to deal with the insidious wage push inflation, which they believed could only be stopped by a showdown with the unions, as the City was demanding. Two influential economic commentators, Oscar Hobson and Professor Paish, called for a cut in public spending and a rise in the number out of work. As will be seen, Eden ignored these calls. He wanted Butler to play cat and mouse with the economy, and Monckton to chat cosily with the unions, while inflation bowled along merrily.

To his followers in January 1956 Eden appeared timid and unable to make up his mind, and his Cabinet was neither loyal nor united. However, the storm was over almost as quickly as it had started. By the end of January the experienced political commentator E. L. Mallalieu MP wrote that Eden was secure in the saddle again, and this was the general view of the lobby correspondents. But his image as the Prince Charming of post-war politics had been dented, if not cracked.[21]

2

Home Policy: Immigration, Secret Ballots, Education and Capital Punishment 1955–6

THE CONTROVERSIAL ISSUE not ventilated in the election was the problem of unrestricted coloured immigration into the UK. The Cabinet had considered putting into their election manifesto a proposal for legislation to curb immigration, but after lengthy discussion decided to shelve it until after the election. The minutes of the Cabinet's Election Business Committee show concern over guidance to candidates over immigration, and several drafts of notes on how to deal with questioners were made. In the first version they were to be told to say: 'I personally would favour taking power to deport people wherever they came from, who are convicted of serious offences . . . a Conservative Government would carefully watch the situation and would not hesitate to put forward proposals doing justice to all, should the circumstances warrant it.' The time spent by the Committee discussing various drafts shows how worried about this issue the Conservative leaders were.[1]

A revised version was submitted to the Prime Minister on 6 May by the Chancellor, Lord Kilmuir. He suggested amendments, including 'a great majority are law abiding citizens but if some are not, this is true of all communities'. This was put in the final version sent to all candidates; and instead of the wording in the first version, which advocated deportation, a more anodyne answer was recommended:

Question   What is the candidate's attitude to the growing influx of immigrants from the Colonies, particularly the British West Indies?
Answer   I know and share the concern which the large number of immigrants is causing. We must remember that all these people are British subjects. The problem is therefore one of great complexity. Any action must affect all Colonial Territories and Commonwealth countries.
   The Government have been watching the situation most carefully.

This is not a matter which should be allowed to become an issue of Party controversy. My own view is that the best course might be to hold a full inquiry to bring out all the facts.

Supplementary Questions and Answers
Question 1   Are not many of these immigrants of an undesirable type?
Answer 1   The great majority are law abiding citizens, but if some are not, this is true of all communities.
Question 2   Are not these people coming to Britain because of the bad conditions in the West Indies?
Answer 2   It is not true to say that these people are coming from the West Indies because conditions are deteriorating there, but because there is full employment and prosperity in Britain. In fact over the last ten years there has been a continuous rise in the standards of living in the British West Indies. It is this which has enabled so many of the population to afford the fare here.

For many years now large sums have been spent by successive British governments on Colonial development. For the West Indies alone Britain has provided over £30 million from Colonial Development and Welfare funds in the last eight years. In addition, the Colonial Development Corporation is committed to expend nearly £9 million.

In 1954 and 1955 the Churchill Government had been worried at the influx of coloured immigrants from the West Indies, although the total of immigrant residents was only 2 per cent of the 1987 level. Secret plans to curb immigration were brought before the Cabinet for discussion. Churchill, as Prime Minister, was ready to legislate. The archives reveal indecision and delay in the face of a mounting problem. At Cabinet after Cabinet the problem was discussed inconclusively; the position was stated with admirable clarity; clear-cut solutions were proposed, but no firm decision was taken. Not until 1962 were laws passed to curb coloured immigration, and in the intervening years the influx had produced difficulties almost impossible to eradicate completely.

The dilemma for the Government in the fifties was that, although an acute labour shortage existed, there was consternation at the influx of coloured workers from Jamaica in certain areas, especially Lambeth in south London. In 1951 twenty-seven Brixton residents complained to the Colonial Office, and in 1952, after reports about Tiger Bay in Cardiff, Churchill, then Prime Minister, asked the Colonial Office for more information, especially about Brixton. Churchill was also alarmed at a report at the same time in the *Daily Telegraph* that Mr Macpherson, Jamaica's Minister of Labour, had said he would take no steps to stop emigration because there were jobs for all in Britain. In December 1952 the Colonial Office told Downing Street that an estimated forty to fifty thousand 'colonial people' (i.e. coloured) were resident in Britain, with the greatest concentrations in London, Liverpool and Cardiff. The main source of immigration was Jamaica, with an average of three thousand immigrants a year from 1945 to 1952.

At Churchill's request his Home Secretary, Sir David Maxwell-Fyfe (before his elevation to the House of Lords as Lord Kilmuir), reviewed the situation in a Cabinet memorandum of January 1954, and reported that colonial governments were trying to stem the flow by tightening up dock control to prevent stowaways. This, of course, was peripheral, but Maxwell-Fyfe continued by saying that immigration officers could be given powers to deport British subjects to their place of origin but 'There could be no question of seeking such power to deal only with coloured people.' His view was that such powers would impose undue burdens on the immigration service and would be 'a complete break with the traditional principle that any British subject had a right to enter freely and remain in the U.K.'. In October 1954 *Empire News* reported race riots in London, and Winston Churchill asked the Home Office for details of the situation in London. He was told that the reports of widespread violence against blacks were exaggerated.[2]

In October 1954 Gwilym Lloyd George succeeded Maxwell-Fyfe as Home Secretary; Fyfe became Lord Chancellor. Lloyd George had inherited much of the charm of his father, the former Prime Minister, but not his strength of character – although in 1931 he had resigned with Lord Samuel from the National Government over the issue of free trade. Soon after he arrived at the Home Office he became convinced of the need for laws to curb coloured immigration. Churchill, too, was ready for action.

In November Lloyd George told the Cabinet that 'the rate of immigration had greatly increased in recent months, and it was now expected that about 10,000 would come to this country from the West Indies in 1954, as compared with a little over 2000 in 1953'. His memorandum to the Cabinet said this 'would in three or four years raise the coloured population to a total of something like 100,000', and as the law stood, there was 'no means of putting any limit on the number of Commonwealth citizens from overseas who may choose to settle here'; the only way to restrict immigration was to impose control similar to that imposed on aliens, but it should not be extended to Ireland. Lloyd George asked for a Departmental Committee to report, and for permission to make a Commons statement, and suggested that the Prime Minister should first mention it to the Leader of the Opposition. The Cabinet agreed to a Departmental Committee, but not to an approach to Attlee.[3]

Lord Swinton, the Commonwealth Relations Secretary, suggested that if Britain excluded Ireland it would be criticized in Commonwealth countries for giving more favoured treatment to Ireland, which had left the Commonwealth, than to the Commonwealth countries. Swinton was a lone voice in this crack at the Irish; though influential and able, he was a relic of the Baldwin and Chamberlain Cabinets with their commitments to the Empire.

Alan Lennox-Boyd, the Colonial Secretary, was one of the rocks on which immigration control foundered. In a paper dated 4 December he told the Cabinet he would have 'the gravest misgivings' if legislation applied predominantly to coloured persons. On 6 December the Cabinet revoked its previous decision to appoint a Departmental Committee on the grounds that it might produce a minority report which would make Government action difficult; instead they asked for a draft Bill.[4]

On 12 January 1955 Norman Brook, Secretary to the Cabinet, minuted to the Prime Minister that the draft Bill would empower immigration officers to prohibit the entry of immigrants unable to support themselves. However, the next day the Cabinet postponed the issue by asking for a White Paper which set out the existing restrictions imposed on the entry of British subjects into other Commonwealth countries. The civil servants found it impossible to draft such a White Paper satisfactorily because of the complexity and number of these regulations. Macmillan was not satisfied, and sent a note to Eden at the Foreign Office proposing a Private Bill in the House of Lords, because legislation 'is hopeless' unless it was agreed beforehand by all parties.

Meanwhile sections of the Conservative Party had become agitated, and Cyril Osborne, a right-wing MP, introduced under the ten-minute rule a Bill restricting coloured immigration, for which he tried to get Conservative backbench support. On 27 January the Conservative Parliamentary Party's Commonwealth Affairs Committee discussed the Osborne Bill. According to the Government Whip present, Osborne explained his draft but 'had not carried the Committee', and the Whip stated that in his opinion debate on the Bill would degenerate into a colour bar wrangle, and 'an administrative solution giving the Home Secretary power to deport undesirables after conviction' would be much more effective than controversial legislation.[5] The Whip continued that an awkward situation would arise if leave to bring in Osborne's ten-minute rule Bill was refused by the House, as was likely, because then the Government's hands would be tied. Osborne had replied to the discussion and lost his temper. There was 'grave disquiet' in the Committee and the feeling that, if Osborne persisted, 'he will, because he is so easily baited by the Opposition, put his foot right in it'. The Cabinet discussed the Whip's report on 31 January, but decided not to act. A fortnight later they revoked their decision to publish a White Paper on restrictions on immigrants to other Commonwealth countries, because it would be too difficult to get all the countries to agree its contents.

On 16 March the Cabinet was informed that at the meeting of the Central Council of Conservative Associations, to be held next day, attention would be drawn to the increasing immigration of coloured workers, and laws requested to enable undesirables to be deported. This was the last time the Churchill Government discussed immigration, and they reached no conclusion.[6]

On 20 April, after Eden had succeeded Churchill, Lloyd George minuted the Prime Minister that although he had a draft Bill ready he preferred a Departmental Committee of Inquiry prior to legislation. Eden asked him to bring the question of Jamaicans to the Cabinet, and found he was in favour of an inquiry. During the General Election Lloyd George wanted to make a speech saying that, if the Government was returned, it would legislate against uncontrolled immigration. The Cabinet would not agree to this at its meeting on 3 May, and decided it was 'ill advised to commit the Government to introduce legislation'.[7]

On 10 June, after the election, Lloyd George in a Cabinet Paper estimated that in 1955 about twenty thousand coloured persons would come from the West Indies to Britain; they tended to congregate in overcrowded streets, especially in the Midlands and certain parts of London, 'which is beyond the resources of the Housing Authorities concerned to prevent or alleviate'. There were no means of controlling the influx, he felt, without legislation.

He continued by saying that his draft Bill would be 'highly controversial', but that controversy would be reduced if the Bill was based on the recommendations of an impartial committee. He considered that the committee could report in time for legislation in 1956, and he suggested a Departmental Committee under the chairmanship of Lord Radcliffe; the Earl of Crawford and Balcarres; John Sparrow, the Warden of All Souls; or Sir David Lindsay Keir, Master of Balliol. He said that the Commonwealth Secretary, Lord

Home, agreed with his recommendation, but that the Colonial
Secretary, Lennox-Boyd, had reservations about the terms of
reference.[8] In a note to the Prime Minister before this Cabinet
meeting Norman Brook minuted:

> The Home Secretary proposes a Committee of Enquiry. Its purpose
> would be, not to find a solution (for it is evident what form control
> must take) but to enlist a sufficient body of public support for the
> legislation that would be needed. . . . Of the Chairmen suggested,
> John Sparrow seems the best . . . a lawyer: though he is untried.'[9]

The Cabinet jibbed at the Departmental Committee and decided
instead to ask the Home Secretary for an Inter-Departmental Committee of officials to prepare a report suitable for publication on the
growing influx of coloured workers, and to resume discussion after
the report. The Committee, chaired by William Cornish, Under-
Secretary at the Home Office, produced on 18 August a long report,
together with an appendix suitable for publication. It pointed out
that reaction in India and elsewhere would be much greater to a
statement about 'coloured people' than to one about West Indians
alone, and that immigration from the 'Old Dominions' had 'never
given rise to difficulties'.

The Irish came within the terms of reference of the Committee: an
estimated 750,000 had emigrated since the end of the war, and were
prepared to live in condemned premises and put up with conditions
which English people would not normally tolerate, but there were
not the same difficulties over the Irish as over coloured people
because 'the Irish are not . . . a different race from the ordinary
inhabitants of Great Britain'. Controls on the Irish were not proposed, and the Committee thought the Government should argue
boldly that the whole British Isles were for historical and geographi-
cal reasons one. The report went on that the absence of laws to
restrict immigration, in a world in which other countries with similar
or better standards of living universally exercised such powers, is
'hard to defend'.

The appendix for publication stated that the recent influx of
coloured persons from the West Indies, probably amounting to
twenty thousand a year, was a new development, and that taking into
account eight thousand Indians and Pakistanis some thirty thousand
coloured immigrants a year were coming to the United Kingdom.
However, there was no evidence that coloured immigrants were
finding it difficult to obtain work, and they had made 'a useful
contribution' to manpower resources. Nor was there evidence that

coloured people were making undue demands on National Assistance, although there was evidence that coloured men in London played a large part in illicit drug trafficking in cannabis and accounted for 'a disproportionate number of the convictions in London for living on the immoral earning of women'. They found no evidence of racial tension, apart from one or two isolated incidents, and coloured workers had made a favourable impression on buses and trains.

However, the report went on that the bulk of coloured immigrants had congregated in relatively few areas, mainly in London and the Midlands, where there was already an acute housing shortage, and there had been 'scandalous overcrowding' with several single people or even families sharing one room. This had created a grave problem for the housing authorities, whose resources were quite inadequate to cope with the problem. It was known that many coloured immigrants hoped to bring their families here, and should any large-scale influx of families take place 'the situation might quickly become critical'. A further significant influx into areas of unsatisfactory housing 'might well lead to developments in which it would be difficult to avoid racial problems arising'. There was no power to prevent any British subject, whatever his origin, from entering Britain, and no control was possible without an amendment of the law, which could be drafted to exclude Commonwealth citizens and the Irish, and to apply only to certain categories, such as West Indians.

The report continued by saying there would be little difficulty in administering a scheme to restrict entry to those who had employment permits and suitable living accommodation, and that such controls ought to be supported by making approved employment or continued residence in suitable accommodation 'a condition of continuing stay'; enforcement of any system of control of entry could be carried out by the Immigration Service, if it was enlarged, although this would involve delays at the airports. The statement emphasized that controls must not prejudice the widespread practice among people of all parts of the Commonwealth from visiting this country for study, business and recreation.[10]

As he was going to be abroad when the matter was discussed in Cabinet on 30 August, Lord Home wrote a memorandum for the Cabinet, in which he emphasized that we did not want to keep out immigrants of good type from the Old Dominions, and that it was politically impossible to legislate for a colour bar. Although prepared to agree to discrimination against West Indians, he took up the cudgels for citizens from India, Pakistan and Ceylon, although he

agreed that the number of working-class Indians coming to Britain had increased in the last year and 'unless checked this could become a menace'. However, he thought the Governments of India and Pakistan were 'genuinely ready to do what they can' to stop immigration. He felt there was a danger that India and Pakistan might introduce retaliatory restrictions on the entry or residence of the British business community, and he wanted the reference to the eight thousand coloured Indians and Pakistanis arriving each year deleted from the published document. Thus Home was agreeable to curb immigration from the West Indies, but not from India, Pakistan and Ceylon.[11]

When the Eden Cabinet met to discuss immigration on 15 September they had before them the Committee report and Lord Home's memorandum. The civil servants were sure that curbs on West Indian immigrants would be put in hand. After all, here was an authoritative report written in sombre, matter-of-fact language which made it crystal-clear that Britain had a problem which was on the brink of becoming critical and could only be solved by legislation. It seemed inconceivable that the Eden Cabinet would flout the civil servants' advice. But that is what happened.

On 15 September the Cabinet accepted the principles of the report and asked Lloyd George to circulate a draft Bill with permissive powers to prohibit the entry of overseas subjects who had neither a home nor a job. On 3 November the draft Bill was discussed by the Cabinet. They had before them a memorandum by Alan Lennox-Boyd, dated 31 October, stating that 'I must go on record that I could not agree to legislation confined to Colonial immigrants [meaning coloured people].' This meant he would probably resign if the Bill was proceeded with, and undoubtedly he influenced Eden against action. Lennox-Boyd was witty and flamboyant and popular in the Conservative Party. He was a firm supporter of the Colonies dealt with by his Department, and a close friend of Eden's.

In Cabinet on 3 November Lloyd George spoke in favour of his draft Bill. Lennox-Boyd argued against it, saying that it was 'inexpedient' and would be criticized as 'social discrimination'. He suggested rather implausibly that 'the preferable course was . . . to disperse the Colonial immigrants more evenly over the UK'. It was stated, almost certainly by Lord Salisbury, Lord President of the Council, that 'if immigration fom the Colonies and, for that matter, from India and Pakistan, were allowed to continue unchecked, there was a real danger that over the years there would be a significant change in the racial character of the English people'. The Cabinet discussed admitting immigrants to work for a period 'not exceeding five years', after which they might be sent home, as this might meet the present need for labour with less prejudice to social conditions. Such a scheme would have resembled the *Gastarbeiter* scheme under which West Germany was recruiting Turkish workers for employment but not for settlement. The view was also expressed on economic grounds that 'immigration was a welcome means of augmenting our labour resources'. Eden summed up and effectively killed the draft Bill by saying that further thought should be given to the problem before the Cabinet could decide whether legislation should be introduced.[12]

Churchill had been ready for strong action, but not Eden, who reversed Churchill's nudge to the Cabinet to close the door on unrestricted immigration. Eden loved his own rhetoric about a new multi-racial Commonwealth, but disliked the prospect of controversial legislation which might spoil his image as a moderate in home politics. Lord Thorneycroft told the author that the Board of Trade view at the time was that the West Indian immigrants were a useful help to industry. He added that the failure to act was a collective Cabinet responsibility, because at that time the extent of the problem was not generally realized, but that Eden would have been the dominant influence and he was never anxious for controversial domestic legislation.[13]

Kilmuir presented his report to the Cabinet on 11 July 1956. It concluded that uncontrolled immigration would have progressively serious implications on housing in the areas affected; a trade recession might have unfortunate consequences, with coloured men thrown out of work; there was a risk that public opinion might become violent: legislation should contain power to deport and to impose an annual quota; Ireland should be excluded, but legislation should apply to the whole British Commonwealth and not to the West Indies alone.

Apart from Lord Salisbury, the majority of the Committee thought that 'control will eventually be inescapable; but that balance of advantage lies against imposing it now'. Salisbury told the Committee that the arguments advanced by it were conclusive in favour of action at some point, and 'the longer we delay, the worse the position is bound to become'.

Kilmuir told the Cabinet that controls would add to the economic problems of the West Indies; the parliamentary timetable was congested, and it would be enough if the problem was reviewed in a year's time. However, after Lord Salisbury had stated that the report disclosed a growing and ominous potential danger the Cabinet decided it must be reviewed in six months' time. The Cabinet also asked the Colonial Secretary to discuss the problem of West Indian immigration with the Chief Ministers of Jamaica and Barbados.

A supplementary report was presented to the Cabinet on 20 November, when Eden was away ill. Kilmuir opened the discussion by saying that the Committee of Ministers' view was that, even if regulation of Commonwealth immigration was decided upon, there were 'solid reasons for excluding the Irish Republic', and the demand for coloured immigrants in employment had not yet reached 'saturation point', while 'the acceleration in the rate of immigration which had been the cause of concern in recent years seemed to have been checked'. Lennox-Boyd said that the reports of conditions in Britain which immigrants were sending to their families and friends were less optimistic now, and this was likely to check the flow.

Lord Salisbury said he remained disquieted, and if regulation was instituted he doubted whether it would be right to continue preferential treatment for the Irish. There was support for Lord Salisbury's anti-Irish view, but the Committee concluded also that the trend of coloured immigration and of unemployment amongst coloured people had disclosed nothing to make the problem more urgent than when it was last reviewed in July, and it was agreed there should be a further report in the following spring. That was the end of the immigration controversy during the Eden Government. The nation might have been spared many tears if his draft Bill had been put to Parliament.[14]

The General Election campaign opened under the shadow of the newspaper strike which only ended on 21 April, while the closing days of the election were darkened by the rail and dock disputes. The dock strike started on 23 May and continued for six weeks. No wage claim was involved. It arose from a dispute between the National Amalgamated Stevedores and Dockers and the Transport and General Workers' Union over a demand for representation by the former as a negotiating body after they had seduced some ten thousand members from the TGWU, for which offence the NAS & D had been expelled from the TUC. The strike was accompanied by a rail strike which had been due to begin on 1 May, but was postponed until 28 May. Its cause was a quarrel over the differentials paid to footplatemen.

Before the election was over nineteen thousand dockers were on strike. Eden did his best to keep the stoppage out of politics, saying in his speeches that it would be 'a grave mistake to make a political issue of the disputes' and that the job of maintaining industrial peace 'must be tackled as a national responsibility'. The moderate Hartley Shawcross declared the bitter opposition of the Labour Party to unofficial strikes, and suggested that they were Communist-inspired. After the election Hugh Gaitskell said that 'strikes were one of the main causes of the Labour defeat'. During the campaign the Conservatives committed themselves to talks with the TUC on the problem of unofficial strikes.

Eden was greatly concerned about the damage to national prosperity caused by the strikes, and set up a Ministerial Committee on Emergencies under Lloyd George, which acted to relieve the breakdowns in the docks. On 31 May an emergency was officially proclaimed. Eden made two broadcasts during the strikes. These were well received and undoubtedly cast oil on the troubled waters, although *The Times* wrote that his second broadcast was 'too eager'. In his memoirs Eden claims credit for these broadcasts, which he felt were evidence of his moderation in home affairs. Happily Walter Monckton, Minister of Labour, was able to settle both strikes without inflationary wage awards, and they were an episode which augured well for Eden's success in domestic politics.

Intent on avoiding further damaging and unnecessary strikes, Eden held talks at Downing Street with both employers and trade unions. Neither side wanted legislation, although both agreed there were far too many unofficial strikes. Discussion at Cabinet level centred on whether a secret ballot should be made compulsory before any union took strike action. Eden himself favoured a twenty-one-day cooling-off period. This had been in existence during the war, but the Labour Government had abolished it in 1951.

On 3 June the Cabinet discussed a memorandum by Monckton on the problems of industrial relations. It began by stating that 'There has been in recent weeks a serious deterioration in industrial relations.' However, Monckton was emphatically against legislation, to Eden's relief.[15] In his memorandum to the Cabinet Monckton wrote:

Secret Ballot

2) To impose a legal requirement of a secret ballot before strike action would in my judgement meet resistance from the trade union movement as a whole. . . .

3) This proposal would be resisted as an interference with the right to strike, and as an interference with the union's management and regulation of its own affairs. In any event provision for a secret ballot would not, of course, help to prevent unofficial strikes which are *ex*

hypothesi against the will and authority of the union. Moreover, a determined union could still pursue its militant aim while keeping within the law. It could arm itself with the necessary authority by vote at an early stage in the negotiations; it could encourage, without formally authorising, unofficial action; and it could engage in lawful obstruction such as going slow and working to rule. . . .

4) Unofficial strikes

Any attempt to make unofficial strikes illegal raises difficult questions of penalties and enforcement. Penal sanctions against individual strikers – there may be tens of thousands of them, as in the recent unofficial coal stoppage in Yorkshire – would be ineffective and dangerous and sanctions could hardly be directed against the funds or officers of the unions whose authority is being flouted.

5) *Compulsory arbitration*

Compulsory arbitration involves the withdrawal of the right to strike. It is not compatible with generally accepted ideas of free negotiation and free contract and is contrary to political pledges given on this subject.[16]

Monckton went on to say that he favoured an inquiry by some body such as a Royal Commission 'into the whole position of trade unions and the system of industrial relations', but qualified this by stating that a Royal Commission would be 'ponderous and slow moving', and in his view an authoritative independent committee 'would prove a better instrument'. If, he said, any form of legislation 'is to be attempted it would in my view be necessary to have some inquiry first to formulate ideas and shape public opinion'; he thought it essential that 'any Government initiative in the field of industrial relations should carry the greatest possible measure of TUC approval and concurrence. Unless we carry with us the responsible elements, who are at present in a majority, we run the risk of uniting the whole movement against us.'

Monckton told his colleagues that he proposed to start informal talks with the TUC and make 'parallel soundings' with the British Employers' Confederation (the forerunner of the Confederation of British Industry). His conclusion was that 'there is no panacea for these ills and, in particular, the scope for remedial action by the Government is limited'.

In face of this negative diagnosis the Cabinet decided to defer action. Eden hankered after progress and appointed a Cabinet Committee (the Industrial Affairs Committee) to consider legislation. Their terms of reference were 'to consider what action should be taken to check strikes and improve industrial relations'.[17] For the first meeting, on 22 July, Monckton repeated his views to the Committee in a long memorandum which concluded: 'I adhere to the view which I have publicly expressed that you cannot legislate for responsibility and I am sure that a legal requirement imposing statutory timing on the calling of strikes would only rarely assist in promoting industrial peace and would raise the usual awkward problem of enforcement.' For the second meeting he added: 'I therefore conclude that legal sanctions against strikers are difficult to enforce and may impede more positive solutions. New restrictions would be strongly opposed by the Trade Unions, and might enjoy little support from the employers.'

The terms of reference were wide and the Committee also considered whether education could improve the attitudes of employers and workers to strikes, or whether profit-sharing schemes might help. Sir David Eccles, Minister for Education, submitted a long memorandum showing how education might help to improve the attitude of both workers and employers to strikes. Although well argued it is, especially with hindsight, unconvincing and unrealistic, and no action was taken on it.

The Committee also considered a memorandum on profit-sharing by Butler. He concluded that the Government should express support for co-partnership schemes in principle wherever a company decided that its own circumstances were favourable to their introduction. 'But we should certainly take no steps to make such schemes compulsory and we should consider carefully before committing ourselves to any other measures which it may be argued that we ought to adopt in order to foster co-partnership.' Butler had been looked on as the apostle of profit-sharing while the Conservatives were in Opposition between 1945 and 1951, but as Chancellor of the Exchequer his enthusiasm had vanished, although it was mainly due to him that co-partnership figured in the Conservative Election Manifesto.[18]

All this was a grave disappointment to Eden, and when on 11 April 1956 Brook minuted to him that the Committee had not got far 'with this intractable subject' and 'both Monckton and Butler wanted it wound up', the Prime Minister reluctantly agreed. Another of his initiatives had withered on the vine because of his colleagues' lack of enthusiasm for any change.[19]

On 8 July 1955 Lord Nuffield, the car magnate, wrote to the Prime Minister asking for an interview because 'I feel so convinced that I should see you to place before you my views on Trade Unions and the strike epidemics over recent years.' Nuffield's political background was slightly clouded by his support for Oswald Mosley in the 1930s, but Eden agreed to see him at Downing Street on the 28th. The day after the meeting Eden sent the following memo to Monckton:

Lord Nuffield came to tell me, and authorised me to pass on to you, that after a lifetime in the motor car industry he believed that the secret ballot would solve industrial difficulties. In his view the men would most of them prefer it. He reminded me that, during the 1926 strike, in 46 establishments which he controlled not one man came out.

I expressed my view that the secret ballot, although useful in some cases, would not cure unofficial strikes. He said that he was speaking not only of a secret ballot before a strike, but also of a secret ballot in elections of union officials. He emphasised that the Electrical Trades Union was in a dangerous situation, being Communist led, and pointed to them as an example of a union which would be much better if its officials were elected by secret ballot.[20]

Within five years scandals showed that the Communist-led Electrical Trades Union was indulging in ballot rigging, and its house was only set in order when Frank Chapple took over. Nuffield was dead right about the ETU, but his warning was disregarded.

A great opportunity for trade union reform was missed in 1955, because at that time the union leaders were moderate and might well have agreed or made little opposition to a sensible package deal. However when Harold Wilson, Edward Heath and Margaret Thatcher later tackled the same problem the union top brass was more militant.

On 10 April 1955, a few days after becoming Prime Minister, Eden wrote to the Minister for Education, Sir David Eccles, a personal letter asking him if he had 'any problems to which we shall have to give our early attention? If so, I should be glad to have a short note from you upon them since I am trying to review the position generally.' Eccles replied on the 14th:

Thank you for your personal letter, asking if I have any urgent problems for the Cabinet. Not as far as I can see.

Rab and I have plans for helping middle-class parents to pay for their children at school and at the University. It is important that these should come off next week.

The most political problem in education is the 11+ examination and the Socialist proposal to abolish it by rolling up all secondary schools into comprehensive schools. I will circulate a paper describing the counter measures which I am taking. No decisions will be required.[21]

The second paragraph must have referred to a scheme discussed by Eccles with the Chancellor of the Exchequer for income tax relief to parents sending children to fee-paying schools. There are no other references to it in the archives, and it certainly would not have appealed to Eden because it was right-wing and would arouse an explosive reaction from the Labour Opposition.

Resentment of the 11+ examination had been growing, and the Labour Party were trying to make a political issue out of the continuance of the grammar schools and the selection system. Labour wanted to abolish selection and convert the grammar schools into comprehensives. The Conservatives were anxious to retain the grammar schools, but were perturbed at the unpopularity of the 11+ selection. Eccles immediately instructed his civil servants to prepare an urgent paper on selection for secondary schools, for circulation to the Cabinet on 19 April. Eccles evidently thought his Department's scheme for replacing 'Selection for Grammar Schools' by 'Selection for All' would defuse the 11+ controversy, about which Eccles sent a note to Brook, Secretary to the Cabinet: 'This bids fair to become a controversial topic in the Election.' However, his scheme was a non-runner.[22]

Eccles prefaced his memorandum by emphasizing that the 11+ was likely to be an election issue, and that parents felt disappointment and jealousy when their children failed to qualify for a grammar school. He appears to have been strongly motivated by the electoral unpopularity of the 11+. He pointed out that a comprehensive school – a combined secondary modern and grammar school – must contain at least two thousand pupils because 'the grammar school element must be at least 400 strong to provide a satisfactory sixth form', and stated that the London County Council had succeeded in doing this at Kidbrooke. However, Eccles pointed out that Kidbrooke was the exception that would prove the rule, that the difficulties of organization were too great to be overcome, that he would not agree to a complete network of comprehensive schools in any area, and that 'although the comprehensive school is certainly not the right answer, we cannot leave the 11+ examination where it is'. Kidbrooke, an adventurous experiment, suffered greatly in the opinion of most educationalists from being too large.

Eccles's solution was to create in secondary modern schools 'special courses with a clear vocational interest', which would mean that each school could offer 'something special that cannot be had elsewhere in the area. Where this is already happening Local Education Authorities are finding that complaints from parents about the selection procedure are strikingly reduced.' He also wanted to encourage more transfers at fifteen or sixteen to and from grammar schools. Eccles now called his policy 'Selection for Everybody', and enthused about developing in each secondary school some special attraction and giving parents the widest possible choice. He added that when he had addressed the National Union of Teachers' Conference the previous week a 'big majority' of the teachers were 'against comprehensives and in favour of building up secondary moderns'.[23]

Eccles's memorandum aroused no enthusiasm with the Cabinet, where it was never officially discussed. After a survey of the documents released in the Public Record Office for 1955 *The Times* wrote in their top leading article on 3 January 1986 that Eccles was 'the greatest of Conservative Education Ministers', and had in 1955 offered an alternative which might have 'saved the grammar schools'. According to *The Times*, the failure to act on Eccles's plan discredited Anthony Eden. This comment does not, however, stand up to a detailed examination of the archives. In the view of most educationalists Eccles was the 'only good' Tory Minister of Education rather than the 'greatest'.

There were many flaws in 'Selection for All', and Eccles did not face up to the virtual impossibility of continuing selection at 11+. Even by 1955 leading educationalists such as A. D. Peterson had seen that the future lay with sixth forms in comprehensive schools combined with two-tier patterns like the Leicestershire plan, with sixth form colleges and finally with tertiary colleges. Eccles's 'far more transfers to and from grammar schools at 15 or 16' was simply unworkable; the academic standard in secondary moderns was too low for massive transfers to grammar schools, while schemes for transfer from grammar schools at thirteen or fourteen were bitterly opposed by parents on social grounds.

In their comments on Eccles's memorandum the civil servants pointed out another flaw in the idea of each modern school developing its own special attraction and encouraging 'parental choice': it could only work in large conurbations where there were a large number of competing schools within a comparatively small catchment area, and could not be operated successfully in rural areas with very large catchment areas for each school. This is true, and is also a reason why the 'vouchers' scheme favoured by Sir Keith Joseph and other prominent Conservatives in the mid-1980s would be so difficult to operate. Eccles also considered 'assisted places' in public schools; he thought this would be difficult politically, and instead he argued for bringing the public school system closer to the state system by implementing changes in entrance requirements designed to give a better chance to candidates educated at state primary schools.

In 1955 the Government did nothing over secondary education, but Eden had his biggest success in domestic policy over technical education. His Government gave it a tremendous impetus, for which the Prime Minister personally deserves much credit. Eden believed strongly that if Britain was to maintain her advance as an industrial nation a proper supply of skilled trained workers was essential. In November 1955 he saw Eccles and told him that he was deeply interested in expanding technical education, and wanted to produce a programme 'which will strike the public imagination as adequate to the demands of the scientific revolution'. Eccles minuted to his civil servants that

> so great was the Prime Minister's enthusiasm for this subject that we can risk unorthodox and drastic methods. One of the mysteries of the post war advance in education is the ignorance of the public about what has been done in further education. The silence must give way now to a series of battle cries. . . . The programme for the next four or five years which we submit to the Cabinet should be what we think should and could be achieved. We can trust the Treasury to cut it down.

Little had been done for technical education in the ten years since the war, despite the mammoth programme of spending on secondary and primary schools initiated by the Attlee Government. Now, with the Prime Minister insisting that technical colleges should be given a powerful boost, the civil servants were delighted. Sir Gilbert Flemming, Permanent Secretary, noted that there were grave defects in technical colleges, and that current progress was much too slow. He surveyed present and prospective needs and produced a programme of a total of 285 building projects costing approximately £72 million. He thought that they should hurry the programme because it would take eight years for all starts for all new technical colleges, and twelve years to finish. He suggested starting 70 per cent of the work within five years, and then pausing to consider how quickly to begin the rest. In the Ministry of Education there was great enthusiasm, and talk about a 'bigger bang' than the 'big bang' of new schools during the Attlee Government.[24] By 19 December 1955 the Eccles Paper for the Cabinet was ready. It recommended stepping up the rate of building for technical education so as to start projects to the value of £70 million during the next five years, planned on a regional basis; it also proposed issuing a White Paper.

On 1 January 1956 Eden sent his Cabinet colleagues a memorandum on technical education, which he said he had been thinking over during the recess because it was 'so vital for the future of the country'. As a result he had asked Lord Cherwell for a report, which Eden now circulated. The Cherwell Report suggested that the topic should be reviewed by 'a small high powered committee'. Obviously Cherwell thought he would be designated chairman. Eden told the Cabinet there 'was much to be said' for such a committee.

This proposal did not, however, meet with Cabinet approval; they preferred the Eccles plan and a White Paper. Butler, the former Conservative Education Minister who had piloted through the 1944 Act, thought it would be 'inappropriate' to have the outside committee proposed by Cherwell. The Cabinet agreed with Butler, and on 4 January 1956 decided to accept the Eccles Report and to publish it as a White Paper, which came out on 1 March.[25]

The White Paper had a good press when it appeared. *The Times* commented that it was 'generous' but it 'started late after a century of neglect'. In the Commons Eccles promised that 'it would be exempt from any cuts', and Eden said in an important speech at Bradford on 18 January that we must produce more technicians and technologists if we were to keep our place in the world. He sincerely believed this, and was ready for deeds as well as words.

Frederick Bray, who had recently retired as an Under-Secretary of Further Education at the Ministry of Education, wrote in the *Journal of Education*:

> Prior to the issue of this White Paper the Ministry of Education operated on an annual programme of capital investment. . . . Local Education Authorities were never sure whether a technical college which had been started would be completed in a continuous process. . . . Now at a time when the Government has been forced to cut investment generally to the bone they produce a plan . . . for a big increase in investment in technical education from an average of £4 million a year since the war to an average of £14 million for the next five years. . . . This is surely a striking change in policy which reflects the greatest credit on the Government in general and on the Minister of Education in particular.

He might have added that the Prime Minister deserved 'the greatest credit' too, and it is pleasant to record this glowing achievement by Eden.[26]

The White Paper was a milestone in the hitherto neglected field of technical education. The colleges of advanced technology became the new universities of the 1970s, and the new polytechnics went on to award CNAA degrees – degrees monitored by the Council for National Academic Awards. In home policy this was the greatest achievement of Eden's premiership.[27]

Eccles submitted a memorandum to the Cabinet, dated 10 December 1956, pointing out that since the war we had just about kept pace with the increase in the number of children, both in providing new schools and in recruiting teachers, but that the effort had left little margin for reducing the size of classes or improving the quality of teachers, and that conditions in the secondary schools were bound to deteriorate in the next few years and attract much unfavourable comment. He stated that, compared with other countries, the proportion of children who went on to university was very low – about 3 per cent, and only about 1 per cent took full-time advanced courses. He asked for an undertaking from the Government that further resources would be forthcoming for extra school building to start in 1957, together with enough money to improve teacher training and 'other plums to attract teachers of the right quality'.

With the Government reeling in the aftermath of the Suez crisis, and Eden in agony over his future, no discussion of the Eccles memorandum took place while Eden was Prime Minister. But there can be no doubt that, if Eden had been fit and well and full of confidence in the future of his administration, as he had been in April 1955, he would have supported Eccles as enthusiastically as he had done over technical education eighteen months before.[28]

In the autumn of 1955 Butler and Eccles had a sharp clash over education expenditure, in which Eccles showed scant respect for the Chancellor of the Exchequer. On 3 August, because of the run on the £, Butler had asked all Departments to reduce their estimates for 1956–7; however in a statement to the Commons Butler said that the Education Building Programme would not be cut by the Government, but that local authorities 'were to exercise restraint in carrying out this and other programmes'.

Eccles and his Department interpreted this rather woolly remark as meaning no cuts in school building. The day after the debate on Butler's second 1955 Budget, on 1 November, Eccles put out the following press statement:

> As stated by the Chancellor of the Exchequer in the House of Commons, the education programme as announced is being maintained. Authorities will, therefore, be expected to carry out all the projects in the approved programme for 1955–1956 and 1956–1957.

This brought a sharp reply from Butler on 2 November:

> When I was about to speak in the House of Commons on Monday [in the Budget debate on 31 October], I was handed a copy of the

[Eccles's] press statement about the education programme. I made no use of it in my speech because it was not in accord with the Message which I had sent to local authorities with your concurrence and that of the other Ministers concerned. . . . You pressed me to exclude Education altogether. . . . I was not willing to do this because it would have increased the difficulties of other Ministers, but I went a long way to meet you. . . .

The intention of the latest Message was that local authorities should be free to defer education projects if they saw fit. You accepted this in your letter to me dated 27 September which specifically said that you recognised that paragraph 5 of the Message might lead to postponement of some rural re-organisation projects, and that if this happened you would not press the local authorities to change their minds. The effect of your Press statement is to instruct education authorities that *all* the projects in the programme are to proceed.

Eccles replied: 'The Country Councils raised a howl when your message reached them . . . it has proved impossible for them to interpret your message in relation to the educational building programme . . . the County Councils could not square your message with our statements on Education.' He also pointed out that the Prime Minister had given a misleading answer about education expenditure when challenged by Hugh Dalton in a debate on 3 October.

Butler replied: 'There is not only a howl from local authorities, but complete perplexity', and asked Eccles to take the opportunity in a speech prominently reported in the educational press, and if possible also in the national press, that the original programme was being stuck to, but that it was important not to try and do everything at once. This bickering between Butler and Eccles was leaked to the lobby correspondents; soon afterwards Henry Fairlie wrote in the *Spectator*: 'It was not a happy Government.'[29]

In 1948 Labour's Criminal Justice Bill proposed no substantial change in the law on capital punishment. However, on a free vote in the Commons an amendment moved by Sydney Silverman MP to suspend the death penalty for five years was carried by 23 votes. The Government proposed as a compromise to 'grade' murders with the death penalty being available only in the worst cases; this was defeated in the Lords, and instead a Royal Commission was appointed in 1949.

In 1953 the Royal Commission recommended important modifications – raising the age limit for capital punishment from eighteen to twenty-one, and empowering a jury to substitute a lesser sentence for the death penalty. Not until 1954 was the Commons given time to debate the recommendations, and then the Churchill Government only wanted to take note of the Report.

Then on 10 February Gwilym Lloyd George, the Home Secretary, said in the Commons that the Government rejected the Royal Commission's main recommendations because capital punishment was an effective deterrent and prolonged imprisonment was not a satisfactory alternative, and there had been no overwhelming change in public opinion about this. However, public anxiety had been aroused by the fear that there had been a miscarriage of justice over the execution of Timothy Evans, who may have been innocent, and over the execution of Derek Bentley when his younger accomplice Christopher Craig, who was under age, had actually committed the murder. Soon after the debate Ruth Ellis was hanged for a *crime passionel* in spite of public demand for clemency; these three cases aroused grave public concern about the death penalty.[30]

The Eden Cabinet first discussed capital punishment on 18 October. Lloyd George stated that the Howard League were campaigning for the abolition of capital punishment, and that as soon as Parliament reassembled 'there would be pressure for some further indication of the Government's intentions'. Eden said that nothing in his view had occurred to warrant any modification of the view which the Cabinet had previously taken, and on 10 November Lloyd George told the Commons that the Government would not accept any of the Royal Commission's recommendations.[31]

Then Silverman put down a Parliamentary Question for 24 November, asking what steps the Government proposed to take to ascertain current public opinion about the death penalty. This caused the Cabinet to debate the subject again on 22 November. Lloyd George thought that no change in public opinion had taken place, although there was widespread concern in the Commons and 'an unremitting pressure for the further discussion of this matter could now be expected'. In discussion, doubts were expressed whether a majority still existed in the Commons for the retention of the death penalty, and it was agreed that Eden should say in reply to Silverman that, although the Government was not opposed to further discussion in Parliament, no time could be found for such a debate. However, the Home Secretary was instructed to prepare a memorandum as a basis for further Cabinet discussion.

This memorandum, discussed by the Cabinet on 3 January 1956, recommended not abolition, but a more extensive use of the prerogative of mercy. The Cabinet agreed to hold a Commons debate but to put nothing on the Order Paper which mentioned abolition. They were determined, it seems, that there should be no division on abolition. Kilmuir strongly supported Lloyd George. In discussion it was thought that it would be 'intolerable if, in consequence of the abolition of capital punishment in this country . . . professional criminals took to carrying firearms and the police had to be armed.' The Cabinet agreed that capital punishment must be retained.[32]

The Labour peer, Lord Chorley, tried to instigate a debate on capital punishment in the Lords for 15 February 1956. Lloyd George told the Cabinet that this was most 'inexpedient . . . for if the Lords declared themselves strongly in favour of retaining the death penalty, moderate opinion in the House of Commons would be more likely to swing in favour of abolition', and he considered there would be a better chance of satisfying them if the Government offered to put into law the secondary recommendations of the Royal Commission, so that provocation by words alone was sufficient to reduce murder to manslaughter, and punishing those who aided or abetted suicide by life imprisonment only.

A report had been published by a Committee of the Inns of Court Conservative and Unionist Society, chaired by Sir Lionel Heald, a former Attorney General, urging the Government to retain capital punishment but to legislate on some of the Royal Commission's other recommendations. Lloyd George emphasized to the Cabinet that such legislation would impress Government supporters, particularly those who favoured retention but were disturbed by the existing scope of the death penalty. Some Cabinet members thought that the Government's case for retaining the death penalty would be seriously weakened if they took no positive steps on lesser points, and the Cabinet agreed that, if Lord Chorley could not be persuaded to postpone his Lords debate, the issue should be debated in the Commons on a motion for retaining the death penalty but advocating legislation to put into law the secondary recommendations of the Royal Commission. This was obviously a ruse to salve the consciences of Conservative MPs with minor doubts, and if successful would put an end to abolitionist hopes during that Parliament.[33]

In early February 1956 the Government tabled a motion: 'While the death penalty should be retained the law relating to the crime of murder should be amended.' The Opposition saw through the manoeuvre and put down an amendment in the name of James Chuter Ede, the former Home Secretary, calling for the abolition of capital punishment for an experimental period. When the debate took place there was a free vote; the arguments followed the traditional lines, but in the division 293 voted for the Labour amendment and 262 against. Eden and ten other Cabinet members voted for retention, but significantly Lloyd, Heathcoat Amory and Macleod abstained – evidence that even at that stage they were probably abolitionists, although there is no record that they expressed such views in Cabinet. Now the Government faced a dilemma; in the debate Butler had pledged the Government to act on the decision of the House, whatever it might be. As a result it was committed to action contrary to the judgment of the Home Secretary.

On 22 February the Cabinet considered a memorandum from Lloyd George on the problem; it pointed out that the Government could hardly now introduce legislation on a matter they had just advised the House to reject, as it would leave them open to criticism for their volte-face; Lloyd George thought it more appropriate that the House which had defeated the Government should sponsor a Bill, and wrote: 'It seems to me far better for the Government to make way gracefully for those who believe in abolition, than to put ourselves into the equivocal position of sponsoring a measure which we have made it perfectly clear we consider to be contrary to the best interests of the country.'

The Cabinet discussed whether the best tactics would be to resurrect the Silverman Bill or to allow the leaders of the Opposition to sponsor a Bill. In favour of Silverman's Bill it was argued that, as it provided for the suspension of the death penalty for five years, and after a further five years its complete abolition, the Government might at the committee stage make amendments which would transform the measure into complete abolition, which would make the Bill 'black and white'; then the Government might be able to whip up enough support for its rejection. Comfort was taken from the thought that, even if the Bill passed the Commons, it was likely to be rejected by the Lords. Eden mentioned that some supporters had said that the issue might be solved by a referendum, 'but he proposed to reply that this was essentially a matter for Parliament itself and that the holding of a Referendum on it would derogate from sovereignty of Parliament'. The Cabinet decided to make time for a second reading of the Silverman Bill, and in the meantime the Home Secretary would consider each death sentence on its merits.[34] A Private Member's Bill, of course, had less chance of success than a Government Bill, and not unnaturally this move was looked upon by many as another trick to thwart the abolitionists.

On 8 March, when a date had been fixed for the first reading of the

Silverman Bill, Lloyd George told the Cabinet that he proposed to make it clear that the Government still thought capital punishment should be retained. It was agreed that Conservative backbenchers should be allowed a free vote, but that Government members should not be free to vote in favour. If the Bill obtained a second reading the Cabinet decided there should be no 'frivolous' or 'wrecking' amendments, because it was the Government's duty to see that the Bill left the Commons in a proper form, but Kilmuir asked that throughout the Commons proceedings 'it should be remembered that the Bill was likely to be rejected by the House of Lords . . . [and] it was desirable that the Government should take as little responsibility for it as they could during its passage through the Commons'.[35]

On the second reading there was a majority of 24 for the Bill. Enough Conservative abolitionists remained true to their consciences to ignore the retentionist views of their constituency associations. In April, in a memorandum to the Cabinet, Lloyd George and James Stuart, Secretary of State for Scotland, recommended that the Government should support, while leaving it to a free vote, amendments designed to retain capital punishment for the murder of a policeman or prison officer and for a second conviction for murder. The Bill passed its third reading in the Commons on 28 June.

Salisbury advised the Cabinet that there should be a free vote in the Lords and that it would be best for the Lords to be advised to reject the Bill on the second reading, and a perfectly constitutional argument for so doing was that no proposal for the abolition of the death penalty had been put to the electorate during the last election. The Cabinet agreed with Salisbury. On 10 July the Lords rejected the Silverman Bill by 238 votes to 95.

The following day the Cabinet agreed that in the next session it would introduce its own Bill to alter the law concerning murder, and narrow the categories of crime punishable by death. Their grounds were that limited retention of the death penalty would command a wide measure of support, and as a result there would be a reasonable prospect that Conservative MPs favouring abolition could be persuaded to vote for it because it restricted the death penalty.[36]

A committee was appointed under Kilmuir to consider the legislation, and he produced a memorandum in favour of limited abolition, with life imprisonment except for the worst categories of murder. However the Cabinet was unable to make up its collective mind on how to proceed, and on 26 July was told that it was open to doubt whether a sufficient number of Conservative MPs would find such a Bill acceptable, and only a narrow majority could be expected.

Eden told the Cabinet 'the Government could not take a final decision . . . until they had a closer picture of the state of opinion among their supporters in the House of Commons', and the Cabinet instructed Edward Heath, the Chief Whip, to take informal soundings to find out whether the proposed Bill could be carried against the votes of the Opposition. Tory abolitionists were subject to considerable pressure not only from their constituency associations, but also from the Whips' Office, to promise not to resist the impending Government legislation on the death penalty.

On 31 July Eden reported to the Cabinet that Heath's inquiries had not progressed sufficiently to enable him to form a reliable estimate, and he feared defeat for the Bill if it was brought before the Commons. In discussion it was pointed out that the Government would be embarrassed if it failed to 'assume' responsibility for a matter which so closely affected law and order. However, in view of Parliament's preoccupation with Suez it was now considered less important to announce the Government's intention; thus when Parliament reassembled at the end of October in the shadow of the Suez war, Kilmuir had persuaded the Cabinet to introduce legislation on the lines of his own further memorandum.[37]

At the Conservative Party Conference at Llandudno in October there were thirty-three motions favouring the retention of capital punishment – more than on any other subject. A resolution in favour of retaining capital punishment was passed with tremendous enthusiasm. One delegate cried out: 'Thank God for the House of Lords.' The only delegate who spoke in opposition was howled down and asked by the chairman to leave the rostrum without finishing his speech.

No Tory abolitionist MP was in evidence. Richard Hornby, who had recently won the Tonbridge by-election, had voted for the Silverman Bill. When the author asked him why the abolitionist MPs kept quiet at Llandudno, he replied that by securing a majority for the Silverman Bill they had forced the Government to take action and that he, like the others, had incurred the wrath of his constituency chairman. 'There was no need for us to put our heads on the block again when we had done the job,' he said.[38]

However, Eden ignored the Conference, telling the Commons on 23 October that the Government would introduce a Bill to curtail but not to abolish capital punishment, and on 21 March 1957, during Macmillan's premiership, this Bill became the Homicide Act 1957. It did not satisfy the abolitionists, but the will of Parliament had in part been accepted by the Eden Cabinet.

3

Budgets and Economic Policy
1955–6

THE FEARS EXPRESSED in April by Robert Hall about a likely deterioration in the economy were soon realized after Butler's expansionist Budget. In the summer of 1955 speculation broke out against the £ which forced the Government to take unwelcome action. When a £124 million trade deficit for June was announced, the total deficit for six months was £456 million. Mainly as a result of the decision to support transferable sterling in February the reserves became stretched, as foreigners did not want to hold the £ when they could sell it at the fixed parity of $2.80. Surprisingly, the archives do not reveal that the Treasury ever concocted a plan to do away with convertibility, which would have reduced the strain; they believed that cancellation of convertibility would weaken the £ even more, but J. C. R. Dow, a member of the Treasury team of advisers until 1954, wrote later that it would have been 'an easy option'.[1]

The sterling crisis came to a head following the OEEC (Organization for European Economic Co-operation) conference in Paris in July, when the UK delegation asked for a recognition of their right to withdraw from the European Payments Union in the event of sterling becoming fully convertible. In conversation some members of the British delegation talked not only of full convertibility, but of the £ being allowed to float. The Bank of England representatives in Paris, even more than the Treasury ones, talked freely of the advantages and probability of a free float.

Foreigners left Paris convinced that either the £ would float freely or there would be full convertibility with 5 per cent bands around the fixed party of $2.80. With the current UK trade deficit and evidence of soaring demand, the experts felt that the £ would sink by at least 5 per cent and holders of sterling sold heavily. Butler was forced to deny rumours surrounding the £, and on 25 July told the House of Commons that 'the policy of the Government will continue to be the maintenance of exchange parity at 2.80 dollars to the £.'

Butler had an impossible task. He was trying to honour the election promise of an industrial boom at the same time as he had to defend a convertible £ with a hopelessly inadequate gold and currency reserve. Making sterling convertible for non-residents in February 1955 had unforeseen pitfalls. Many British companies were international and could obtain 'non-resident' entitlement to convertibility whenever they wanted. There was not exactly a black market, but resident companies were managing to make their sterling convertible, and without a vast new apparatus of exchange controls it was impossible to stop them. In Basle a kind of club of central bankers met each month to conduct the Bank of International Settlements. Here, whispers abounded about the British intention to float or put wide bands around the parity because of the strain on sterling, and bankers all over the world advised their clients in the summer of 1955 to sell sterling before it sank. Unfortunately, further remarks by various influential Bank of England officials encouraged suspicion that wider bands might be in the pipeline, and there was insufficient liaison between the Treasury and the Bank.[2]

In the lead up to convertibility in 1953 and 1954 foreigners had bought and held sterling happily in the expectation that they would soon be able to convert it into dollars, and during 1953 and 1954 the British reserves received a windfall of at least £250 million worth of gold and dollars from this source. This went dangerously into reverse in February 1955, and to the Government's complete surprise the £ stayed under severe and continuous assault as foreigners took advantage of convertibility.

The Bank of England and the Treasury had convinced Butler that making the £ convertible would restore the strength of the Sterling Area, from which the British economy had benefited so enormously before the war. Their argument ran that sterling was the most widely used international currency, but it would not be attractive to foreigners if it was hobbled by regulations; however once the pre-war freedom of exchanging sterling into dollars or any other currency was restored foreigners would make much more extensive use of it for international trade.

In 1955 it would have been the most effective international currency, and all countries would want to hold large sterling balances to have a supply of ready cash. Thus they would have to buy sterling from Britain, which would being enormous benefits to the City of London and also increase demand for British exports. But above all this, demand for sterling ought to boost Britain's sadly depleted gold and foreign exchange reserves and enable the Conservative Government to follow their declared policy of continuing economic expansion and a sharp rise in living standards. All would have been well if Britain had had sufficient gold and currency reserves to withstand temporary speculation against the £ by supporting sterling in the market. The whole policy broke down because of bad judgment by the Treasury.

Butler's faith in credit control and a high bank rate, which he had expressed in the Budget, soon proved misplaced. The pressure of demand released by income tax cuts could not be curbed by his monetary policy. Imports soared, and the balance of payments showed nasty deficits while the £ stayed under continual pressure.

After the Paris Conference in July 1955 economic controversy in Whitehall centred on convertibility and the advantages and risks of a free floating £. Economic journalists speculated about absolute convertibility soon and a free floating £, and there were informed leaks that the Bank of England was pressing for more flexibility on exchange rates. The impression built up that British official opinion was on balance favourable to floating rates. City editors continually echoed this.

Harold Macmillan, the Foreign Secretary, was never reticent in discussing likely Government policy in knowledgeable circles. He was a convinced floater and made no secret of it. No doubt he contributed to the spate of rumours by his indiscretions. On 21 August he sent to the Prime Minister and Chancellor of the Exchequer a memorandum misleadingly titled 'Dizzy with Success'. The important part was about sterling. He emphatically wanted the Government to 'take the plunge' and float, as the following excerpt reveals:

Exchange

5. Convertibility is the logical end of our policy since 1951. I have never been very happy about it, because I have always had sneaking doubts about the whole 'free trade' policy which we have followed. However, it has certainly worked out pretty well and I am not unduly alarmed by the inflationary situation. I believe it is marginal and can be checked by some, or all, of the means already described. But, with full employment and an expanding economy, there must be some 'give' somewhere. In the years between the wars we took it on the level of employment. We can't do that again, and survive politically. Our currency (having freed commodity markets and decided to support

transferable sterling) is virtually convertible – if you know how, and a lot of people do know how.

6. Having done, or shown that we intend to do, some or all of the things set out in (i)–(v) above, we might well take the plunge. At present, we are in the absurd position that no foreigner will buy sterling against his future commitments until he needs it, because of the fixed rate. Since he doubts whether we can maintain the 2.80 dollar rate, he holds off. He can't lose by doing so, and he may gain. But do *not* devalue, to a *fixed* rate. You won't be able to hold it. Get some flexibility.[3]

In his autobiography *Tides of Fortune*, Macmillan quotes from 'Dizzy with Success' with pride, but does not comment on the pros and cons of a floating £. Probably this is because when Macmillan was Prime Minister and Chancellor of the Exchequer he was under strong pressure to float the £ but always resisted the proposition.

Ten days later, on 2 September 1955, Peter Thorneycroft, President of the Board of Trade, and like Macmillan soon to be Chancellor, 'put certain thoughts into the pool'. He was against a floating rate because he thought it could only be supported by import controls; instead he wanted a strong monetary policy with bank rate raised to a 'realistic level'; abolition of the bread subsidy, rent control and the investment allowance, and reduced state spending on coal, including cuts in atomic energy which some of his colleagues thought should be exempt. He also wanted a capital gains tax. Thorneycroft was advocating policies which appealed to the Treasury.[4]

In July the Chancellor asked the banks to restrict their lending even further, and it was announced that investment in the nationalized industries would be pruned. Credit and hire purchase restrictions were strengthened. The price of coal was raised by 18 per cent – partly to fund the Coal Board's losses and partly to mop up excess consumer spending.

The Cabinet discussed the state of the economy on 28 July when Butler told his colleagues that 'much of the recent pressure on sterling could be attributed to the rumours arising out of the Paris discussions, that we intended to introduce a floating rate of exchange'.[5] He went on to state that the anti-inflationary policy would be continued during the recess, and that he would not make an important statement on exchange policy at the meeting of the International Monetary Fund fixed for early September in Istanbul. On 15 August Butler told the Cabinet that 'the economic situation continued to be somewhat uneasy'; and on 26 August that there was 'no cause for alarm though the time of year was approaching when the balance of trade and payments were seasonably unfavourable'. He thought that the abolition of the bread subsidy should be considered, that increases in bank rate should be held in reserve, and that there should be no further moves towards convertibility. The Prime Minister agreed with Butler about a higher bank rate and convertibility and wanted a comprehensive plan ready for Parliament. Other points raised were that work on some large Government buildings should be postponed, and steps taken to make savings more attractive to small investors.

According to the Cabinet Minutes of 26 August the view was expressed that 'the Chancellor's present plan was not sufficiently balanced', and that, if house rents were increased, the bread subsidy abolished and reductions made in the subsidy on school meals, further restraints should be put on profits and dividends. The capital gains tax proposed in Thorneycroft's memorandum was discussed, as were compulsory limitation of dividends and a withholding tax on the Canadian model. Butler told the Cabinet that all these would be extremely difficult to put into effective operation.[6]

Butler reported what had been said to Bridges, Permanent Secretary to the Treasury, who dictated for his Treasury colleagues that the majority of the Cabinet were against CGT and thought that the balance of the package deal was not fairly held ('Rather a bore this' was Bridges's comment). On bread he said 'We may have to leave it out' because Eden had said there would be much opposition; the Chancellor had made it clear he was willing to do so. Bridges went on that an increased tax on beer was mentioned and supported by Macmillan, and that everyone was keen on lower taxes on savings.[7]

Eden and Butler toyed with the idea that a swingeing increase in profits tax should be announced before Parliament reassembled. Sir H. Hancock, head of the Inland Revenue, and Mr Fiennes, parliamentary counsel, replied to Bridges's inquiries that they were strongly against this and that it should be announced to Parliament only, as otherwise it would be resented by MPs. The Treasury were not impressed by the Cabinet's note about the Canadian withholding tax, which would have meant a double tax – one on net profits and another on dividends distributed. According to the Treasury minute the Cabinet had discussed it without a proper understanding of what a withholding tax was.[8]

Eden now became jittery and began to badger Butler over details of the corrective package, and this may well be the reason why in his autobiography Butler criticized Eden for interfering with his Ministers. The Treasury files reveal Eden's meddling. Eden insisted on seeing Butler on 7 September, just before he left for the International Monetary Fund conference in Istanbul. The Prime Minister now wanted to recall Parliament as early as possible, but Butler insisted that he could not cancel his trip to Istanbul because that 'would really cause a stir and do a great deal of harm on the exchange front'. So they agreed on the recall of Parliament on 27 September, with an emergency Budget which would have to be concluded before 30 September because of the October Party Conferences.

During Butler's absence in Turkey, Eden asked the Treasury on 9 September whether everything was ready for the recall of Parliament 'at a moment's notice'. He was afraid that Hugh Gaitskell, the Shadow Chancellor, might seize the initiative and ask for an early recall of Parliament before the Government had made any economic announcement, and he wanted to be 'ready to move instantly if any rumour reached him or the Chief Whip'.

Eden's interference in the details of the proposed economic package was hectic and not appreciated by the Treasury, as the following minute by Louis Petch, dated 1 September and marked 'Top Secret', shows:

Sir Edward Bridges

c.c. Sir Leslie Rowan
Sir Robert Hall

I had the Chancellor on the telephone at lunch-time, reporting the gist of a call he had had earlier from the P.M. It is important in that it reveals that there is still quite a job of education to be done with the P.M., and a great deal clearly hangs on the effectiveness of Sir R. Hall's commentary on his recent minute.

According to the Chancellor the P.M. is ready to accept 'anything which is necessary in order to help exports'. Such elements in the purchase tax package as do so should, therefore, get through. But the Prime Minister remains strongly opposed to 'impositions for their own sake' because of the effect on the cost of living; this bodes ill for the bulk of the purchase tax plan and for the cuts in transfer payments (bread subsidy, school meals, etc.)

Further than this, the P.M. put forward the idea of making the 'package' a mixed one by putting in something to reduce the cost of living. The proposal he mentioned was a reduction in the duty on beer.

Unless the P.M. can be convinced that we have got to take some of the money out of the consumer's pocket, it may well be better, as I think you felt this morning, to put the bread subsidy and the other things forward as cuts in Government expenditure rather than attacks on excessive demand.[9]

Eden had become alarmed at the runs on the £, and he was determined to maintain the expansion of the economy which he had so eloquently promised in his election campaign. Probably all the economic measures could have been introduced in the House of Commons by way of ordinary business, but the Prime Minister wanted a Budget to show dramatically that he had put his house in order. In a minute to Butler dated 30 August, Eden wrote: 'We must put the battle against inflation before anything else. After all, if we win out the other problems, for example the gold and dollar reserves, will take care of themselves.' However, Eden only imperfectly understood the economic crisis, and the impossibility of combining convertibility of sterling with all-out expansion while too high wage settlements were causing inflation. In various telephone conversations in early September Eden had told Butler that he was worried about the effect of purchase tax, and wanted detailed examples of the sort of things which would be affected. He told Butler that he still toyed with the idea of including in the package a reduction in beer duty, and was unhappy that we no longer had control over building, saying: 'Anyone who wishes can now build a cinema and it may be possible to restore building controls on projects over £250,000.'[10] Butler clearly did not appreciate this interference over details just as he was about to go to Istanbul, and anyhow the effects of the measures for which the Prime Minister expressed his personal preferences would have been minimal.

Butler reported the talk to his Treasury advisers on 7 September, playing down the Prime Minister's fears and adding that he had received a letter from Roy Harrod, the distinguished Oxford economist, taking the line that he need not worry 'unduly' about the internal situation and certainly not to the extent of an autumn Budget, and that most of the present troubles would be remedied if the Chancellor were to announce now the spread which he had in mind for the sterling exchange rate after convertibility. It was a cogent argument that once the £ floated it would remove most of the worries amongst holders of sterling. Butler added to his advisers that Harrod had not caused him to change his mind, 'but that he felt the weight of the responsibility he was carrying'.[11]

Butler's final note to Eden on 8 September, before leaving for Turkey, was: 'Decision on bread subsidy saving £40 million (effect on cost of living index of 1.33 points) should be taken on my return. Distributed profits tax should be increased from 22½% to 30% and perhaps bank rate increased simultaneously with recall of the House of Commons.'

On 26 August the Cabinet had suggested that steps might be taken to make savings more attractive to small investors. Lord Mackintosh, chairman of the National Savings Committee, expressed the view that 'small savers are not interested in yields but are deterred by the fall in the value of money.' Eden had asked Butler for a report on what measures he contemplated in the Budget to stimulate National Savings. The Treasury reply in Butler's absence stated that new forms of small savings were not required, 'the existing media being adequate', and repeated Mackintosh's view that small savers were not interested in yields but were concerned about stopping the fall in the value of money. Henry Brooke, Financial Secretary, wrote on these lines to Eden on 12 September, making it clear that the Chancellor did not intend to include any measures for savers in his forthcoming Budget, and that all that could be done was to advance the date of the new issue of Defence Bonds.[12]

Eden's reaction to Brooke's memorandum was to instruct David Pitblado, his private secretary, to write to Bridges the next day, 13 September, saying that the Prime Minister was 'much disappointed about savings because from conversations he had with Butler, and from Butler's minutes, he had understood that some positive savings proposals would be brought forward' and that there would be 'widespread disappointment' in Parliament if nothing was proposed on savings. He wanted positive proposals to be ready for consideration when the Chancellor returned. Pitblado added that Eden wanted reduced travel allowances and a scheme for restraining large buildings as part of the package, and suggested that Bridges went over the ground again.

Bridges replied on 14 September that an income tax rebate on life assurance would 'give away quite a lot of money without necessarily attracting a very large volume of new saving', that he had 'recoiled fairly soon, rebuffed by the difficulties and complexities' from income tax relief on savings, and that the only practical proposal for 27 September was to announce a new issue of Defence Bonds.[13]

The Inland Revenue had reported that giving concessions on life assurance of £6 million a year would involve 400,000 man hours or extra overtime of five hours a week for six weeks in October and November, making a working week of 55½ hours for six weeks in late autumn. 'This would impose very severe strain on staff physique and staff relations.' The Prime Minister was crying for the moon over savings as far as the Treasury and Inland Revenue were concerned, and anyway, even if his wishes had been met the net result could not have made any real difference to the sterling crisis.

As a result of Pitblado's letter, while Butler was still in Istanbul Bridges replied to the Prime Minister in a long note on 14 September: 'I am sorry you are dissatisfied with the report sent to you on 12 September. As instructed by you I have gone over the ground again from the point of view of finding what proposal about savings could be announced in Parliament as part of the "package". There is, I think, only one proposal, which is a clear starter, Defence Bonds.' He went on: 'For the rest, I am afraid I have nothing to report which will give you much satisfaction, but I hope when you have read what I have to say you will feel that the obstacles to doing anything in the Autumn Budget are real obstacles.'

The next day, the 15th, Cairncross, Eden's private secretary, telephoned to say that Eden had read Bridges's note and was 'dissatisfied' with it and the Treasury proposals on savings. 'Advancing the date of the next issue of Defence Bonds was not at all his idea of a satisfactory solution.' He pointed out that 'other measures were going to bring in a lot of extra money, so why should not some of it be used to give relief (e.g. life insurance?)?' He wanted to talk about it to Bridges later in the day. When they met, Eden told Bridges that he did not want to pursue the idea of abolishing the bread subsidy unless compensation could be given to those most seriously affected. Bridges's reply was that the increased cost was very small, on average 5d a week or an increase in the retail price index of 1 per cent, which the economy could take in its stride, with average earnings rising by 13s per week, and that National Assistance scales could be increased by 4s a week for a married couple.

Bridges showed Eden a minute by Sir Robert Hall which expressed the opinion that restoring people's confidence in the value of savings by a successful deflationary movement would be more likely to encourage savings than anything else. Yet right up to ten days before the Budget Eden would not give up the fight for tax relief on savings, and discussed it with Butler as late as 17 October, when he said he would give way, provided the maximum holding of savings certificates was raised from £750 to £1000. He was fiddling while Rome burned.

While Butler was away Bridges had also written to the Prime Minister on 12 September saying that it was impracticable to put controls on buildings of over £250,000, and that the Government ought to hold in reserve any decision to reimpose specific controls on building projects. Eden discussed this note with Macmillan on 13 September, and wanted controls on buildings; they were going behind Butler's back. Macmillan sent Eden a note saying that the

Government ought to ask insurance companies and banks not to lend on new building projects, but Macmillan's plea was shot down by William Strath of the Treasury, who pointed out in a memorandum that the great bulk of new building was taking place in London, and that a substantial proportion had been started and could not be left unfinished. 'The amount therefore which is capable of being postponed must be comparatively small and by itself could make only a trifling contribution to an anti-inflation drive; as regards the other types of buildings mentioned by the Foreign Secretary there are only 3 new cinemas being built in the country.'[14]

Bridges delivered this message to the Prime Minister and received support from Nigel Birch, Minister of Works, who minuted to Eden on 15 September that he agreed with the Treasury and that we should restrain new building in the public sector and 'leave private building to the credit squeeze'.

None of Eden's horses had become runners; fortunately when Butler returned from Istanbul the Prime Minister was less jittery. However, the following memorandum from Bridges to the Chancellor, dated 21 September and marked 'Top Secret', is proof that the Treasury were seriously worried about the crisis over the £, and wanted to cover up what they considered an imminent economic crisis.

The Timing of the Package

1. This is a matter of such importance that I have thought it right, after our discussion this evening and further reflection, to let you have my views in writing. I have not shown this to my colleagues, but I am sure that they agree.

2. We have in any case to face a difficult situation made more difficult by the conjunction of the date of publication of the September gold and dollar loss, the announcement of our inability to go to 90% liberalisation in Europe, your Mansion House speech and the Party conference.

3. At the moment you have the initiative; the exchanges are quiet. The recall of Parliament, after Istanbul, will be interpreted by foreign opinion (and it is this that can break our reserves) as a brave and resolute act and as a logical sequel of your policy. It has the great merit that it leaves the position at risk for the shortest possible time, draws the sting of the September gold and dollar figures, and gives a realistic basis to your Mansion House speech and the Party conferences.

4. By delay
    (i) you lose the initiative and appear to act under force majeure;
    (ii) you prolong the period of risk.

5. We are dealing here with confidence – an incalculable factor. We

cannot predict how it will act, but we know that it tends to work to extremes. I am bound to advise you that, to allow the September figures to appear without having made clear beforehand the corrective measures which you propose to take, runs great risks. At the worst, there could be very great losses of reserves, and a marked deterioration which would certainly ensure that the package was less effective – perhaps insufficient. At best, we believe that the position would continue to get worse.

6. Delay therefore runs risks with the economy – risks which I admit seem to be unjustifiable.

7. If, however, the Cabinet decide to delay, then it is best to say nothing at present about an Autumn Budget, and to defer any announcement until nearer the time when it can be judged in the light of developments.[15]

Butler took Bridges's warnings seriously, and at the Cabinet meeting on 2 September repeated some of Bridges's words. At Istanbul Butler had asserted categorically that the value of the £ at $2.80 would be defended, and there would be neither a floating rate nor further moves to convertibility. He pointed out that the September gold and dollar losses would be serious, and said that the immediate recall of Parliament would take the sting out of them and be interpreted by foreign opinion as a logical sequel to the declaration he had made at Istanbul. The Prime Minister said that public opinion at home was not prepared for such a step, and that foreigners might infer that we were on the point of collapse. Majority opinion in the Cabinet was against recall, and Eden had clearly recovered his nerve, which he had almost lost at the beginning of the month. Budget Day was set for 26 October, with a normal recall of Parliament.

On 20 October the Cabinet had their Budget meeting. Butler told them he would cut down local government and state industry capital spending and increase purchase tax sharply, and it was 'for consideration' whether the profits tax should be raised to 27½ per cent to yield £38 millions or to 30 per cent to yield £57 millions.

Butler also emphasized that the bread subsidy was 'economically indefensible' and 'its removal would be taken as a sign that the Government were determined to check inflation'. Eden would not have it. He said that an increase in the price of bread would be represented as unfair, and insisted that Butler discuss this measure with him further and submit his final proposals on all matters at the next Cabinet meeting.[16]

On 25 October the Cabinet was told by Butler that the bread

subsidy would be kept, though he remained of the opinion that it should be abolished; profits tax was only to be increased by 5 per cent, and there would be no change in the foreign travel allowance. Eden told the Cabinet that 'the delay in introducing the Government's measures to deal with the economic situation had been justified' since it had avoided an atmosphere of crisis and allowed sterling to be strengthened by the assurances which the Chancellor had given in Istanbul. Eden had interfered mercilessly with Butler over the details of the package; he was to find it more dangerous to treat in the same way his next Chancellor, Harold Macmillan.

While Eden was fussing over the inessential details of the package he was planning to replace Butler by Macmillan. In his autobiography Eden is unenlightening as to why he wanted this change. Not so Macmillan, who devotes nine pages to it. On 23 September Eden asked Macmillan if he would move from the Foreign Office to the Treasury, telling him he had suggested it the day before to Butler, who had agreed. According to Macmillan, Eden felt that Butler after 'four years of slogging work with many ups and downs had become depressed', and had also 'suffered a grievous personal loss through the death of his wife, so that he had temporarily lost his grip'. If Macmillan is correct Eden had lost faith in Butler and did not feel he was sufficiently resolute to tackle the economic crisis. There is evidence, however, that Butler had not 'lost his grip'.

Sir Leslie Rowan accompanied Butler to Istanbul, and on 18 September sent a long, handwritten letter to Bridges in which he wrote that at the IMF the Chancellor

> was much the most notable figure, and, in his own language, he has certainly regained any lost initiative in the field of international economic policy. The Secretary of the US Treasury is, of course, listened to; but it is *our* policy they want to hear; it is Butler whom they respect and will follow. And he has done an excellent job and created the best impression – by frankly saying that the UK was too inflationary and he was going to put it right – by the classical measures of internal policy not by import cuts. This goes equally for the Commonwealth; we had an excellent meeting yesterday.[17]

Andrew Shonfield, then the leading economic journalist in London, also accompanied the Chancellor to this IMF meeting in Turkey and recorded that he was astonished at his jauntiness. Thorneycroft, who had plenty of opportunity to watch Butler at close quarters, told the author that Butler was no different in the autumn of 1955, after the death of his wife, from any other time. According to Thorneycroft the able and intelligent Butler was also always 'wishy washy, indecisive and weak', and that was why he put up with so much meddling by Eden in the autumn Budget of 1955.[18]

The Prime Minister wanted Macmillan to give him an immediate reply about accepting the Treasury. With strange impertinence Macmillan refused to give a decision for a month, and then only accepted on terms which amounted to insolence. Clearly, Macmillan now had his eye on 10 Downing Street: having witnessed at close quarters Eden's tension and nervousness, he had probably decided that the Prime Minister was putting himself under such pressure that he would not be able to stand the strain much longer. Macmillan wrote that he would only move provided that Butler did not remain Deputy Prime Minister, adding: 'Incidentally this post does not exist constitutionally and was invented by Churchill to suit quite exceptional circumstances.' This was a red herring, because there is no written constitution, only precedent. Eden had operated for a long period as Deputy Prime Minister during the war, and Butler had been Deputy Prime Minister in Churchill's last period and during Eden's eight months of premiership. Eden must have been sorely tempted to rid himself of Macmillan, but weakly he accepted his terms, although he insisted that Butler should preside in Cabinet when he, the Prime Minister, was absent. So Butler became Leader of the House, and Macmillan Chancellor of the Exchequer, on 23 December 1955.[19]

Macmillan believed that Eden wanted the change so that he could have foreign policy more under his own control. This is almost certainly true. Macmillan was toying with a different approach to Europe, to which Eden was entirely opposed. Eden secured a compliant Foreign Secretary in Selwyn Lloyd, but in Macmillan he had a Chancellor whom he could not boss around as he had done Butler. Indeed, when Eden wanted to refuse to allow Macmillan to abolish the bread subsidy, instead of complying, like Butler, Macmillan threatened resignation. There is no doubt that Eden regretted accepting Macmillan's humiliating terms instead of letting him go to the backbenches.

In his Budget on 26 October Butler increased purchase tax by one-fifth and included certain goods previously exempt; tax on distributed profits was raised from 22½ per cent to 27½ per cent; lending for capital projects to local government and nationalized industries was curbed; the housing subsidy was reduced; and telephone charges were increased. This produced savings of £112 million in a full year. There was no need for a Budget – it could all have been done by Regulation. The greater part of the tax cuts of April were removed, and Butler was violently attacked by Gaitskell, the Shadow Chancellor, for having introduced an electioneering Budget six months before. However, Butler and Eden performed well in debate when under attack. Butler's forthright declaration at Istanbul that 'we' would not devalue the £ probably did more to strengthen it than the October Budget.

With considerable reluctance Macmillan left the Foreign Office and shouldered the nation's economic problems. Immediately Eden sent him a memorandum with ideas for action on the economic front. As Prime Minister he was always worrying about the economic situation, and wanted Macmillan to consult him continually. But Macmillan wanted to steer his ship on his own, and Eden found in him a far less co-operative Chancellor than Butler. 'A British Chancellor', wrote Dow, 'is in a position of unique strength among the financial Ministers of the world . . . he has barely to consult his colleagues, except the Prime Minister himself, about his Budget.' Unfortunately, Macmillan and Eden were to clash hard and frequently. To Eden's first memorandum Macmillan replied that there was 'a great deal to absorb, and I would hesitate to give you a considered view', and asked to be forgiven if he refrained from comment for a little while.

At the end of 1955 the balance of payments gave certain grounds for concern, and Britain had suffered some loss of reserves; this was due to strong home demand arising from full employment and higher wages. Inflation stayed at a low level. Butler's 'pots and pans' Budget in October appeared to be having the necessary corrective effects, and according to Dow 'though corrective measures seemed necessary, the atmosphere was not one of crisis'.[20]

On 29 January Eden, on board the *Queen Elizabeth*, wrote to Macmillan that he wanted 'one grand Budget' in place of last year's several economic statements, 'culminating in the Autumn Budget'. Macmillan's reply was truculent:

Of course it would be nice if we could do everything in a single operation. But I am sure we can't. . . . We must act soon for three reasons:

First, from the broad political angle, because the country will forgive mistakes but not inaction. Everyone is expecting speedy action.

Secondly, from the narrower House of Commons point of view because there is great pressure from the Opposition for a debate on the economic situation. We can't hold this till the Budget, even if we bring the Budget forward to March.

Thirdly, because of the broad financial and economic needs of the country we must not lose time.

We could theoretically have a March Budget.

Macmillan went on to say that a March Budget coming after the (1955) autumn one would be generally regarded as a crisis Budget; therefore he proposed that he should make a statement on 15 February setting out proposals for bread and milk subsidies cuts; this to be followed by a 'possible' increase in bank rate from 4½ per cent to 5½ per cent, and 'a Budget on 10 April (?) by which time he hoped to be far enough away from the bread and milk row'. Macmillan added that he hoped to avoid 'import controls or other physical controls', but was not hopeful about tax cuts. Macmillan's last words were ominous for Eden: 'I must ask you to accept this programme without which I could not feel that I was doing my duty to you and the country.'[21]

Eden was rigidly opposed to cuts in the bread and milk subsidies and wanted to defer a decision until the spring Budget, mainly because it would raise the cost of living and have an adverse effect on important wage negotiations, particularly those of the engineers. Macmillan insisted that a statement must be made on 15 February, and felt so strongly that he threatened to resign if he did not have his way. He wrote to Eden on 11 February, as soon as the Prime Minister returned from America:

> I don't want to appear to threaten the Cabinet; I have never tried such tactics in all my service. But I would not like you to be under any misapprehension and afterwards perhaps blame me for not letting you know the depth of my feeling. I must tell you frankly that, if I cannot have your confidence and that of my colleagues in handling this problem which you have entrusted to me in the way that seems to me essential, I should not feel justified in proposing measures which seem insufficient for their purpose. Nor should I be any good to you and the Cabinet in such circumstances. One can compromise about minor points of policy that come up all the time in Cabinets, but I would not be any good if I were trying to defend policies in which I had no belief.[22]

Macmillan took a pessimistic view about the prospects for the economy, particularly over the reserves and the strain on the £. It may be that he had an innate streak of financial caution deriving from his Highland ancestors, but his advisers, particularly Bridges, influenced him to gloom. The Treasury had been shocked and chastened by their failure to warn Cripps in time of possible disaster for the £ in 1949, and were determined not to be responsible for another similar forced devaluation. Bridges wrote a report for Macmillan, which the Chancellor incorporated into a memorandum for the Cabinet on 5 January:

> It is clear therefore we are faced with the necessity of taking further immediate action over a wide field of a more drastic character than has hitherto seemed necessary. Time is running out. . . . Gold and dollar reserves are therefore approaching the critical level which is between 2,000 and 1,500 million dollars, at which experience shows that speculation against sterling can be expected. When this happens the reserves themselves are in danger of falling so low that confidence in our ability to maintain the value of sterling may be lost.

On 18 February a Treasury report on the balance of payments stated: 'We have used up our time and run down the reserves and have now little room for manœuvre. We could expect a position of great gravity by the summer or early autumn . . . deflation is needed.'[23]

In conversation Macmillan used these Treasury arguments with his colleagues to justify his resignation threat, and told Butler, Heathcoat Amory and Thorneycroft on 14 February that if the Prime Minister would not 'give in' on bread and milk 'he must find another Chancellor'. Macmillan's colleagues persuaded Eden to offer a compromise – to take 1d off the 2½d bread subsidy immediately, and the rest later; milk subsidy was to end in July. Right up till the last moment Macmillan's resignation was in doubt. Macmillan relates in his memoirs that he had drafted his letter of resignation and there is a copy in his archives. His statement was due on 16 February, and the day before he had had discussions with Bridges and the Governor of the Bank of England, C. F. Cobbold, as to which would do most harm, 'his resignation or a compromise'. The Governor told him that his resignation would cause a panic in the City.

In his memoirs Macmillan records that after this talk he was content because he had been given 'four-fifths of his demands', and the next day he made his statement to the House about the bread and milk subsidies; raised bank rate from 4½ per cent to 5½ per cent; made some marginal cuts in state spending, and tightened hire purchase.[24]

Macmillan relates the tale of this minor economic contest with Eden with some pride, but wrote nothing in his memoirs about two further clashes concerning far graver decisions. The first was over defence expenditure on aeroplanes. On 23 March Macmillan minuted to the Prime Minister:

> . . . We also know that it is defence expenditure which has broken our backs. We also know that we get no defence from the defence expenditure. When the story of the aeroplanes finally comes out it will be the greatest tragedy, if not scandal, in our history.
>
> The only way that I can see by which we could restore our economy is by really getting down to the defence problem. The Minister of Defence and I sent you a minute on this on 20th March which no doubt you are now considering. What I should like to be able to do is to renew in the Budget Speech the declaration that I made in February that although the estimates for the year were agreed we should go on seeking for economies. I would like to go further and to make some precise reference to a new approach to the whole defence problem. This would hold the situation and give us a little time. But if I cannot do that I think I shall have to abandon all ideas of giving some reliefs in the Budget and content myself with a swingeing increase of taxation. I am wondering whether we could have a talk with the Minister of Defence before you go for your holiday.[25]

Macmillan felt strongly that spending on the RAF must be cut, and in his memoirs wrote that he was exceedingly doubtful of the value of Fighter Command in Britain, however valuable such squadrons might be overseas. In his diary for 29 January 1956 he put: 'We go on wasting immense [sums] on the design, development and production of "fighters".'

Eden replied to Macmillan's minute:

> I should like to have a talk with you on Monday evening . . . I do not think it would be useful to talk then about the long term shape of the defence programme. There is still much to be done before we can reach any useful conclusion about that. And I do not see how we could say anything responsible which could help you with the Budget which you have to introduce as early as 17 April.

When they met on 26 March it was *à deux* after dinner; there is no record of their conversation, but Eden refused out of hand to agree to the defence cuts. Later he dictated the words Macmillan was to use in his Budget speech on 17 April, which were that the Prime Minister and Minister of Defence were undertaking a comprehensive study of the whole programme which he (the Chancellor) felt sure would produce 'worthwhile savings'.[26]

Having been refused his defence cuts Macmillan fell back on the 'swingeing increases in taxation' referred to in his note to the Prime Minister of 23 March. He decided that in order to defend the £ the 6d reduction in income tax made twelve months before should be rescinded in the April Budget. He even discussed the matter with Butler, who was sensitive to the issue because this direct contradiction of his income tax cuts would have made a nonsense of his whole economic policy.

On 5 April Macmillan sent the Prime Minister the following revealing minute, which finds no place in either the Avon or Macmillan memoirs:

The present view of my advisers is that the crisis will come between August and November. I would say that on present form the betting is pretty heavy odds on compulsory devaluation. Most foreigners are sceptical even now of whether we can avoid it, although our recent measures have shown a determination to risk unpopularity in order to save the £. . . .

The Government must do one of two things. It must either make impressive reductions in expenditure – of the order of £100 million or £150 million, or it must increase taxation. . . . I propose, therefore, to add the following:

Bread	£10 m.
Tobacco (2d on packet of cigarettes)	£27 m.
Income Tax 6d on standard rate	£74 m.
Income Tax 3d on reduced rate	£33 m.
	£144 m.

In my view this demonstration of absolute determination to overcome the inflation would have a great effect abroad. It would also have a large – perhaps decisive – psychological effect at home. . . .

What will be the political effect?

1) The Party in the House of Commons will be shocked at first.

2) The Party supporters in the constituencies will be depressed – we shall lose some subscriptions and some members. But they will recover and may even draw strength in due course from sense of pride that we have shown such resolution.

I must not disguise from you that this is the real test for the Government and the Party. If we live up to it, you and your administration will earn first respect and then renewed confidence. No personal considerations or national hesitations should stand in the way.[27]

Eden refused point-blank to agree to increases in income tax to reverse Butler's spring Budget of twelve months before, and

Macmillan accepted the decision. There were no income tax changes in the Budget.

It is strange that after Macmillan had threatened to resign over the comparatively minor bread and milk subsidies, he later toed the line over major decisions about defence and income tax. Eden called his bluff, having decided that he would rather accept Macmillan's resignation than suffer another humiliation. Faced with the Prime Minister's firm line over major aspects of economic policy Macmillan must have decided that discretion was the better part of valour, because he knew Eden would let him go.

In his Budget speech Macmillan announced with a flourish that he had something 'new' for the saver through a state lottery – a Premium Bond on which the saver could not lose. Harold Wilson described it as 'a squalid raffle – hundreds of thousands would be outraged'. Henry Brooke, Financial Secretary, declared that Premium Bonds were 'a dazzling plan for savings'. The wind was taken out of Macmillan's sails by letters to *The Times* from Professor George Trevelyan, the Cambridge historian, and Professor Heathcote Garrod, the former Oxford Professor of Poetry, who revealed that state lotteries were nothing new in Britain.

Macmillan also said: 'Monetary policy cannot go it alone – you cannot restrict credit without high interest rates', although he had been told that if he appointed a committee he might find out how to do it. It has taken recent Conservative Governments many years to find this out, although Macmillan and his Treasury knights knew it in 1956. Macmillan was able to say that the economy was running at a high level with more jobs than men to fill them; more orders than industry could meet, easy profits and rising costs. Yet Macmillan was not happy because inflation, running at 3 per cent, was a threat to the value of the £: he curtailed Government spending by £100 million, a large sum for those days. But then Britain had the thankless task of being banker to the sterling area – a large part of the world – and this was a millstone around her neck.

After the February measures the April Budget changes were minor. Tobacco duty and profits tax were increased by around £30 million, and against this relief was given on national insurance contributions to the self-employed. Eden was clearly justified in his preference in January for 'one good Budget' in place of the February statement.

4

Messina and the Common Market
1955–6

EDEN WAS PRIME Minister during a period when momentous decisions had to be made about Britain's future association with the
other countries of western Europe. Like Attlee and Churchill before
him, he shied away from any European institution which required
supra-nationality and pooling of sovereignty. The result was that in
1955 Britain turned down the invitation to join the Common Market,
and in the process so antagonized the participants that they rejected
out of hand Britain's proposals for a European Free Trade Area
when Macmillan succeeded Eden as Prime Minister. Eden's priority
was Britain's special relationship with America and her position as
the head of the Commonwealth; although he wanted Britain to play a
key role in European post-war institutions he did not share the
mounting enthusiasm for federalism and supra-nationalism in western Europe, which came to a crescendo in the early fifties.

From 1948 onwards the countries of western Europe which had
been defeated by Hitler at the start of the war had started their own
organizations for international co-operation; the Brussels Treaty
organization in March 1948, followed by the Organization for European Economic Co-operation just a month later, and by the Council of Europe in 1949. These did not involve any supra-nationality
and Britain played her full part. On the continent of Europe there
was popular support for a Federal or United Europe with pooling of
sovereignty; it had become an emotional issue after being discussed
widely in the closing stages of the war. The British Government,
although enthusiastic for the OEEC, which administered American
economic aid for Europe under the Marshall Plan, tended to be
dismissive of a united Europe, and deprecated any proposals involving supra-national institutions or a European customs union which
might be difficult to reconcile with the existing Commonwealth
preference tariff system. In contrast the French politicians Jean

Monnet and Robert Schuman, and the Italian Alberto Spinelli, were enthusiasts for a Federal Europe with common social and economic policies and a customs unions.

Their idea was that Europe should be a third great power of comparable standing to the USA and USSR. This had little attraction for the majority of post-war British politicians. Winning the war and liberating western Europe had left a feeling of triumph and a fatal illusion of power. The close wartime partnership with America was highly prized, and a major object of British foreign policy was to preserve this 'special relationship'. In the immediate post-war years Britain was still the third world power – albeit puny in relation to the USSR and USA, and did not want to share this role with the European countries which it had delivered from Nazi tyranny.

Few were ready for Britain to join supra-national European institutions which would limit Britain's freedom of action and impinge on the important relationships with America and the Commonwealth. Nor was there at that time much confidence in the skill of the continental countries in handling their economic problems. On the other hand the Six – the French, Italians, the Benelux countries and the Germans – thought increasingly that those of their economic problems which were difficult to solve on the national plane would be more tractable on a European plane. 'Europe' had a different meaning on the Continent from the one it had in Britain.

On 9 May 1950 the French Government suddenly and unexpectedly launched the Schuman Plan, named after their Foreign Secretary. It contained dramatic proposals for pooling the coal, iron and steel resources of France and Germany and of any other European countries willing to join in putting them under the control of an independent high authority. In October came proposals for a European Defence Community, which involved placing each country's armed forces under a supra-national authority and bringing West Germany into NATO. These two proposals were the watershed for Britain, who stood aloof because of her distaste for yielding any sovereignty to supra-national European institutions.

The initial reaction of the Foreign Secretary, Ernest Bevin, to the Schuman Plan on 10 May 1950 was that it was 'difficult to see how British iron and steel industry under public ownership could be integrated with the continental combine', and a Committee of Ministers chaired by Attlee concluded that it showed 'a regrettable tendency to move away from the conception of the Atlantic Community and in the direction of European federation'. The only senior Cabinet Minister in favour was Stafford Cripps, Chancellor of the

Exchequer. He told Monnet on 15 May that, although he realized his proposal might lead to political federation, in his personal opinion the UK should accept to negotiate at once on the basis proposed by the French. As Cripps had been at the ministerial meeting five days before, this volte-face was a surprise to the civil servants. Roger Makins, later Lord Sherfield, who accompanied Cripps, minuted: 'This plunge by the Chancellor took Edwin [Sir Edwin Plowden, economic adviser to the Treasury, was also there] completely by surprise' and the Foreign Secretary 'must be told of it'.[2] Unfortunately for Attlee both Cripps and Bevin were suffering from fatal illnesses. Shortly afterwards they both had to resign and without Cripps the Labour Government spurned the ambitious and wide-reaching French plans. On 7 June Attlee told the French Ambassador in London that it was impossible to sign 'a blank cheque', that because of the importance of iron and steel to Britain's economy 'this country could not consent to hand over to irresponsible persons such wide powers over essential matters', and that there was already great pressure from the Commons to control such organizations as the Coal Board even though they had been set up as 'independent bodies'. This was slamming the door. A revealing comment from Bevin on his sick bed in the London Clinic was 'We cannot buy a pig in a poke.' The Labour Party were not going to agree to federal control of the recently nationalized British steel, and the French insisted that countries participating in the Schuman negotiations must accept in advance the 'principle' of removing coal, iron and steel from national control and putting them under a 'supra-national' high authority.[3]

Monnet tried to bypass the Foreign Office and negotiate direct with Plowden at the Treasury – obviously feeling from his talk to Cripps that the Treasury were more sympathetic to his plan. This was resented by the Foreign Office. With Cripps absent on holiday in France, on 2 June the Attlee Government formally decided not to take part in the conference which was to draft the Treaty bringing the European Coal and Steel Community (ECSC) into existence in April 1951, the signatories being Italy, France, West Germany and the Benelux countries. When Cripps heard of the decision he demurred and wanted to open the door again by having talks in Paris with Monnet on his journey home; the Foreign Office objected, and Attlee would not allow it.[4]

In October 1950 René Pleven, the French Prime Minister, outlined to the French Assembly his plan for a European army within the European Defence Community (EDC). It was not just a plan for

achieving the rearmament of Germany, but a military counterpart to
the Schuman Plan with a European Minister of Defence responsible
to a European Assembly. The idea had been given great encouragement by Churchill at the Council of Europe at The Hague in August
1950, when Churchill even accepted an amendment adopted by the
Assembly envisaging a European Defence Minister with responsibility for the army. The Labour Government firmly rejected the
Pleven Plan in November 1950.

When the Conservatives under Churchill returned to power on 26
October 1951, there were high hopes that with the change in
Government Britain would now participate in the Schuman Plan and
the European army. On 26 and 27 June 1950, during what amounted
to a vote of censure on the Attlee Government for refusing to enter
the negotiations over the Schuman Plan, Eden had said in the
Commons that subject to safeguards 'we would be prepared to enter
discussions as a result of which a high authority would be set up
whose decision would be binding upon the nations who were parties
to the agreement'. Churchill said in the same debate: 'Without
hesitation we are prepared to consider and, if convinced, to accept
the abrogation of national sovereignty provided we are satisfied with
the conditions and safeguards . . . national sovereignty is not inviol-
able.'

High hopes in Europe aroused by such words were quickly
dashed. In office, like Labour, the Conservatives were not prepared
to yield power to the supra-national institutions desired by Europeans; Churchill and Eden ate the words they had uttered in
Opposition. Within three days of becoming Foreign Secretary Eden,
without consulting his colleagues, minuted on a Foreign Office
internal note about a supra-national political authority: 'I am against
this.'

On 28 November Eden held a press conference in Rome. To the
great disappointment of the EDC powers he stated that British units
and formations would not participate in a European army, although
there might be some other form of association. On 6 December
Churchill made an equally negative statement to the House of
Commons.

On the 30th, when reports came to the Foreign Office that there
had been discontent with the British attitude to the Schuman Plan
and the European army at the Assembly of the Council of Europe
at Strasbourg, Eden minuted: 'Strasbourg was always a misfortune;
it is now nearly a calamity.'

Early in December, in a memorandum to all overseas Embassies,

Eden defined the stand which he was to take consistently both as Foreign Secretary and as Prime Minister: 'We want a united Europe. . . . It is only when plans for uniting Europe take a federal form that we cannot ourselves take part, because we cannot subordinate ourselves or the control of British policy to federal authorities.' On 17 December Eden and Churchill met Pleven and Schuman in Paris. Churchill's summary of Britain's attitude towards the plan 'was that they should be *with it though they could not be of it* [author's italics]'.[5]

This inconsistency between the policy of the Conservative leaders in office and their attitude while in Opposition not unnaturally caused some concern to pro-European Conservative MPs who were delegates to Strasbourg. On 3 December the seven Conservative delegates (Julian Amery, Tufton Beamish, Robert Boothby, Dick Harden, Christopher Hollis, Charles Mott-Radclyffe and Priscilla (Lady) Tweedsmuir), supported by Lord Layton, the sole Liberal delegate, sent a round robin to the Prime Minister drawing his attention to 'the great and increasing difficulty of our present position as Conservative delegates to the Consultative Assembly of the Council of Europe', and stressing that 'the attitude of the UK towards the Schuman Plan and the proposal for a European Army' had assumed great importance 'since it was widely regarded as the test of our sincerity'.[6]

The letter went on that the refusal announced by the Foreign Secretary in Rome on 28 November to participate in a European army came as 'a shattering blow to most members of the Assembly'. The writers drew Churchill's attention first to his speech to the European Assembly on 11 August the previous year, when he had said that Britain should delare herself 'in favour of the immediate creation of an European Army under a unified command in which we should all bear a worthy and honourable part', and second to similar declarations of intention in European Assemblies debates in August and November 1950 by the Minister of Supply, Duncan Sandys, the Secretary for Overseas Trade, Henry Hopkinson and the Minister of Housing, Harold Macmillan. The letter concluded that 'there are doubtless formidable reasons against our participation in a European Army at this juncture, but we do not know them', and they appealed to Churchill 'to take some positive action to restore British prestige in the Consultative Assembly' and 'to show that HMG mean to play their part in the military defence and economic development of Europe'.[7]

Churchill showed no signs of embarrassment at this rebuke, and replied that he had talked the matter over with the Foreign Secretary and 'We fully understand the difficulties under which you have been labouring at Strasbourg and we trust things will work out better later on when our full policy is understood in Europe.'[8] It is perhaps typical of the loyalty of backbench Conservative MPs that this reply did not produce from these Strasbourg delegates an outburst in favour of joining the Schuman Plan and the European army, nor open criticism of the Prime Minister and Foreign Secretary. Back-bench Tory MPs were in no mood to rock the boat while their party had only a precarious majority over Labour.

In a note to the Cabinet, Churchill wrote: 'I never contemplated Britain joining in this plan [European army] on the same terms as Continental partners.' It is impossible to reconcile these words with his much-publicized declaration at Strasbourg on 11 August 1950. Robert Boothby also wrote personal letters of protest to both Churchill and Eden from Strasbourg during December, but these too did not have any success. Boothby stressed how American Congressmen visiting Strasbourg wanted Britain to take a lead over European federalism to counter the possibility of West German domination.[9]

Henry Hopkinson was the leader of the British delegation to Strasbourg; he wrote to Churchill on 13 December that

> things boiled up . . . at a dinner given for [Spaak] by the European Movement where Spaak [former Prime Minister of Belgium and President of the Council of Europe] and Reynaud [former Prime Minister of France and Chairman of the Economic Committee of the Council of Europe], who seemed to be working hand in hand, bitterly attacked the British Government's attitude particularly in relation to the European Army. . . . Everyone recognised that Britain would not federate. One or two of the more extreme Federalists called for a full political authority for Europe without Britain . . . Spaak had given no indication of his intention to resign. . . . But I think he has sincerely convinced himself that the only course now is for the Continental countries to go ahead with some form of federation on their own and has made himself the leader of the federal element in the Assembly. The violence of his speech may also have been partly due to the very provocative attitude of [Patrick] Gordon Walker [later Foreign Secretary in the Wilson Government] who led the Socialist group after Glenvil Hall went home and showed a remarkable lack of tact and courtesy.[10]

Here was prima facie evidence that the rejection of the European army by Britain was making the country unpopular in Europe, but

Churchill did not reply, merely passing the letter on to Eden, who ignored it.[11]

Macmillan, then Minister of Housing and Local Government, struck another dissentient note writing to Eden on 16 January 1952. In his letter he voiced his fears that without Britain, West Germany would dominate the union created by the Schuman Plan, and that they might in certain circumstances side with the Russians. He agreed that Britain could not join any 'Federation', but wanted Britain to give a lead to Europe in the creation of a confederation organized on the same lines as the Commonwealth, with a common currency and a European customs preferential area 'interlocking with imperial preference'. Eden was not interested in these suggestions; his assistant private secretary wrote on Macmillan's covering letter: 'The S of S knows of this letter and the enclosures but does not want to read them at the moment.'[12]

Macmillan brought his suggestions to the Cabinet, also without success. Eden's response was that Macmillan ignored that 'much of Europe wants to federate', which was true. After the Cabinet discussion Macmillan wrote to Churchill on the same lines as the Conservative delegates to Strasbourg had in December, stating that 'the Government's continued opposition to the whole movement for European unity was inconsistent with the pronouncements [while in Opposition] by Churchill and Eden on the Schuman Plan and the European Army, and with the conduct of the Conservative delegates to the Council of Europe at Strasbourg.' All Churchill did was to reply that he had referred the letter to Eden with the comment 'I doubt if we can do any more than he is now planning.'[13]

Macmillan was right. Churchill had completely changed his attitude to the Schuman Plan and the European army, and took the identical line to Eden. He was not going to have a brush with his Foreign Secretary, and he sadly disappointed the federalists and enthusiastic Europeans on the Continent and at home, because while Leader of the Opposition he had had inspiring flashes of vision about a united Europe. Then he showed great enthusiasm for the Council of Europe, which he envisaged at first as a European parliamentary political authority. In May 1948 he had played the leading role in the first Congress of Europe at The Hague, and he had launched the European Movement, which brought together various groups in Britain and western Europe working for European unity. At The Hague he called for European unity in high-faluting although imprecise terms, playing down his reservation that Britain, while working closely with Europe, would never become integrated. He equated

Britain and the British Commonwealth of nations with the United States and the Soviet Union as 'friends and sponsors of a new Europe'. And in May 1950 Churchill had called for the 'immediate creation of a European army under a united command'. When René Pleven, the French Foreign Minister, had announced in 1950 the Pleven Plan for a European Defence Community, which would bring German troops into NATO, Herbert Morrison, the Labour Foreign Secretary, was non-committal; but when Churchill had returned to power in 1951 he astonished his European friends by refusing to take Britain into the proposed European army. This caused gloom and anger in Europe, and Spaak resigned in protest as President of the Council of Europe.

In Opposition Churchill had been so successful in inspiring others with the ideal of an united Europe that it is hard to explain his later ambivalence. Either he was guilty of muddled thinking, or he thought that he could establish a political ascendancy over Attlee by re-evoking his role as a great wartime European leader. He was definitely inspired by the vision both of the Council of Europe as a European parliamentary political authority and of a European army. Perhaps the most realistic way to look at his attitude is that he wanted the best of both worlds, and while Leader of the Opposition and out of touch with the civil servants he became carried away by his own oratory. Anyway, as Prime Minister from 1951 to 1955 he refused to support the unity of Europe if it was to involve Britain in supra-nationality.

The British Governments in the fifties were ready for a free trade area with Europe, but not a customs union. A customs union entailed a common external tariff against all outside countries including the Commonwealth, and this meant the erosion or abolition of prefer-ences for colonial and Commonwealth imports to the UK and inevitable similar downgrading of preferences for UK exports to them. A free trade area would have no common external tariff, and thus Imperial Preference could continue. A European customs union was the original objective of OEEC when it was formed in 1948, but because of British opposition it was not pursued. The British invariably took the line that OEEC could plan to remove quotas and quantitative restrictions on trade, but that tariffs must be left to the General Agreement on Tariffs and Trade (GATT).

In the early fifties the architects of the Schuman Plan would have welcomed Britain with open arms and were ready to adjust their plan to meet British requirements. Without Britain the High Authority of the ECSC took office on 10 August 1952. Monnet, its first President, was by now the driving force behind an ever-strengthening move towards a united Europe with supra-national institutions, and during 1951, 1952 and 1953 he led Europe along the road which was to end in the Common Market. However, just as the re-created West German coalmines and steelworks came under European control within the ECSC there was a serious setback to European unity. The French Assembly rejected EDC by 55 votes at the end of August 1954.

Italy, Germany and the Benelux countries were ready to go ahead, but the concept encountered strong opposition in France. The Americans put pressure on France to join, and Dulles made a statement that if France did not ratify the EDC Treaty there might be 'an agonising re-appraisal' of American defence policy. The French Prime Minister, Mendès-France, met Churchill and Eden on 23 August at Chartwell, and told them he feared that the French Assembly would not ratify. The British urged him to do his best to push it through. Mendès-France asked whether Churchill would help by bringing Britain in, but Churchill and Eden refused out of hand. Churchill conveniently forgot that his original proposal for a European army was close to the current EDC Plan. However, both the French and the British leaders were agreed that if the EDC was not ratified and nothing put in its place, the Adenauer Government would be at risk and any successor West German Government might want to play the USSR off against the West. Mendès-France floated in vague terms the idea of another organization to replace the EDC, one which would include Britain but without any of the supra-nationality involved in the EDC. This was not pursued at Chartwell because Eden and Churchill concentrated on pushing Mendès-France into a supreme effort to get the EDC Treaty ratified; the British helped only with exhortation, not promise of action.[14]

After the French Assembly had rejected EDC, the Mendès-France idea was revived. Dulles and Eden for once worked well together, and Britain offered to station permanently on the Continent four British divisions and the Tactical Airforce. Thus was born Western European Union (WEU) which was accepted by the French Parliament and consisted of the Six, plus Britain. WEU was primarily a sub-division of NATO with a few other minor functions, and much more to Eden's taste than EDC with its supra-nationality. It is an interesting footnote to history that the original concept of WEU came from Mendès-France, and not Eden.

Ratification of EDC by France would have been a major advance in terms of progress towards European unity. With its strong supra-national element, it went beyond the 1951 Coal and Steel Community and beyond the Treaty of Rome, which was concluded three years later. It was this supra-national element which Churchill and Eden wholly rejected and which probably was in part responsible for Mendès-France's unwillingness to stake all on trying to get the EDC through the French National Assembly. It is a sobering thought that, had he succeeded, it would have been far more difficult for Britain to get herself into the mainstream movement towards European unity after she missed the EEC bus between 1955 and 1957 during the Eden and Macmillan premierships.[14] In some ways WEU seemed the start of a new relationship between Britain and Europe, but for Eden and the Foreign Office the failure of EDC was considered proof that the Six would never agree on supra-nationality, and therefore Britain need not fear a European customs union coming into being.

In 1955 Monnet, as President of the High Authority of ECSC, was determined to extend European co-operation to atomic energy (Euratom) and to create a customs union. Fortunately for his aspirations the Mendès-France Government in France, which was opposed to more integration and had rejected EDC, fell in February 1955 and was replaced by the Faure Government which included several convinced federalists, among them Schuman.

On the initiative of the Benelux countries the Assembly of ECSC called on the six Foreign Ministers to meet at Messina at the beginning of June 1955 to discuss a 'Common Market'. There they relaunched the European ideal in the economic field and decided that atomic energy and a customs union free of all tariffs and quotas was the best line of advance with 'the development of common institutions and the progressive fusion of national economies and the progressive harmonisation of their social policies'.

Spaak, the Belgian Foreign Minister, was designated chairman of a committee to formulate plans, and to report by 2 October; he drove ahead with tremendous vigour. It was another watershed for Britain. At Messina the Six wanted Britain to participate from the start. No British civil servant went to Messina, and the Foreign Office and the British Cabinet were taken completely by surprise. A myth has grown up, largely because of a well-publicized BBC radio programme, that Russell Bretherton, Under-Secretary at the Board of Trade, went to Messina. Bretherton told the author categorically that this was untrue, and neither he nor any other civil servant went to Messina. In the same BBC programme Anthony Nutting claimed that he 'begged Eden' to let him go to Messina.[15]

Finally the Old Guard bows out. Churchill hands over to Eden, April 1955.

Eden, Butler (right) and Woolton plan the Conservative Election Campaign.

Queue at Euston as the rail strike threatens Eden's election campaign.

Eden returns to Smith Square to see the details of his triumph in the election.

Eden speaks at Fulham in support of Keith Joseph, who did not win.

Nye Bevan was the most effective critic of Suez in the Commons.

Selwyn Lloyd and Eden outside Lancaster House during the Suez Canal Users' Association Conference.

Eden, now Prime Minister, still dominated foreign policy and underestimated the importance of Messina; his stand remained that Britain had a special relationship with both the USA and the Commonwealth and therefore could never accept equal status with the Six. Nothing would induce him to contemplate Britain pooling sovereignty with other European countries or entering a customs union subject to supra-national control. A complete barrier to British co-operation was the 'gut feeling' of Eden, Macmillan and Butler that there were still three 'great' powers. After Eden's death, Butler stated publicly that Eden was 'bored' with the Messina powers' plans; 'even more bored than I was'.[16]

Eisenhower and Dulles expressed themselves strongly on the desirability of Britain joining the proposed European Common Market. This caused Eden displeasure, because it made clear that in US eyes Britain no longer had a unique role to play as a bridge between North America and Europe. Eden still had an inflated idea of Britain's standing in the world, and resented Americans denigrating it; the Americans thought that the Commonwealth was obsolete and felt that Britain should admit she was nothing more than an important European state. The US State Department tried hard to push Britain into the European Common Market, mainly because they thought it would bind West Germany to the West; de Gaulle later actually expressed his feeling that the EEC was an American creation.

Macmillan made it clear in his memoirs that in 1955 he did not want a six-power Europe with a customs union and supranationalism, and took the Eden line. Lord Thorneycroft, then President of the Board of Trade, told the author that in 1955 and 1956 the predominant attitude inside the Treasury and the Foreign Office was anti-European, and that only in his Department were the civil servants pro-Europe. At Whitehall there was a general feeling that the Messina project would never come to fruition. Lord Gladwyn, later the most enthusiastic supporter of European unity, told the author that in 1955 he believed it would fail.[17]

The British were far ahead of the Six in the development of atomic energy, and were much wanted in the atomic energy field. This contributed to miscalculations by the British Government about their bargaining strength when later they proposed a free trade area as an alternative to the Common Market of the Six. However, in the summer and autumn of 1955 much goodwill towards Britain was shown by the Six, who had high hopes that Britain would establish at least a form of close association with the Common Market and Euratom, and were prepared to make concessions for the Commonwealth and Colonies.

Beyen, the Dutch Foreign Minister, came to London with Spaak, the leading promoter of the Messina plan, for a meeting with the British Ministers on 21 June 1955. Butler took the chair and the other Ministers present were Thorneycroft, Geoffrey Lloyd, Minister of Fuel, John Boyd Carpenter, Minister of Transport and Civil Aviation, and Lord Reading, Minister of State for Foreign Affairs. Beyen stated that the Messina powers felt that progress towards economic integration would best be made if it was initiated by the Six and not through existing organizations such as OEEC, and that they had decided to ask the British to participate and to seek expert assistance from OEEC. He emphasized that the Six were intent on a supra-national institution, and he went on that 'they realised that the UK could not accept the supra-national principle and could not therefore become a full member of any body of that nature'. Clearly he envisaged a close association of the United Kingdom with the Six, rather than Britain becoming a full member.

Butler replied that he was 'disturbed by the prospect of considerable duplication of the OEEC', but Beyen countered that the invitation to OEEC to participate in the work of the Spaak Committee 'should serve to avoid any duplication'. Thorneycroft asked if it was envisaged that the Common Market should be protected against the outside world by a tariff wall, and that Britain should be invited to join such a market. In reply Beyen said that the Benelux countries were not in favour of a tariff wall, but that it would be easier to persuade other countries to join if there was one.

Butler summed up by saying again how important OEEC was in the British view, and that he could give no indication of what UK policy would be. Butler's emphasis on OEEC was obviously an obstructionist tactic. The Six had wanted originally not to make the OEEC the main instrument of European economic recovery, but the British view was that it was only an inter-governmental organization on the traditional pattern, and in 1952 on a British initiative the OEEC budget was drastically cut; this led to an emasculation of OEEC. Further evidence of British loss of interest was that the British plans for restoring convertibility to sterling were discussed almost exclusively with the USA and the Commonwealth and not in OEEC, which by 1955 had declined in importance.[18]

On 30 June Beyen issued a formal letter of invitation to the United Kingdom to participate in the work of the Spaak Committee, and stated that the first session would be on 9 July. A high-powered committee of civil servants worked at speed on the problems involved in the Messina initiative. Their report was circulated to the Cabinet for its meeting on 30 June, when Butler was to comment orally. It pointed out that the Messina powers were intent both on creating a common organization for the peaceful development of atomic energy, and on a European customs union, and that at the meeting with Ministers at the Treasury on 21 June Beyen had made it clear that the Six were 'inspired as much by political as economic motives', and wanted supra-national institutions to run the Common Market subject to a common political assembly. On atomic energy the civil servants stated: 'We would have much to give but little to gain.' They felt a customs union would damage the OEEC and GATT and might lead to a 'discriminatory bloc' in Europe against the rest of the world.[19]

The report went on that the Six could not be prevented from doing what they wanted, but if their invitation to participate was accepted 'we can seek to ensure that their actions are as little prejudicial to our interests as possible'. Still, they agreed that Britain had strong interests in 'any new links binding Germany with the West', but it would be 'better not to become too closely identified with the deliberations of the Preparatory Committee'. Therefore if the Cabinet agreed on 'participation' in Brussels with the Spaak Committee they should accept, but as 'observers only'.

On 30 June the Cabinet agreed with the report, except that Macmillan felt the British civil servants at Brussels should be 'representatives', not 'observers', saying that we should preserve full freedom of action, but might be able to exercise a greater influence in discussions if we were to enter them on the same footing as other countries concerned and not as observers. It was decided that Butler and Macmillan should have discretion to decide on the status of the British at Brussels; Macmillan won the day. At that stage Macmillan intended British influence to be as strong as possible in preventing the designs of the Messina powers succeeding.

Sending 'representatives' rather than 'observers' was getting off on the wrong foot, because Beyen's and Spaak's interpretation was that Britain was seriously considering associating itself closely with the Common Market, and it increased their indignation and anger later when the door was suddenly slammed. When Beyen came to London after the discussions had made progress he told Lord Reading that he was glad that the representatives of HMG had not been merely observers but had been enabled to take a valuable part in the discussion.[20]

Macmillan wrote formally accepting an invitation to appoint a

British representative to take part in the studies, but emphasized that Britain did not want to see the work of OEEC duplicated. The chief representative was Russell Bretherton, Under-Secretary at the Board of Trade. Thorneycroft explained to the author that Bretherton was very much in sympathy with the aims of the Six. He stayed in Brussels in close touch with Spaak and Beyen and was on cordial terms with them and the others concerned in the work of the Spaak Committee. Bretherton's instructions from the Cabinet were: 'to leave open the possibility of our joining or entering into a close association while avoiding any positive commitment; and to try to avoid expressing any views on the issues being discussed in the Preparatory Committee'. Bretherton was told 'if driven into a corner and forced to show his hand or some of the cards in it' to say there would have to be proper safeguards for, and consultation with, the Commonwealth and Colonies, and that a free trade area would probably bring fewer difficulties for the UK than a customs union; also:

> (c) That we would find great difficulty in accepting limits on national sovereignty beyond those which would be essential to ensure the major benefits of a common market (we would not, for example, contemplate any abrogation of the right to impose or vary duties for revenue purposes).
> (d) That in view of (c) above we could not be parties to the creation of a supra-national authority to organise the formation of a common market, and could only consider participating if the move forward was to be along the road of international consultation that has been tried out in OEEC.
> (e) That we should have to be satisfied that the common market would not develop into an inward-looking discriminatory trade bloc following policies at variance with a 'one-world' approach.[21]

These instructions, which did not seem to rule out a customs union or some form of supra-nationality, seemed to go beyond anything the Prime Minister was prepared to approve. The suggestion, too, that a free trade area might meet the aspirations of the Six was evidence of a lack of realism in Whitehall; the Six were determined on a customs union.

Almost immediately Bretherton reported that he was confronted with 'something of a dilemma' because

> if we take an active part in trying to guide the final propositions into a form which is acceptable to us it will be difficult to avoid later on the

presumption that we are in some sense committed to the result. On the other hand, if we sit back and say nothing it is pretty certain that many more things will get into the report which would be unpleasant from the United Kingdom point of view whether we in the end took part in the Common Market or not.

He also wrote: 'We have the power to guide the conclusions of this conference in almost any direction we like, but beyond a certain point we cannot exercise that power without ourselves becoming in some measure responsible for the results.' His letter was discussed at the Cabinet's Mutual Aid Committee on 9 August, but no guidance was given to him, even though he had correctly pinpointed at this early stage the risk of antagonizing Spaak and his Committee by taking part in deliberations about the shape of a vital new European grouping which Britain had no intention of joining.

In October Bretherton reported (erroneously as it turned out) that the Spaak Committee were placing 'little emphasis on supra-national authority'. He wrote also: 'Although conclusions cannot be drawn at this stage it seems that current thought about institutions is on more reasonable lines than we first expected, and if there is no supra-national authority U.K. association or even membership might become more attractive than at present seems likely.' The Foreign Office minutes on this report read: 'Whether or not we eventually establish some kind of relationship with a European Common Market we have a general interest in seeing any such arrangement run on inter-governmental lines'; and 'The institution looks as if it will be almost indistinguishable from O.E.E.C.'

Bretherton also sent a note of a talk with the French delegate on the attitude of the French Cabinet, which provoked this comment from A. H. Ross in the Foreign Office on 19 October: 'French participation in any Common Market seems increasingly unlikely.' When a French memorandum was forwarded Ross minuted: 'These conditions come very near to being a declaration that France will not participate on any terms likely to be agreed.' A. J. Edden added: 'In the face of this it is difficult to imagine that even agreement in principle to set up a Common Market will be reached at the Ministerial meeting in December (if there is one).' Clearly the French Assembly's rejection of the EDC in August 1954 had produced scepticism about the ability of the Six to conclude a far-reaching agreement.[22]

Ministers discussed the Messina proposal at meetings of the Cabinet's Mutual Aid Committee and Economic Policy Committee.

The Foreign Office sent reports that the French were cool towards the Common Market and that some West German industrial in- terests were hostile, but that the Americans welcomed the initiative and would much like Britain to join. The Treasury advised that 'an entirely new situation' would arise if the Six were to go ahead on their own and establish a genuine Common Market without the United Kingdom, and 'There seems no doubt that this would be contrary to our interests.' We should then need to consider the question of whether we could afford to stay out, but we should be doing this from 'a disadvantaged negotiating position'. A report to the Cabinet Economic Policy Committee stated that the Spaak Committee was meeting with the UK representatives on 7 November, and Ministers 'will have to make a decision in December about the proposals for a six power initiative which will duplicate OEEC', and 'if the Common Market comes into existence it can be argued with some reason that the disadvantages of abstaining outweigh the advantages'.[23]

The Cabinet's Economic Policy Committee was told that the Common Market would be disastrous for the UK chemical industry, which had been protected for thirty-four years by Key Industry Duties of 33 per cent (the MacKenna duties of the First World War to keep out non-essential imports) on most synthetic chemicals. Without protection UK firms would not be able to subsidize exports out of home sales. In general the Common Market would damage UK exports to Europe, but 'this is expected to be much less disastrous than freedom for European competition in UK markets'. The cotton industry and those handling rayon and synthetic fibres, wool yarn and cloth would be better off out; engineering would lose; and for the motor industry, currently protected by a 33 per cent tariff, the common market would be neutral. The advice given to the Economic Policy Committee was that if the Common Market were formed without Britain 'the interests of the United Kingdom would almost certainly be adversely affected by the establishment of a Common Market in which we did not participate'. On the political question the civil servants reported: 'If we were hostile or even lukewarm and the idea collapsed we should certainly be blamed' and that 'we do not want the colonies to feel that we are joining it for our own narrow economic advantages while the colonies would lose'. The civil servants' view was that the Common Market 'would offer no clear and definite prospect of such political benefits in terms of our external relations as would compensate for the weakening of the Commonwealth'.[24] Macmillan, Butler and Eden accepted the Treasury briefing that the Market would damage the economy and decided to make every effort to stop it being formed without appearing to be hostile. Spaak and Beyen were quickly to find out what the British were up to.

During November 1955 they both came to London and had separate interviews with Butler at the Treasury. Unfortunately Butler, while trying to be evasive, gave his visitors the impression that Britain was seriously considering joining the Six in the Common Market. This was untrue, and had unfortunate consequences later because both Beyen and Spaak felt that Butler had misled them, and if he had been frank he should have declared that the Prime Minister and the Government were opposed to the creation of the Common Market.

Butler and Beyen met on 2 November. Butler said to Beyen that HMG regarded the work of the Six as a 'powerful and imaginative initiative' and that 'we in the UK understood their long term aims and as good Europeans we were sympathetic to it'. He 'felt bound to point out that a decision to join the Common Market would call for such major adjustments in UK policy as to rule it out as a short term possibility', and 'enlarged on the importance to the U.K. of our trade and continued good relations with the Commonwealth' which would be affected by the proposals of the Six. He summed up that UK accession to the Common Market presented British Ministers with a problem 'involving a huge and long term test of statesmanship'. Butler went on to emphasize the importance of avoiding harm to the OEEC, the need for the Six to go slowly to avoid crossing wires, and above all to maintain contact throughout with HMG and OEEC. Beyen said there was no prospect of an early worthwhile agreement being reached between the Six, and 'went out of his way to praise the contribution which Mr Bretherton had made to the Brussels conference'. He said 'no-one knew what France would do, and Western Germany's attitude was schizophrenic'. Butler was non-committal on nuclear energy, saying that 'it was the most difficult and most delicate sphere of all'. He summed up that the Six would always find us 'sympathetic' and 'European', but there could be no question of our taking any definitive step in the short term. Long after, on BBC Radio, Ernst van de Beugel of the Dutch Foreign Office said Beyen got the impression that 'Britain was likely to change her mind', and in the same programme Butler said he felt a personal repugnance for Beyen 'who was a very pushing man . . . always telling you what to do'.[25]

On 18 November Butler saw Spaak. Here is an extract from the note of the interview made by Edward Boyle MP, then Economic Secretary to the Treasury:

The Chancellor went on to say that he had no doubt M. Spaak was well aware of the difficulties from the point of view of the United Kingdom – in particular, the special relationship with the Commonwealth. The Chancellor laid special emphasis on the problem of the future relations between the Six and the O.E.E.C., and in this connection he appealed to M. Spaak as former O.E.E.C. Chairman. He hoped that the Six, in any further moves toward consolidation, would at the same time turn in the direction of the O.E.E.C., and he was particularly keen that the wires should not become crossed. Could not M. Spaak attend the next meeting of the O.E.E.C. which would take place in February 1956?

M. Spaak, in reply, remarked that the O.E.E.C. was something of a 'boutique', and that the Six hoped to enjoy a more intimate and wider union. He certainly recognised the U.K. problem, but hoped that it might be possible for the Six to have a special association with the U.K. at a later date, on the analogy of the Standing Council of Association between the U.K. and the E.C.S.C.. At this point the discussion turned in the direction of admitting Spain to O.E.E.C., and M. Spaak remarked that this constituted a formidable political problem from his point of view. His party felt equally strongly about not recognising Spain as it did about recognising Communist China.

With regard to Euratom, M. Spaak said that the question of control was all-important, and exactly the same problem arose from the point of view of the O.E.E.C. Working Party.

M. Spaak admitted that France was not easy from the point of view of her partners in the Six, but that Germany was really the basis of the difficulty, because opinion within Western Germany was so divided. The Chancellor once again asked M. Spaak to consider attending the O.E.E.C. in February, but M. Spaak did not give any commitment. Both M. Spaak and the Chancellor agreed that a number of members in the Commonwealth, especially Canada, took a considerable interest in the affairs of Europe, and M. Spaak assured the Chancellor that, for his part, he had no desire at all that the activities of the Six should put Britain in a difficulty with regard to her relations with her Commonwealth partners.[26]

Robert Rothschild, Belgian Chef de Cabinet, accompanied Spaak and later recorded that 'the warmer Spaak became, the colder and colder Butler obviously became'.[27]

Butler was in a particularly difficult position at this meeting because the week before he had presided at a meeting of Ministers which had not only decided to tell the Six firmly we could not join them but also made plans to wreck the project. Later Spaak heard of this, and it may well be that he never forgave Butler and the British for what was said at this interview. This decisive Ministers' meeting was the Cabinet's Economic Policy Committee on 11 November; they agreed that they should order their representatives at Brussels to be non-committal until December, and then explain in clear terms our inability to join a Common Market. The meeting also decided that the West German and US Governments should be informed immediately that the UK Government rejected the Common Market. This was to be done with a view to lessening West German and American enthusiasm for the project. 'If we were to give them a lead, the Germans might decide not to join a common market and to concentrate on co-operation through OEEC'; that was why they were to be informed in advance. The same reason lay behind the decision to tell the USA in advance.

Butler told the Committee that 'it seemed clear that the UK should avoid joining a European common market, at any rate for some time to come' and the Committee were in general agreement with him on the grounds that it would lead to a 'division in Europe', and 'to the creation of a bloc discriminating against the United States', and our participation would 'eventually mean the end of the present system of Imperial preference'. However, it was pointed out that

in the much longer term, it was not impossible that the United Kingdom might be able to follow a policy of closer economic association with Europe, without inconsistency with our responsibilities to and relations with the Commonwealth. Certain Commonwealth countries, notably Canada and Australia, for different reasons had considerable and growing interests in Europe.

Butler stressed his attachment to OEEC, saying the Six would 'infringe the wider interests of OEEC. As the holder of the leading position in OEEC [chairman] it should therefore be the concern of the United Kingdom to divert as far as possible the activities of the Brussels Conference into the wider framework.' This specious emphasis on the supreme importance of the not very successful OEEC continued to dominate the British arguments with the Six, to the annoyance of Spaak and Beyen.[28]

At this key meeting neither Thorneycroft nor any other pro-Europeans in the Cabinet entered any note of dissent. Indeed, Thorneycroft saw Winthrop Brown, US Ambassador to Britain, on 2 December as Brown was about to return to the USA for two months, and sowed in his mind the idea that the UK was not blowing cold on Messina because of the Commonwealth, but because of the fear of a central discriminatory bloc in Europe. Here is the note of Thorneycroft's conversation with Brown, which was clearly intended to damp down American enthusiasm for the Messina project:

> The President [Thorneycroft] said he had always argued in favour of widening the basis of trade and payments and against advocators of a central discriminatory block [*sic*] in Europe (which some circles in this country contended should be set up as a counter to what they described as 'United States restrictionist policies'). He thought that the danger in the present common market proposals was, that in falling short of a real common market – which would require not only a common tariff policy but also a common monetary policy with common fiscal measures and investment programme – a central discriminatory block in Europe would result. If this should happen it might well prove to be a serious setback to the anti-discriminatory policies of the United Kingdom and the United States. While he realised the strong appeal any move to unite Europe was bound to have in the United States, he thought that the practical effects of the strictly limited type of a common market which he was sure would result from the current European proposals would require much more serious study in this country and the United States. Mr. Brown said that it was very important for the reasons behind the United Kingdom's attitude towards these proposals to be clearly stated so that there could be no risk of misunderstanding in the United States. If it was thought that the United Kingdom was withholding her support solely because her Commonwealth preferences were at risk, then United States opinion would be unsympathetic, but if her real reasons, as outlined by the President, were made clear, he thought this would lead to much better understanding of the problem in his country.

Ross minuted on the Foreign Office file: 'The reason advanced by the President of the Board of Trade is perfectly genuine and also much more acceptable to informed opinion than any other.' He noted also that Thorneycroft was carrying out the Prime Minister's intention that we should discourage American support for the Messina powers. Another minute (signature indecipherable) read:

> There is every reason for disabusing the Americans of the idea that it is only because of the Empire that we are fighting shy of the Common Market, particularly so when members of the administration and Mr. Dulles are saying favourable things about the Brussels proposals. Perhaps we might add some sentences to the letter to the Germans indicating the need to explain ourselves to the Americans along the lines of Mr. Thorneycroft's statement.

D. S. Lasky, Head of the Economic Relations Department, added: 'Yes, but don't let us overstate our case. The main reason why we dislike the Common Market – certainly the one which weighs with the Cabinet, is its effect on the Commonwealth. But the discrimination point is a valid one which we should certainly air with the Americans.'[29]

In a letter to the author Thorneycroft emphasized that when he saw Winthrop Brown the Government had already decided to reject the Messina powers initiative, and in those days collective Cabinet responsibility was accepted, so that it was his duty to defend their decision. Our obligations to the Commonwealth were eroding, and he felt it was a far better argument that the Six might be inward-looking.

Macmillan and Eden decided the British démarche against the Common Market should be made at a meeting of permanent delegates to OEEC in Paris on 7 December. Almost certainly they wanted to do it at an OEEC meeting to emphasize the importance of OEEC in British eyes. But this was to recoil on them, because Beyen and Spaak correctly saw it as designed to sabotage Messina.

The British permanent delegate to OEEC in Paris was Sir Hugh Ellis-Rees, who had spent eighteen years with the Inland Revenue before joining the Treasury. He was appointed permanent delegate to the OEEC, with the rank of ambassador, in 1952. Lord Gladwyn told the author that Ellis-Rees was a 'typical' Treasury officer without imagination, who understood only English, an opponent of the supra-nationalism advocated by the Messina powers and jealous of anything which might diminish the role of OEEC. Bretherton confirmed to the author that in conversation Ellis-Rees was always pro-OEEC and anti-Spaak's Committee. On 7 December Ellis-Rees telegraphed to the Foreign Office: 'European Common Market. I have taken action as instructed. At an informal meeting of the permanent delegates on the Council of OEEC I made a statement and we had a first debate. I was satisfied with the result.'[30] Why Ellis-Rees was 'satisfied' is obscure. The démarche was a bombshell to Beyen and Spaak and produced an explosive reaction. There is every reason to believe that their fury at their cavalier treatment on 7 December after Butler's soothing interviews with them, and the dedicated co-operation of Bretherton in Brussels, permanently altered their attitude to Britain. From the anger generated at this meeting stemmed the Messina powers' refusal to associate Britain with the Common Market through a Free Trade Area when Macmillan was Prime Minister in 1957 and 1958.

On 10 December the British Ambassador, Sir Paul Mason, telegraphed from The Hague that Beyen had summoned him urgently that morning.

> I found him in a state of great perturbation and indignation. . . . He said he could understand neither its purpose nor its timing. He had always been aware that common market plan was one which HMG was most unlikely to join . . . he had understood when he saw the Chancellor in London in November that the one thing which we wanted was to avoid being pushed into having to take up [an] attitude towards the common market scheme. Why, then, had we now reversed our view on this point? He said that in his view our statement . . . amounted to a direct attack on the work which the six were trying to carry out. . . .
>
> The timing could not have been worse. What was the hurry in making our views known? M. Spaak's committee was not to produce its final report until January, and the six Foreign Ministers would not consider that before March. Why could we not have approached the subject in a more tactful manner? As it was, the whole work of the six would be thrown into confusion; . . . he simply could not follow the argument about cutting across the work of OEEC. As we knew, he was a convinced protagonist of that body, but it was idle to suppose it could carry on within its framework the kind of closer operation which the common market plan envisaged, and he could not accept that, in pursuing their aims, the six were damaging OEEC's prestige and efficiency.

The follow-up letter from Mason about the 'row' explained that Beyen was particularly bitter against Butler for giving him the impression that the UK was benevolent to the Common Market; it also stated:

> We must, I am afraid, accept that Beyen's confidence in our general attitude towards European co-operation, and in his special position, as he likes to think of it, of close co-operation with ourselves, has been shaken. This is primarily, as I see it, a matter of the timing of our démarche. I remember telling you, when I was in London, that if we had at some time to make it clear that we could not go along with the Messina Common Market plan, i.e. if we could not ourselves join in it, he would be sorry but not surprised. . . . Ideally what should have been done . . . is that, as soon as we had decided that we should have to formulate our position . . . Beyen should have been specially taken into our confidence and his views invited as to how best to set about making our point clear. His feelings would then not have been hurt and he might perhaps have had some useful advice to give us as to the

modus operandi. The main unsatisfactory residue is that Beyen will, I think, for some time to come, doubt how far he really remains in the confidential relationship with ourselves.[31]

Mason was right. Britain had destroyed Beyen's belief in Britain's good faith.

Probably Ellis-Rees handled the meeting of the permanent delegates to OEEC badly. He was opposed to the ideals of the Messina powers, believing that all moves towards European integration and a customs union should be dealt with by OEEC. A letter from him to the Foreign Secretary (with copies to the Board of Trade and Treasury) dated 11 October made his attitude clear. 'Secretary General of OEEC at Brussels has been made to feel most unwelcome . . . there has never been any effort at consultation or avoidance of duplication.' The Messina powers were 'by passing OEEC completely and Messina powers will either duplicate the work of the OEEC or cut across it'. He went on: 'If it is not our intention to become members of the Common Market or be associated . . . it is far better to be outspoken at the outset. . . . I would regard it as a fatal mistake to abandon our present status in order to become a member of a purely European grouping which by implication would require some abandonment of sovereignty.'[32] Pro-OEEC and anti-Messina, possibly he was so glad to be the instrument which prevented Britain from making what he considered 'a fatal mistake' that he failed to appreciate the reaction of the representatives of the Messina powers during what he called a 'satisfactory' discussion. Bretherton in Brussels had caught the Messina spirit, and the contrast between the two must have been a shock to Beyen and Spaak.

A further letter from Mason to the Foreign Office stated: 'There is evidence that the choice of the OEEC meeting and Ellis-Rees to make the démarche was ill chosen.' Significantly, the Ambassador in Paris, Gladwyn Jebb, reported from Paris that a French Foreign Office spokesman had told him that the French felt the OEEC had not led to the 'desired economic co-operation and integration', and that the French 'would do their part in completing the Messina exercise'.

On 2 December Spaak had told Sir George Labouchere, the British Ambassador in Brussels, that 'if the Messina project were to be put on to practicable lines then this involved in his opinion a supra-national authority. For this reason he did not foresee anything useful emerging from discussion in O.E.E.C.' Soon afterwards,

Labouchere informed the Foreign Office that Spaak's favourite theme was that 'only the Common Market under a supra national authority combined with Euratom would keep Germany sufficiently interested to prevent eventual flirtation with the Soviet Union', and that Spaak made it clear that he deprecated OEEC dealing with such questions as the Common Market, largely because it was a question of too many cooks; also that Spaak felt it was 'in the relative privacy of W.E.U. that European linen should be washed rather than in the public eye of O.E.E.C.'. Spaak wanted Macmillan informed of these views.[33] The Foreign Office did not comment on Labouchere's note, which made it clear that Spaak had no use for the OEEC in the Common Market context, and it was tactless for Britain to keep on repeating that OEEC was all-important – as if it was the divinely chosen institution for all European co-operation – when the Messina powers so clearly thought differently.

Beyen and Spaak soon rumbled the British decision, disclosed in the minutes of the Economic Committee on 11 November, described above, to change from 'indifference' to 'positive hostility'. This created ill-will and mistrust which was not dissipated for years. Macmillan was due in Paris for a meeting of WEU on 14 December, but before that Lord John Hope MP, Under-Secretary at the Foreign Office, had to appear there at the meeting of the Council of Ministers of the Council of Europe. The Foreign Office were distinctly perturbed by the anger of Beyen and Spaak; a telegram to Hope stated that he must be careful 'not to attack the Common Market as such, whether off stage or in public', and that we must insist that the Six come to Paris and work out with the OEEC how their objectives could be fitted into an all-European framework so that it 'does not disrupt the co-operation of the nineteen' (all the powers in OEEC). The telegram concluded: 'In general our advice is that as little should be said as possible. If there is to be a row we ought to have it in OEEC.'

A long brief was sent by diplomatic bag to Hope, stating that 'in the *coulisses* we shall hear the usual mutterings about the U.K. stabbing Europe in the back'. Hope was urged to reply that the Common Market must conflict with our interests as a member of the Commonwealth, and might encourage regionalism and discrimination and the erection of new tariff barriers in other parts of the world. The main theme of the Hope brief was that OEEC would be a far better organization than the Common Market, and 'If we are to unite Europe and not divide it, Europe must not lose on the OEEC swings what it gains on the Messina roundabouts.' This brief ignored the rejection of OEEC as a forum by Spaak, and was likely to anger Spaak and Beyen even further. Fortunately John Hope, who possessed not only great charm but also tact, decided to ignore it.

On 13 December Hope met Beyen at a dinner for the Foreign Ministers at the Irish Embassy. Earlier in the day Beyen had asked him if they could then have a talk about 'the famous démarche over the Messina plan'. Sensibly, Hope suggested they should talk after dinner when they would both feel more mellow; in the morning he had told Beyen 'how frightfully distressed we were that he had been so upset'. After dinner Beyen reiterated all his familiar arguments about the Ellis-Rees démarche – adding a new one, that it was adding insult to injury because he should have been told personally by the Ambassador. Hope thought this was 'wholly' reasonable as 'Beyen had been playing a very personal role', and agreed with him. Beyen also said that when he met Butler he had seemed to express 'rather more than a neutral interest in the Messina plan' and that 'Sir Hugh Ellis-Rees had been "very silly in the OEEC"'.[34]

The Foreign Secretary faced the full rage of Beyen and Spaak at the WEU meeting on 14 December. In his memoirs Macmillan makes light of it, but the official account show that the architects of the Common Market were furious with Britain. Spaak led off by saying that HMG had adopted an unfavourable, even hostile, attitude towards the plans of the Messina powers as being contrary to the true interests of Europe, and had indicated their opposition to these plans. He thought it particularly unfortunate that this opposition should have been expressed in another international organization. Beyen followed by saying that he had been

> greatly surprised by the British démarche in which the United Kingdom had indicated that they felt compelled to inform the Messina powers that they could not participate in the Common Market for three reasons; first, because of their links with the Commonwealth; second, because a common market could not be reconciled with a one world system; third, because a common market would impede the workings of the OEEC. The Messina powers had not asked for the view of Her Majesty's Government and the present British initiative had been spontaneous.

Beyen concluded by asking Macmillan if the declaration made by Ellis-Rees 'constituted condemnation of the Messina plans'. In reply Macmillan emphasized that the British declaration

> meant exactly what it said . . . we felt that our responsibilities and our associations ruled out British participation in the Common

Market. . . . Our declaration was not condemnation of the six power
plans but it was a warning that we must not divide Europe in the
course of trying to unite it. We felt that it would be useful to discuss
this matter corporately and see how the six power plans could be
recognised and harmonised with the activities of OEEC.

This reference by Macmillan to OEEC was not calculated to soothe
Spaak in face of his often reiterated view that the Messina powers
wanted a supra-national authority which could not be enacted
through OEEC. Spaak returned to the attack on the British Foreign
Secretary, saying that the Ellis-Rees declaration had not been
'merely a proposal for a study, but had been in fact a declaration
against a Common Market, and the Six could not pursue simultaneously two policies, one on a six power basis, and the other in
O.E.E.C.'

Macmillan refused to comment further, which provoked Beyen to
another attack, saying that the timing of the British declaration had
benefited nobody. On a more conciliatory note, he added that he
hoped that the UK 'would not feel bound by their present declaration
when the six power plans had been finalised and the question arose of
working out some form of association with the U.K., and that the Six
had no objection to other O.E.E.C. countries participating in their
plans'. He thought it would be a good thing for the whole subject to
be discussed at the next meeting of the Council of OEEC. Spaak
'indicated dissent' at this last suggestion.[35]

In telegrams to his ambassadors in Bonn and Washington
Macmillan instructed them to stress that in the British view 'the
political cohesion of Europe [the adhesion of the Federal Republic of
Germany to the West] would be damaged by the Six, and it would be
deplorable if all O.E.E.C. stands for were to be jeopardised for the
shadow of a Common Market which either never came to anything or
if it did, proved harmful to the world wide movement towards freer
trade'. This was sabotage, and contradicted Spaak who, as had been
seen, was continually stressing that only the Common Market would
stop West Germany flirting with the Soviet Union.[36]

In Washington the British Ambassador, Makins, implemented his
Government's instructions to try and 'lessen American enthusiasm'
for the Common Market in two conversations with Livingstone
Merchant and Burke Elbright at the State Department on 21 and 22
December. He wrote a personal letter to Macmillan:

One of the main attractions which the State Department evidently
sees in any scheme of European integration is that it should somehow

tie Germany up with the West or at least appear to the other European countries to do so, and thereby increase their confidence. If, as I understand it, your real object is to hasten the end of the Common Market, it might be as well to sow doubts at least in the minds of the Americans about the beneficial effects of tieing Germany to Europe.

He added that he had already done so as far as the French angle was concerned. When the author showed the archive to Lord Sherfield, he said that he had no brief about the German aspect, so that he could not sow seeds of doubt with the Americans on this issue.

No briefing to Makins about West Germany was given by the Foreign Office. By now some Foreign Office officials were impressed by the argument that 'we could not afford to stay out', and had reservations about taking up too hostile an attitude. Merchant would make a written record of his conversation with the British Ambassador, which would be given wide circulation within the State Department, where there were plenty of officials passionately keen on the Common Market. As a result Makins's remarks would quickly be leaked to the Spaak Committee in Brussels. This happened, and it fanned the rage of Beyen, Spaak and his colleagues. From Bonn German diplomats would have made similar leaks to the rest of the Six. R. W. Munro realized the danger that the instructions to Washington and Bonn would come to the knowledge of the Spaak Committee, and minuted: 'As the Germans have now stated they intend to pursue the Messina objectives of the Common Market they will do their own research and reach their own conclusions irrespective of our views. I think we have now gone as far as we *safely* can in sowing doubts in the minds of those concerned.' Other comments were, from A. J. Edden: 'The exercise suggested by Sir R. Makins seems to be to sow doubts in the minds of the Americans. This may still be desirable seeing that they wish, and the case of Euratom may be in some position to give, their encouragement to supranational Six Power integration if and when this becomes practical politics'; from C. H. Johnston, 'The most encouraging development in Germany since the war has been the genuine attraction of the European idea – particularly for the younger generation' and . . . if we frustrated this it would be 'very serious'; and from D. S. Lasky: 'If the Common Market becomes a reality and if it is decided we cannot afford to stay out, we shall obviously have to reconsider our present attitude.'[37]

The letter below from Harry Crookshank, Lord Privy Seal until the December reshuffle, typifies the Cabinet's attitude to the Messina

Plan; he wrote it to Macmillan on 23 September 1955, sending copies to Butler and Thorneycroft:

> I am concerned that our continued presence at the Brussels talks is arousing to an increasing degree hopes among Europeans that we would participate in a common market. If a practicable scheme emerges we are going to be faced with an embarrassing decision. . . . Failure . . . would earn us opprobrium among the Europeans, whereas if we join in these later stages we would be in danger of finding ourselves drawn . . . into a European Customs Union which would require us to give priority to . . . Europe at the expense of our trade with the Commonwealth. This would be bound gradually but inevitably to have a most profound effect on our political relationship with other Members of the Commonwealth. The longer our decision is delayed, the more awkward a one it may prove.
>
> I do not wish to suggest that our representatives at Brussels should be withdrawn at this particular stage or to urge any revision of the instructions which have been given to them. I do however hope that the situation will be closely watched, and that if any unexpected opportunity presents itself for us to disengage ourselves during the next few weeks, the matter will be brought at once to the notice of Ministers for a decision whether to avail ourselves of that opportunity.

Macmillan replied that he understood Crookshank's preoccupations 'over the potential embarrassment in our relations with the Commonwealth', but thought it 'most unlikely that we shall have to face any decision until the French elections have taken place next year'. In their letters of reply not Macmillan, Thorneycroft nor Butler expressed divergence from Crookshank's views.[38]

Crookshank was right, because Britain had earned 'opprobrium' when Bretherton was summarily withdrawn from Brussels in November, and he was accurately presenting the strongly held view within the Conservative Party that they wanted close relations with the Commonwealth and disliked the idea of a trading partnership with Europe which would erode Commonwealth preference. Consciousness of party opinion is evident in the Government's dealings with the Messina powers during 1956.

Eden, due to go to Washington for talks with the President early in February, asked for a detailed brief from the Foreign Office, the Treasury and the Board of Trade. Several diplomats, influenced by Jebb, had now become convinced that Messina was likely to come to fruition. The Treasury, on the other hand, were sceptical and hostile. A Treasury memorandum by R. W. Clarke on 16 January, and agreed by Macmillan three days later, summed up their views:

Two months ago the Foreign Office was insisting that there was not the slightest possibility of the Messina 'Common Market' coming into existence and that the only troublesome question was whether we should strive to kill it or let it collapse of its own weight. Now there is a strong body of opinion there which appears to have been convinced by Mr Dulles that the Messina plans are essential in order to 'contain' Germany. I suspect that the Foreign Office view would prefer this brief to be more forthcoming towards Messina . . . if the extreme Foreign Office . . . were accepted this would in effect ditch O.E.E.C. (at the moment our 'chosen instrument' in European economic policy under the Chancellor's chairmanship). We hope therefore that if there is pressure from the Foreign Secretary or the President to tilt the balance of the brief, the Chancellor will feel able to resist it.

Treasury fears that the Foreign Office would influence Eden and Lloyd in favour of Messina were groundless. The final brief was negative – reiterating that it would weaken OEEC, fail to strengthen Europe, and undermine the future of European co-operation by setting up a discriminatory bloc contrary to our interest.[39]
Thorneycroft wrote to Eden about the brief:

I am convinced that the Americans are in a fool's paradise about Messina, and I strongly recommend that you and the Foreign Secretary should seek to bring home to President Eisenhower the gravity of the dangerous situation which is rapidly developing against the interests of both our countries and all our joint work since the war to build up a 'one world trading system'. . . . If we joined the Six I do not see how any British Government could afford . . . to go on with existing Anglo-American policies of non-discriminatory multilateral trade as enshrined in the G.A.T.T. Certainly the Conservative Party would not stand for it. Our businessmen would be ousted from the European markets through discrimination in favour of their German competitors . . . I think it is vital that you should give a plain and unmistakeable warning to President Eisenhower.

Eden's opinion coincided with Thorneycroft's, and within the Foreign Office it produced this response from R. W. Munro:

If the Six decide to go ahead on the Common Market and we are to avoid the dangers described, we will have to devise some *modus vivendi*. In the meantime we have to see if we can discourage the Six from going ahead without risking incurring their displeasure by coming out in open opposition to their ideals.
The Americans have already fairly openly expressed their feelings that we will not subscribe to the Common Market idea for selfish

national and Commonwealth reasons. I very much fear that they may interpret a warning from the Prime Minister on the lines of the minute written in the same way.[40]

Edden minuted: 'The minute by the President of the Board of Trade is, however, fresh evidence that he, at least, will continue to oppose any *voluntary* [sic] abandonment by the U.K. of our existing "one world" policy.' Geoffrey Harrison minuted: 'The brief could hardly be set out more unattractively and less effectively than it is in some of the paragraphs.'[41]

Meanwhile it became clearer and clearer that the Foreign Office was right and the Brussels powers were on course for an agreement. The warning light for the Treasury should have been a note to Figgures from Edden on 16 January that he had heard that Spaak had written his report in such a way that 'it can with very few adjustments be re-written in the form of a draft Treaty'.[42]

Macmillan was concerned lest the Six would conclude a Treaty. In his memoirs he wrote: 'Britain might be excluded from the benefits of a large European market which seemed likely to develop . . .' although it was clear to him that the weight of British opinion in the Conservative Party, in the Opposition, and in the Press was against our joining as a full partner in the Common Market. Anyway, he asked his Treasury officials to study a plan for an alternative which might prevent the Messina proposals being implemented. On 6 February he asked for an internal Treasury study which might be 'a rearguard action or an advance'.[43]

His instruction was ill received by the Treasury, who still thought the Messina Plan unimportant. Figgures's minute of 8 February shows their aloof attitude:

(a) It involves the preparation of a completely new external policy. It is a huge task.

(b) The ground was gone over very carefully by officials before the Prime Ministers Conference in 1952 when the Government decided in favour of 'one world.'

(c) The only regional bloc we could then see was a Europe/Commonwealth bloc. It was doubtful if this could be achieved politically (the Brown Dominions) and doubtful whether it could be viable for many years. In addition, of course, it would gravely damage the position of Canada in the Commonwealth and eventually – whatever their present views may be – would undermine our relations with U.S.A.

(d) I am sure that if this is to be examined it should be done first inside the Treasury alone but I hope we could confine it to re-examination of the case submitted in 1952 to see whether it still fits.

(e) Anything more than this is a major job. In 1952 the preparation of a new external economic policy involved the officials concerned for the bulk of their time over a period of months. If we are to prepare a new policy it would be most undesirable to try to do this while we are still facing a possible crisis. We simply haven't the resources to do it; we are at full stretch under normal conditions and under great strain at times like the present. I do not see how we could take on another 1952 examination at present.

Macmillan brusquely over-ruled Figgures and set his civil servants to work with the guidance that he did not like 'a European bloc excluding Britain, but he would not join the Six'; he was seeking an initiative which would block the Messina powers' plans, although he was not opposed to their customs union; and 'he wanted to join it with the Commonwealth but to have no part in any supra-national or federal tendencies'.[44]

On 9 February Eden reported to the Cabinet about his talks in Washington:

On the main questions of policy in Europe there was a complete identity of view between the two Governments. . . . The discussions had, however, revealed some difference in the attitude of the two Governments towards the new projects for economic integration in Europe – the proposal resulting from the Messina Conference and the project for an European Atomic Authority. The U.S. Government entertains for these projects an enthusiasm similar to that which they had shown to the European Defence Community; the Canadian Government, on the other hand, were much more alive to the risk that these associations would lead to creation of a high tariff group in Europe.

In Cabinet there was no discussion of the Common Market; the record of the Eden–Lloyd–Pearson conversation in Ottawa on 7 February shows that all three had talked disparagingly of the Messina proposals and favoured more important roles for OEEC, NATO and WEU.[45]

Macmillan persuaded the Prime Minister to agree that the search for an alternative to Messina should not be confined to the Treasury, and that the Working Party should include the Foreign Office and the Board of Trade. Nutting had made an effort to convert Lloyd to the Messina ideas. On 10 January he wrote to him enclosing a long memorandum: 'Of one thing I am sure, that we should not take the present period of quiet in Europe to mean all is necessarily well and should be left alone. . . . I am certain that some way must be found – and found by Britain – if we are not to witness serious deterioration in the European scene in the alarming near future.' In the memorandum Nutting set out detailed reasons for his fears on the future of Europe, and suggested that Britain should take the lead in initiating some new policy for the integration of Europe by extending the Commonwealth to include European countries. It implied that the Six, Britain and the Commonwealth would be locked in a customs union.

Nutting invoked the help of the charismatic and influential Jebb, who from the British Embassy in Paris had a ringside view of the Messina negotiations. Enclosing another memorandum commenting favourably on Nutting's suggestions, Jebb wrote to Lloyd:

> The Minister of State's most able and far seeing paper raises issues of the first importance which as I believe will have to be faced in the fairly near future . . . and if I am right in thinking that we shall one day have to make a future move 'towards the Continent' then I think as a matter of practical politics it is clear that the sort of thing involved will be the United Kingdom membership of the Coal and Steel Community, of Euratom, and no doubt also of a 'Common Market'. . . . All or any of these proposals may be anathema now; but what would our attitude be if we really thought that there was a prospect of the Governments of Rome, Paris and Bonn coming directly or indirectly under the influence of the Soviet Union.[46]

Denis Wright commented:

> At the moment we have put our money on O.E.E.C. in Europe. Officials in Whitehall are searching desperately for new initiatives which we might introduce there and thereby make O.E.E.C. more appealing both to the Europeans and to the Americans. . . . We may eventually be forced to join a Common Market; we hope, however, that the idea will be still born. . . . It is for consideration, however, whether it might not pay us in terms of good relations with the Six (and the Americans) to announce fairly soon that we would be ready to enter into an Agreement of Association such as we have with E.C.S.C. Such a step would cost us nothing although it would not be liked by the other members of O.E.E.C. The virtue of taking this step would be that it would help dispel existing beliefs that we are determined to sabotage both the Common Market and Euratom.

Nutting commented on Wright's minute: 'This is not very encouraging. But it is better than the Washington brief which is the bleakest document I have seen in years.'[47] There is no evidence that Lloyd ever replied to Jebb or took either his or Nutting's memorandum seriously; he did not see it as part of his job as Foreign Secretary to be innovative over Europe. Nutting told the author that the only reply he received from Lloyd, who had a facetious streak, was a written note saying: 'Much ado about nothing.'[48]

The archives show that the inter-departmental Working Party beavered away at speed to find new European counter-proposals which might spike the Messina guns. However, the Spaak Committee in Brussels worked even faster and were a long way in front. Their Report, made public in April, was not only a detailed plan for the customs union and the supra-national institutions, but a statement of its motivation and economic philosophy. It held out a friendly hand to Britain, suggesting that states which did not feel able to join should establish relations closer than 'those they previously had with each of those States individually'. For the British Government one of the unattractive features of the Spaak Report was its declaration that all obstacles to trade in agricultural products must be 'eliminated'. This meant that, if Britain were to join, preferential duties on imports of food from the Commonwealth would eventually have to be abandoned unless the Commonwealth could be included on the lines recommended by Jebb and Nutting.[49]

The Foreign Ministers of the Six decided to meet in Venice at the end of May for formal consideration of the Spaak Report. By 13 April the Report of the British Joint Working Party was ready, but unlike the Spaak Report, which was a blueprint for a Treaty, it presented only interim conclusions and asked Ministers to give them a 'tilt' to show in what direction they should continue their efforts. It was realistic, stating:

> 8. There are thus two threats – one that Germany will dissociate herself from the West, and the other that Germany, while remaining with the West, will establish a domination over Europe.
>
> 9. . . . If the proposal for a common market of the 'Six' came into being, it would be so dangerous to our economic interests that we should have to make special arrangements with it. If . . . it did not come into being, this would mark one more failure of the European countries to work together – and a highly publicised one – and by creating a vacuum in Europe, would be one more step towards the disruption of Europe, unless something new could be found to replace it.
>
> 10. . . . If it were possible for the United Kingdom to develop a closer economic association with Europe, without weakening our links with the Commonwealth and the United States, this would be a powerful reinforcement for the West. Our weight would balance

Germany's, and the closer link between our world-wide economic associations and the Continent of Europe would extend the opportunities to be derived from the association – and thus the attractions in it and the likelihood of success on the main object. . . .

13. . . . It has generally been agreed, for example, that to join a European common market would be incompatible with the United Kingdom's Commonwealth and world-wide interests. The European market has been increasing in importance in the last few years, for it has been expanding steadily at a time when the markets in primary-producing countries have been stagnant. But less than one-third of our trade is with Europe; entry into a common market would be bound to damage much of the other two-thirds (particularly that with the Commonwealth). This course would take us too far towards Europe.

The Working Party put forward six alternative propositions:

a) Active policy of co-operation [with the Six] in O.E.E.C.
b) Merger of the Council of Europe and O.E.E.C.
c) 'European Communities' Tariff scheme for a general reduction in import duties on commodities which countries derived predominantly from O.E.E.C. sources.
d) Free Trade Area in Steel.
e) Partial Free Trade Area with Europe by which tariffs would be removed on imports from the Six to the U.K. on a list which excluded goods in which the Commonwealth was significantly interested and agricultural products.
f) 'Strasbourg Tariff Scheme.' A system of common preference between Europe and the Commonwealth ultimately replacing Imperial Preference altogether, but with no question of supra-national authorities or economic integration as implied with 'Common markets, free trade areas, etc.'

No decision on the Report was taken until 31 May, after the Venice Conference, when a meeting of Ministers – Macmillan, Salisbury, Lloyd, Heathcote Amory, Lennox-Boyd and Boyle – was held at the Treasury. They decided against all the schemes except (e), and ordered a further study of (e) to be made with 'an expansion on the lines suggested by the President of the Board of Trade to make it more attractive to the Commonwealth, involving maintenance of free entry into the United Kingdom for manufactured products, continuation of preferential arrangements for agricultural products'; a detailed study of 'the implications for U.K. industry of abolishing over a period of time existing protective tariffs against Europe on manufactured goods'; and 'the probable timetable of events if we decided to launch such a scheme'. It was over the 'timetable' where the Ministers were furthest astray; the Working Party's plans were developing slowly and carefully, while the Six were galloping ahead fast.[50]

The Venice Conference was outstandingly successful. The British Government had not been invited even to send an observer, although such an invitation had been envisaged in Whitehall. Sir Leslie Rowan commented on 16 May, the eve of Venice,

> . . . it is quite likely that the Six will not progress very much further in fact at Venice, and it may be thought that the risk is negligible of our receiving any embarrassing invitation to join. Unless the French run very contrary to form it is not very likely that there would be any very clear cut decisions to which we could possibly be asked to subscribe or show our sympathy.

Rowan could not have been more wrong about 'clear cut decisions', and his minute reveals how out of touch the British politicians and civil servants were with the mood of the Six.[51]

At Venice the Heads of Government of the Six agreed to draft a treaty based on the Spaak Report, and to reconvene for this purpose at Brussels on 26 June. In the communiqué attention was drawn to the problems of the inclusion of overseas territories and countries in the Common Market, and in the hope of being able to secure the collaboration of other countries the Six issued invitations to all members of the OEEC to Brussels, stating that the treaty would provide for the adherence of, or accession of, other states.

For the British the snag was that if they accepted the invitation to go to Brussels it meant that they had to accept also the principles of the Spaak Report. Figgures was clearly horrified. On 8 June he minuted the following (Plan (e) of the Working Party Report had now been christened Plan G):

> So far as Euratom is concerned, the invitation – if invitation there ever is – to O.E.E.C. countries to attend the meeting in Brussels is largely a tactical question.
>
> But on the Common Market, this seems to me to be potentially of great importance to the United Kingdom. Given the vital importance of the Common Market to Plan G, it is highly desirable that we be as fully informed as possible of what the Six are doing and how they are thinking. This will all become comparatively easy once we decide to do Plan G: we can then talk to M. Spaak and he will, no doubt, fall over himself to make arrangements for us to be associated as closely as we wish thereafter. In the meantime, we merely wish to know as much

as we can without being obliged to say a word, i.e. we want, it appears to me, to be an observer in the ordinary sense of that word.

If no action has been taken by M. Spaak during the next ten days or so, I think we ought to consider asking the Ambassador in Brussels to find out whether we are likely to receive an invitation to be present as an observer. Obviously it would be quite impracticable for us to attend as an observer if that were conditional on our having accepted the text of the Experts' Report. It would be a pretty monstrous condition to make given the fact that France at least is in no position to say that the Government, i.e. plus Parliament, has accepted it either.

Is not this a question which we could usefully raise at an early meeting of your new Committee on Plan G?

I realise that invitation is nebulous and that if the six countries were joined at Brussels by other members of the O.E.E.C., in however restricted a capacity, there would be some risk of their appearing to be merely 'hangers-on'. But the proposals of the Messina Powers, in particular on the Common Market, are potentially of immense importance both to us individually and to the O.E.E.C. as a whole. We consider it of vital importance to know what is going on and that we should miss no opportunity of ensuring that the inter-relations of the Messina plans and O.E.E.C. is [*sic*] not neglected. I consider therefore that the message to M. Spaak should not only seek to obtain clarification but should indicate that H.M. Government would be willing to attend without commitment.[52]

Spaak had to make it plain later that he was not asking other members of the OEEC to join in on equal footing in the drafting of the treaty, and there were to be no observers on the model of Bretherton. They would, if necessary, ask for help at any stages of their work where the need might arise. The Foreign Office gave hints to Spaak that HMG would be willing to attend without commitment. The Venice implications of an early treaty being signed by the Six galvanized the British into speedier action on Plan G, and conversations with Commonwealth Governments were initiated urgently. On 15 June Ellis-Rees objected that other members of OEEC would be alarmed if observers went to Brussels, saying that it would be a transfer of authority, that OEEC would be seriously weakened, and that, if British observers went, it would be a shock to OEEC because it would be a hint of 'a special relationship of the U.K. with the Messina powers'.[53]

Ellis-Rees need not have been worried. On 15 June Maurice Faure, head of the French delegation to the Spaak Committee, came to London and made it clear to Nutting that Britain could only be represented at Brussels if it was ready to negotiate on the basis of the

Spaak Report. Spaak made a statement that any OEEC countries could join in the Brussels Conference on an equal voting basis, but must first accept the Report as a basis for negotiation. There was no chance of Britain accepting this; instead the Ministers felt confident, like Figgures, that Spaak would make arrangements for Britain to be associated if they decided on Plan G. On 18 June Spaak was told that Britain declined regretfully to accept those terms. The European train was starting off without Britain.

At Venice the Six had decided to try to enter into a formal treaty ignoring Britain. However the British Government was now alarmed at the pace of events, and after talks with Commonwealth Governments the Cabinet jointly agreed a memorandum written by Macmillan and Thorneycroft to

> arrange discreetly for the Secretary General of O.E.E.C. to prepare a proposal for . . . a study covering the whole possible range of co-ordination and co-operation between O.E.E.C. and the Group of Six countries; . . . We then at the Council, at what seemed the right moment, would indicate our readiness to take part in such a study. We would hope thereby to secure agreement to *adjourn* [author's italics] consideration of the tariff issue in O.E.E.C. until the results of the study were reported to a subsequent Ministerial Council. . . . We shall be able to keep the discussion going until we have time to make up our minds.[54]

At the OEEC Council it was agreed to set up a special group to study all possible forms of co-operation between the Messina Group and the other European countries in OEEC. Spaak and the other keen Europeans saw through the British duplicity and realized that it was, in the British Cabinet words, 'a move for adjournment' and a 'diversion' which the British hoped to keep going for some time to prevent the Six agreeing to a formal treaty.

On 27 July, the day on which the Suez crisis erupted, Macmillan and Thorneycroft jointly circulated a note on the Common Market prepared by officials from the Foreign Office, Treasury and Board of Trade, who had now been joined by civil servants from the Ministries of Agriculture and Commonwealth Relations, the Colonial Office, the Board of Customs and Excise and the Bank of England. It said: 'We shall shortly be faced with the need to make decisions on commercial policy because of the proposal to create a Common Market in Europe and from the difficulties into which we are running on Imperial Preference with Australia', and they expected to submit these matters to the Cabinet for decision early in September.

The Report, entitled *U.K. Initiatives in Europe, Plan G*, ran to fifteen pages. It was naïve over the likely reaction of the Six:

> We should expect the Plan to be enthusiastically received by some European countries, particularly the more highly industrialised. The Plan would be a major encouragement to the 'European Movement' and to the supporters of the Messina initiative who would see their hopes of tying Germany into Western Europe and creating a greater coherence in Western European economy greatly strengthened.

The Six did not see it that way. They recognized the Plan as a delaying tactic contrived to wreck the Common Market, and, intent on a customs union with supra-national institutions, they would not accept instead a free trade area. Particularly obnoxious to the Six was the fact that the Plan envisaged the continuation of Imperial Preference over foodstuffs. The Messina powers would never agree to abolish tariffs against Britain, and to meet the competition of British industry if she continued to enjoy cheap food and a lower cost of living as a result of low-priced Commonwealth food imports.[55]

The Plan needed a positive decision by the British Cabinet to change from being a high tariff country to being part of a free trade area. This meant abolishing protection for British industries, which had been cushioned against competition from other industrial countries since 1932 by the Import Duties Act plus other out-of-date high duties like the 33 per cent Key Industries Duties dating back to the First World War.

In a further Cabinet memorandum Macmillan and Thorneycroft explained the reasons which led them to support the Plan. They emphasized the Commonwealth aspect:

> It would leave us free to retain for the Commonwealth free entry to the United Kingdom market, together with the agricultural preferences which the Dominions now enjoy, and on manufactured goods any preferences over imports from foreign countries outside Europe. . . . We have a chance which might not recur of gaining the general support of what may be described as both the European and the Imperial wings of the Conservative Party.[56]

On 14 September Macmillan told the Cabinet that

> the arguments for and against proceeding with the Plan were evenly balanced, and the decision must be taken in part on the attitude of the Commonwealth countries. Neither of the two major political parties

now had a well founded economic policy or coherent economic policy. This the Plan would provide, but it would also involve the need for making more rapid and effective adjustments than we had hitherto achieved. . . . Nevertheless our economy could not be sustained indefinitely on the basis of a protected and well insulated market, and the Plan would open the way to those competitive pressures which would force the economy to become more efficient.

This was lukewarm advocacy, but Thorneycroft enthusiastically supported Plan G to the Cabinet. Thorneycroft told the author that he was much the most convinced European in the Cabinet and that the civil servants in the Board of Trade under him were much keener on Plan G than were the Treasury or the Foreign Office. Edden wrote in a Foreign Office file at the end of July: 'The President of the Board of Trade is known to be very keen on Plan G.'[57]

Because of the Suez crisis no decision was taken by the Cabinet before November, but meanwhile the Cabinet gave Macmillan authority, without coming to a definite decision, to discuss Plan G in general terms with the Commonwealth Finance Ministers at their meeting in Washington at the end of September. Macmillan has recorded: 'The younger Ministers seemed favourable; some of the older ones doubtful or hostile.' Eden, according to Macmillan, was favourable, although he warned there would be trouble in the Cabinet and within the Party.[58]

On 3 October the Cabinet was informed by Macmillan that in Washington he had explained to the Commonwealth countries the proposals for a free trade area, and as this had been leaked a press statement was now necessary. Macmillan added: 'we must be satisfied before we would contemplate entering a Free Trade Area in Europe that agricultural products were excluded and we preserved both the interests of Commonwealth agriculture in the United Kingdom Market and of the system of Commonwealth preferences.' On this 'agricultural' issue Plan G was doomed to failure, because the Six were now determined to include agriculture in their treaty.

Macmillan must have had high hopes of Plan G because he wrote to Spaak, who was in New York on 3 October, entreating him 'to keep things as fluid as possible at the meeting of the Foreign Ministers of the Six on 20 October, so as to permit us and other countries to associate with the Customs Union in a wider free trade if we can do so. Binding decision at this stage might make this difficult.' This letter left Spaak unmoved; he was determined to conclude a treaty at the earliest possible moment, and was not going to be diverted from his purpose by British spoiling tactics.[59]

On 18 September the Cabinet deferred a decision on Plan G. Then Macmillan said that the UK had declined in importance relatively; 'The basis of industrial production must be large enough to carry the overheads which modern industrial techniques made necessary, and the home market was now relatively too small to provide this, but because it would expose sterling to new strains . . .' a decision could not now be taken on whether to proceed with the plan until future events could be clearly foreseen (for instance the result of Suez).

The Prime Minister said it was a dilemma.

> . . . there seemed no alternative but to base our policy on the proposed plan for closer association with Europe or some suitable variant or extension of it. The French Prime Minister had recently asked whether we might be prepared to revive the offer of common citizenship made in 1940, and we now had to consider our reply. In his opinion . . . although the Conservative Party had traditionally been a Commonwealth Party the younger generation were conscious of a need for new policies and might prove responsive to an initiative in these directions.

The Cabinet decided that no final decision was possible because of the Suez dispute; they ignored the fact that to prevent the Six concluding a treaty there was no time to lose.[60] Fourteen days later they rejected common citizenship with France.

However, Eden had advanced a long way from his rejection of Europe in 1955 under Churchill when he was Foreign Secretary. If, with his popularity in Europe and his powers of debate and negotiation, he had taken Plan G under his wing and argued for it enthusiastically, he might have convinced Spaak and his associates of Britain's sincerity and changed the course of events in Europe. But he was submerged by the Suez crisis and unable to find time to take the initiative.

Because of French involvement in the Suez crisis an important ministerial meeting of the Messina powers due to begin on 10 October had to be postponed. When it took place on the 20th it did not go well. Both the French and the Germans made reservations; it was the first real setback Spaak had experienced. For a short period British hopes were raised that Messina would not come off, and the French and Germans might be tempted to opt for Plan G.

Telegrams from the British Embassy in Paris stated that at midday on 21 October

> Spaak was distinctly gloomy about the lack of progress. . . . Preliminary talks on the previous day had seemed satisfactory but when the

experts had tried to record the results on paper for submission to Ministers it was apparent very considerable difficulties still subsisted. M. Spaak spoke sadly about the French whose impossible demands, he stated, were preventing any further progress. France's partners were all doing their utmost to help out but every time they made a concession, France demanded something more until they came to the point when one or another of the Five refused to go any further. . . . M. Schumann had commented to a British Embassy official that the meeting had gone badly and that the blame lay with Britain. The German Liberals, he said, were coming to think that a satisfactory agreement on the Common Market with France was impossible and that it would be more sensible to work for a British style free trade area. . . . Dr Adenauer, of course, was still strongly in favour of the Common Market.

On 16 October Macmillan sent another personal message to Spaak:

There will be much discussion whether the Colonial Territories as opposed to Commonwealth Territories should be in or out. I hope that we may be able to discuss the technical problems of this in the O.E.E.C. working party and that no premature decision will be taken by the Six. . . . I know that the French have certain views. . . . I am not pleading for a decision. I am pleading for a little time before final decisions are made.

Macmillan was thoroughly alarmed at the danger of Britain being excluded if the Six went ahead.

In an internal Foreign Office minute G. F. Rodgers wrote: 'I am almost (but not quite) of the opinion that the French are now embarking on conscious sabotage of the Common Market'; Edden wrote: 'Perhaps they are just waiting for us to show our hand. They too may really prefer a Free Trade area. Please note also that from the German side Dr Erhardt is prompting from the wings.' In a further minute Edden wrote: 'Little seems to have happened to justify our fears that the Six might commit themselves in various ways before our plan could be launched.' However, just as it seemed as if French intransigence might provide an opening for successful free trade area negotiations, Spaak gave France all the concessions she wanted, explaining to the British that

the trouble was that France was undergoing serious economic strains and if certain concessions were not made to her, then she would definitely refuse to join the Common Market. In the circumstances he was obliged to yield, particularly as speed in signing the treaties was essential. This must be done before the German elections and while M. Mollet continued at the head of the French Government.[61]

Once Spaak had overcome the French and German objections raised on 20 October, the Six concerted their plans to include agriculture in their treaty, and the Common Market took shape quickly with draft clauses being agreed to cover overseas territories, arbitration, voting rights and other matters. The British Cabinet looked on this progress as sinister, and, despite being preoccupied with the preparations and aftermath of the Suez war, on 13 November it considered a memorandum from Macmillan and Thorneycroft proposing an announcement in Parliament that Britain would negotiate through OEEC for a mutual free trade area on the lines of Plan G. This stated that the response to discussions with other Commonwealth countries had been 'unexpectedly favourable', although their attitude would change if the danger emerged of concessions on their foodstuffs, and that there had been an unexpected measure of support from the Conservative Party and the TUC. A decision was deferred, but on 20 November the Cabinet decided to embark on negotiations. It was an important move towards Europe because the Government had agreed on the vital move from being a high tariff protected economy to low tariffs or free trade with Europe.

A Commons debate was held on 26 November. Macmillan and Thorneycroft argued in favour with conviction, and the Labour Party, strongly influenced by Harold Wilson, concurred. However, Government spokesmen continued to emphasize that agriculture must be entirely excluded. This categorical blanket exclusion of food products (for man or beast, drink and tobacco) the Six 'would not swallow' (Roy Jenkins's words in the debate). They felt that, although Britain was making a gesture towards Europe, the country's main reason for the change of front was the feeling that 'we cannot afford to stay out', and fear of the Plan G proposals prompted Spaak to press on even faster with his negotiations to complete the Treaty of Rome as soon as possible; it was signed on 27 March 1957.

On 7 January, two days after Eden resigned, Spaak came to London and had discussions with Macmillan (now Prime Minister) and Thorneycroft (now Chancellor of the Exchequer); they concentrated on agriculture and overseas territories within the Common Market and the proposed free trade area. Spaak was aware that these two had taken the lead under Eden in pressing for Britain to be associated with the Common Market through the free trade area. However, the British Ministers again stressed that agriculture must be excluded. Macmillan overplayed his hand by stating that this was 'non-negotiable'; it was another miscalculation of the strength of the British bargaining position. Unfortunately it was also the sticking point for Spaak, and the British made no headway with him on this issue. The visit was a failure. The Six had not yet formulated complete plans for the Common Agricultural Policy, and the British objected to the imposition of a common external tariff on food imports from the Commonwealth. Spaak insisted that if there was agreement on Plan G all British food imports must pay the common external tariff, and objected to Britain keeping down the price of food by deficiency payments to farmers because with this cheap food Britain had an economic advantage.

The OEEC Council meeting in February 1957 did not go smoothly. Britain again contested that agricultural products must be excluded, and was in a minority of one. The Six would have nothing to do with any proposal which might slow down ratification of the Treaty of Rome, although they agreed that the negotiations about a free trade area should be continued in OEEC.[62] A 'wave of suspicion' of Britain swept the Six during the early months of 1957. They feared that the British negotiations were purposely aimed at delaying the signing and ratification of the Treaty of Rome. The continental press was continually reporting that Britain was trying to torpedo the Common Market, despite repeated statements that it wished the community well.

Thus when the European Economic Community came into being on 1 January 1958, after the Messina powers had ratified the Treaty of Rome in their national Parliaments, the British efforts to create a free trade area in association with the Community through OEEC were stillborn. The damage done by the hostility of the Eden Government to the Messina powers after they had been encouraged by Bretherton as a 'representative' to the Spaak Committee in Brussels could not be repaired. Macmillan and his Cabinet, alarmed at the threat to the economy inherent in the customs union of the EEC, tried hard for the next two years – but in vain – to achieve association with the Six through a free trade area.

In 1958 de Gaulle came to power in France and, much to Macmillan's annoyance, firmly vetoed any more negotiations for the proposed free trade area. In 1955 the Eden Government could have sailed freely into the still malleable Common Market, and obtained substantial concessions for the Commonwealth. Not for another twenty years was Britain able to negotiate entry, and then on worse terms than would have been available under Eden's Prime Ministership.

The Far East
1954–6

GRAVE DISPUTES OVER policy towards Indo-China and Formosa clouded relations between Dulles and Eden in 1954 and 1955. Therein lay the seeds of the quarrels which were to bedevil Anglo–US relations and lead to America behaving with surprising harshness towards Britain over Suez in 1956.

Dulles feared that Communist China would launch far-ranging attacks in the Far East, over-running the independent states; Eden – correctly, as it turned out – believed that Communist China would not risk a third world war. Eisenhower used his friendship with Churchill to put forward the Dulles view in personal letters, and Churchill tended to side with the Americans. This produced tension between Eden and Churchill, which was aggravated by Churchill continually putting off the date of his resignation. Overcoming many difficulties, Eden had considerable success when in July 1954, at the Geneva Conference, agreement was reached with Communist China and France for a ceasefire and the partition of Vietnam. Dulles had wanted American military intervention to aid the French and an immediate military coalition to include Britain to stop the Communist Chinese helping the Vietminh; Eden refused to countenance either until all diplomatic efforts had failed.

In 1954 and 1955 the Far East was in turmoil, with fighting both in Vietnam and between the Communist Chinese and the Formosan Nationalists. The Korean Armistice had been signed in July 1953, but talks on a Korean political settlement, begun at Panmunjon in October 1953, had collapsed in December, mainly over prisoner exchange.

The French war against the Nationalist Vietminh under Ho Chi Minh had started in December 1946, and after seven years had been internationalized with the Communist Chinese supplying ever-increasing help to the Vietminh over the border, while the USA stepped up their help to the French and their Vietnamese army. The

Vietnamese and Chinese were traditional enemies, but they sank their differences because of their common socialist ideals. American assistance to the French began under President Truman when the Chinese People's Republic came into existence and the Korean War started. At first it was looked on with disapproval in America as a French colonial war. However by 1954 it was regarded with approval as a fight against Communism, because in 1948 France had established a sort of independence for its former colonies; the ex-Emperor Bao Dai was created head of an independent Vietnam, while Laos and Cambodia were given independence within a French union. On the other side Moscow and Peking granted recognition to the Nationalist Vietminh revolutionaries in North Vietnam.

At the end of 1953 there were hints that China wanted peace in Vietnam. However Mendès-France, who was in favour of peace negotiations, missed becoming Prime Minister of France by 13 votes and instead Laniel, who took a hard line, formed a Government. By the end of 1953 the Nationalist Vietminh controlled around half of Vietnam, but the major cities in the north, Haiphong and Hanoi, and Cochin-China and Saigon in the south, were still in French hands. Considerable alarm was caused in the West when in 1953 the Communist Vietnam General Giap occupied about half Laos and areas in northern Cambodia.

Laniel backed the Navarre Plan (called after General Navarre, GOC in Indo-China) for the build-up of French forces to over half a million men. The major snag was that over half would be Vietnamese recruits, and with their troubles in Algeria, Tunisia and Morocco France was in no position to commit more troops in the Far East; also, under French law conscripts could not be sent to Vietnam.

The Americans became alarmed at the French lack of success and feared that Chinese Communists would occupy not only all Vietnam, but also Cambodia and Laos. This would pose a threat to Thailand and also to British Malaya, where the Americans had strong economic interests through their purchases of tin and rubber. Dulles and Eisenhower were very conscious of the strategic importance of Indo-China and were determined to do everything they could to prevent a French collapse, and by the end of 1953 America was paying half the French costs of the war.

President Eisenhower, Prime Minister Churchill and French Foreign Minister Bidault held a meeting in Bermuda in December 1953, where they all agreed that the French war effort in Indo-China was of 'vital importance'. They decided to hold a four-power conference with Russia in Berlin, but the French position in Indo-China

Peking ■

KOREA

Sea
of
Japan

Yellow
Sea

C H I N A

Shanghai ●

● Chung-king

⦂ Taichen

● Matsus

Battle of
Dien Bien Phu

Quemoy

FORMOSA
(TAIWAN)

BURMA

Hanoi ■
Haiphong
Gulf of
Tonking

Hong Kong

L
A
O
S

NORTH
VIETNAM

HAINAN

CEASE FIRE LINE, JULY 1954

THAILAND

● Hue

Bangkok ■

SOUTH
VIETNAM

South

CAMBODIA

China

Gulf of
Thailand

Saigon ■

Sea

Mekong River Delta

M
A
L
A
Y
PENINSULA

The Far East
1954-1956

Singapore ●

0   500   1000 km

deteriorated seriously before the conference began in January 1954. Stalin had died nine months before, and in Berlin Molotov, the Foreign Minister, suggested a five-power conference including China to discuss Korea and Indo-China. Urged on by Bidault, Dulles eventually agreed, but only on the understanding that the USA would not recognize the People's Republic of China. The conference was to meet in Geneva on 26 April.

Meanwhile General Giap halted his successful Laotian campaign and began to besiege the French stronghold at Dien Bien Phu on 26 February 1954. Chinese fighter aircraft appeared over Dien Bien Phu, although there is some doubt whether they actually entered into combat. Within two days of Giap's attack on Dien Bien Phu General Navarre concluded that the fortified position would be lost without early American intervention. On 20 March General Ely, President of the French Chiefs of Staff, flew to Washington in an effort to get an assurance of air support if Chinese aircraft attacked French positions, and also to speed up American military aid. Meanwhile Field Marshal Harding, British Chief of the Imperial General Staff, reported to the Cabinet that the French were in a very dangerous situation. The American Chiefs of Staff told Ely they were sure a properly equipped French/Vietnamese army could defend Indo-China against the Communists, and promised to accelerate their aid.[1]

By now the American Government believed a French disaster in Vietnam was imminent, and in Dulles's words 'the imposition on South East Asia of the political system of Communist Russia and its Chinese Communist ally . . . and that possibility . . . should be met by united action' which 'might involve serious risks'. Eisenhower emphasized that he agreed with Dulles. Admiral Radford, the US Chief of Staff, suggested to Ely 'a limited tactical aerial bombardment of Vietminh positions around Dien Bien Phu', which would require several strikes from B-29s stationed at Clark Field in the Philippines, supported by fighter aircraft. How the pilots would identify the targets after their marathon flight was unclear; there would have been a grave danger of them bombing the French positions. The French asked the USA to undertake the air strike, known as Operation Vautout, on 5 April. Radford brought his plan to a secret meeting of Congressmen and said that if the bombing failed to relieve the garrison US ground troops would be used. This meeting virtually vetoed the Radford plan, and it was clear it would not get Congressional support unless Britain agreed to support it. Dulles knew that Eden and the British Cabinet would oppose it. So he dispatched notes to Britain and France, New Zealand and

Australia, asking for a 'defence coalition' to warn China against intervening in Indo-China. Eden was not averse to such a warning, but did not want to announce it before the Geneva Conference.

When Dulles came to London for talks at the Foreign Office on 11 April 1954 a strange misunderstanding arose between Eden and him. Eden stated firmly that he would not agree to the use of British armed forces in Indo-China, but left Dulles with the impression that he would agree to start discussions on a defence organization. As soon as he got back to Washington Dulles invited the ambassadors of nine countries to a meeting on 20 April to consider the proposed South-East Asia Defence Organization. Contrary to Dulles's understanding of their 11 April talk, Eden now claimed he had not authorized even preliminary discussion of this and ordered his Ambassador in Washington, Makins, not to attend. Dulles was forced to turn the meeting into a briefing session for the coming Geneva Conference – much to his annoyance.

Some commentators suggest that Eden had second thoughts after his talk with Dulles because he was worried by attacks on him in the House of Commons by Bevan, who accused the Foreign Secretary of toadying to the Americans and ignoring India and the Common-wealth. There is little evidence to support this view, and how this misunderstanding on 11 April arose remains a mystery. Dulles believed Eden had gone back on a promise and wrote to his sister: 'Eden has double crossed me. He lied to me.'[2]

According to Evelyn Shuckburgh, Eden's private secretary, the American record showed that Eden 'did indicate that we should be willing to start such talks at once provided we were not committed to any action against Indo-China, but ours was obscure and AE has always denied it'. Makins reported that 'the State Department's full record is clear and unequivocal, whereas the only record I have is ambiguous'. Eden replied to Makins: 'I am not aware that Dulles has any ground for complaint . . . he is creating difficulties for anyone in this country . . . who wants to maintain close Anglo–American relations. We at least have constantly to bear in mind the Common-wealth even if U.S. does not like some of them.' Eden wrote the telegram scrawled around the incoming message from Makins when he was week-ending at Binderton, and according to Shuckburgh this illustrated Eden's personal irritation with Dulles, and his growing sense of indignation over the lack of deference which, he felt, the Americans were showing towards their British ally. Eisenhower wrote in his diary that at Geneva Eden would press for a ceasefire, that the British attitude would be deeply resented by Australia and

New Zealand, and that America might have to form a coalition with the Philippines, Thailand, France and Indo-China to the complete exclusion of the British.

Before the Geneva Conference opened Eden and Dulles attended a meeting of NATO in Paris on 22 April. Communist successes in attacks on Dien Bien Phu were arousing acute anxiety, and the French renewed their plea to Dulles to undertake Operation Vaut-out. In order to overcome Congress opposition Dulles wanted immediate British participation, and he again suggested to Eden that a united defence organization should be formed at short notice with France, Britain, Australia and New Zealand. Eden rejected this, saying that 'conditions in Indo-China could not be remedied by outside intervention at this hour'. There was a quarrel, and it did not help matters when Admiral Radford arrived from America and was even keener than Dulles on intervention, proposing immediate air raids on China.[3]

Radford asked Eden if RAF units could be sent into Tonkin from Malaya or Hong Kong, and asked if Britain had an aircraft carrier in the area. To Dulles's irritation Eden told him he must have forgotten the Russo–Chinese alliance, and that if we went into Indo-China we might be fighting the Chinese as well as the Vietminh and heading for a third world war.[4] The two Foreign Secretaries were poles apart. Eden was bent on partition and a ceasefire, and would consider neither armed intervention nor a long-term major anti-Communist regional alliance while the Geneva Conference had any chance of success.

On 24 April Dulles told Eden that the Americans would not intervene at Dien Bien Phu because 'no intervention could now save the fortress'. (Dulles quickly changed his mind about this.) He went on to say that 'if the French were confident that we would join in the defence of Indo-China they might not capitulate altogether on the fall of Dien Bien Phu', and that assurances to this effect would keep the French in the fight (in southern Vietnam). He feared that without Anglo–American backing France might abandon the whole of Vietnam to the Communists.

Churchill became so alarmed at this rift between Eden and the Americans that he telephoned to Eden to say he would fly to Paris to talk to Laniel and Bidault. This was anathema to Eden, who knew that once he was in Paris Churchill would take charge of the negotiations, so he decided to fly back to England, arriving at Chequers late on the evening of the 24th. The next day, Sunday, the Chiefs of Staff were summoned to a meeting of Ministers to discuss whether Chinese support of the Vietminh should be checked by 'vigorous military action against the Chinese mainland' – in other words a blockade of the Chinese coast and air attacks on military targets in China, which Radford believed could be taken without risk of drawing Russia into the contest. Eden argued, and Churchill and the Cabinet agreed, that anything like open war against China might well involve the Soviet Union and lead to a third world war.

That afternoon Eden was told by the French Ambassador, Massigli, that Dulles had suddenly changed his mind and now wanted an immediate US air strike against Dien Bien Phu following an urgent request from the French Government; and that Dulles had told the French that if the UK would associate themselves with a declaration to use military action 'to check communism', Eisenhower would ask Congress for emergency approval so that US aircraft might be able to launch an attack on Dien Bien Phu as soon as 28 April. Massigli urged on Eden that the British should immediately join the Americans in such a declaration. The Chiefs of Staff were recalled to an emergency second meeting of Ministers, which decided they could not join in such a declaration, and Eden was authorized to snub Dulles by saying, 'Our military advice gave us no confidence that the fortress of Dien Bien Phu could be effectively relieved by air intervention of the kind now proposed . . . we ourselves had no forces which could assist in such an operation.'[5]

The next day, on his way to Geneva, Eden saw Bidault in Paris and told him that the Cabinet had turned down the American request. Bidault told him (erroneously) that reports from Dien Bien Phu were slightly better, and that was why the French were asking for an air strike, which Radford had told them would be 'of the order of 450 tons per sortie'. Late that evening Eden and Dulles had an acrimonious meeting in Geneva, at which Eden gave the American the Cabinet's message. Dulles replied that 'an inglorious end to the Indo-China campaign would affect the French position in Morocco, Tunis and elsewhere', and that he was sceptical of Britain's ability to hold Malaya if Indo-China were lost. Dulles was now against an air strike on Dien Bien Phu – a quick change of mind – but he still wanted to support the French militarily, and said that if an experienced American general such as General van Fleet was put in charge of reorganization of operations and training 'much might be achieved'. Eden reiterated to Dulles that first they must try for a respectable settlement at Geneva with the Chinese.[6]

The same evening, 26 April, Churchill surprisingly gave Radford dinner at Chequers with the British Chiefs of Staff. Winston told

Radford that the loss of Dien Bien Phu must be faced and that 'after we had seen what had come out of the Geneva Conference the Cabinet would be willing to consider the situation in the closest consultation with their American allies'. Churchill warned that war with China who would invoke the Sino–Russian pact might mean an assault by hydrogen bombs on these islands because of the American Air Force bases in East Anglia. Radford told Churchill that Navarre, the French Commander in Vietnam, was 'a disaster'.

Colville, who had been at the Chequers dinner, reported to the Foreign Office that Radford thought the British Chiefs of Staff unrealistic in believing that Malaya could be held if Indo-China went; when Radford got back to Washington he told Makins he was 'depressed but pleased with his reception at Chequers, and unconvinced by what he was told by the British Chiefs of Staff at the dinner'. Makins wrote: 'I am sure he is a strong advocate of going ahead without us but plus the South Koreans, the Formosans and *ad hoc genus omne*. There is a distinct possibility of an American decision on these lines.'[7]

When the Conference opened, the atmosphere at Geneva was cold. The French were defeatist; Dulles was reproachful of the British and would not speak to the Chinese or shake hands with any of them. At first Chou En-lai, head of government of the People's Republic of China, was aloof and refused to consider any compromise. Fortunately Molotov was helpful, and he and Eden agreed to be co-chairmen. Gradually Eden softened Chou En-lai. But Dulles rigidly refused to speak to Chou or to any member of the Chinese delegation.

On 27 April Dulles complained that Eden was pressing the French towards a ceasefire which would in his (Dulles's) view be fatal to their whole military position in Vietnam. Eden denied this and said a ceasefire was only possible within a political settlement. Dulles countered by postulating that there was no chance of the French staying in the fight without 'a common defence system', and in London on the same day the British Chiefs of Staff were told that the American plan was for Super-Fortresses from Manila, 1200 miles away, to bomb the Vietminh supply lines leading to Dien Bien Phu; the object would be to free the French Air Force so that it could concentrate on close support of the fortress of Dien Bien Phu; the British Chiefs of Staff advised that such attacks would 'not be effective'.

At a dinner on 1 May in Geneva relations between Eden and Dulles reached their lowest point when Dulles told Eden that Britain and America were in 'complete disarray'. Eden replied that he had no idea what Britain was being asked to do; we had refused to intervene with armed forces, and if America entered the Vietnam war the next stage would be that the Americans and Chinese would be fighting each other 'and that was in all probability the beginning of the third world war'. Nettled, Dulles replied that he was only asking Britain for 'moral support'. According to Eden it was 'a highly disturbing conversation' because the Americans were deeply aggrieved at 'our refusal to support them in military measures', and according to Shuckburgh Eden foresaw himself after American forces had landed in Indo-China getting up in the Commons to answer the question: 'Did you know of and approve this move?'[8]

On 3 May Dulles left Geneva in a huff; Walter Bedell Smith, Under-Secretary of State, was put in charge of the American delegation, and immediately the atmosphere improved immensely. Dulles left a letter to Eden proposing secret talks between the USA and Britain about Siam and the South-East Asia position generally, which he wanted kept secret from the French. His last message to Eden was: 'Could not the British Government reconsider its position at least to the extent of enabling us to help and provide Bidault with some hope which might enable him to gather the political strength to hold off from the surrender which otherwise seems inevitable?'

Bedell Smith and Eden got on well. Eden reported that on 3 May, when he had dinner with him, he was most receptive and eager to find some way of ending the misunderstanding, and told Eden that there could be no question of sending American ground forces. 'They will go in over my dead body,' he said. On 7 May Dien Bien Phu fell and Eden's plan for partition and a ceasefire became more acceptable to both French and American opinion. Eden's attitude to Dulles is revealed by his telegram to the Prime Minister on 12 May:

> The situation here gets steadily more confused and difficult. The French have their thoughts in Paris, but we are doing everything we can to try to get them to make up their minds upon their minimum terms, so that we can go into action in support of them.
>
> Washington, until very recently, has been trying to get wholly unrealisable terms. Meanwhile Dulles' daily commentary multiplies confusion and exasperates everybody.

Churchill gave orders that this message was not to be shown to other members of the Cabinet; he was determined that his 'special relationship' with Eisenhower should not be wrecked by the Eden–Dulles row. Winston wanted Bedell Smith to fly to London to talk to him; Eden curtly refused this suggestion.[9]

A telegram from Makins to the Foreign Office from Washington on 21 May referred to 'the racket here about the existence of a major rift in Anglo–American relations (said to have been officially confirmed by a Foreign Office spokesman)'. Churchill wrote on it: 'Is this so?' The Washington reports of an Anglo–American rift sprang from what Eden termed 'a disconcerting incident' on 15 May when Swiss newspapers reported that the Americans and French were having talks about American intervention in Vietnam. Dulles had ruled that the British should not be informed of this, but when Eden taxed Bedell Smith the latter confirmed that such talks were taking place behind Eden's back. Bedell Smith promised that in future Eden would be 'fully informed', and managed to soothe him.[10]

According to Evelyn Shuckburgh, by mid-May Eden was 'enjoying the conference in the fullest sense because he is really running it and recognised to be the King of the Conference'. Eden was also pleased by the good press he was getting in Britain for standing up to the Americans and keeping Britain out of war with Indo-China.

On 21 June the Conference adjourned. To Eden's intense disappointment the Prime Minister had refused to resign in July, as he had promised. Churchill had become disturbed at the ill-will between Eden and Dulles, and had far more sympathy with the American's viewpoint over the Indo-China crisis than with that of his own Foreign Secretary. Eisenhower had written personally to Churchill on 27 April inviting him to come to Washington in June, saying: 'I am deeply concerned by the seemingly wide differences in the conclusions developed in our respective governments especially as these conclusions relate to such events as the war in Indo-China and to the impending conference in Geneva.'

On receipt of this letter Winston sent a message to Eden in Geneva: 'Ike's message . . . speaks about grave divergences entirely contrary to everything Dulles said about his visit over here', and enthusiastically accepted Eisenhower's invitation. Eden was annoyed with Churchill about this, and also because Churchill suggested he should come to Geneva, telling Eden that 'I should like to have met Molotov again and Chou en Lai for the first time. I have many prejudices to get over about the Chinese.' The last thing Eden wanted was Churchill in Geneva with his prejudices about the Chinese, just as he himself had become the 'King of the Conference' and was making headway with both the Russians and the Chinese.

On 16 May Eden told the Prime Minister: 'I confess that at the moment I view any visit to the U.S. in June without enthusiasm. But it may well be that if we can get no agreement here it will become imperative.' On 24 May Winston wrote to the President: 'Our meeting may brush away this chatter about an Anglo–American rift.' On 25 May, in a telegram to the Prime Minister, Eden voiced further opposition about the Washington meeting:

> I believe that it would be a grave mistake for the visit to be announced before the position here is clearer. Whatever the terms of the announcement, it would, if made now, be assumed to be connected with Anglo–American differences about Indo-China. It would be thought that these differences had attained such serious proportions that you felt it necessary to visit the United States yourself in order to compose them.
>
> This would put us into a most embarrassing position. And apart from personal considerations it might have a serious effect on the Conference itself and therefore increase those dangers which we discussed together during the weekend. . . .
>
> Having been away so much from England you will know how reluctant I am to set out again. But if I am to be with you, do not you think I should be with you all the time in Washington?

On 1 June Eden tried again to persuade the Prime Minister to drop the US visit, writing that 'the main American concern is not now, if it ever has been, for the success of the Conference, but with preparations for intervention', and that 15 June was the 'danger period' for Hanoi; they might arrive in Washington just as the French were in grievous trouble and the American desire to intervene at its height. Eden went on that the Conference would not be finished by the end of the next week and

> We might be over the worst, but we are more likely to be in a dangerous phase. If I were then to leave this work and go with you to Washington wouldn't that seem all wrong? . . . I only put these thoughts to you because they are in my mind as part of the most troubled international scene I can ever recall.

This clash between Eden and Churchill came to a head on 11 June when Dulles attacked Eden in a speech in Los Angeles, saying that Eden had not kept his word after the 11 April meeting. Eden telegraphed to the Prime Minister:

> These charges must be answered, and I shall have no difficulty in answering them. I am concerned, however, about the timing of my reply in relation to the announcement of our impending visit. I think

that it will seem very strange if it is announced that we are going to Washington in the face of Dulles' unanswered charges.

Eden wanted the announcement of the visit deferred until after he replied to Dulles in the Commons; he also told Churchill that, although the Communists wanted to keep the Conference going, he and Bedell Smith wanted to break it up because Russia and China were 'so divided', and 'taking it all in all I have never known such a tangle'. Churchill then forbade Eden to reply to Dulles's charges, exercising his authority in a way which must have been maddening to Eden, coming so soon after Churchill had refused to hand over the reins of government. He wrote to Eden:

> I am sure the House would not want to hear from you a refutation of this chatter by Dulles, and they very earnestly desire the full statement which only you can make about the Geneva conference. . . . You might or might not think it worth while to refer to this particular floater in which Dulles has indulged, but I hope you will consider very carefully whether a personal wrangle with your fellow Foreign Secretary in Washington would be a wise feature to introduce into a situation already, as you say, a tangle such as you have never known. I therefore cannot agree to repudiate my proposal to the President. . . . This would only be raking up a fresh dispute with our only powerful ally at a moment when so many differences and divergences of a serious character are alive between our two countries.

Perforce Eden accepted this ruling by his superior, and to console him Winston told him: 'Dulles, in British public opinion, stands nearly as low as McCarthy, but the latter is better found on TV', 'I am sure Dulles will grovel when we meet him', and 'Dulles evidently does not like our White House meeting. What he says counts for absolutely nothing here and the more he says it, the more harmless does it become . . . the Dulles "Aunt Sally," few have noticed it, and fewer still have bothered to try and understand it.'[11] Churchill brought his doctor, Lord Moran, to Washington with him. According to Moran, on the air journey the Prime Minister said to him: 'I hope Anthony will not upset them; they are so kind and generous to their friends'; and on 27 June, while Dulles and Eden were closeted at an evening meeting, Churchill was in a state of anxiety and said to Moran: 'Eden must be back . . . oh, go and see. Christ! I hope they haven't quarrelled and killed each other!'[12]

The cause of the Dulles–Eden current quarrel had been removed when on 13 June Mendès-France had replaced Laniel as Prime

Minister of France, and had declared that the French would not continue fighting in Vietnam, thus making American intervention impossible. Temporarily the two Foreign Secretaries had nothing to quarrel about.

Still there remained another long-term controversy between Eden and Dulles. The Americans intended to use atomic weapons in the Far East against the Chinese Communists if they broke the armistice agreement in Korea, intervened in Vietnam or attacked Formosa. Eisenhower had agreed at the end of 1953 that in principle these weapons should be as available for use as any others, and Dulles was eager to have this point agreed internationally. He tried to do this in private conversations and in NATO presentations, and was continually prompted by Admiral Radford to get approval for atomic bombs in various eventualities. Eisenhower was more cautious, but the Americans believed that nuclear weapons were there to be used in the Far East; Eden and Churchill did not like this at all.

At the Bermuda Conference on 5 December 1953, between America, France and Britain, Eden and Churchill had been shocked when the Americans categorically told them they intended to use atom bombs in Korea if the Chinese came to the help of the North Koreans. This was strongly resisted by the British. The next day, in private, Eisenhower told Colville that 'Whereas Winston looked on the atomic weapon as something entirely new and terrible, he looked upon it as just the latest improvement in military weapons.' According to Colville, 'He implied that there was in fact no distinction between "conventional weapons" and atomic weapons; all weapons in due course became conventional weapons. This, of course, represents a fundamental difference of opinion between public opinion in the U.S.A. and in England.' With difficulty Winston succeeded in persuading the Americans to leave out the words 'free to use the atomic bomb' and substitute the phrase 'reserving the right to use the atomic bomb' in the official communiqué.

Eisenhower told the British that 'the United States public would not understand failure to use weapons on which so much had been spent, and which are evidently now regarded in the United States as established weapons of war.' In his report on Bermuda to the Cabinet, Eden wrote: 'In communicating with the Old Commonwealth Governments . . . we should affirm in particular that the consequence of the use of atomic weapons against an enemy in the Far East might be so serious for the United Kingdom that we cannot agree to such action in advance and must insist on being consulted at the time before it is taken.'[13]

Five-power military talks on the Far East were held in Washington from 3 to 11 June 1954. The participants were America, Britain, France, New Zealand and Australia. In the agreed report, which did not commit the Governments of the respective delegations, came these ominous words: 'To achieve a maximum and lasting effect [against the Chinese Communists] nuclear as well as conventional weapons should be used from the outset.' In their report the British Chiefs of Staff added: 'Although the use of nuclear weapons in war against China would from the military point of view obviously be more effective than the use of conventional weapons their employment would have a serious effect on Asian opinion generally.'

Churchill and Eden could not veto the use of atom bombs in the Far East by the Americans, and at that time Britain was committed to using atomic weapons if Russia attacked western Europe. Macmillan, Minister of Defence, had reported to the Cabinet that 'In regard to Europe, if war comes in the next few years the Allies would have to make immediate use of the full array of nuclear weapons with the object of containing Russia's overwhelming superiority of man-power. We must therefore plan on the assumption that global nuclear bombardment will become general.' With the Churchill Government ready to use atom bombs in Europe, it was not such a far cry to doing the same in the Far East. China had an alliance with Russia, who had already tested a nuclear weapon and might have retaliated on behalf of the Chinese, but during that period Russian nuclear weapons were less devastating than American ones.[14] Evidence of Eden's anger with Dulles over atom bombs comes in a telegram to Makins:

I have also not forgotten Mr. Dulles' remarks to me last September [1954] that Quemoy was indefensible except with the use of atomic weapons. Have the Americans really weighed the dangers of having to use them to defend useless islands simply to support Nationalist morale by compensating them for the loss of the equally useless Ta Chens [*sic*]?[15]

The Washington Conference accomplished nothing, and on 14 July Eden was back in Geneva after meeting Mendès-France and Dulles in Paris. There was doubt whether Dulles would return to Geneva; to Eden's relief he decided to stay away, and instead Bedell Smith returned alone. Thus the way was clear for Eden to secure a diplomatic victory; Mendès-France had stated he would secure agreement within a month or resign; Molotov had become much easier, and Chou En-lai, probably scared by US atomic power, was now ready for a settlement based on Eden's plan for partition.

Right up until the end the result was in doubt. On 17 July Eden reported that Chou En-lai had told him he was concerned that the Big Three meant to split South-East Asia, and he insisted that 'the three associated States must be independent, sovereign and neutral', and that there was still doubt whether Dulles would insist on Laos and Cambodia being incorporated in a regional security organization. This would mean US military bases in those countries, which Chou En-lai would find unacceptable. On the same day Churchill wrote to Eden: 'I am sorry to read in the newspapers that things are looking adverse on your front.' The press had reported fears that Molotov might break off negotiations and denounce the non-Communist delegations or make unacceptable demands.

The next day, 18 July, Makins cabled from Washington:

> We still face, as we have faced since April, the prospect of a serious rift with the Americans over Asian policy. It would be a profound mistake to underrate the intensity of their feelings on these matters. . . . Some of the intensity of their feelings is, of course, attributable to domestic pressures. They see the Communist tide rising in Asia and are determined to do something now to try and stop it.

The same day Eden cabled to the Prime Minister:

> In my view we still have no more than a fifty-fifty chance of reaching agreement here. The time limit which Mendès-France has set himself is Tuesday, 20 July. If we get no agreement the Americans think it very important that the Governments concerned should be ready to issue with the least possible delay some clear statement of their intention to press forward with the conclusion of a collective defence agreement for South East Asia and the South West Pacific. I think there is much value in this idea.[16]

Over this Eden and Dulles were on the same tack.

Frenzied last-minute negotiations by Eden were successful, and agreement was reached between all parties on 21 July. Dulles instructed Bedell Smith not to sign; instead America took note. There was to be a ceasefire; Vietnam was to be partitioned at the seventeenth parallel; Cambodia and Laos were to be independent; and elections were to be held in Vietnam within two years. In addition, an International Supervisory Commission (ISC), presided over by India and composed of representatives of Canada, Poland and India, was to prevent 'revocations' of the Treaty.

On 22 July Eden told the Commons that the 'only alternative was continued fighting and suffering'. The *Times* leader commented that 'the future depends on both sides'; that Eden and Mendès-France had 'avoided one of the most acute dangers of a great war', and that 'Eden showed imaginative skill in talks with Molotov and Chou En-lai often when the chances of success seemed small.' This praise was justified. Eden had attained his diplomatic end; and the long war in Vietnam was temporarily over.

Eden showed his continued resentment towards Dulles by reporting to the Cabinet: 'at Geneva they had to overcome difficulties which occurred as a result of the attitude adopted by the representatives of the USA who attempted to interfere with the successful completion of the Conference's work.'[17] Eden had persuaded Chou En-lai for the first time to take part in negotiations with the West, and in addition Molotov had played an important part in securing a compromise solution which gave a chance of peace to the Far East in face of Dulles's warlike stance. Eden proved his ability as a negotiator triumphantly, and the French had been enabled to withdraw from a militarily impossible position by agreement in good order.

On the other side of the coin Geneva produced only a breathing space, and the war was to flare up again after a long truce. Nor did the promised elections take place. Nearly a million voted with their feet by crossing the frontier from North to South Vietnam. The supervisory capacity of the ISC was so limited that, despite the dedication of the Indian Government, it became non-effective – the Canadians always took the non-Communist view and the Poles the Communist one. In the sixties a large-scale resumption of hostilities in Vietnam began, with the Americans taking on the French role but casting themselves as defenders of the free world against Communism. The USA then became involved in a prolonged struggle which produced politically unacceptable losses.

An American-sponsored South-East Asia Collective Defence Treaty followed the Geneva Conference, and a pact was signed by eight nations (the UK, France, New Zealand, Australia, the USA, the Philippines, Thailand and Pakistan) in Manila on 8 September. Dulles went to Manila, but not Eden. Surprisingly Dulles did not try to spell out America's exact military commitment, and a Council, the South-East Asia Treaty Organization (SEATO), was established to keep the military situation under review.

The Treaty was a Declaration of Intent, and only authorized military action under closely defined circumstances. However the Manila powers were satisfied that it gave adequate protection to the non-Communist states in Indo-China, and the guarantees by America and Britain made Chou En-lai aware that there was a joint Anglo–American policy over Indo-China. With Manila the Eden–Dulles differences over Vietnam appeared to have been buried.

As the dust settled on the 1954 Geneva Conference a further clash between Eden and Dulles began which was to last into Eden's days as Prime Minister; it came over Formosa and the offshore Chinese islands. When the Chinese Nationalists under Chiang Kai-shek had been forced to evacuate mainland China by the Communists in 1948 they retreated to Formosa (now Taiwan), the Pescadores and the offshore islands of Quemoy, Matsos and Tachen. From these bases Chiang Kai-shek threatened to invade the mainland, while the Communists threatened to liquidate Formosa.

On 11 August 1954 Chou En-lai made a vicious anti-American speech, saying: 'It is imperative to liberate Taiwan and the traitorous Chiang Kai-shek group. Taiwan has been converted into a U.S. colony and they have the wild ambition of restoring criminal fascist rule and converting the whole of China into a U.S. colony.' Eisenhower retaliated by stating that any invasion of Formosa 'would have to run over the American Seventh Fleet'.[18]

In September General Hull, commanding Far East American forces, reported to Dulles that 'atomic bombs' would have to be used against the Chinese mainland to break up Chinese dispositions if the offshore islands of Quemoy and Matsos were attacked by the Communists. Dulles then wrote a memorandum for Eisenhower stating 'almost certainly a committal under present circumstances to defend Quemoy etc. would alienate world opinion and gravely strain our alliance both in Europe and with ANZUS [Australia and New Zealand]. This is the more true because it would probably lead to our initiating the use of atomic weapons.'[19] Dulles was on edge when he came to London for talks with Eden on 17 September, because on 5 September the Chinese Communists had begun to shell Quemoy and Matsos, which lay only five miles from the mainland. The Nationalists replied with their own artillery and announced that they 'would fight to the finish'.

Dulles told Eden that the US National Security Council was in favour of United States forces defending Quemoy because 'any further Communist success coming so soon after the Indo-China settlement would suggest that the United States was not willing to stand and fight at any point in Asia and damaging inferences would be drawn both by the Communists and by America's allies . . . withdrawal from Quemoy . . . would have a disastrous effect on morale in Formosa', which was essential to US Pacific defences and needed the aid of the Chinese Nationalists for its defence. Eden was antagonistic and replied that he wanted the neutralization of Quemoy, leaving Formosa and the Pescadores under Chiang Kai-shek, and direct negotiations with the Communists for a guarantee that, if Quemoy was abandoned to them, they would leave Formosa 'in peace and quiet'.

Dulles suggested that the offshore islands would have to be defended by atomic weapons even at the risk of a third world war; this alarmed and angered Eden, who had just been given a secret report by the British Chiefs of Staff that Quemoy and the offshore islands were indefensible 'except at the cost of great exertions by the U.S. Fleet', and they were not essential to the defence of Formosa. Still, as a result of their harmony over WEU, Dulles and Eden dined together in Paris on 17 December, and Eden reported to Churchill: 'I had a pleasant and confident feeling that Anglo–American relations are as they should be and really cordial.' Alas, this did not last, and in January 1955 the dispute boiled up again as Eden prepared to meet Dulles in Bangkok to set up SEATO.[20]

In January 1955 the Cabinet approved Eden's proposal that the British should refuse to support Dulles in any American guarantee to Chiang Kai-shek to defend Quemoy and Matsos. The Americans, with New Zealand backing, wanted the offshore islands dispute to be considered by the United Nations. According to Humphrey Trevelyan, the British representative in Peking, Chou En-lai would not hear of this and refused to separate the question of the offshore islands from Formosa. On 20 January 1955 Eden instructed Makins to put it to Dulles 'very strongly' that the Chinese would never acquiesce in the coastal islands remaining in Nationalist hands; that the United Nations could take no effective action; and that as long as the Nationalists occupied the islands 'there will be a continuing danger of friction and fighting'.[21]

This drew a personal letter from Eisenhower to Churchill, obviously drafted by Dulles, dated 25 January: 'We are convinced that the psychological effect in the Far East of deserting our friends on Formosa would risk a collapse of Asiatic resistance to the Communists', and also decried Churchill's opposition (in a previous letter to the President) to the use of atomic bombs in the Far East. 'We believe that the consequences would not be as far reaching as you describe. I refer to the extraordinary increase in the value of tactical or strategic surprise brought about by the enormous destructive power of the new weapons and the probability that they could be delivered over targets with little or no warning. . . .' According to the President, the Kremlin and Peking were driving forward with plans of political and military nibbling in relative safety, 'knowing we in our democracies abhor the thought of mass destruction', and added ominously: 'there can be "local" deterrents as well as "global" deterrents.' Before the Bangkok Conference Eisenhower wrote again on 10 February to Churchill in an effort to persuade him to soften Eden:

> certain groups in the USA wanted us to take a much stronger even truculent position. The number that would like to see us clear out of Formosa is negligible. I know that on your side of the water you have the exact opposite . . . the Nationalist troops and Chiang himself are not content now to accept irrevocably and permanently the status of 'prisoners' on the islands. They are held together by a conviction that some day they will go back to the mainland.

He argued that Quemoy and Matsos must be defended. Both Churchill and Eden felt the idea that Chiang Kai-shek's forces might attack the mainland was 'arrant nonsense', and it must be doubtful if Eisenhower really believed this himself.

Churchill replied to Eisenhower that a war to keep the coastal islands for Chiang 'would not be defensible here' and he could see 'no decisive relationship' between the offshore islands and an invasion of Formosa. 'It would surely be easy for the U.S. to drown any would-be Chinese invaders of Formosa whether they started from Quemoy or elsewhere. . . . I do not think it would be right or wise for America to encourage him to keep alive the reconquest of the mainland to inspire his faithful followers.' He also urged Eisenhower to use the present lull to remove the fifty thousand Nationalist troops from Quemoy and Matsos.[22] On 16 February Dulles made a speech containing the phrase that 'further one-sided concessions are not the way to proceed'. On reading it, Eden brusquely instructed Makins to tell Dulles: 'It may not be possible for me to avoid saying what the views of HMG are.' Dulles had sent a draft of the speech to Eden, who had replied that he could not remain silent if it was made; but Dulles only toned it down slightly. Eden also sent a message that there was no chance of world or UK opinion supporting Chinese Nationalists remaining on Quemoy.[23]

On 19 February Eisenhower replied to Churchill: 'What we have done has apparently been interpreted by the Chinese Communists merely as a sign of weakness . . . further retreats become worse than a Munich.' He continued that he suspected the Chinese of being really interested in Formosa and later on Japan, that the coastal islands were marginal, and that the Americans had not the 'capacity' to drown anybody who tried to cross the Formosa straits and therefore had to rely on 'a loyal and dependable force of Nationalists on Formosa to deal with the attackers'. The letter ended with what Eisenhower obviously thought would be a cogent argument: 'It would surely not be popular in this country if we become involved in possible hostilities on account of Hongkong or Malaya which our people look on as "colonies" which to us is a naughty word. Nevertheless I do not doubt that if the issue were ever framed in this way, we would be at your side.'

Churchill wrote to Eden in Bangkok: 'It is a much better letter . . . it is a real and sincere attempt to make us understand the American point of view. They do not mean to let Japan go red.' Churchill enclosed a paper he had had prepared by his staff on the abuse that Chiang Kai-shek and Chou En-lai had been hurling at each other. This included a statement that Chou had said he would wipe the Americans off the face of the earth. If Churchill took it seriously that Chou En-lai might carry this out, his judgment had gone. More probably he was filled with nostalgia for his comradeship with Eisenhower during the war, and wanted Eden to be more accomodating to the Americans and to pander less to the Chinese Communists; but as he had agreed to resign within a few weeks his influence over his Foreign Secretary was now almost nil. There could be no repetition of the incident the previous July, when Churchill had vetoed Eden replying publicly to Dulles's criticisms.

With Dulles angry at Britain refusing to join in a guarantee of Quemoy and Matsos, and Eden thoroughly alarmed at the Americans' intention to use atomic weapons to defend what he considered unimportant islands, their Bangkok meeting on 23 February produced another clash. Dulles refused point-blank to have anything to do with Eden's plan that the Nationalists should withdraw from the islands in return for a pledge by China not to attack Formosa. Dulles told Eden aggressively that surrendering Quemoy and Matsos would increase the potential for a successful Chinese attack on Formosa, and 'greatly weaken the morale of the Nationalists'. There was no meeting of minds, and Eden became seriously concerned that Dulles might precipitate a third world war.[24]

On 25 February Eden reported to Churchill that his conversation with Dulles 'had convinced him the situation was so grave and urgent, and action so imperative, that I should at least offer to meet Chou en Lai half way if there is any prospect of finding a basis for negotiations. You will realise my reluctance to go to Hong Kong to meet Chou en Lai.' Churchill was not in favour of such a meeting, but with Eden about to take over the reins of government had to give a reluctant assent. After consulting with Butler he told the Foreign Secretary that he and his colleagues 'would wish him to act upon his own judgment'.

In Peking Chou En-lai told Trevelyan that he was angered both by Churchill's statement to the Commons ('There was a great difference between the coastal islands and Formosa') and by a misleading agency report that at Bangkok Eden had said HMG might fight alongside the Americans in defence of Formosa. The interview was acrimonious, but Trevelyan carried out Eden's instructions by asking Chou En-lai whether the Chinese Government would state privately or publicly that, while maintaining their claim to Formosa, they did not intend to prosecute it by force, and that if China was prepared to give such assurance 'we would be ready to inform the U.S. Government and approach them with, we believe, a good hope of finding a basis for a peaceful settlement in the various islands.' On 1 March Trevelyan reported that Chou En-lai would welcome a visit to Peking by Eden only if he would discuss the cessation of US aggression against China and the withdrawal of US forces from Formosa. Eden replied that 'a common basis does not exist and a meeting would serve no useful purpose'.

Churchill was relieved and telegraphed to Eden, who was in Rangoon: 'I was very glad to see your telegram to Chou en Lai, and so were the Cabinet. We are so glad you are coming home according to plan. Chou en Lai's suggestion that you should come to Peking seemed a pretty impudent response to your friendly offer to meet him in Hong Kong.'[25] Eden's proposal to visit Chou En-lai was kept secret, and Eden did not mention it in his memoirs. There have been references to Eden's 'flirtation with the Chinese Communists', and this was part of it. Given the impasse between Britain and the Americans nothing helpful could have come out of the meeting, and it would have been a red rag to the Americans.

As Eden prepared to become Prime Minister he did nothing to mend his bridges with Dulles. He was determined that the offshore islands question should not be raised in the Security Council (such a move had been suggested by New Zealand and was called Oracle), instructing Makins on 12 March: 'It is bad enough that we should have our present disagreement with the Americans over the coastal islands, but it would be far worse if the disagreement were to be exposed in the United Nations. . . . I see no good and much harm from Security Council action.' Dulles told Makins he was convinced that the Communists wanted a major showdown both in Formosa and South-East Asia . . . 'the Chinese Communists' intentions in South East Asia are even more menacing than their attitude on Formosa'; and that the UN should debate the Formosan crisis before the end of March because he was disquieted by Communist military preparations opposite Formosa on the coastal islands.

Eden replied to Dulles: 'Public opinion in this country and I believe in Asia, would not support action that seemed designed to confirm Chiang Kai Shek in Quemoy and Matsos. . . . I am sorry to go on disagreeing with you about the question of next move,' but he was adamant that the matter should not go before the Security Council. With bad grace Dulles agreed to postpone action in the Security Council and wrote to Eden: 'The risk of hostilities is very real and if they break out there can be no assurance that they will not become extended.' From the viewpoint of Anglo–American friendship it was an inauspicious moment for Eden to become Prime Minister.[26]

Dulles and Eisenhower knew that the ageing Churchill was perturbed over the estrangement and wanted at all costs to preserve Britain's special relationship with America. Accordingly, at Dulles's instigation the President wrote a further series of personal letters to Churchill designed to undermine the Prime Minister's confidence in Eden's Far Eastern policy. After Eden had criticized American policy in the Far East in the Commons in March, Eisenhower wrote to Churchill on 29 March. The President had no idea that Churchill was within days of resignation and thus a spent force: 'The existence of differences is so clearly and sadly recognised on both sides of the water. We see eye to eye on Europe, but not on the Far East . . . the time to stop the advance of Communism in Asia is here now.' Churchill made one last attempt to influence Eden, minuting to him that it was 'a serious statement of [the US] position', and he asked Eden to talk to him about it. But Eden knew he was now the sole arbiter of British policy in the Far East, and he no longer needed to pay attention to his aged mentor who had annoyed him so much over the years.[27]

After Eden became Prime Minister on 6 April 1955, with Macmillan as Foreign Secretary, the Anglo–American quarrel over the Formosan straits continued. Eden remained convinced that the American refusal to allow the evacuation of Quemoy and Matsos was likely to start a third world war, and with Churchill out of the way he was ready to antagonize the Americans even further rather than alter a policy in which he believed so sincerely. On 19 April he told his Cabinet that we must be prepared for a Chinese Communist attack on Quemoy and Matsos during the election campaign, and on 4 May the Foreign Office produced two drafts of alternative press statements to be issued in the event of such an attack. One was to cover the eventuality of the Americans coming to the help of the Nationalists; the other in case the Americans decided not to oppose the attack. Both stressed that Britain had no commitment. Eden minuted to Macmillan: 'I would think that it would be better not to show them to Dulles at least while S.E. Asia climate lasts.'[28]

On 22 April the new Prime Minister minuted on a report in New York newspapers that the Americans might persuade Chiang to pull out of the coastal islands in exchange for a pledge from Britain, Australia and New Zealand to guarantee them against a Communist assault: 'Foreign Secretary, I am sure we must be careful of this one. A.E.' When on 11 May Makins reported that Dulles seemed to be 'edging away from the idea of a guarantee' Eden minuted: 'F.S. I hope this is so. We could not give it. A.E.' Strong evidence of how far Eden was prepared to put Anglo–American friendship at risk because of his rooted conviction that a deal must be done with Chou En-lai comes in his minute to Macmillan dated 23 April: 'It is only too clear that so long as the Americans are unable to get Chiang out of the coastal islands a Chinese attack on them would place our alliance in jeopardy.'[29]

Macmillan had a much better personal relationship with Dulles, but the archives reveal that he toed the Eden line at first, knowing that any attempt to depart from it would be ill received by his temperamental master. In his memoirs he is unenlightening over his attitude to the Formosan straits controversy, although a hint that his views were at variance with Eden's is given in an extract from his diary which states that he had thought Eisenhower's reply to 'our suggestion' that Quemoy and Matsos should be evacuated and a stand made only in Formosa and the Pescadores was 'certainly a powerful well argued and persuasive document'.

Suddenly a ray of light appeared. At the end of April delegations from twenty-nine nations assembled at Bandung in Java. Representing at least 1.4 billion people from the countries of Asia and Africa, it was the first authentic meeting of the emergent regimes. President Nehru of India and Chou En-lai were the dominant figures. Chou En-lai had gone to Bandung expecting to hear little but abuse of the former colonial powers and America; instead he was surprised at the amount of pro-Western sentiment, and he had a change of heart during the proceedings which culminated in his making an offer to sit down with the United States to seek a solution to their differences. Coming at the time of extreme tension over Formosa, this was dramatic. Unfortunately the acting Secretary of State, Herbert Hoover, with Eisenhower's approval, immediately replied that such a meeting could not be held without Chiang Kai-shek. As soon as he returned to Washington, Dulles tried to undo the damage done by Hoover; on 26 April he stated, much to Eden's relief, that direct talks would be acceptable and might be useful. Macmillan did his best to get negotiations started, arguing with Dulles that Chou En-lai would be unlikely to attack while a conference was in prospect.

Nehru was anxious that India should play the role of intermediary, and accordingly Krishna Menon, the leader of the Indian delegation to the United Nations, went to China for prolonged talks with Chou En-lai. Eden was delighted, and convinced himself that Menon's intervention could be the key to a solution of the dispute between America and Communist China. Menon came to London on his way to Washington, and Eden insisted that they should have a long private talk at 10 Downing Street; Eden also urged Eisenhower to see Menon personally. Menon arrived in Washington on 10 June just as a Cincinnati poll had shown overwhelming support for defending Quemoy and if necessary using nuclear power.[30]

Eden's faith in Menon as a peacemaker was misplaced. Makins reported that there was a 'profound incompatibility of temperament between Dulles and Menon', and although the Indians thought he was a roving ambassador he did 'harm' with Dulles. According to Macmillan, Dulles disliked Menon. Nor was Menon's interview with Eisenhower – so desired by Eden – rewarding.

Macmillan arrived in America on 16 June for preliminary talks with the Americans about the four-power summit meeting with the Russians and French, scheduled to start in Geneva on 18 July. Macmillan and Dulles met both in New York and San Francisco, where the tenth anniversary of the founding of the United Nations was being celebrated. Their talks were friendly, and Macmillan noted that Dulles 'did not show any resentment at least to me'. Dulles told Macmillan that he really wanted to get Chiang off the offshore islands, but he could not do it 'although he had sent Robertson [Under-Secretary of State] and Radford to see Chiang some weeks ago, but they had failed'.[31]

On 17 June Macmillan noted in his diary: 'The Americans could not understand Menon's plan and did not like it as far as they understand it. I have a feeling that Dulles would like to change his approach to the Chinese problem but is just waiting for public opinion in the U.S. to allow him to do so.' In his memoirs Macmillan states that Menon's plan was 'only' for a series of talks to settle minor causes of disputes, but the archives disclose that it was for a gradual withdrawal from Quemoy and Matsos and that Chou En-lai was not insisting that the Nationalist garrisons on these islands should surrender, but was prepared to see them withdraw to strengthen the defence of Formosa.

With the failure of Indian intervention the next hope for a solution lay in the Geneva four-power summit. Unfortunately the Far East could not be put on the agenda. The Permanent Under-Secretary at the Foreign Office, Ivone Kirkpatrick, summed up the difficulty: 'The Americans will not discuss the Far East at a high level meeting in which Communist China takes part; whilst the Russians will not discuss the Far East unless China is present. So the best we can do is to utter some generalisations . . . and hope that the Russians will not declare us out of order.'[32]

The 1955 Geneva four-power summit aroused great expectations all over the world because it was the first gathering since the end of the war of the Communists and the free nations. With Stalin dead and new Soviet leaders in charge there were high hopes of a new atmosphere of conciliation. These were not fulfilled, although during the six days of proceedings the Russians exuded a certain amiability which became known as 'the Geneva atmosphere'.

The main items on the agenda were reunification of Germany and disarmament. No progress was made with the Russians on either. Nor did a follow-up conference of Foreign Ministers in Paris in the autumn achieve anything. The West insisted unrealistically on free elections for all Germany, regardless of the fact that these would sweep away Communism in East Germany, which would clearly be unacceptable to the Russians. Over disarmament both Eden and Eisenhower put forward plans which failed to interest the Soviets and are best described by Robert Blake as belonging to the 'debris of history'.

At Geneva Eden and Macmillan had discussions with the Russians and Americans on the Far East; these talks are fully documented. On 17 July Eden and Eisenhower talked alone, and both agreed there was no immediate danger of war in Europe. Eden told the President that the Indians had 'worked hard to persuade the Chinese to moderate their attitude'. Eisenhower replied that this might be true of Nehru, but he had not much use for Krishna Menon who 'concealed intellectual arrogance under the cloak of humility'.[33] After an inconclusive discussion of Quemoy and Matsos the President repeatedly told Eden he was anxious to be 'quit' of the islands. He said he would like another talk on the same subject after he had consulted Dulles.

On 22 July Dulles and Eisenhower came to breakfast with Eden and Macmillan. Eden commented that 'the outcome of the discussion was not encouraging'. Dulles and Eden went over all the old ground about Quemoy and Matsos, without coming to any agreement; Dulles admitted that the position was highly dangerous and we 'might be said to be living on a volcano'. But Dulles would not agree with Eden that the Nationalists must abandon the islands, although he emphasized how hard Radford had tried – unsuccessfully – to get Chiang to agree to evacuate.

Eden also had two talks with the Russians about the Far East; these got nowhere. At a dinner with Bulganin and Krushchev on 22 July Macmillan repeated Eisenhower's remark that the Americans would be very happy if Quemoy and Matsos were sunk under the sea. According to Eden, 'this suggestion appeared to receive universal approbation except possibly, we all admitted, from an absent Chou en Lai. The Russians commented "The master of the house is absent."' On 23 July Eden had his last conversation with Bulganin and Krushchev, at which he stressed that the Americans were being patient and trying to calm things down. Krushchev replied: 'Traditionally the Chinese were a patient people, and he believed they would not take any rash action at the present time.' This was true; the Formosan straits crisis was coming off the boil. Fortunately arrangements had been made for meetings to be held in Geneva between the Ambassadors of the United States and China, and Krushchev said he hoped 'some fruitful result would come from their meetings'.

On his return to London Eden reported to the Cabinet that Eisenhower was resolved to do his utmost to restrain Chiang Kaishek from 'any rash or provocative course of action', and that it was also evident from his conversations at Geneva that the Russians would use such influence as they had over the Chinese Communists to dissuade them from taking any action which might precipitate a major conflict in the Far East. Eden was right. The danger of a conflict in the Far East was receding, and the American–Chinese talks in Geneva could be expected to produce beneficial results. On 20 October Macmillan was able to tell the Cabinet 'in the Far East there had been a relaxation of tension in the area of the Formosa straits'.

Although no clash had taken place between Eden and Dulles at Geneva, there was no improvement in their personal relationship. Evidence of this comes from Eden's behaviour when the Americans suggested publishing the principal Geneva statements of the President and Dulles. Macmillan objected, saying that copies might get into the hands of journalists, as had happened with the Yalta documents. Dulles replied: 'No doubt there will be a demand for the publication of an account of the restricted sessions.'[34]

Macmillan thought Dulles's note 'somewhat obscure, but satisfactory'. Not so Eden! He scrawled on the letter: 'The last sentence is far from satisfactory. There can be no more conferences if Americans even think of publishing restricted sessions. I think you should take Dulles up sharp on this. The phrase "not expected to comply" is typical. A few months later he will say we did not object.' This betrays Eden's attitude to Dulles after Geneva, which was not a good omen for the remainder of his premiership.

When in November the Foreign Office asked the Prime Minister for permission to send records of his private conversations with the President about the Far East to the Ambassadors in Washington, Peking and Moscow, he was reluctant to authorize distribution outside the country; however he eventually agreed that copies could go to Makins in Washington for his personal information, with a note drawing attention to their special secrecy. The Prime Minister also gave instructions that the Foreign Office should not quote anything that the President had said to him in confidence at Geneva. The records of the conversations give no grounds for considering such secrecy justified.[35]

Throughout the Formosan straits crisis, both as Foreign Secretary and as Prime Minister Eden rigidly refused to give any guarantees to Chiang Kai-shek, and insisted that the Nationalists ought to evacuate the offshore islands. He was convinced that the Dulles policy was risking war with Communist China, which might escalate into World War III with atom bombs, and this at all costs must be avoided. Unlike Dulles, he appreciated from his contact with Chou En-lai at Geneva in 1954 that the Chinese leader would not risk provoking a nuclear war, although his ground forces could have conquered territory as he willed. He stuck steadfastly to a policy which put at risk Britain's special relationship with America. It can be argued that his judgment was at fault because Quemoy and Matsos remain today in Nationalist hands, but it is more important that he prevented a disastrous war in the Far East.

6

Cyprus and Malta
1955–6

CYPRUS, ORIGINALLY PART of the Venetian Empire, became by conquest part of the Ottoman Empire in 1571, and under a convention with Turkey in 1878 Britain took over her government. When Turkey joined Germany in the First World War Britain, as an enemy power, formally annexed the island, and after the war by the Treaty of Lausanne Turkey surrendered all her rights over Cyprus; in 1925 Cyprus became a Crown Colony. This did not please the Greek Cypriots, who formed two-thirds of the population while the remainder were Turkish and hostile to Greece. The Greek Cypriots wanted Enosis or union with Greece – an idea much disliked by the Turkish minority. Soon agitation for union with Greece began; it reached a peak in the early fifties.

By 1955 Cyprus had become a grave problem because with the decision to evacuate the Suez Canal base the island was essential as an alternative base for a British military presence in the Middle East. Britain too needed to keep on good terms with Turkey, who had joined both NATO and the Baghdad Pact, and was vital for the success of the latter. Turkey would not countenance the secession of Cyprus to Greece nor a constitution which gave dominance to Greek Cypriots. As a result it was impossible for Britain to negotiate with the Greek Cypriots on relinquishment of sovereignty in return for British use of airfields, ports and army installations.

Proposals for a liberal constitution had been made by the Attlee Government in 1948, but they had been publicly withdrawn and a more limited constitutional plan proposed. Outlining this new plan in the House of Commons on 28 July 1954, Henry Hopkinson, Minister of State for Colonial Affairs, tactlessly stated: '. . . there are certain territories in the Commonwealth which, owing to their particular circumstances, can *never* [author's italics] expect to be fully independent.' 'Never' was a gaffe which had far-reaching consequences.

It certainly exasperated Field Marshal Papagos, Prime Minister of Greece, who now decided to support wholeheartedly the campaign by Archbishop Makarios, the elected spiritual and political leader of the Greek Cypriot people, for Enosis. Greece attempted to inscribe a resolution about Cyprus on the Agenda of the United Assembly, which was quashed only by a procedural wrangle and US support for Britain; the British Government then accepted that unless it made some progress over constitutional reform there would be an annual conflict with Greece at the United Nations.

A crisis erupted on 1 April 1955 when an underground organization, EOKA, under the leadership of Colonel Grivas (a Cypriot by birth and wartime leader of a right-wing Greek terrorist group) proclaimed their aim to be the liberation of Cyprus from British rule, and started a series of bomb attacks and acts of sabotage. The Governor of Cyprus, Sir Robert Armitage, urged a more democratic constitution and a statement 'bolder than anything made hitherto' describing where constitutional development might eventually lead. A joint Eden–Lennox-Boyd Cabinet memorandum in early April 1955 suggested a legislature with a majority of elected over nominated and official members, and looked forward to full internal self-government. The Cabinet deferred consideration until after the General Election, and on 14 June discussed a new approach, suggested by Macmillan (now Foreign Secretary) and Lennox-Boyd, which was to invite Greece and Turkey to a Tripartite Conference in London with Britain. Old-fashioned colonialism was still current in the Eden Cabinet, and in discussion it was noted that such a conference might establish 'a dangerous precedent' by inviting foreign Governments to discuss future constitutional developments in a British colony, and might for example result in neighbouring South American states tendering advice on British Guiana or British Honduras, or India on colonies where there were substantial Indian minorities. Furthermore, it might be regarded as 'an admission that two foreign Governments had a right to be consulted on the internal affairs of Cyprus'. The Cabinet decided that sovereignty must not be on the agenda, and that the invitation must emphasize that Greece and Turkey were 'co-partners in the North Atlantic Alliance, and that Cyprus was of strategic importance to the members of that Alliance'.

Eden declared that, were it not for the embarrassment of the UN, he personally would have preferred to take no further initiative for the present. Greek claims to Cyprus were ill-founded and we were on strong ground in resisting them. The policy of firmness . . . had already had some effect on public opinion in Greece. We had hitherto declined to discuss this question with the Greek Government, and it might be taken as a sign of weakness if we now offered to consult them on it.

This was to be Eden's attitude during the remainder of his premiership; he wanted a hard line against terrorism and an uncompromising attitude to Enosis. Because of Eden's lukewarmness a small Cabinet committee reconsidered the proposed conference but eventually invitations were issued and accepted by the Greek and Turkish Governments for a conference in London to start on 27 August. But no Cypriot delegation was invited.[1] Meanwhile the situation in Cyprus was deteriorating fast. EOKA launched a second major offensive on 19 June 1955, with attacks on police stations in Nicosia and Kyrenia, and Athens Radio, despite protests from the British Ambassador, Sir Charles Peake, made what the Foreign Office called 'subversive and inflammatory broadcasts which amount to an open glorification of the acts of terrorism'.

Armitage reported that he might feel compelled to declare a State of Emergency and possibly arrest Makarios, who had refused to condemn violence, connived at the use of force, and allowed church funds to be available for the purchase of arms from Greece. From New York the permanent representative at the United Nations, Sir Pierson Dixon, reported: 'I hope that it will be soon possible to take a decision about . . . Cyprus. . . . Time is, I am afraid, running out on us if we wish to mobilise the Americans in our support.'[2] On 25 June Armitage stated that 'purely repressive measures . . . may well result in widespread disorders which would have adverse effects internationally', and it would be more prudent to consider the principle of 'self determination'. Against this Eden minuted: 'No.' Armitage's considered view was that: 'Whatever statement may be made about future policy, EOKA must be crushed', and he proposed the declaration of a State of Emergency some time after 1 July. The Government refused to do so pending the tripartite talks.[3]

Although the Greeks had accepted the invitation to the conference they jibbed at the date and wanted it brought forward, because 29 August would be too late for Greece to lodge an appeal at the United Nations; the USA backed their complaint. The Greeks went ahead and filed an appeal about Cyprus at the United Nations without waiting for the conference. Meanwhile Athens Radio stayed so viciously anti-British that Macmillan and Eden considered jamming it.

Two days before the Tripartite Conference opened a request was received from Armitage for seven police officers with experience of emergency conditions in Malaya or Kenya to be recruited as a result of three policemen being killed by EOKA. The Cabinet agreed, after Macmillan told them on 26 August: '. . . unless the administration showed themselves firm and resolute, the situation in Cyprus might easily get out of hand. Prompt action should therefore be taken to strengthen the police and security services in the Island. The Prime Minister endorsed this view.'[4] By now Macmillan had lost faith in Armitage and minuted the Prime Minister that he was 'really worried about Cyprus' where he thought the real trouble was 'at the top' and asked: 'Could we not have a new Governor?' As there was 'almost bound to be a lot of trouble after the Conference and we must have somebody with guts and imagination', Macmillan suggested the former diplomat and Conservative MP, Fitzroy Maclean, who had distinguished himself with Tito during the war. Eden cast doubts on Maclean's suitability. Macmillan then minuted:

> Do you not think that we ought to have a man at the top in Cyprus who radiates the impression that he knows what he wants and can get it? I do not think it would be wise to appoint a soldier. Apart from the misrepresentation of military tyranny, etc., which would follow, I am sure that we want somebody with political and diplomatic gifts to set Cyprus going on the road towards self government.

The Prime Minister replied that this was 'the first item' on his agenda with the Colonial Secretary. Eden rejected Macmillan's advice not to appoint a soldier and plumped for Field Marshal Harding, the retiring Chief of the Imperial General Staff, who was appointed to succeed Armitage on 23 September 1955. Harding certainly had the 'guts', but his 'political and diplomatic gifts' were unknown quantities.[5]

Michael Stewart, Counsellor at the British Embassy in Ankara, forecast that at the conference Turkey 'was likely to be rigid and violently anti-Greek' and said he had been given hints that any change in the status quo would allow Turkey to reopen matters supposedly settled permanently at Lausanne. Eden minuted on the message: 'I am sure that it is in our interest that Turks shall speak out because it is the truth that they will not let Greeks have Cyprus.' The Foreign Office had already told Stewart that the Turkish case was going by default in the United States, and suggested that discreet

Butler goes to the House of Commons to announce his 'pots and pans' budget.

Dulles (left), Pineau and Eden in London for talks on the Suez Crisis immediately after the Canal nationalization.

Ben-Gurion, after his re-election as Prime Minister of Israel, talks to the British Foreign Secretary, Selwyn Lloyd.

General Sir John Glubb with his wife and adopted Arab daughter the day after he was dismissed by King Hussein.

Pineau, head of the French delegation to the Suez Conference, with Jebb, British Ambassador to France.

Ruth Ellis, who was sentenced to death for the murder of her lover in June 1955.

The Hon. D. Mintoff, Prime Minister of Malta, visits No. 10 Downing Street on 29 June 1955.

hints should be made to the Turks to put this right. The British Embassy in Athens thought that with circumspect handling Stephanopoulos, the Greek Foreign Minister, 'might be brought to agree to a formula involving self-determination at some future date'. Against this Eden minuted: 'But we can't be brought to agree.'[6]

For Eden the Tripartite Conference was shadow boxing. He wanted to give the impression that Britain was designing a liberal, self-governing constitution but was prevented by Turkish intransigence, whereas in fact the Prime Minister was determined not to give an inch to Greek claims. Macmillan accepted this, explaining to the Cabinet on 15 August that at the conference a wide difference of opinion would be revealed, and it would have been proved 'that the deadlock was due, not to British colonialism, but to the irreconcilable attitudes of the Greek and Turkish Governments', while the British aim was 'to safeguard the eastern Mediterranean against Russian aggression'. The Tripartite Conference duly revealed the impossibility of Turkish and Greek agreement. Afterwards Dulles, when consulted, said he did not know what had occurred at the conference, still less what HMG's proposals were. This annoyed Eden, but Dulles had seen through the British pretence.[7]

The most realistic assessment of the conference was published in the *Economist*:

> The London Conference on Cyprus is officially said to stand 'suspended'; but it is hard to avoid the conclusion that it has, in fact, failed. The British Government put forward constitutional proposals that were a great advance on anything offered to the island before, and would give the Cypriots full self-government in all spheres except foreign affairs, security and defence. But Mr Macmillan effectively damned even these liberal proposals in Cypriot eyes by coupling them with a categorical statement that he could see no prospect of self determination for Cyprus 'in the foreseeable future'. And he failed to offset this by making any constructive suggestion calculated to appeal to the Greek Government and induce it to cooperate in making a go of Cypriot self-government. . . . If the Government was not prepared to make a bid for the support of the Greek Government in some more striking and imaginative way, it is difficult to see how it could ever have hoped that the Conference would succeed.
>
> One most unfortunate by product of the London meeting is the sad deterioration of Greco–Turkish relations. . . .[8]

Macmillan's 'categorical statement' criticized by the *Economist* was made in his conference speech on 30 August, when he said:

British sovereignty over Cyprus was beyond dispute; there was no prospect of any change in the foreseeable future and HMG did not accept the principle of self-determination as one of universal application. Here Macmillan was in breach of the United Nations Charter, and he had to withdraw the last part of his remarks. The Turks, anxious to preserve the status quo, were delighted; the Greeks furious.[9]

The Tripartite Conference did harm, not good. However Anthony Nutting told the author that one 'incidental' benefit arose because he was able to argue at the United Nations that Britain was prepared to negotiate, while the Turks and Greeks would not, and this enabled him to persuade delegations from outside countries of the righteousness of the British position. Obviously this was the cynical reason why the Government decided to call the conference, because on 28 June Eden had told the Cabinet that a conference had 'certain tactical advantages' on the grounds that the British position in the UN would be improved, and moreover it would provide a valuable opportunity for Greco–Turkish differences to 'be revealed for all to see'.[10]

Alarming news reached London about EOKA's increasingly violent activities, the stranglehold they were exerting over the population and the inadequacy and low morale of the police force. On 3 September a message was received from Armitage that the situation was likely to deteriorate rapidly and that urgent consideration must be given to the provision of troop reinforcements. On 5 September Eden chaired a small meeting of Ministers to evaluate the recent telegrams, and the next day Head sent a note to Eden that Second Commando and an extra infantry battalion were being sent to Cyprus, while 50 Brigade was to remain at fourteen days' notice. Eden minuted: 'I agree, excellent.'

After the Turkish Consulate at Salonika in Greece had been bombed, anti-Greek riots broke out in Turkey at Izmir and Istanbul on 7 September, the day after the Tripartite Conference was suspended. There were suspicions that the bombing at Salonika and the riots had been stage-managed by the Turkish Government. Considerable damage was done to Greek property and churches in Turkey, which the Turkish authorities did little to prevent. Peake reported that the Greek Government was evidently extremely worried about relations with Turkey. Against this Eden wrote: 'Only hope. Let medicine work', and he wrote the same phrase on two other telegrams from Athens on 9 and 12 September.

While the British Ambassador was on leave A. E. Lambert of the

Athens Embassy warned that too strong an anti-Greek line at the UN might force the Greeks to 'neutralism', in other words to leave NATO. Eden minuted: 'F.S. I shall be glad when Sir C.P. [Sir Charles Peake] gets back. I hope that we shall then stop taking the Greek pulse so often.'[11]

As Greece tried to inscribe the Cyprus issue on the Agenda at the United Nations, Macmillan urged Nutting to impress upon Dulles 'how deeply hurt we shall all be here if we cannot rely on American help in matters of this kind', and stressed how often Britain had subordinated her own view to 'the common interest of the team'. In the debate Nutting spotlighted that the Tripartite Conference proposals were 'a fair and generous basis for advance', and stressed that they went 'too far for Turks, but not far enough for the Greeks'. Thus while Britain was using repressive military measures to crush EOKA, she was proclaiming to the world how anxious she was for a settlement between the Turks and Greeks, and as a result of successful lobbying the General Committee of the UN recommended that the Cyprus item should not be inscribed.[12]

Harding took over as Governor from Armitage on 3 October. Eden impressed on him that he was to be essentially a 'military' Governor, and his instructions made it clear his priority was to restore law and order, while a political settlement and social and economic advance were secondary issues. Harding immediately held a series of talks with Makarios. Although at first Harding was hopeful of an agreement Makarios was adamant over the Cypriot right to self-determination, and the talks faltered. Harding stepped up his security programme, and asked for and secured the dispatch of more troops to the island. Eight days after Harding's arrival there was a complete breakdown in his negotiations with the Archbishop. When this was reported to London Eden commented to the Colonial Office:

It is not our position that we will never grant self-determination to Cyprus. It is our position that we cannot grant it now, both on account of the present strategic importance of the island and because of the consequences . . . on relations between NATO powers and the Eastern Mediterranean. We have offered a wide measure of self-government now . . . at some later date unspecified, when self-government has proved a workable proposition, we are prepared to discuss . . . stages in the island's political future. These stages would not exclude self-determination, nor can we pledge ourselves now that they will include self-determination but there is no objection to the Cypriots at that time raising self determination and arguing for it.

Since an immediate commitment to self-determination was the sticking-point for Makarios and the revolutionaries, prospects of an agreement were virtually nil. On 17 October Eden asked Harding if he would favour a fresh statement of the British position, whilst assurances were given to quash Turkish fears that Britain was preparing for a volte-face over self-determination. Macmillan commented that 'in this already metaphysical realm of argument about self-determination, restatements often have valuable results'. Harding had previously been reluctant to countenance another approach to Makarios unless he had 'some enticement to offer him to move in the direction of compromise', he now (i.e. mid-October) thought that, with certain modifications, this new statement 'might prove the answer to Greek-Cypriot aspirations and allaying Turkish fears'.[13]

Harding was asked to meet Makarios secretly and put to him a 'formula', which meant that Britain supported the 'principle' of self-determination but that this was not now a practical proposition in view of the strategic and political situation in the Eastern Mediterranean; Britain instead offered a wide measure of self-government, and intended to 'work for a final solution' which would satisfy Cypriot wishes and yet be consistent with existing British treaty obligations and strategic interests. When Makarios and Harding met, the Governor found the Archbishop 'obdurate' and insistent that the 'formula' meant a denial of the principle of 'self-determination'. However, the Greek Government's reaction was more favourable, and on 30 November Eden appealed to Karamanlis, the Prime Minister, 'to take a bold initiative and recommend our statement to the Archbishop'. The Greek Government's eventual reply was that it welcomed the British initiative but that the statement was 'so encumbered with considerations of strategic interests and treaty obligations as to render the promise implied therein almost imperceptible'. Against this unpromising background Harding declared a State of Emergency on 26 November, taking wide-ranging powers to restore order.[14]

On 21 December 1955 Eden, Macmillan and Lennox-Boyd met at 10 Downing Street. Lennox-Boyd said that if the security situation continued to deteriorate it would probably be necessary to deport both bishops [Makarios and the Bishop of Kyrenia], and he gave a written note of the measures he contemplated. They included powers of detention and interrogation of suspected EOKA members, collective punishments, and severe restrictions on movement by air and sea to prevent arms smuggling. These were approved, but shooting down of unidentified aircraft at night was not agreed (Greek planes were bringing in arms for the terrorists). The removal of more extreme elements of the ethnarchy was agreed if necessary, as was the jamming of Athens Radio and the possible breaking off of diplomatic and economic relations with Greece.

Harding wanted to impose 'collective whipping' for offences such as rioting or unlawful assembly. Eden would not have this, and it was authorized only in individual cases. However, he did not suggest rescinding the Governor's powers to whip. In 1956, as will be seen, Harding reported that terrorists were escaping from detention camps and he asked for permission to put anti-personnel mines around the perimeter wire fences to stop this. By going outside the circle of the Colonial Service and politicians, Eden had found in Harding the tough Governor he wanted.

On 9 January 1956, after the Greek Government had sent a special envoy to Makarios to recommence negotiations, Harding and Makarios had an 'inconclusive discussion', but agreed to meet again. At the Cabinet's Colonial Policy Committee on 12 January it was stressed that concessions to the Greek Cypriots would only be given if Makarios promised to co-operate in stopping the violence. After further meetings with Makarios, Harding reported that the Archbishop and his Council seemed determined never to accept any 'formula' which recognized Turkey's right to participate in discussions about self-determination for Cyprus. He told London that the next meeting should be the last. The Foreign Office agreed, replying: 'The Archbishop's shiftiness over a promise to denounce violence is particularly unpromising.'[15] In Athens, Peake urged the Greeks to persuade Makarios to see reason, but both he and Bowker, the Ambassador in Ankara, were pessimistic about the possibility of any agreement to which both Greece and Turkey would subscribe.

On 18 January Harding returned to London for consultations. There were press reports of a row between him and Eden; still, a strategy was agreed. Makarios was to be asked to condemn violence and in return a consultative conference on a constitution would be held. This was put to Makarios, who replied at great length in writing on 2 February. As Harding had predicted, he now shifted the emphasis from self-determination to self-government and promised co-operation in framing a constitution provided its basic principles had been agreed in advance. Significantly, he remained evasive over denouncing violence, suggesting that pacification of Cyprus might best be achieved by ending the emergency regulations and declaring a general amnesty. Harding diagnosed Makarios's letter as not 'a genuine acceptance of the proposals' and, disgusted with the Archbishop, reported that it would be 'most unlikely that he will give a really firm and effective lead to the Greek-Cypriot public' and would 'always find ways of blaming us for any failure on his part to honour his side of the bargain'. The Field Marshal insisted that it was useless to continue bargaining with Makarios, and wanted to publish all the correspondence.[16]

On 14 February the British Government sent a communication to Makarios reiterating that a constitution could not be defined in advance, but could only take shape after full discussion with both Greek and Turkish Cypriot communities. It also suggested that if Makarios would now use his influence to stop the violence, then, once law and order were restored, Britain would repeal the emergency laws and initiate a consultative conference on the constitution.

Now Francis Noel-Baker, a Labour MP and a descendant of Byron, with strong Greek connections, took a hand. He persuaded Makarios to begin further negotiations, and as a result Harding and the Archbishop met again on 23 February. Once again the talk was abortive. Makarios would only co-operate in the proposed conference if Britain now granted an amnesty for all those convicted of political crimes. In London Eden agreed that if Makarios 'makes his appeal for non-violence, and if this has its effect, there will be an amnesty for strictly political offences', and that Makarios must be told that 'this is our final offer and that we must make our position clear to the world'. Makarios replied that his conditions were a Greek elected majority, a revocation of the State of Emergency, an unlimited amnesty, and transfer of internal security to Cypriot representatives as soon as law and order was restored. Eden's reaction was that to give responsibility for law and order to Cypriots was 'clearly unacceptable'.[17]

Lennox-Boyd was dispatched to Cyprus with a briefing from Eden: 'It seems to me that we have gone as far in concessions to Makarios as it is reasonable to expect the Turks to accept at this stage . . . my own instinct in this business is that we should let the world know what we have offered and see how the medicine works.' A talk on 29 February between Lennox-Boyd and Makarios in Cyprus marked the end of negotiations and immediately violence increased. On 3 March EOKA blew up a Hermes aircraft – an incident which, but for a delay in take-off, would have killed sixty-eight passengers.[18]

When Lennox-Boyd returned to London Eden felt he had come to the end of the road because five months of discussions with Makarios had been abortive. The Cabinet decided to deport the Archbishop, and discussed bringing him to London, where they thought he might soon become a 'bore' for the world press. Harding disagreed, feeling that Makarios would become a 'martyr' wherever he was. Instead Makarios and the Bishop of Kyrenia were intercepted while en route for Athens and deported to the Seychelles.

With Makarios out of the way, the Government toyed with involving NATO; Harding wrote that he could see no end to the present strife unless Greece modified her demands to take account of Britain's and Turkey's legitimate interests, and NATO might persuade Greece 'to accept half a loaf'. After Lloyd and Eden had turned down the idea of NATO, throughout March Harding bombarded London with his proposals, even suggesting that the Chiefs of Staff should re-examine Cyprus's role in British strategic planning otherwise 'we shall run a real risk of either giving something away on the political side to the prejudice of our military requirements or of unnecessarily cramping our political style by holding on to something which is not crucial on the military side'. Harding thought that, in its desire to go for a constitution, Britain was putting the cart before the horse and would merely complicate the situation, because once the constitution was granted it would be much more difficult to resist the demand for Enosis. The Government disagreed, and insisted to Harding that once terrorism was overcome they would try to launch a new constitution. This would create a good debating point for the United Nations, but it was a non-runner with EOKA, who were stepping up their violence.[19]

In Athens Peake despaired of co-operation from the Greeks: 'One cannot make a silk purse out of a sow's ear, and it is this latter with which for too long we have had to deal.' Greek indignation arose when Harding refused to commute the death sentence on two terrorists, Karaolis and Demetriou, who were hanged on 10 May. Harding insisted that the executions must take place, writing to the Colonial Office: 'if we are to restore law and order here and bring about a solution . . . we have got to face all (repeat all) the consequences of firm government . . . and see this business through.' Eden and Lennox-Boyd agreed. Riots in Athens followed the executions; a wave of violence erupted in Cyprus, and two British servicemen were captured by EOKA and executed as a reprisal.[20]

Noel-Baker went to see Karamanlis in Athens and reported to the Foreign Office that the Greek Prime Minister was 'genuinely (indeed desperately) anxious to settle the Cyprus problem'; if Britain would propose a reasonable solution, the Greek Government would back

it. Peake was sceptical of the genuineness of the Karamanlis over-
ture, and the Foreign Office comment was that the Karamanlis
message had acquired a good deal in the telling, due to Noel-Baker's
anxiety to help. Eden disliked Noel-Baker assuming the role of
intermediary, and replied coldly to the Greek Prime Minister: 'I
would like you to know that I shall always be glad to receive any
views or thoughts you may wish to express to me through our
Ambassador.'[21]

In Cabinet on 5 June Eden expressed concern about public
opinion in Britain and abroad about Cyprus. Home, recently returned from Canada, said that opinion there was adverse to Britain
over Cyprus, and Eden thought Greek propaganda effective while
the Turkish machine had yet to be fired.

The next day Eden wrote to Eisenhower:

> . . . the offer which we made to Makarios at the end of our last
> negotiations went beyond what the Turks themselves thought we
> should have offered. . . . To attempt to get results by offering more
> . . . would inevitably entail strong Turkish reactions which would
> have very serious consequences for the security and stability of the
> Middle East as a whole. Nor would I feel confident of facilities in
> Cyprus under the present conditions unless we had control of internal
> security. Athens Radio has made it plain enough that the Greeks
> would not in any event be willing to allow our facilities in Cyprus to be
> used for any purposes connected with the Middle East. That is just
> what we might want them for. A N.A.T.O. base by itself would meet
> only part of our needs. . . . I am working hard and will attempt to find
> some means of reconciling our needs with rival Greek and Turkish
> aspirations in the island.[22]

Dulles criticized British policy to Lloyd and thought that Britain
should break the deadlock by resuming negotiations with Makarios.
The Americans did not realize how insuperable the problem was:
Britain needed Cyprus as a military base to replace Suez, and was
finding it impossible to restore law and order without antagonizing the Turks, who were so vital for the Baghdad Pact policy of
encircling Russia – which was endorsed by the United States.

In June the Cabinet decided that a constitutional Commissioner
should be appointed to draw up a constitution in consultation with
Greek and Turkish Cypriots; the issue of self-determination should
be put to the NATO Council ten years after the introduction of the
constitution and, subject to a two-thirds majority of the Council
and the conclusion of a tripartite defence arrangement, might be

granted. This had the grave disadvantage of giving Turkey a virtual veto on self-determination, a point which was not lost upon the Greeks and Cypriots.

From Cyprus Harding issued solemn warnings against introducing a liberal constitution without first having 'frozen' self-determination for ten years; he also strongly opposed partition (now favoured by Turkey), which he regarded as an admission of failure, only to be considered as a last resort. He argued that work should be started on a constitution which made it clear that self-determination could not be applied.

The Cabinet reconsidered the grisly problem on 5 July, and discussed a draft statement which stated that it had proved impossible to devise a solution which safeguarded British interests and was satisfactory to both Greece and Turkey, and it therefore had no option but to suspend seeking an international solution. The Cabinet was asked to decide between two alternative endings to the public statement; the first was that Britain intended to introduce a constitution once law and order was restored; the second merely stated Britain's intention of keeping 'constitutional advance' under consideration. The Cabinet decided on the first alternative, over-ruling Harding's advice that it would be disastrous to introduce a constitution without first 'shelving' the issue of self-determination. Eden explained the decision in a personal message to Harding: 'I have given full weight to it [Harding's view] but do not feel that it is over-riding . . . no ban on discussion of Eunosis could be effective internationally.'[23]

An official statement was made on 12 July that Lord Radcliffe would go to Cyprus to start work on proposals for a constitution. The Americans were delighted, and Dulles promised support, apologising for his refusal to back earlier action on the grounds that Turkish reaction had been so strong that it would probably have made no difference. Dulles's announcement of his support for Radcliffe's mission, according to the British Embassy in Athens, greatly alarmed the Greeks, who tried in vain to get the Americans to make a further statement in a contrary sense.[24]

Harding reported that amongst other things he was 'impressed by the necessity for Anglo–American agreement as the foundation for any solution. . . . The lack of an agreed Anglo–American policy has certainly produced an atmosphere of doubt and uncertainty which leaves the field wide open to selfish and irresponsible jockeying for position by the various parties interested in Cyprus.' He hoped that 'a plan of campaign will now be worked out as a matter of urgency and that the operations will be begun soon and that there will be no let up in their tempo until success has been achieved'. This produced a note from Downing Street stating that the Prime Minister was worried that 'the Governor's thinking appeared to be out of step with our own'. The Prime Minister wanted to let the tempo fall because the statement 'had been comparatively well received and we should let the medicine work'; he thought the Governor should be told that we were disinclined to take the initiative, and that American support could not be expected until after the Presidential Election in November.[25]

The militant Enosis supporters, including the mayors and the ethnarchy, refused at first to meet Radcliffe, and EOKA relaunched their campaign of violence, killing seventeen people and wounding eleven others in July alone; nine EOKA terrorists had been sentenced to death; two had already been executed and three others followed shortly; seventeen had been sentenced to life imprisonment. Athens Radio propaganda became viciously anti-British when the Suez crisis erupted at the end of July, and Greece refused to attend the Suez Canal Users' conferences in London; she was determined to keep Nasser's support at the United Nations. A Foreign Office minute pointed out: 'If Greece is not even prepared to attend a Conference because of the offence which might be given to Egypt, how much less could she be expected to agree to British use of Cyprus for military purposes contrary to Egyptian policy.'[26]

On 16 August, during the Suez crisis, EOKA announced the suspension of violence to allow talks with Makarios to begin again, and the Greek Government suggested that an agreement might now be reached. When the British Embassy in Athens cabled that the Government might have made this move because they had been shocked by the Suez situation, Eden expressed the hope that 'there will be no question of making any nice noises to the Greeks at present'.[27]

The 'peace' was short-lived. Although the Greeks approached the Americans and asked them to mediate, and an American diplomat, Julius Holmes, went to London, Athens and Ankara, his efforts came to nothing. The Greek Government told him that it would only accept an agreement which stipulated self-determination within three years, although they would allow Britain to retain control of defence and foreign affairs, but only initially of public security. Eden minuted that he was 'bewildered by this Holmes negotiation . . . I do not understand on what grounds the Americans are in this special position. It could not be by virtue of the help that they have given us over Suez.' On 9 October the Cabinet considered Holmes's and the Greek Government's proposals and firmly turned them down.[28]

On 6 October Harding declared that the EOKA ceasefire had been only an excuse for them to lick their wounds, regain their breath and plan a fresh campaign, that up until 1 July he had been pressing EOKA hard, but that the Suez situation had had a marked effect on Britain's ability to keep up the offensive and had put the campaign back two or three months. Now he needed 'a very strong and efficient force available for use anywhere in the island'. Whilst it was difficult to estimate how long it would take to eliminate EOKA, Harding believed that if he could make up the lost ground and 'keep up the pressure on all fronts, I am confident that a distinct improvement should be apparent by the end of this year and I believe that Grivas's terrorist organisation can be put out of business as a major factor in a matter of months'.[29]

At the end of November Harding wrote a paper, entitled *Strategic Aspects of Future British Policy for Cyprus*, in which he argued that Britain must retain sovereignty 'at any rate until the communist threat in the Middle East has been held and defeated'. He also suggested that Britain should use Cyprus as a base for military operations only with the agreement of a majority of the member nations of N.A.T.O. or the Baghdad Pact'. The Foreign Office reaction was that HMG could not accept that military action from Cyprus should depend upon NATO and Baghdad Pact agreement: 'Such agreement would not have been forthcoming for our recent intervention in Egypt.' The paper was rejected.[30]

Meanwhile the internal situation in Cyprus was deteriorating and Harding's promise to put the Grivas operation out of business in a few months was over-optimistic. The Governor asked for harsher repressive measures. Detainees had been escaping from the concentration camps and, as mentioned earlier, Harding wanted to put anti-personnel mines around the perimeters. On 9 September he wrote:

Security of Detention Camps

An effective deterrent to persons contemplating escape from the detention camps would be to lay anti-personnel mines in the area between the external face of the main perimeter wire and what is known as the 'thirty yard wire' (which is an extra obstacle for an escaper to get through after he has broken out of camp).

2. The detainees themselves would be made aware that the area had been mined and notice boards would be erected on the outer limit to the mined area to inform the public.

3. I am advised that inasmuch as there is no clear legal provision for taking this action it would be difficult to avoid responsibility under ordinary criminal law (e.g. Sections 222 (f) and 226 of the Criminal Code, Cap. 13) if some escaper or member of the public was injured by one of these mines. Clear legal authority would therefore be necessary. There may also be certain obligations in international law which have been assumed towards political detainees which would render the use of mines open to objection.

4. I should be grateful to have your early views on this proposal. An alternative, but less effective, deterrent would be the Army type trip flare which is not dangerous and which I would be prepared to consider if in your view there are overriding objections to using A.P. mines.

On the telegram Nutting wrote: 'We really must stop this. What a pretty story it would be in U.N. debate. (Have we gone mad?)' Permission to use mines was refused.[31]

On 12 November, as EOKA attacks on defenceless civilians mounted, Harding wrote that the time had come for more drastic measures and requested the mandatory death penalty for any person convicted of possessing firearms, ammunition or explosives, and for those who associated with such persons. When the Colonial Office did not reply, Harding repeated his request, whereupon Lennox-Boyd asked him to reconsider it in the light of the imminent publication of the Radcliffe Report. Harding persisted, possibly influenced by the fact that thirty-three people had been killed by EOKA in the first three weeks of November. The Government then concurred in this extension of the death penalty at a time when, as has been seen, a Commons majority had been secured for abolition of capital punishment at home. Later Harding justified himself by pointing out that the number of murders fell fast after the introduction of this harsher legislation.[32]

The Radcliffe proposals, which were released simultaneously in Cyprus and the Commons on 19 December 1956, offered nearly total self-government but not self-determination nor control of internal security. They were rejected by the Greeks. Shortly after Eden left office the Macmillan Government released Makarios and the Bishop of Kyrenia, even though they would not promise to condemn terrorism. They immediately returned to Cyprus, and then followed throughout 1958 the worst terrorism of all. Finally Makarios abandoned Enosis, the Turks yielded over partition, and an agreement was signed at Zurich in February 1959. But it did not bring permanent peace to the island.

* * *

It must have been a relief for the Eden Cabinet to turn away from the insuperable problem of Cyprus to the lesser difficulties of Britain's other island colony in the Mediterranean, Malta. After being conquered by Napoleon in 1798, and recaptured by the British in 1800, it had been bartered over in the Treaty of Amiens with Napoleon in 1802, and then formally annexed by Britain at Malta's request in 1814. Thereafter it became a vital cog in British Mediterranean defence, and was awarded the George Cross in 1942 for its courageous resistance to the Nazis. Limited self-government had begun in 1921 with a series of constitutions, but these did not produce the hoped for results and Crown Colony rule was restored in 1939. In 1947 a limited form of self-government was introduced; internal affairs were administered by the Maltese while defence, foreign affairs and related matters were still under the British.

At the coronation of Queen Elizabeth II in 1953 the Maltese Nationalist Prime Minister, Dr Borg Olivier, had objected to his proposed seat in Westminster Abbey and insisted that he should have 'his rightful place alongside the other Prime Ministers of the Commonwealth'. As a result he was given equal recognition with the Prime Minister of Southern Rhodesia, but told that this was only due to Malta's special position as a holder of the George Cross, and not because of his political claims.[33]

While he was in London for the coronation, Olivier presented a memorandum suggesting that responsibility for Malta should be transferred from the Colonial Office to the Commonwealth Relations Office. The view of the Colonial Secretary, Oliver Lyttelton, was that Malta could never qualify as a full member of the Commonwealth because she was too small and too poor. Over one-third of her income was derived from Britain, and this could be disastrously reduced if there were contractions in British defence requirements in the Mediterranean. However, Lyttelton told the Cabinet that the situation was becoming intolerable as 'dissatisfaction with their constitutional status' was 'poisoning our relations with a people to whom we owe much', and he proposed to put Malta on a par with the Channel Islands and the Isle of Man by placing the island under the Home Office. This did not satisfy Olivier who, in the autumn of 1954, pressed for an early date to be fixed for full self-government within the Commonwealth. However in the General Election of February 1955 Olivier was replaced by Dom Mintoff the Labour leader.[34]

Mintoff fought the election on a platform of close integration with Britain, and floated the idea of Maltese MPs in the Westminster Parliament on the lines of the French colonial MPs in Paris and the

Hawaiians and Puerto Ricans in the Washington Congress. On 15 April 1954, while Churchill was Prime Minister, the Cabinet had considered this. Lyttelton was against it and the Cabinet agreed that 'representation of Malta in the Parliament at Westminster could not be contemplated'. Lennox-Boyd, who replaced Lyttelton as Colonial Secretary, felt differently, and in Cabinet on 30 June 1955 argued strongly for integration, which would be 'a considerable constitutional innovation', and warned of the possible danger of a Maltese alignment with Italy, which would be 'gravely embarrassing'. In the discussion the Cabinet was divided. Some members supported 'an imaginative gesture' to satisfy Maltese constitutional aspirations, since in view of Britain's bad press elsewhere – especially over Cyprus – she could not afford a crisis in relations with Malta. On the other hand serious concern was expressed about the risk involved in having Maltese MPs at Westminster, because they might hold the balance between Labour and Conservative, gaining disproportionate influence. To solve the impasse a round table conference was suggested.

Evidence of the Cabinet division lies in a Macmillan note to Eden on 2 July:

> Although the proposal to have Maltese members in the House of Commons is novel, or even, to use Lord Salisbury's expression, eccentric, I hope the Cabinet will accept it, at least in principle . . .
> I feel at this moment in our history, the voluntary and patriotic desire of Malta to join us is something we ought not to repel. Centrifugal forces are very strong at the moment. Let us cherish any centripetal movement that we can find.

Both Eden and Macmillan had a romantic feeling towards Malta, but it was not shared by the civil servants and all their Cabinet colleagues.[35]

Brook was strongly opposed, sending two long notes to the Prime Minister on 4 July. He recommended the Cabinet to 'weigh very carefully the possible long term consequences' of allowing Malta representation in Parliament; Gibraltar, Cyprus, Bermuda, the Bahamas and Mauritius, to name only five, might desire the same status as Malta.

> What effect would this have on the Parliament at Westminster? It is not enough to measure the effect in terms of three Maltese members. Once this pattern was set, we must assume that a number of small Colonies would secure similar representation – we should then be

headed towards a Parliamentary Assembly representing not the United Kingdom but the United Kingdom and Colonies. . . . What the Maltese really want is an assurance that their economy will be made viable – or, more honestly, as that is impracticable, that there will be subventions from outside sufficient to produce the same result. They ask for representation at Westminster because they think that it will mean, or at least will enable them to press more effectively for, economic integration with the United Kingdom – in which they hope to have all the special advantages of a 'depressed area.'

Brook went on that there was doubt about the opposition of the Roman Catholic Church and of Olivier's party, and asked: 'When all this is taken together, is there not much to be said for trying to do a deal on "money" which appeals to men of all Parties in Malta and creates no constitutional precedents?'

Brook had summed up the problem accurately, and it would have saved the Government much time and trouble if they had followed his advice. The project of integration foundered not just on opposition to the idea of having Maltese MPs at Westminster, but because the precedent would have made it impossible to refuse similar representation to other colonies, and on the economic question that Malta wanted larger subsidies from British taxpayers so that they could have the same social services and the same standard of living as Britain. In the end the cost of this was more than the British Government could stomach.[36]

To Mintoff's delight, on 6 July – ignoring Brook – Eden announced that a round table conference on Malta would be held on 19 September under Lord Kilmuir's chairmanship. In Malta Archbishop Gonzi told the Lieutenant-Governor, Trafford Smith, that he was against integration – not so much because of fear of Britain interfering with the position of the Church in Malta, but of a 'progressive' Maltese Government which might at some stage interfere with the powers of the Church, and he wanted assurances about this which were outside the power of the British Government to give. Trafford Smith reported that the Archbishop intended to oppose integration 'tooth and nail'. In another dispatch the Governor, General Sir Robert Laycock, mentioned worries that the Archbishop might seek the support of the Vatican and even Roman Catholic circles in Britain for his campaign. As a result, hasty telegrams were sent to the British Legation to the Holy See, instructing them to reassure the Vatican that the proposals formed no threat to the position of the Church in Malta.[37]

The British Cabinet remained divided, frequently reiterating the same arguments in favour and against, and becoming more and more concerned about the cost of the Maltese social service if there was integration. At first Kilmuir had grave doubts about the wisdom of allowing Maltese MPs at Westminster, and asked: 'Is there not, therefore, much to be said for making it clear from the outset that Maltese representation in Westminster *is not possible* [italics in original] ?' Against this Eden minuted: 'How can we? We have said the opposite.' On 15 September Kilmuir asked the Cabinet to give him guidance on 'handling the Conference' by coming to a decision as to whether they were in favour of, or against, Mintoff's proposals. This was refused. Once the Conference started Kilmuir shifted his ground, writing to Eden on 26 October: '. . . the Conference is virtually unanimous in the view, which I share, that representation at Westminster is likely to provide the most promising basis for a satisfactory and permanent solution of the constitutional problem of Malta. . . . The greatest potential obstacle in the way of integration is the attitude of the Roman Catholic church.'

The report was ready on 9 December 1955. It concluded that further economic assistance from Britain would be required, but that only £4–5 million could be spent productively, and recommended the presence of three Maltese MPs at Westminster – provided the Maltese people 'demonstrated clearly' that this was their wish. Mintoff now bombarded London with requests that the report be published quickly. He wanted to cash in on the current popularity of his Government and to hold a referendum on the proposals before Lent in mid-February, which coincided with the peak of the Church's influence. The Governor was told to inform Mintoff that there was no certainty that the main recommendation of the Conference would be accepted automatically by the United Kingdom Parliament, and that 'if he goes plunging ahead in this headlong way, he may seriously prejudice [the] reception by Parliament of, and its final decision on, the Conference's report'; while Lennox-Boyd sent a personal message to Mintoff saying that it would create a deplorable impression in Britain, where it would be thought that he was making unreasonable haste in order to forestall criticism and to force the hand of the United Kingdom Government and Parliament.

Mintoff prevailed, and despite opposition from the Cabinet scheduled the referendum for 9 February 1956; once again the Cabinet was divided, with some members thinking it would be an advantage if Parliament knew where Malta stood before debating the report.[38] Now Mintoff blotted his copy book seriously with the Prime Minister. He visited Egypt privately in late December 1955 and invited

President Nasser to take a holiday in Malta. As will be seen, Nasser at this stage was very much in Eden's black books. Trevelyan reported this to the Foreign Office, adding that Nasser was agreeable. Philip de Zulueta, Eden's private secretary, told the Colonial Office that on discovering this the Prime Minister had become 'very distressed', and wanted to know urgently what action could now be taken 'to prevent Colonel Nasser's visit or at least to minimise its effects'. Mintoff agreed to cancel his invitation, but said he thought the visit would have improved Anglo–Egyptian relations. Lennox-Boyd ordered Laycock to vet Mintoff's letter to Nasser, writing: 'I need hardly say that it is very desirable that Nasser should not get the impression we have stopped his visit.' A minute was sent to Eden from the Colonial Office to the effect that Mintoff's letter had more or less disposed of a visit, though it contained some unhappy gratuitous comments which provoked Eden to minute: 'Mintoff falls steadily in my opinion. A.E. 1 March, 1956.' The Cabinet was so split over the Conference's main recommendation that there should be three Maltese MPs at Westminster that they could not reach a decision on what date to debate it in Parliament.[39]

Meanwhile Mintoff went ahead with his referendum amid quarrels with the Archbishop, who roundly condemned the integration policy. On 14 February the referendum results were announced; 59 per cent of the electorate voted, and 75 per cent of those voting were in favour of integration – corresponding closely to the numbers supporting Mintoff in the General Election. Laycock had been to Rome to talk to the Pope, and the Vatican began to influence Archbishop Gonzi to reach a concordat with Mintoff. Lennox-Boyd told the Cabinet that 'the longer the delay in holding the debate, the greater the danger of serious consequences in the political situation in Malta and of an irremediable breach between the Maltese Government and the Roman Catholic Church in Malta'. Laycock's view, which was also reported to the Cabinet, was that it was unlikely that a serious security situation like Cyprus would arise in Malta, although 'If his co-operation ceases, however, Mr. Mintoff can undoubtedly make it exceedingly hot for the British in Malta and the efficiency of the base is bound to suffer.' If Mintoff did not get his way, it was always open to him to demand full self-determination and rent for the use of the bases. The Governor wanted the debate as soon as possible. In Cabinet on 13 March, doubts were expressed by some as to whether there had ever been a majority of Government supporters in favour of the principle of Maltese representation at Westminster; 'it was probable that in recent weeks opinion had hardened against representation', but after the same old arguments, with the Cabinet still divided, 26 March was fixed for the debate.[40] This brought a threat of resignation from James Stuart, Secretary of State for Scotland, who wrote to Eden on 14 March:

> . . . I cannot force myself to believe that anyone has any right to wield powers without responsibility . . . I might, possibly, be able to consider – (but *most* unwillingly) – 'integration' *after* Malta has reached a state of equality with the UK as regards general standards of living, e.g. social services, etc. . . . I cannot agree that Mr. Mintoff and Company should be allowed to force us into agreeing to integration, and to electing MPs to this House, until they have built up their own standards. The people of Malta are divided and I am assured they have not the slightest idea as to what the plan involves: they have no knowledge of P.A.Y.E. or Insurance and will only squeal like silly half wits when they are asked to contribute a share, however small: they will say that we (the British) have swindled them and let them down. . . . I felt it to be my duty to write to confirm what I said verbally yesterday.
>
>   Yours ever,
>   James Stuart.
> P.S. To be 'crystal clear', I should add that I would have to resign before I agree to 'integration' on present conditions. Sorry. J.S.[41]

The debate duly took place on 26 March; the Government Whips delivered the votes, and two days later Eden announced that the Government would proceed with legislation for integration, but that representation at Westminster would depend on the Maltese people showing their desire for it by a General Election.

Once the British Government were commited to integration Mintoff began to raise his demands for economic assistance, demanding £8 million for the coming year even though it had been assumed at the conference that the UK contribution would not exceed £4–5 million. When the Government refused, Mintoff came to London and saw Lennox-Boyd and Eden, who categorically refused to raise the ceiling on British subvention. Mintoff was angry, and Laycock was told by the Colonial Office: 'You are going to have a most difficult task in handling Mintoff when he gets back.' In fact on his return to Malta Mintoff announced that negotiations had broken down, and the Colonial Office were told that Mintoff and his Cabinet were in 'a mood of utter despondency', maintaining that the £5 million ceiling would have 'politically unacceptable consequences, especially on unemployment' and would make working towards integration impossible. Laycock reported: 'It will almost certainly

not be possible to prevent widespread acceptance of the view that
H.M.G. are spoiling the ship for a ha'p'orth of tar.'

The Cabinet remained adamant against increasing the financial
contribution to Malta. Lennox-Boyd, originally the most enthusiastic
supporter of integration, wrote to Eden on 27 June:

> . . . To concede ground to Mr. Mintoff on this issue will convince him
> finally that H.M.G. is ready to meet all his terms for the sake of
> integration. . . . I have become convinced in these negotiations that
> Mr. Mintoff is either unwilling to make, or incapable of making his
> contribution to that co-operative endeavour. . . . Having carefully
> weighed up the situation with which we are now faced, my conclusion
> is that we must stand by the decision to limit our financial aid this year
> to a maximum of £5 million and face the consequences. . . . The Lord
> Chancellor is firmly behind this proposal of mine.

The Cabinet agreed with Lennox-Boyd.[42]

It would have been better if Eden had accepted Brook's advice of
4 July 1955. When Macmillan, whose romantic support of Maltese
MPs in July 1955 must have influenced Eden, was Prime Minister,
he would not give in to the Maltese demands for higher subsidies,
and the integration proposal died a natural death.

7

The Middle East
1955

WHEN EDEN BECAME Prime Minister Britain still had heavy responsibilities in the Middle East arising out of her former Mandate for Palestine, her military occupation of Egypt and heavy dependence on the Suez Canal. The Palestine Mandate originated in a Declaration by Arthur Balfour, then Foreign Secretary, on 17 November 1917, that the British Government 'viewed with favour the establishment in Palestine of a national home for the Jewish people', although he qualified it by saying that 'nothing shall be done which may prejudice the civil and religious rights of existing non-Jewish communities in Palestine'. The Turkish Empire, of which Palestine had been part, collapsed in 1918, and at the San Remo Conference in 1920 Britain assumed the role of mandatory power.

A strong section of the British Cabinet would have preferred the responsibility to be undertaken by the USA. However Winston Churchill, who became Colonial Secretary in 1922, was an enthusiastic Zionist, and thanks largely to his spadework Jewish capital and immigrants flowed into Palestine, at first without any significant injury to the Arab population. Farming techniques were improved vastly, and factories sprang up. By the 1930s Jewish immigration was increasing so fast that Britain could not discharge her obligations to both Jews and Arabs, whose interests had become incompatible. As the two races would never agree to joint government even within the British Commonwealth, partition or control of immigration were the only solutions.

Accordingly in 1937 a Royal Commission under Lord Peel was set up; it recommended that limitations on Jewish immigration must be imposed. The report coincided with an escalation of Hitler's persecution of Jews within Germany, which created an urgent demand from hundreds of thousands of Jews to go to Palestine. Yet the Chamberlain Government imposed quotas on German Jewish immigration both to Palestine and to Britain. The USA also restricted Jewish immigation, and as a result vast numbers of would-be Jewish fugitives from Nazi tyranny had nowhere to go.

Unfortunately for the Jews in Germany, and later in Austria and Czechoslovakia, the Prime Minister, Neville Chamberlain, and his Colonial Secretary Malcolm Macdonald were anti-Zionist, and felt that, in the event of war with Hitler, Moslem friendship would be vital. Chamberlain recorded in the Cabinet Palestine Committee on 19 April 1939: 'If we must offend one side let us offend the Jews rather than the Arabs', and on 19 November 1938 the Chamberlain Cabinet had rejected partition of Palestine on the grounds that Britain must keep the friendship of the Arab world.[1]

After an abortive London Conference of Jews and Arabs early in 1939 a White Paper (Cmd 6019) in April stated that no further Jewish immigration into Palestine should be allowed against Arab wishes. It was a British rejection of the Balfour Declaration at a moment when European Jewry faced disaster. The Commons were divided on non-party lines. Churchill (out of office), pro-Zionist as ever, opposed the White Paper. In the division the Government majority sank to 89, although its normal majority was 240.

During the war the Labour Party demanded the rejection of the White Paper and reaffirmed its support for a Jewish national home in Palestine, but its policy changed when Labour came to power in 1945. Ernest Bevin, as Foreign Secretary, was pro-Arab and anti-Zionist. In 1948, because of the plight of so many Jews in Europe after the war, President Truman demanded the immediate entry of a hundred thousand of them into Palestine. Bevin would not agree, and instead engineered the appointment of an Anglo–US Committee of Inquiry. However, on 1 May 1948 this Committee recommended that a hundred thousand Jews should be admitted to Palestine immediately. At that time the position of the British Army and Police Force in Palestine was becoming intolerable. Dissident Jews in Palestine had created Haganah, an illegal private army of eighty thousand, which was inflicting mounting casualties on British soldiers and police.

It was the end of the road for the Attlee Government. In July 1946 the Cabinet accepted a report from the Colonial Office advocating a partition solution which would relieve Britain of her financial and political commitments under the pre-war Mandate; the Chiefs of Staff opposed it. In the Commons debate Churchill defined his and the Conservative attitude to the Middle East by saying that, unless the Americans shared the burden, Britain should relinquish the

Mandate and give it back to the United Nations, and that 'we should inform Egypt that we stand by our Treaty rights, and will by all means maintain our position in the Canal Zone'.[2]

Truman would not agree that America should 'shoulder the burden'; instead the United Nations appointed a Special Committee on Palestine (UNSCOP) to visit the Middle East and decide what recommendations should be made to Britain as the mandatory power. Meanwhile the British seizure of ships containing illegal immigrants, and their return to Germany and other parts of Europe, produced adverse publicity and also created a bad impression on UNSCOP, who recommended that the British Mandate should be terminated and that Palestine should be partitioned and made independent under United Nations control for the interim period.

Because of Bevin's intransigence there was a long British policy vacuum over Jewish immigration just when European Jewry desperately needed an open door to Palestine. On 20 September 1947 the Cabinet, after considering the UNSCOP report published earlier that month, announced its intention to surrender the Mandate and fixed 1 August 1948 as the date for British withdrawal. Eden supported the Government in the Commons debate and, surprisingly, suggested a federal solution: no more was ever heard from him on federalism.[3] There was doubt as to whether the United Nations would agree, but, with both the Americans and Russians in favour, on 29 November 1947 the UN General Assembly voted for partition by 33 to 13. The Jews rejoiced.

However, ahead lay both a battlefield and a political minefield. The American State Department decided that partition was wrong, and instead wanted UN trusteeship. They foresaw the inevitability of war after partition – and were proved right – but Truman over-ruled them. Then, as the Jews in Palestine prepared to celebrate their independence and the creation of the State of Israel, Arab armies mobilized to destroy it at birth. Even American Jewry lost their nerve in face of the Arab military threat, and the issue hung in the balance, but Truman and Marshall, the American Secretary of State, stood firm in favour of partition.

On 14 May 1948, while the UN Political Committee was still debating a new trusteeship, the Jewish leaders took the plunge and, defying the Arab threat, proclaimed the Jewish State of Israel. The same day Truman recognized it *de facto*; not so the British, who delayed *de facto* recognition until 30 January 1949 and *de jure* recognition until 27 April 1951. Stalin gave Israel recognition. In the Commons debate Churchill attacked Attlee for not giving recognition, and in the division the Government were 150 votes short of their normal majority.

Immediately fighting started. The Arab Legion, with British officers led by General Glubb, supported by the Iraqi Army, tried to drive the Israelis out of Jerusalem and Galilee; Egyptian troops penetrated to within twenty-six miles of Tel Aviv. As a result of UN intervention the fighting stopped and an eleven-month truce was agreed on 11 June; in spite of this, hostilities started again on 9 July. On 17 September there was another truce, and Count Bernadotte was appointed by the Security Council of the United Nations as mediator between the Jews and the Arabs. Unfortunately he was murdered by recalcitrant Jews, and fighting broke out again in October 1948. Then the Israeli Army had some dramatic victories, and probably only the threat of British intervention saved the Egyptian Army in the Negev from complete destruction. In February 1949 a ceasefire was concluded, which lasted until the Israeli attack on Egypt in collusion with France and Britain in October 1956.

When the Jewish leadership accepted the UN partition resolution of 29 November 1947 they believed that the Great Powers would enforce its acceptance. This was an illusion. However, as a result of the fighting Israel not only kept all the territory awarded by the UN resolution, but gained 5000 square kilometres which under the partition agreement should have gone to the new Arab state. Between 24 February and 20 July 1949 Israel signed separate formal armistices with Egypt, Lebanon, Jordan and Syria. Nearly all the territory won by her military successes was allocated to her under the 1948 armistices, but the Arabs looked on them as only temporary interruptions to the fighting, which implied no political settlement. Israel desperately wanted a permanent peace settlement with each of the Arab states, which would be guaranteed by the Great Powers; however only King Abdullah of Jordan was willing to negotiate, and just when he had reached agreement with David Ben Gurion, the Israeli Prime Minister, pressure from other Arab states made him withdraw. But there was no more organized fighting after 1 June 1949, and Israel retained her territorial conquests during seven and a half years of unease and friction.

In the early 1950s Britain had to reappraise her attitude to Egypt in light of the surrender of the Palestine Mandate, the Israeli War of Independence and internal events in Egypt. Britain was still the dominant power in the Middle East. In addition to the huge military base on the Suez Canal, a naval base at Aden, air squadrons stationed in Iraq and rear bases in Cyprus and Malta, Britain paid for and provided the commander of the Arab Legion in Jordan.

Since 1882 Egypt had been under British domination and thus protected against the Turks, who had ruled from 1517 to 1879. This protectorate ended and Egypt was proclaimed an independent kingdom in February 1922, but defence and other policy were still dealt with by the British. (This caused Mussolini to seek similar privileges in Abyssinia in 1935.) In 1936 a perpetual Treaty of Alliance was signed, and provided for the stationing of British forces in Egypt for twenty years. In 1945 Egypt declared war on Germany, became a founder member of the United Nations and, after hostilities were over, demanded the withdrawal of all British forces and the revision of the 1936 Treaty. As a gesture Britain evacuated the Cairo citadel and the naval base at Alexandria, but refused to leave her great military base on the Suez Canal.

After her humiliating defeats in 1948 and 1949 in the Israeli War of Independence, Egypt was more determined than ever to prevent Israel becoming an independent state, and refused any compromise settlement. With Egypt unilaterally abrogating the 1936 agreement with Britain in 1951, violence against British troops accompanied a campaign for the evacuation of the Suez military base, and on 23 July a military coup d'état was carried out by General Neguib and Colonel Nasser. King Feisal was sent into exile; attempts at economic reforms to improve the standard of living made the new regime popular, and soon Nasser emerged as a dictator determined not only to rule Egypt single-handed, but to be the leader of the Arab world.

In January 1953 Eden, as Foreign Secretary, decided to try to negotiate with the Egyptian Government the evacuation of the eighty thousand British military personnel in Egypt, provided the Suez base could be available in a future war. In return he suggested a programme of military and economic assistance to Egypt by the United States and the United Kingdom.

After an exchange of letters in late December 1953 Churchill asked Eisenhower not to give moral and material support to Egypt while they 'threaten and assault our troops and conduct a campaign of hatred against us'. Winston proposed that the Americans should join in the Egyptian negotiations about the base. The two leaders met in Washington in March 1954, when a sympathetic Eisenhower agreed to send General Hull to Cairo for six weeks to help negotiate a settlement, but would not go as far as Churchill wanted over joint command in the Middle East.[4] In the end there was no American participation, because the Egyptians refused to consider it before all British troops had been evacuated from Egypt, and without an invitation from Egypt Eisenhower would not send Hull. If America and Britain could have acted jointly over Egypt in 1954, the whole history of the Middle East would have been different.

In the spring of 1953, when Eden was ill, Churchill took charge of the Foreign Office and hence the negotiations with Egypt. Thirty Tory MPs, led by Charles Waterhouse, Ralph Assheton, Fitzroy Maclean and Julian Amery (the Suez Group), campaigned against withdrawal from the Canal and were backed by the elderly but still influential Lord Hankey. Churchill had hardly moved from the views he had given to the Commons in 1948 – that Britain must stand by her Egyptian Treaty rights – and not surprisingly no progress was made on the Eden initiative during his enforced absence. When Eden returned in October he insisted, against Churchill's opposition, that British interests in the Middle East, and especially her growing need for Middle East oil, must be protected by negotiated agreements with the Arab states and not only by military strength. The Foreign Secretary particularly wanted to remove the Suez base 'irritant' to Egypt, because he believed that only Egypt had sufficient strength to give a lead which would produce a permanent Arab settlement with the Jews.

Churchill still hankered after US participation, but was shocked by a report from Makins on 19 June 1954 that Dulles had been telling friends that American policy in the 'oil rich Middle East', as well as Asia, had been badly handicapped by 'a tendency to support British and French "colonial" views' which had 'caused the United States to be identified in the minds of the people of that area as a colonial power despite its long tradition as a champion of freedom and independence', and as a result Dulles believed the Arab people were 'turning more and more to Russia as an advocate of their drive for self rule and eventual freedom'. This was not a good portent for American co-operation over the base agreement. Accordingly Winston wrote to Eisenhower:

> Now is the time the Middle East front should be considered together by the United States and Britain. I had hoped more than a year ago that the United States would act to join with us in negotiating an agreement with the Egyptian military dictatorship in accordance with the terms already agreed between the British and American staffs. Since then there has been a deadlock . . . I am obliged by the way in which you have so far withheld arms and money from the Egyptian dictatorship.[5]

In late June 1954, when Eisenhower, Churchill and Eden met in Washington, the Americans agreed that future US assistance to Egypt would be conditional on Egypt fulfilling the terms of a 'Base Agreement'. Eden had opposed the Prime Minister's renewed pressure for American participation in the Egyptian negotiations on rather flimsy grounds, minuting on 21 June 1954 that amongst other things he was 'apprehensive of the effect on other Middle East countries (especially Iraq and the Persian Gulf) if we appear unable to settle this business ourselves and have to ask help from the Americans'.

As a result of Dulles's objections, on 26 June Eisenhower firmly refused to be a signatory of any agreement over the base, although he agreed that a way would be found to indicate to the Egyptians that US arms and loans would be conditional upon Egyptian fulfilment of the agreement.[6] With this American carrot to the Egyptians Eden's negotiations prospered. Anthony Head, Secretary of State for War, and Anthony Nutting, Minister of State, Foreign Office, went to Cairo. Without much difficulty agreement was reached on 26 July; twenty months was allowed for evacuation of the British military personnel, and after that for seven years the base was to be held and staffed by British civilians. Amery declared in the House on 29 July that it was 'virtually unconditional evacuation of the Canal zone'.

In the Commons debate on the Base Agreement Eden said: 'I . . . say plainly to Egypt tonight that we are going to enter into this new era with a real determination to make it succeed. If they will do the same by us they will find full reciprocity and understanding here.' The effect of Eden's speech was rather spoilt by Attlee pointing out that, if the Foreign Secretary had stood up to his backbenchers two years earlier, the Base Agreement could have been settled on better terms then. This was not fair on Eden; Attlee should have put the blame on Churchill.

Unfortunately Nasser pursued two will o'the wisps which were to foul his relations with Britain. They were the elimination of Israel, and the leadership of the Arab world.

During a brief period of friendship, on 17 December in Paris Dulles and Eden agreed, in Eden's words, 'to try and do some work with the utmost secrecy on the Arab–Israel problem, though none of us are optimistic as to what we can make of it'. Shuckburgh, Under-Secretary for Middle Eastern Affairs, was summoned to Paris and found both Eden and Dulles 'amenable' to the idea of concessions from Israel. Secret Anglo–US talks began with Francis Russell of the State Department co-operating well with Shuckburgh. Eden wanted Israel to make concessions, and Dulles, in spite of the importance of the Jewish vote in the USA, agreed, believing that the immense advantage to Israel of Great Power guarantees far out-weighed any loss of territory.[7]

A leading British international historian, F. S. Northedge, has written that after America in late 1954 at Churchill's request had given Egypt a $40 million grant for development, Nasser 'seemed set to become a firm friend of Britain and the West if not an Ally'.[8] The archives reveal that Eden as Prime Minister was at first enthusiastic for Nasser's friendship and ready to ask Israel to make large terri-torial sacrifices in exchange for a guarantee of Israeli frontiers by the UK and USA. Unfortunately the Baghdad Pact soured the friendship with Egypt which Eden wanted. After a tour of potential trouble spots in the Middle East, Dulles had said in a well-publicized speech: 'Many of the Arab League countries are so engrossed with their quarrels with Israel or with Great Britain or France that they pay little heed to the menace of communism.' With encouragement from Dulles Eden negotiated the Baghdad Pact, and eventually Britain entered into a military alliance with Turkey, Iran, Iraq and Pakistan, the countries around the Soviet southern frontiers in order to keep Communism at bay; but the Americans shilly-shallied and would not join.

In his autobiography Macmillan is non-committal about the Baghdad Pact, writing that it was arguable how far it was 'a prudent move' or how far 'a hazardous adventure'. But as Foreign Secretary in 1955 he showed enthusiasm for it, was anxious that all signatories should receive weapons from Britain and America, and tried hard to persuade the USA to join. The snag was that the Baghdad Pact infuriated Nasser, who viewed it as a continuation of colonialism and a threat of his leadership of the Arab world because he felt it would split the unity of the Arab states now tenuously grouped in the Arab League. In the end the Baghdad Pact turned out to be a broken reed, although originally it appeared a plausible *cordon sanitaire* to re-strain the Kremlin. On 10 February 1955 Shuckburgh noted: 'The Egyptians are in a state of fury about Nuri's [Prime Minister of Iraq] determination to sign a pact with Turkey. . . . I am counting on AE's visit to Cairo to put some sense back into Nasser.'[9]

Eden met Nasser in Cairo on 20 February 1955 at a dinner given by the British Ambassador, Sir Ralph Stevenson. Eden was on his way to the Bangkok Conference and about to succeed Churchill as Prime Minister. There have been inaccurate and highly coloured reports of the meeting; in fact it went reasonably well. Shuckburgh, who was not present, noted: 'It was not the success we hoped for, though there were friendly moments'. Heikal, who accompanied Nasser, writes plausibly that the Egyptian Prime Minister told Eden how glad he was that Britain had agreed to evacuate the Canal Zone, but said the Baghdad Pact was a threat to Anglo–Egyptian relations.[10] Eden countered by asking why Nasser was attacking people like Nuri es Said, Prime Minister of Iraq. Nasser argued that the Baghdad Pact must lead to a division of the Arab world and the isolation of Egypt, who would be left alone to face the Israeli danger. Eden replied that Britain wanted to defend the Middle East against Communism, whereupon Nasser said 'the proper defence of Egypt against Communism must come from inside the country'.

Eden went on that there was nothing Nasser could do to stop the Bagdhad Pact, and he was not worried by Nasser's opposition to it; although Britain was ready to negotiate with Egypt on Egyptian problems, he could not accept Nasser's stand about the overall situation. Eden's report to the Foreign Office ran: 'No doubt jealousy plays a part [in Nasser's hostility to the Pact] and a frustrated desire to lead the Arab world.' On 7 March Eden told the Cabinet that

> In Cairo he had found that the P.M. [Nasser] was not personally hostile to the idea of a rapprochement with Israel. It had, however, been evident that the Egyptians would have strong views on the timing of such a move; and in view of the recent incident at Gaza [where thirty-eight Egyptians had been killed in an Israeli raid] it was unlikely that any progress could be made at the moment.[11]

Field Marshal Lord Harding, who as CIGS accompanied Eden, told the author that Lady Stevenson had made a mistake in inviting women to the dinner, which resulted in the serious discussion starting too late; Eden did not show off in any way, and the discussion was sensible. According to Harding, Eden argued that Egypt should join the Baghdad Pact to stop the spread of Communism into the Middle East, and offered Nasser a NATO type of organization. Nasser refused, courteously enough, on the grounds that he wanted instead an Arab defence coalition without the USA or the UK playing any direct role. Harding did not feel that at that stage Nasser was on bad terms with Nuri, and emphasized that nothing went wrong at the Nasser–Eden meeting.[12]

Eden felt, as he prepared to become Prime Minister, that although the agreement to evacuate the Canal Zone was a step in the right direction, its weakness was that there was no clause to restrain Egypt from attacking Israel, with whom Egypt still proclaimed herself at war. At that time Egypt was preventing Israeli ships using the Suez Canal and sailing into the Gulf of Akaba and up to the port of Eilat, because Egyptian forts with coastal guns controlled the mouth of the Gulf at Sharm-el-Sheikh.

Meanwhile Russell and Shuckburgh were implementing the instructions given by Dulles and Eden in Paris and working out a detailed and ingenious plan for an Egypt–Israeli settlement; given the codename Alpha, it was enthusiastically endorsed by the British and American Governments. Alpha was a plan for a land link between Egypt and Jordan across the Israeli-held Negev. Israel was to be asked to concede two triangles of land in the extreme south of the Negev, a few miles north of Eilat – one to Egypt, with its base on the Egypt–Israel frontier, and the other to Jordan, with its base on the Jordan–Israel frontier. The points of the two triangles would meet under complete Egyptian or international control, while a road from Egypt to Jordan would pass over the road to Eilat, which would remain under Israeli control. In addition there were to be minor frontier adjustments and an international zone at Jerusalem, and Israel would pay compensation to Arab refugees, with Britain and USA contributing besides facilitating Israeli loans in New York and London.

The Israelis attached great importance to their possession of Eilat, because with its land link through the Negev and Beersheba it could be developed as a port for trade with South Africa and the Far East without ships passing through the Suez Canal. The over-riding problem, therefore, was to provide a land link between Jordan and Egypt without destroying the connection between Eilat and the rest of Israel. Curiously neither Eden in his memoirs nor his authorized biographer refers to Alpha, although Eden as Prime Minister expended a great deal of time and energy on it.

In his memoirs Macmillan is dismissive of Alpha, describing it as 'fantastic' and 'Dulles' pet idea'. This is misleading. The plan was as much British as American, and the archives reveal that Macmillan took it seriously during his term at the Foreign Office. Macmillan is also incorrect in stating that the plan was reported on adversely by 'both the American and British Ambassadors in Cairo'. They both enthusiastically tried to get it accepted by Nasser, and had high hopes of it.

On 14 April Shuckburgh had his first meeting with Macmillan 'about Alpha. He was very polite about the paper . . . and discussed the whole problem helpfully'. Macmillan read the Foreign Office brief in detail, despite the General Election claims on his time. On 22 May he minuted:

1) This is a truly long paper for exhausted Cabinet Ministers to read.

2) If the present Government is returned to power could we not make it easier by putting all or most of Para 8 in an appendix? Para 8 could just say '£100 million will be needed to compensate the Arabs [refugees]. The Jews will say it is too much, the Arabs too little. Our contribution – by way of loan – will not be more than £15 million.'

3) When ought this to be circulated? Perhaps on polling day? It might be a prologue or an epilogue – Alpha or Omega.[13]

On 2 February Dulles had sent a message via Makins that he was attaching the greatest importance to Eden's forthcoming interview with Nasser on 20 February. He and the State Department hoped that at this meeting Eden 'would be willing to sound Nasser in a preliminary way', and 'impress upon Nasser the need to take advantage, while there is still time, of the relatively favourable policy of the present U.S. administration towards the Arabs', and let him know that Dulles's argument was that Israeli confidence and pretensions 'have been reduced to a comparatively low ebb by the policy of the U.S. Government in refusing arms, security guarantees, etc. over the past two years, and that as Election year approaches it will be increasingly difficult for the administration to hold this position'.

There is no evidence of how much Eden repeated to Nasser. However, as almost his last act as Foreign Secretary, on 6 April Eden presented to Churchill's Cabinet a long paper giving details of the Alpha plan with its crossing points, and stating that the settlement should include minor adjustments on the Jordan and Syrian borders, plus internationalization of Jerusalem, loans to Israel to pay compensation to refugees, and an agreement on the use and distribution of the Jordan waters over which Eric Johnston, as Eisenhower's special representative, had worked out a plan 'which has very nearly gained acceptance on both sides'. Eden commented that secrecy was vital, and

I recognise the risks of any Anglo–American initiative in this matter and I am not over optimistic about our chances of success, but I think that the approach if properly timed and pressed with all the weight of our two Governments, offers the best chance of success and should be tried. The dangers of inaction are so great that some risks must be taken and some financial burdens accepted.[14]

At this stage there were high hopes of the Johnston Plan for the Jordan waters. The scheme, initiated by experts from the Tennessee Valley Authority, had become known by the name of Senator Eric Johnston, who had been sent by President Eisenhower to persuade Israel, Jordan, Syria and the Lebanon to agree on it. Israel had already begun work to divert water from the River Jordan by a canal and pumping works at Jisr Banat Yakub, with the intention of irrigating the distant Negev desert and turning it into a green and fertile land. Unfortunately Jisr Banat Yakub lay in the demilitarized zone between Israel and Syria. Syria objected to the engineering work and took the matter to the UN, so that Israel was forced to suspend work. There were problems over the apportionment of the waters and the proposed storage of surplus water in Lake Tiberias in Israeli territory, but by the end of 1954 all four countries had been persuaded by Johnston to acknowledge the benefits inherent in his plan. Britain and the USA felt that if agreement could be reached on the Johnston Plan the way might be paved for a general Arab–Israeli settlement which could be guaranteed by America and Britain.[15]

On the prospect of a treaty between Israel and the Arabs, Eden informed the Cabinet in a written memorandum:

> I need only say here that the key to the whole project is thought to lie with the Egyptian Government. None of Israel's other Arab neighbours would dare to participate in a settlement unless it knew that Egypt was sympathetic. Jordan, which is most directly concerned and which more than any other would benefit from an easement of the tension is too dependent upon Arab League supported to make any move alone. Iraq is not a neighbour and is particularly fanatical on the subject. Egypt, on the other hand, is strong, not fanatical about the Jews, and seriously inconvenienced by the tension on the Gaza frontier. When I spoke to Colonel Nasser in Cairo in February I found him not entirely negative. He thought it was a matter of timing and that any settlement must be comprehensive. Mr. Dulles and I have therefore agreed that the first soundings should be made in Cairo and that the plan could be unfolded to the Israelis only if Colonel Nasser shows a disposition to help.[16]

There the matter rested as Eden became Prime Minister. There was little discussion of Egyptian policy during the election, and Alpha was a closely guarded secret. But Eden still felt as Prime Minister that Alpha was his own personal plan.

After the General Election Macmillan produced a further paper on Alpha for the Eden Cabinet on 11 June, beginning: 'I now continue the story', and stating that Nasser, shortly before he left Cairo for the

Bandung Conference, had sent a message that 'in spite of many misgivings he was ready to do his best', and had emphasized that his main interest lay in the restoration of the land link between Egypt and the Arab states to the east. Macmillan claimed that 'Solomon could do no better' than Alpha, and 'there can be no solution except by the principle . . . of a point at the junction of two triangles where the sovereignty appertains to both or neither.' His memorandum emphasized that any settlement must provide for the payment of compensation by Israel of £100 million maximum to the Arab refugees; that Britain would find not more than £15 million by loan to Israel (probably on unattractive terms) and the United States about £50 million; and that the Israelis could raise about £30 million from their own resources or by contributions from the international Jewish community (permission might be given to raise £15 million by the sale of Israeli Government bonds on the London Stock Exchange).[17]

Alpha required taxpayers' money for the British contribution to the Israeli fund to compensate Arab refugees, and the Chancellor of the Exchequer had to be present when the Cabinet approved it. Shuckburgh wanted it taken as early as possible, optimistically hoping that progress would soon be made. Macmillan, who was about to go to America, minuted on 9 June:

> If it can be taken on Tuesday so much the better. But I want to give Cyprus the preference. Cyprus is *my* plan. *Alpha* is really an *inherited* plan and no-one will be a better advocate than the P.M. It can quite well be taken in my absence. Mr. Nutting can speak for me. P.M. will probably be on our side. Explain this to Sir Norman Brook. It's the sensible way out of the difficulty.[18]

In Macmillan's absence in America, Nutting brought the Macmillan memorandum on the Alpha Plan to the Cabinet on 15 June, when it was approved in principle, even though Butler demurred about loans to Israel because of the balance of payments problem. Finally Butler said he was 'reluctantly prepared to co-operate', but hoped Britain would take no initiative in offering Israel special facilities for raising money in London. Nutting replied: 'If the plan is shorn of its financial features it is unlikely to succeed'; it would cost the UK no more than 'their present expenditure on Arab refugees through the United Nations Relief and Works Agency' (UNRWA).[19]

Unfortunately for hopes of a speedy solution to the Arab–Palestine quarrel, on 28 February 1955 there was a nasty violation of the 1948

Armistice in the Gaza Strip, the narrow finger of Egyptian territory jutting into Israel from the south-west along the Mediterranean. Regular Israeli troops attacked Egyptian positions, killing thirty-eight and wounding eighty Egyptian soldiers; while Israel lost eight dead and fifteen wounded. Israel argued that the action was justified by unbearable Egyptian provocation, but on 29 March the Security Council of the UN unanimously condemned Israel for this armistice violation, and stated: 'No progress can be made unless the parties comply strictly with their obligations under the General Armistice Agreement and the Security Council's cease fire resolution of 15 July 1948.' Shootings and reprisals continued on both sides for weeks, just when Anglo–American efforts on behalf of an Alpha settlement were at their peak.[20]

At a Dulles–Macmillan meeting during the summer of 1955 Macmillan, armed with Cabinet support and the reluctant approval of the Treasury, told Dulles he wanted 'to persevere' with Alpha. Dulles stated that his political opponents – Mr Truman, Averill Harriman and Mayor Wagner – were all going to Israel to help them with the Jewish vote and might make very damaging statements. His original intention had been that the UK and US Governments should present a joint memorandum containing specific proposals to both sides, but he had now been persuaded instead to make a 'statement' which would be 'less specific'. Dulles and Macmillan agreed that the terms of the Dulles statement should be discussed between Russell and Shuckburgh.

Russell came to London early in July with a draft of the proposed Alpha speech to be made by Dulles; this included a public explanation of how the land connection between Egypt and Jordan would be achieved by means of the double triangle in the Negev. As Russell explained, Dulles felt that only by getting the US Government publicly committed to the Alpha policy could he insure himself against being compelled later on, in the atmosphere of the US elections, to take a much more pro-Israeli stand, and Dulles was not weakening at all on the Alpha demand for sacrifices from Israel.[21] On 12 July Eden told Macmillan that his impression was that 'the main difficulty was that Nasser would not appoint a sufficiently senior officer to negotiate effectively with the Israelis. Could not Mr. Nehru push them to this?'[22]

Nutting now had cold feet about Dulles's speech, mainly because of the Jordan waters negotiations. On 13 July he wrote to Macmillan that he was sorry to be 'always confronting him with awful dilemmas', but his advice was not to mention it in Cabinet until there had been further discussion with Dulles, and that if the statement came before Johnston had clinched his waters agreement it was pretty certain that there would be no waters agreement. If it came after, Nutting thought the agreement 'might hold'. Macmillan did not think it 'an awful dilemma' and on 13 July calmly minuted: 'The first thing is to get this problem discussed in Cabinet *on its merits*. After this we can discuss the new problem which is important but not fundamental. I shall therefore proceed in Cabinet as planned.'[23]

Macmillan presented a memorandum on the 14th: 'Our efforts to induce the Prime Minister of Egypt to enter into discussion of a possible settlement had not achieved results, and there seemed little prospect in view of deteriorating conditions in Gaza, of any progress. . . .' Therefore the time had come for Dulles to make a public statement of the outlines of the Alpha Plan, which would be supported by a similar British statement. Macmillan pointed out that the statement would be 'highly unpalatable' to the Israeli Government 'because it will destroy their hopes (now apparently running high) of securing a guarantee from the U.S. in advance of any settlement and without sacrifices on their part'. The main points of the Dulles statement, which had already been agreed by the Foreign Office, had been circulated to the Cabinet in advance.

Macmillan said that Dulles must make his statement around 18 August because of the forthcoming US elections. There was real danger that, under pressure of the election campaign, Dulles might be led to proposals which would be more favourable to Israel and consequently even more objectionable to the Arab states. Macmillan's judgment was: 'Fundamentally, the proposals represent a courageous and, I think, right attempt to break the deadlock between Israel and the Arab States.'[24]

On 28 July Macmillan told the Cabinet that Dulles had modified his statement so as to meet many of the British objections. The Cabinet agreed that Macmillan should issue a statement in support of Dulles, provided that the USA agreed in advance to join the Baghdad Pact and pay for British tanks for Iraq if there was a settlement. Eden emphasized that tanks for Iraq would soften both the Iraqis' and the general Arab attitude towards Alpha. Makins was told to make this clear to Dulles, and he reported that Dulles had confirmed to him 'by a nod' that the USA intended to adhere to the Baghdad Pact once a settlement was reached.

Dulles's speech was scheduled for 26 August, and all British Embassies in the Middle East were given copies of it and Macmillan's supporting statement to show in advance to their accredited

Governments, but they were told that the code name Alpha must remain top secret as Dulles's statement did not reveal the existence of the proposal. Dulles and Macmillan co-operated excellently, as is shown by the following letter from Dulles:

Dear Harold:
I am about to leave for New York, first to make the Davis Cup draw and then to launch 'Alpha'. I hope and believe this latter will turn out to be a constructive move, although obviously we are taking some risks. However, risks are inherent in the situation.
One thing is, however, already a good result – that is the close cooperation between our two Governments in preparing this project. I want to thank you very much. Yesterday Francis Russell showed me the copies of your instructions to your Near East posts with reference to follow-up. I was greatly impressed by the high quality of these instructions – both as regards substance and lucid expression.
I do not know of any joint project that has been better prepared and if it does not succeed that will not be due, I think, to any lack of care on either of our parts.
Faithfully yours,
John Foster Dulles

Against Paragraph 1 (on his copy) Eden wrote: 'F.S. We are taking the risks.'[25]

Unfortunately Eden did not see it as a 'well prepared joint project', and tried to throw spanners into the works. A week before the scheduled date for the speech, Andrew Stark, Macmillan's private secretary, minuted Kirkpatrick:

The Private Secretary at Chequers has just given me by scrambler telephone an indication of the Prime Minister's thoughts about the new development in Alpha.
2. The Prime Minister thinks that the Americans are behaving disgracefully. This is their third change of plan over this operation. He naturally cannot assess what is involved until he sees Mr. Dulles' proposed text and he certainly cannot undertake to give H.M.G.'s support to a statement which we have not yet seen. Sir A. Eden feels that we should hold the Americans responsible for any flare-up which may occur in the area.
3. The Prime Minister considers that it is desirable in conveying our thoughts to the Americans to maintain the link between Alpha and the tanks for Iraq. (This thought as conveyed to me by Mr. de Zulueta was somewhat elliptical but I think that what the Prime Minister would like us to convey to the Americans is that if they go at

their Alpha statement like a bull at a gate, Nuri will not have had the *quid pro quo* to which we attach importance.) If necessary the Prime Minister is prepared for us to have a row with the Americans about all this.

4. I gave Mr. de Zulueta the text of the telegram which you had already sent off this morning – the Prime Minister had, of course, already been given the gist of this – and I pointed out that we had been pressing hard for the text of Mr. Dulles' proposed statement. I added that we had reason to believe that the text might be on its way to us now and that I felt sure the sensible thing to do was to see it before firing off more ammunition at the Americans.

Kirkpatrick wrote on Stark's minute 'Secretary of State to see'. He did not want to be involved.

On 25 August, the day before the speech was due to be made, Eden interfered again. J. N. Graham sent the following to Macmillan:

> I have been told by No. 10 that the Prime Minister is now feeling more than ever doubtful of the value, on balance, of Mr. Dulles's statement on Palestine. He feels that, as originally drafted, the statement contained positive advantages to off-set the obvious disadvantages which would follow its publication. In its present watered-down condition, however, little will be gained and much may be lost by making it. If you feel that nonetheless the balance of advantage lies in going ahead, he would be content, but if not, he would be willing to send a message to the President asking for the operation to be called off. The Prime Minister, I understand, considers that there is a chance that President Eisenhower will be willing to do this as he gained the impression in Geneva that the President was not particularly keen on the operation any way.
>
> I have consulted the Department & Mr. Shuckburgh and there are two considerations. In the first place, there is one positive gain in the statement – the undertaking by the United States, given the solution of the Palestine problem, to guarantee the boundaries of Israel and the Arab States. Secondly, from the practical point of view it would be extremely difficult, if not impossible, to draw back at this stage. We have told a large number of other countries what is intended in general terms and of our support and it would not be easy to explain a decision not to go ahead. Moreover in at least one instance – Iraq – the reaction has been most encouraging.
>
> If you agree that we should go ahead, I will inform No. 10 and despatch the attached telegram.

Macmillan, accustomed to his chief's sudden changes of mood, wrote on the minute: 'Please inform No. 10 accordingly. It's no good trying it call it off now.' 'Accordingly' a telegram was sent to Washington, saying that Her Majesty's Government approved the final text of the Dulles speech. This incident denotes a bizarre relationship between the Foreign Secretary and the Prime Minister. In his memoirs Macmillan quotes from his diary: 'Dulles' proposed speech has caused No. 10 to flap.'[26]

The author showed these surprising minutes to Makins (Lord Sherfield) and Stark. Sherfield commented: 'A good example of the petulance to the point of unreason to which he [Eden] was always prone and which was intensified after his illness and when he was Prime Minister.' Stark (now Sir Andrew) was kinder and wrote:

He may well have doubted Dulles' ability to appreciate all the nuances of relations between Middle Eastern countries like Egypt and Iraq or that Nuri would have a built in mistrust of a Nasser infiltration in Jordan; the provision of tanks, whether American or British, for the armoured division Iraq wanted would have been the quid pro quo that might have made Alpha easier for Nuri to live with.[27]

In his speech Dulles emphasized the pressing need of Israel for frontier guarantees, and held out the bait of the USA entering into formal treaty engagements guaranteeing Israel's frontiers: 'If there is to be a guarantee of borders now there should be prior agreement upon what the borders are. . . . The existing lines . . . were fixed by the Armistice Agreements of 1949. They were not designed to be permanent frontiers in every respect.' He advocated the fixing of permanent boundaries, and in a clear allusion to the Negev said: 'The difficulty is increased by the fact that even territory which is barren has acquired a sentimental significance.' He made it plain he was advocating substantial territorial concessions by Israel to Egypt and Jordan, and given his and Eisenhower's sensitivity to the Jewish vote it was both courageous and an encouraging example of Anglo–American accord.

In the supporting statement Macmillan said: 'The US statement was a welcome development which offers the prospect of real security to the peoples and States concerned' and Britain 'would be ready . . . to guarantee by treaty or treaties . . . any territorial settlements so agreed'.[28] Shuckburgh noted in his diary on 31 August:

Macmillan is suffering from prime ministerial interference by A.E.! He said, 'He has got the habit of writing minutes on telegrams. It is a nuisance, especially as he is not in London – or even in Chequers, but at Broadchalke where he has no room for a Private Secretary. But I am biding my time. I ignore most of them.' This afternoon we had a scene exactly identical (though more restrained and discreet) to hundreds I have witnessed with A.E. in the different role. My draft telegram to Dulles about next steps in 'Alpha' had to go to A.E. in the country and he suggested all sorts of changes. We met most of these but when M was told that A.E. wanted the text cleared again with him he threw the papers on the desk and murmured 'I might as well give up and let him run the shop.'

This reveals that on the previous day Eden had sent instructions that the draft telegrams to Dulles about Alpha must not be sent until he had approved the final alterations. Shuckburgh sent back the finalized drafts to 10 Downing Street with a note to Eden's private secretaries that 'they must be approved by telephone by 5 p.m.' as Dulles was going on holiday to Duck Island and the telegrams must be sent off by that hour. They were approved.

Macmillan wrote to the Prime Minister politely: 'I have amended the telegrams about Alpha to take account of your suggestions, for which I am grateful. . . . Dulles is going to Duck Island for a fortnight's rest so I hope to benefit from this pause in the flow from Washington to London.' In red ink Eden scrawled further messages to Macmillan on this note, which the Foreign Secretary ignored. It was bizarre that the Prime Minister was unwilling to trust his Foreign Secretary to conduct the important Alpha operation; not unnaturally Macmillan resented Eden's incursions into his field.[29]

Initial reactions to Dulles's speech from both Israel and Egypt were encouraging. Byroade, the US Ambassador in Cairo, saw Nasser after he had presented him with a copy of the speech before it was delivered, and told Trevelyan that 'he thought the interview had gone well'. Trevelyan also saw Nasser, who told him that there had been a better chance of a Palestine settlement seven months ago, but emphasized that he was a man of peace, although Egypt felt her flank was insecure and thus spent on armed forces money which should go into development. Fawzi, the Egyptian Foreign Minister, told Trevelyan that the main difficulty would be over the Negev and they would not agree to corridors, but he 'insisted on re-establishment of territorial continuity, by which he meant the Negev (and I understand Beersheba as well)'. However Fawzi encouragingly said that the British and Americans should jointly put their more specific ideas to Nasser. Shuckburgh commented: 'This is no worse than we expected. The Egyptian price is the Negev. That we knew. On the rest they will not make difficulties. That we suspected, but the confirmation is encouraging.' He was derisory about Byroade's discussion with Nasser, minuting: 'Byroade had no business to discuss crossing points with Nasser if that means the triangle solution. But I am not surprised to hear he has done so. However, probably not lucidly enough to convey to Nasser what we were in fact proposing.'[30]

In Washington Abba Eban, the Israeli Ambassador, told the State Department on 6 September that the Israelis regarded the statement 'as a serious act of public statesmanship' and thought the proposed United States guarantee 'would contribute greatly to the peace of the area'. But he urged the USA to separate the 'guarantee' from frontier adjustments, and declared that Israel would not give up all or even part of the Negev. On 12 September the State Department reported that the attitude of American Jews to Dulles's speech was favourable.[31] On 5 September Macmillan told the Cabinet that the Dulles speech and his supporting statement had 'a reasonably satisfactory reception', and Eden said 'he was anxious that everything possible should be done to ensure speed delivery of tanks to Iraq.'[32]

On 14 September Trevelyan estimated the Egyptian position was that they wanted secret conversations and were not prepared to take a lead with other Arab states until 'they think they will be able to get a settlement which they can politically justify'; there would be no insurmountable difficulty over refugees and Jerusalem, and their present position on the territorial settlement was probably not the last. He felt there were no grounds for supposing that the Egyptians would accept a solution which would leave Eilat in Israeli hands or anything in the way of corridors or cross-over points.

Russell came to London on 19 September, and he and Shuckburgh produced an agenda for talks with Israel and Egypt which they agreed that Byroade should try and get Nasser to accept, and then British and American representatives would make a tour of the Middle East capitals 'for some other ostensible purpose and start the reconciliation progress'.[33] Russell emphasized that what Nasser most wanted was 'arms supplies', and as he could not pay, America might offer him long-term credit if he committed himself formally to negotiations with the Israelis.

British and American confidence that they could solve the Egyptian–Israeli dispute in 1955 has never been revealed. In a letter to the author Shuckburgh wrote:

> Alpha was always kept very secret because the very idea of proposing a settlement was highly controversial and risky. Both Governments

were afraid that if any such ideas leaked out before there was a
modicum of acceptance from Nasser and the Israelis there would be a
fearful outcry. In particular Eden and Dulles were frightened of their
Zionist lobbies. The Israelis threw icy water on any suggestion that
they might make the smallest concession for the sake of an agreement
(and a guarantee of their frontiers). The only hope seemed to be if
confronted with a fully worked out proposal and with evidence that
Egypt and other Arab States were prepared to recognise Israel with
the firm offer of Great Powers Guarantee Israel might take a more
favourable line. We were working to prepare such a situation.[34]

Nasser and Fawzi scrupulously obeyed the British and American
request that the Alpha proposals should be kept completely secret.
Heikal, the Cairo journalist, claims he was Nasser's closest friend and
confidant in 1955, but it is clear from his published books that even
he had no idea that Alpha discussions were going on in secret with the
British and American Ambassadors.

Optimism was shattered when, early in the morning of 21 September, a telegram from Trevelyan was deciphered which showed that
Nasser had become truculent and had told Trevelyan 'the present
was no time for a Palestine settlement'. What had happened was that
Nasser had secretly concluded an arms deal with the Soviet bloc,
which enormously increased Egypt's military potential; with the
resulting euphoria his attitude had toughened.

When they talked that same day Russell told Shuckburgh that if

Nasser remained so obdurate Byroade should be instructed to point
out that his [Nasser's] attitude amounted to in effect the first negative
response we have had from any Government to Mr. Dulles' statement, and the US Government who had not expected this of Egypt
were seriously disturbed and might be forced to reconsider their
whole policy in the Middle East.[35]

On the 22nd the news of Nasser's arms deal burst around the
world. The Alpha talks were 'abandoned'. However, Nasser had
done the deal and there was nothing that Dulles and Macmillan could
do about it. On 3 October Shuckburgh recorded that he and Russell
went over all the ground again with Dulles and Macmillan, and
decided 'we must "live with" the Czech contract tho' we will try to get
Nasser to limit it and offset it with political concession, e.g. support
of the Johnston Plan' (for the Jordan waters).

The Israelis had warned Johnston that if agreement over the
waters was not reached soon with Syria, Lebanon and Jordan, they

would resume their engineering operations at Jisr Banat Yakub regardless of the hostility of their Arab neighbours. All hope of success for the Johnston Plan lay with Nasser. If he gave it wholehearted support the Arab states might accept it. Although Nasser tottered on the brink, he never fully endorsed the plan, which perished despite determined British and American efforts.[36]

At the Cabinet on 4 November Macmillan said: 'the right policy now was to accept the existence of the [Soviet] arms contract . . . it was perhaps unfortunate that our own deliveries of arms to Egypt had been disappointing and behind promises', and Eden said 'he saw no advantage in attempting to put pressure upon the Nasser régime e.g. by withholding the release of sterling balances or obstructing Egyptian policies in regard to the High Dam.' Six days later there was another alarm. It was announced in Cairo that the Russians were offering development finance for the Egyptian Aswan Dam and other projects in Arab countries.[37]

In early October a Foreign Office report on Middle East oil pointed out to the Cabinet that UK fuel needs would treble within the next twenty years, and the Middle East was the only source; there was a serious danger that the Middle East 'will slip away from us . . . the Egyptians, the Saudi Arabians, and now the Russians are making great efforts to undermine our position and spending large sums of money'. The paper stated prophetically that the Middle East oil-producing countries

> question the right of Western Governments to derive large revenues from taxing the refined products. Pressure can therefore be expected from time to time to increase their share of profits, i.e. the price at which they allow us to have their oil, and since they have a virtual monopoly they are well placed to extract more from us . . . it is important to maintain the principle of equal profit sharing . . . if it were breached there is no knowing where the rapacity of the Middle East States would end and there would be an increased cost to our balance of payments including an increase in the net cost of our oil imports.[38]

This forecast of the deadly danger to Britain's balance of payments and cost of living was proved 100 per cent correct in the early 1970s. However, in 1955 the economic danger was a minor worry compared with the threat to the defence of the Mediterranean against Russia.

Such thoughts on the precariousness of British oil supplies, coming on top of the announcement of Soviet finance for the Aswan Dam, provoked Eden to send a telephone message on 12 October from his weekend cottage at Broadchalke to the Foreign Office: 'Do you think we could get an estimate from our Ambassador in Cairo as to Nasser's present position, the extent of his support, and the chances of any rival, e.g. Ali Maher?' A telegram was sent that evening to Trevelyan, who replied:

> There are at present no reliable signs of the régime losing its grip of the situation or of its opponents gaining ground. The acceptance of Soviet bloc arms has added to Nasser's prestige and has perhaps given him to some extent at least temporarily what he has always lacked, a measure of personal popularity. . . . There are no signs that Nasser's personal predominance in the CRC [Nasser's political party] is seriously challenged and the popular applause for the arms deal will have further strengthened his position in it. . . . Little has been heard for some time of any of Nasser's potential rivals. General Neguib is generally considered to be a broken reed and his name is now rarely mentioned even when the question of an alternative to Nasser crops up. . . . We do not hear the Independents such as Ali Maher mentioned in a political context. If the régime broke down as a result of the assassination of Nasser, disunity in the armed forces, or defeat by an outside Power it is probably only the WAFD [the former ruling Conservative Party] which has the organisation and popular appeal necessary to take over. Whether the army can throw up another military leader cannot even be guessed, but if it did his policy might well be similar to that of the present régime.[39]

Here was irrefutable evidence of the unassailability of Nasser's position. It would have been better if Eden had recalled Trevelyan's advice in 1956 when the Canal was nationalized.

Eden now fell back on another line of attack, and decided to confront Nasser with a request to declare his intentions. After corrections in Eden's own handwriting, Kirkpatrick produced a draft message for Trevelyan saying that the Prime Minister was disturbed at the gradual deterioration of Anglo–Egyptian relations and that the time had come to confront Nasser with a request to declare his intentions. Trevelyan was to seek an interview and make it clear that he was conveying a personal message from Eden.

> You should say that when we met in Cairo after the conclusion of the Anglo–Egyptian Treaty, Nasser assured me that Egypt wanted a new relationship with us. We, for our part, were very ready to make a fresh start. But since then, the course of Anglo–Egyptian relations, and indeed of Egypt's relations with the West in general, has been a deep disappointment. The continuing vituperation against us in the

Egyptian press and on the Egyptian radio has naturally led us to doubt the value of Nasser's assurance, and the attitude of the Egyptian Government over the Sudan has strengthened this impression. Now we are faced with the apparent determination of Egypt to go through with the Egyptian–Czech arms deal and to permit the Russians to carry the cold war to the Middle East.

We do not question the right of Egypt to pursue a policy of neutrality. But it cannot be in Egypt's interest to cut herself off from her potential friends in the West and to lean towards the Russian bloc. It is idle to expect that Russian influence will not, in the long run, be dangerous to Egypt and to Nasser's régime. He cannot be unaware of the potential dangers of communism in the Middle East.

We for our part are still willing to do what we can to help Egypt. . . . But Nasser is making it almost impossible for us to be friends with Egypt. In particular, public opinion here will not tolerate the supply of arms to a country which daily denounces us and which seeks supplies from the East.

We are determined to defend our position in the Middle East in face of the Russian threat. In this situation, we are entitled to ask Egypt where she stands. If Nasser wishes to continue to denounce Britain and to oppose British policy in every way, let him say so. If not, let him make a demonstrable effort to carry out the promises which he made to me and he will find me more than willing to meet him half way.

To Kirkpatrick, Shuckburgh described this proposed personal message as 'worse than useless' and 'sharp and inquisitorial', and on 27 October Kirkpatrick minuted to the Prime Minister:

This communication would be made in the hope of bringing about an improvement in Egypt's conduct. So we must proceed on the assumption that it might be successful. In that event, what would or could we do for Egypt?

If we reach the conclusion that, with an eye on Israel and our financial situation, there is nothing much we could offer by way of inducement or recompense, then it would probably be better not to make the attempt. And all we should have to consider is whether we should be wise to undertake a propaganda exercise for the record.

The next day Guy Millard, Eden's private secretary, spoke to Shuckburgh and then minuted to the Prime Minister: 'Would this not increase Nasser's self importance and make him think he can frighten us? Would he listen? Should we not be making ourselves look rather silly? How would we look if it became public?' On

Millard's note Eden scrawled in his own handwriting: 'Could you try your hand at a shorter effort.'[40]

When he was Foreign Secretary in Baldwin's Cabinet Eden had sent a similar questionnaire to Hitler about his intentions after the remilitarization of the Rhineland in 1936. This received great publicity, and Hitler humiliated Eden by refusing to acknowledge it or reply. Perhaps Millard's note 'How would we look if it became public?' triggered off Eden's memory about the failure of the same technique with Hitler. Anyway, on 1 November Eden changed his mind about the message to Nasser, cancelled it, and instead decided to try for a diplomatic solution favouring Egypt against Israel.

At the Cabinet on 20 October Macmillan said that 'initial reaction to the Soviet arms deal might be expected to give place eventually to a more balanced view . . . we should adopt a policy of moderation in our dealings with Egypt and we should endeavour to persuade the Americans to do the same'; Eden took an even more conciliatory line, saying that

> the main objective of our policy should be to protect our vital oil interests in the Middle East. From this point of view strengthening the Northern Tier defence arrangements was more important than the attitude of Egypt. . . . It must be admitted that Egypt had not received any large supplies of arms from the UK. . . . In view of Nasser's dependence on the support of the army in Egypt his decision to accept the Soviet offer was understandable if regrettable. The allocation of the Egyptian High Aswan Dam project to the European consortium, if it could be secured, would be of immense importance in restoring the prestige of the West, and particularly of the older European powers in the Arab world generally. In our dealings with Egypt it could be a trump card.[41]

This revealing Cabinet discussion contradicts impressions given in Eden's and Macmillan's published memoirs.

After an interview with Nasser on 2 November Byroade told Trevelyan: 'A few months should be given to try for a Palestine settlement before further efforts were made to increase membership of the Turco/Iraq Pact [Baghdad Pact] on the grounds that if it is enlarged Nasser will be annoyed again and far less likely to co-operate on Palestine.' Eden wrote on Trevelyan's telegram: 'I don't agree at all, the stronger the Northern Tier the better Nasser will behave.' This shows his nostalgia for Britain's role as the predominating force in the Middle East.[42]

On 4 November the uneasy peace was threatened by fighting at El

Auja between Israelis and Egyptians, with casualties on both sides, but according to Shuckburgh on that day Eden decided to take a hand to show he was a 'great man' and wanted 'to go to Cyprus in a broad and generous gesture of Peace and summon the Egyptians and Israelis to his side'. When it was pointed out to him that Cyprus was not in a proper condition for such a meeting he fell back on the idea of 'a stirring declaration' in his Mansion House speech on 9 November. Shuckburgh told Eden that if it was to have any effect in the Arab world it would have to be 'something which the Israelis will detest'. That did not deter Eden, and Shuckburgh was told to draft part of his speech mentioning the UN 1947 partition frontiers as a factor in any settlement.[43] This showed that, despite the Russian arms deal with Nasser, Eden was determined on a settlement in favour of the Arabs and considerable sacrifices by Israel.

Eden agreed the text of his speech with Dulles beforehand. It included this passage:

> We have only one desire in this, if our Arab and Israeli friends would but believe us, and it is to help to find a means of living which will enable the peoples concerned to dwell side by side in peace. Let us give one instance. *If there could be an accepted arrangement between them, about their boundaries, we, Her Majesty's Government and, I believe, the United States Government, and perhaps other Powers too, would be prepared to give a formal guarantee to both sides, and that might bring real confidence and security at last; and our countries would also offer substantial help, financial and other, over this tragic problem of the refugees* [author's italics]. . . .
>
> The position today is that the Arabs on the one side take their stand on the 1947 and other United Nations resolutions – that is where they are. They said they would be willing to open discussions with Israel from that basis. The Israelis on the other side; they found themselves on the later armistice agreement of 1949 and on the present territories which they occupy.
>
> Now, my Lord Mayor, between those two positions there is, of course, a wide gap, but is it so wide that no negotiation is possible to bridge it? It is not right, I agree, that United Nations resolutions should be ignored, but equally can it be maintained the United Nations resolutions on Palestine can now be put into operation just as they stand?[44]

The day after the Mansion House speech Trevelyan talked to Fawzi, who told him that 'the Egyptian Government welcomed the statement and would associate themselves with the task of seeking a settlement'. He promised that Egypt would do its best to see that reaction in the press and radio was not too critical, but 'it would be a tactical mistake for the Egyptian Press and radio publicly to support the speech. Everybody would suspect that there was some conspiracy with the British.' Fawzi thought a multi-lateral negotiation with the Israelis which brought in other Arab states would 'kill' all possibilities of a settlement, but they would be prepared to discuss the details of a settlement with the British and Americans if the conversations were 'extremely confidential', and would be prepared at the right time 'to stick their necks out more than was prudent for them' as they had over the Jordan waters. Macmillan told Eden: 'This is encouraging. I only met Fawzi once and I thought him smooth and false. Perhaps he is a Liberal.' To Dulles he said: 'This shows how worthwhile your Alpha exercise had been.' Four days later the USA confirmed that their Ambassador in Tel Aviv had been instructed to tell Ben Gurion in general terms that 'the US endorses Sir Anthony's speech in its support of Mr Dulles' speech in August'.[45]

On 16 November Shuckburgh wrote in his diary that he saw 'glimmerings of hope. Nasser and Nuri have taken A.E.'s statement very well and both talk of a settlement. Jack Nicholls [UK Ambassador to Israel] thinks even the Israelis would like to be forced into a compromise despite Ben Gurion's flat and absolute rejection.' On the same day in Cairo Trevelyan, Byroade and Fawzi met at a dinner party. The Egyptian Foreign Minister told the Ambassadors that informally Egypt would accept a settlement if it included 'full territorial continuity between Egypt and Jordan without corridors which would mean the Negev for the Arabs, but gave the impression that if Eilat became Arab, some facilities for Israeli trade there might be negotiated perhaps in return for corresponding facilities at Haifa'. Over Jerusalem he said the Egyptians would agree to almost any solution acceptable to the parties including internationalization or partition, with guaranteed rights of access to the Holy Places, and he saw no difficulties over compensation and repatriation of displaced Arabs. If the outstanding points could be settled, according to Fawzi it would automatically be followed by an immediate removal of the restrictions on Israeli shipping using the Canal and on third parties trading with Israel, and Egypt wanted the Jordan waters scheme agreed independently of the Palestine question. Shuckburgh interpreted this as: 'Nasser and Fawzi are nibbling strongly at Alpha.'

Byroade considered Fawzi had produced 'the most favourable Arab starting point we could possibly have hoped for'. On reading the reports of the dinner party, Macmillan agreed 'to try and persuade Mr. Dulles that it is enough of an opening' and wrote to him on 19 November:

> I have studied the account of the Cairo dinner party. You may wonder, as I do, whether the opening is wide enough for us to explore the ground with the Israelis. There are, of course, risks in going ahead without some firmer base, but on the whole I think we should take the chance as both our Ambassadors seem to advise. There doesn't seem much hope of getting anything further from Nasser at this point. I would be grateful for your views.[46]

The reference to the Ambassadors' advice is in complete contradiction to Macmillan's statement about Alpha in his memoirs.

From Tel Aviv Nicholls reported that the Israelis would not negotiate unless they could be satisfied that 'it is *not* the intention of H.M.G. and the US Govt to press Israel to surrender the Negev'; while Ben Gurion and Sharett, the Foreign Minister, made public statements that they would never make territorial concessions, suggesting that Dulles was not backing Eden in this new initiative and alleging that Eden intended to extract the whole of the Negev from them. Ben Gurion went off on the wild tack that Eden's plan was to use the Negev as a British Army and Air Force base, basing his assumption on a conversation with Ernest Bevin in 1947 which the Foreign Office could not trace. Dulles again said he could not support Eden publicly because of the Jewish vote, but would do so privately in all discussions with the Egyptians and Israelis.[47] In Washington Dulles saw Sharett on 21 November and handed him a memorandum which included the words 'the territorial adjustments referred to in Secretary Dulles' August 26 speech may have to include concessions in the Negev to provide an Arab area joining Egypt with the rest of the Arab world'. Sharett was then given details of the Alpha plan. The Americans told London that the next step should be to follow up the Dulles–Sharett talk by informing the Israelis of the Egyptian attitude to negotiations and urging them to accept an agenda for discussions.[48]

Eden got impatient at the delay after his speech and asked Macmillan for action. Kirkpatrick minuted Shuckburgh on 2 December: 'Alpha seems to have got stuck. The Secretary of State would like us to make another push.' Shuckburgh replied: 'I think we must really await Mr. Sharett's response to Mr. Dulles' memorandum. It is expected on 6 December.' Macmillan, now in his last few weeks as Foreign Secretary, agreed, writing on the 3rd: 'All right. Wait until 7 December and then consult me again.' In

Washington Dulles told Makins that, although the Israeli Foreign Minister had sounded very intransigent, he thought 'he perceived some chinks in the armour'. Sharett left with Dulles an aide-mémoire, which turned out to be less rigid than his spoken words. However, the important thing was that Sharett told Dulles that 'Israel was prepared to negotiate either direct or through a mediator.' Foreign Office minutes were that the Israelis had not excluded territorial concessions by negotiation, and that 'this is perhaps the first time that Israel has accepted the idea of negotiation through a mediator'.[49]

Eden decided to send a message to Nehru through Malcolm Macdonald, the High Commissioner in India, asking him to 'express sympathy' with the Guildhall speech. The Prime Minister thought this was of considerable importance and made several amendments to the Foreign Office draft letter, but Macmillan would not be drawn into it, minuting on the 5th: 'Send it to the PM to approve or amend.'

The Iraqi Foreign Minister, Taufiq Swaidi, went to Cairo with friendly messages to Nasser. The visit was a success and, according to Swaidi, Nasser told him: 'If some solution could now be found to the Palestine question he would be willing to co-operate and perhaps associate himself in some form with the Baghdad Pact.' Wright, HM Ambassador in Baghdad, noted that Swaidi was far from being always reliable 'but on this occasion struck me as telling the truth'. Iraqi–Egyptian relations had been bad ever since Nasser had come to power, and Arthur in the Foreign Office minuted 'too good to be true'. Probably it was.[50]

On 29 November Elath, the Israeli Ambassador in London, wrote a letter to *The Times* accusing Eden of anti-Israel bias, saying: 'co-operation can exist only on a basis of complete impartiality and equal treatment for and from all parties concerned'. He pointed out the unfairness of Britain's refusing both to supply arms to Israel, and to take effective action to prevent the Arab economic boycott and the Egyptian denial of free passage through the Suez Canal and the Straits of Tiran which led to the Gulf of Akaba. Eden was furious, and told Millard to write to the Foreign Office:

> The Prime Minister notes that there are precedents for contentious letters to the press by foreign representatives. But is it not a most improper proceeding for an Ambassador to make what amounts to a public attack on a speech by the Prime Minister of the country to which he is accredited? Surely the Israelis would be incensed if Nicholls made an attack on a speech by Ben-Gurion.

The Prime Minister thinks that, subject to the Foreign Secretary's views, it might perhaps be a good thing if Sir Ivone Kirkpatrick were to send for Mr. Elath and point this out in appropriate terms.

Macmillan squiggled on the bottom of the 10 Downing Street letter: 'Sir IK. I should be against this. What do you say?' Kirkpatrick minuted:

I think this is a marginal case. If an Ambassador wrote a letter to the newspapers really attacking the Prime Minister for a speech by the Prime Minister, I think we should protest.

But I do not think that this speech can be fairly described as 'a public attack on a speech by the Prime Minister,' as Mr. Millard alleges. I have read the letter carefully, and it seems more accurate to describe it as a letter explaining that the Israeli Government's first unfavourable reaction to the speech is maintained and has not been modified. If any of us were to see the Israeli Ambassador in the next day or two, I think it would be appropriate to tell him in a friendly way that he had been sailing rather close to the wind. But I should not advocate summoning him to the Foreign Office in order to administer a rebuke.

Macmillan squiggled on the Kirkpatrick minute: 'I agree. I should do nothing unless P.M. returns to this topic.' That was the end of it, but this incident was typical of Eden in Downing Street.[51]

On 29 November Lord Reading, Minister of State Foreign Office, sent a long memorandum to Macmillan about the Mansion House speech. He clearly looked on himself as a mouthpiece for British Jewry, and wrote that the Zionist element in the Jewish community had always felt they could count on Winston Churchill because of his long-standing and often-proclaimed Zionist sympathies. His resignation filled them with a certain amount of apprehension, and their first emotional reaction to the Guildhall speech had been one of shock because they felt the Prime Minister had thrown his weight into the Arab scale, and they regarded it at first as a death warrant for Israel although their worst fears had since been assuaged. He went on that the Israelis and their supporters found the Prime Minister's reference to the 1947 UN resolution deeply disturbing. Macmillan merely acknowledged it, and it is doubtful if it went to Eden.[52]

On 15 December Russell and Shuckburgh met in Paris and were as optimistic as in September before the Egyptian–Soviet arms deal. They agreed that the US Government should be mainly responsible for dealing with Israel, 'whereas when the time came for an approach to the Egyptians it might be that Sir H. Trevelyan should take the lead'. Russell emphasized that Dulles had made it plain to Sharett that a concession in the Negev was regarded as 'the touchstone of Israel's sincerity in seeking a settlement'. The two diplomats thought that Israel should be given the Gaza Strip if she relinquished a big section of the Negev.

Streibert, an American diplomat, went to the Middle East and saw both Nasser and Ben Gurion shortly before Christmas. Nasser told him he was definitely interested in a settlement with Israel, provided it covered both compensation for refugees and frontier rectifications. In Tel Aviv Ben Gurion said he was ready to talk to Nasser and would accept rectification of frontiers on a 'basis of give and take', and would stop violence pending the outcome. He also said he would not object to a mediator. After the Streibert–Ben Gurion conversations Nicholls reported to the Foreign Office that Ben Gurion was thinking in terms of ceding territory in the Negev and taking the Gaza Strip instead.[53] As 1955 came to an end prospects of a settlement were reasonable, and it would have been difficult to believe that within eight months Eden would have a volte-face and become passionately pro-Israel and anti-Nasser.

8

The Aswan Dam and Jordan
January–July 1956

IN JANUARY 1956 Dulles and Eisenhower sent Robert Anderson, a close personal friend of the President and a former Secretary of the Navy, secretly to the Middle East to meet both Ben Gurion and Nasser with the idea of fixing a meeting between the two heads of state. Anderson found Ben Gurion co-operative, but Nasser cold and distant; he gave the gloomiest possible report of his efforts. Whereas after Dulles's August speech and Eden's Mansion House speech Nasser had appeared to desire a compromise peace, now the roles were reversed, and clearly Nasser's involvement with the Soviet Union was making him conscious of the strength which Russian support was giving him vis-à-vis the Western powers.

Eden, who had said in March 1955: 'Nasser is the man for us', now began to be hostile to him. By the end of January Eden was comparing Nasser with Mussolini and said that 'his object was to be a Caesar from the Gulf to the Atlantic and to kick us out of it all.' Eden even hinted that he might try to revise the agreement for the evacuation of the Suez base, but early in 1956 Eden and Dulles were still hoping for a permanent Arab–Israeli settlement linked to Anglo–US financing of the Aswan Dam, which Eden still believed would produce a change of heart in Nasser.[1]

The Aswan High Dam was to be built south of the existing Aswan Dam, and would be able to store the entire surplus water of the Nile from one year to another. This would not only irrigate a huge area, but also provide power for industrial development and rural electrification for Egypt. For the Sudan it would provide additional water in the low season, but in 1955 the amount of Nile water that the Sudan could take was still limited by the Nile Waters Agreement of 1929. In 1952 the Egyptians decided on the Aswan High Dam, and German firms carried out exploration work and made preparatory drawings. After the Anglo–Egyptian Agreement of 1954, British and

French firms joined with the Germans and the resulting consortium began negotiations with the Egyptians at the beginning of 1955. However Egypt needed a giant international loan to finance the scheme.

In November 1955 the Egyptian Government made it plain that they would seriously consider offers from Russia and Poland unless the West made satisfactory comprehensive proposals for financing the project. The British and Americans suggested to the Egyptians that Britain should advance $80 million; the USA $130 million; and the World Bank $200 million. This was dependent on agreement between Egypt and the Sudan over the division of the Nile waters, over which no great difficulty was anticipated. By January 1956 Britain and the USA had drawn up their proposals in aides-mémoire to the Egyptian Government, and the World Bank had drafted a letter of intent setting out the conditions on which they would make the loan to Egypt. Unfortunately Nasser jibbed at the terms of the letter of intent, and told both Trevelyan and Byroade that the conditions of the bank loan amounted in effect to control of the Egyptian economy; in view of the country's recent history Egyptian public opinion was very suspicious of 'strings', so that it would be politically impossible for him to accept the conditions without amendment.

Nasser also raised other objections, the chief of which was that he must feel quite sure that all the money needed to 'see the project through' would be forthcoming before he embarked on it. The Bank drew up a 'draft Memorandum of Understanding' designed to meet Nasser's objections. Byroade thought Nasser would be content with this, but the Foreign Office and Trevelyan were less confident.[2]

The Bank insisted that Nasser should sign an agreement containing the clause 'subject to review if exceptional circumstances should intervene'. Macmillan told the Egyptian Ambassador in London that this was no more than 'ordinary caution', but this phrase was to become a stumbling block. On 31 December in Cairo Abdel Kaissouni, Egyptian Minister of Finance, told Trevelyan that the chances of acceptance of the World Bank's terms were more than 50 per cent, but that the West must accept some of the points that Nasser was putting forward, such as Nasser's reluctance to agree to a number of small contracts with the Bank for individual advances, saying 'Only when they got the contract for the whole advance would they feel safe.' When Trevelyan saw Nasser the next day, the Egyptian Prime Minister told him that public opinion was very suspicious, and they must be careful not to ignore this; it was politically impossible for him to accept the letter of intent as it stood. He wanted 'extraordinary circumstances' replaced by 'Force Majeure', and went on that some Americans had said in Cairo that the Egyptian Government was only pretending to negotiate, being already committed to the Russians, 'which was completely untrue and had upset him'. Trevelyan unequivocally advised the Foreign Office to press the World Bank for 'one loan at once for the lot'.[3]

Eugene Black, President of the World Bank, was not malleable, and at a tripartite meeting in Washington with the Americans, British and Egyptians made it clear that in no circumstances would the World Bank agree to amend the terms. Byroade had told the State Department that Nasser 'meant to do business with the West but would not agree to reviews of his national budget'. Trevelyan summed up the impasse by telling the Foreign Office on 21 January that 'Only Mr. Black can dispel the suspicions by coming to an understanding with Nasser which convinces him the Bank is not going to try and run the Egyptian economy, and that in spite of the language of the Bank's lawyers Nasser is going to get his loan.'

Black stuck to the line that he must insist on 'normal conditions' for a loan, because if the Bank modified their conditions for Egypt other countries would seek similar modifications and 'an important part of the Bank's protection would be lost'. This rigidity was a serious error. It was not a normal commercial loan. Instead it was the key to Anglo–American Middle Eastern policy and vital for keeping Nasser out of the Russian camp. It can well be compared with the need to keep Mussolini out of Hitler's arms prior to the remilitarization of the Rhineland and the Anschluss in 1936. A briefing letter from the Treasury to the Foreign Office on 25 January said: 'There is no normality because the Bank do not normally enter into a preliminary agreement with a member country in advance of formal negotiation . . . the whole project is quite exceptional . . . the largest [loan] the Bank has proposed to undertake.'[4]

En route to Cairo Black came to London on 25 January and had a conference with Macmillan. According to the record of the meeting made by the future Head of the Civil Service, Robert Armstrong, then a rising Treasury star, Macmillan did not press the Treasury point of view, agreeing that the Bank were only asking for 'normal' conditions, and said: 'Our concern has been to do all we can to secure that Egypt follows the western route . . . we are anxious to do all we can to smooth the negotiations. We have told the Bank we see no procedural difficulties.'[5] Macmillan did not impress on Black the political reasons for agreement with Nasser, and when Black got to

Cairo his face-to-face negotiations with Nasser were abortive. Thus a great opportunity of bringing peace to the Middle East was lost.

As soon as Black arrived in Cairo Trevelyan emphasized to him that Nasser wanted a publishable document that did not appear to infringe Egyptian sovereignty, and did not give the Bank the right to control the Egyptian economy; therefore the letter of intent should be redrafted, although the Egyptians would agree to competitive tendering. 'Colonel Nasser wants to be able to say that the Egyptians can spend their money where they like; although they would include a written agreement that no proportion of the scheme should be financed or carried out except by countries which were members of the International Bank.'

By 4 February alternative drafts of letters between the Bank and the Egyptian Government were ready. Agreement was on the cards, but when Black met the Egyptians on 6 February he told them their drafts were unacceptable because inter alia they provided only for a statement of intentions by the Government of Egypt in return for a commitment by the Bank. Trevelyan then told Black that there must be 'a document coming out of these negotiations or all was lost'. Black replied that he did not share this fear. Trevelyan was right, and the February negotiations in Cairo foundered when they were on the brink of success, to the grave detriment of Egypt's relations with the West.[6]

In January and February 1956 Cairo Radio continuously broadcast vicious anti-British propaganda, and Nasser did everything he could to prevent Jordan or other Arab states joining the Baghdad Pact. Eden was outraged when on 1 March King Hussein of Jordan sacked General Glubb, commander of the British-trained and -subsidized Arab Legion, peremptorily and without notice. In his memoirs Eden claimed that this was a complete surprise. It should not have been.

In May 1955 the Foreign Office had received reports that Hussein and Glubb were not on good terms. Generals Templer (CIGS) and Keightley (Commander, Middle East Forces) went to Jordan at the end of May 1955; the visit was not a success. Templer reported that he had 'formed a very poor impression' of Hussein, who had kept him waiting fifty minutes for his dinner, and then 'pointedly took leave of him without allowing him the opportunity of half an hour's private talk which had been arranged'. Although Templer had been impressed with Glubb, he found much to criticize about 'the attitude' of the British troops in Jordan. Although some Arab officers had served for fourteen years, Glubb told Templer he did not consider any would be fit to command even brigades for another three years, and it would be ten years before any Arab officer was fit to take command of a division, although he recognized that to meet Hussein's wishes he might have to go faster than that. Glubb told Templer that senior officers had 'no grievances' about this and recognized that they could not yet fill the highest posts. He was incorrect. The British Ambassador, Charles Duke, had already urged Glubb 'to make it clear there were better prospects of promotion for Arab officers to satisfy both them and the King'. However Templer took Glubb's side. Duke told the Foreign Office of complaints by Hussein that Glubb tried to keep everything in his own hands, did not co-operate with the Jordan Defence Minister, and 'had his own favourites' whom he encouraged and supported. The King had pointed this out to his Defence Minister, Farhan Shbeilat, who reported it to Duke, adding that 'many of them were incompetent and unworthy'.[7]

According to Duke, the principal cause of the King's 'ill humour' towards Glubb was the insistence of the British Government that Wing Commander Jock Dalgleish, since June 1953 head of the Jordan Air Force, should be replaced when his tour of duty came to an end in February 1956. Dalgleish had little in common with Glubb, but he was a great crony of Hussein's. The King adored flying; Dalgleish encouraged this and flew with him all the time. Hussein, educated at Harrow and Sandhurst, was anglicized, and found in Dalgleish the easygoing close friend and companion he needed. He could escape from the formal atmosphere of the Palace and relax with Jock and his wife in their home, where he would help with the cooking. Dalgleish's flying log reveals that during one month he flew with Hussein on all but five days.

On 26 October Duke reported that Glubb was extremely depressed and that one of the King's Ministers had told him the King was 'bad tempered with Glubb because of his irritation over the decision to replace Dalgleish in February'. On 6 October Duke had written that Hussein was behaving in a manner calculated to undermine the 'organisation and discipline of the Arab Legion', and his attitude to Glubb had deteriorated. Hussein had told Glubb that the Legion was 'a rabble, lacked any proper organisation' and that Glubb 'was promoting bad men and keeping back good men'. Glubb complained that the King was giving written orders for transfers and promotions without even consulting him.[8] The Foreign Office wondered whether Dalgleish was impervious to Foreign Office advice and would not help because he was a 'King's man', and thought it would be 'really useless' to ask him or expect him 'to influence the

King in any way we want unless that way happened to coincide with the King's whim'.

On 6 December Templer arrived in Amman again, charged by Eden with the task of persuading Hussein to join the Baghdad Pact. In return Templer was to offer to re-equip the Arab Legion with a fourth infantry brigade, a regiment of tanks and an artillery regiment, plus a large increase in the annual subsidy. Hussein offered to sign a note to say that he would join the Pact, but at the last moment withdrew because of Nasser-organized demonstrations and riots in which many were killed. Glubb and the Arab Legion crushed the uprisings to a barrage of hate from Cairo Radio. British reinforcements were flown to Cyprus to be ready to go to Amman, while Egypt, Syria and Saudi Arabia offered Jordan an Arab subsidy to replace the British one. Hussein's position was precarious, but he survived thanks to the Arab Legion restoring order. However, at the end of December the Egyptians were again organizing country-wide demonstrations to demand Glubb's dismissal. When Glubb reported this to the Foreign Office, they commented that his 'intelligence' was usually quite good if at times melodramatic.[9]

With this background it should have been clear in London that Hussein might get rid of Glubb soon, because apart from politics he found the General out of date and governessy. He also wanted to counter Nasser's propaganda that he was under British influence. He may have felt, too, that sacking Glubb would increase his popularity in the Arab world.

Dalgleish told the author that he was certain that if he had not left Jordan on 28 February 1956 he could have prevented the sacking of Glubb or had it postponed and done in an orderly manner. Without success Hussein had asked Duke several times for Dalgleish's appointment to be extended, and when Shuckburgh, the King and Dalgleish met at the Dorchester Hotel in London on 24 October the main theme of the talk had been that Dalgleish should stay on, although Hussein did tell Shuckburgh that he had reservations about Glubb, which caused Shuckburgh to consider 'gathering names' for a replacement. Yet Shuckburgh made no request to the Air Ministry to get Dalgleish's appointment extended. This was a fatal mistake; the Foreign Office failed to appreciate how vital Dalgleish was for good Anglo–Jordanian relations, and instead thought he did harm.

Dalgleish believes that Major Ali Abu Nuwar, Hussein's chief ADC, was entirely responsible for Glubb's abrupt dismissal. He was anti-British and pro-Nasser (the 'arch villain', in fact), and had boasted to Dalgleish two days before he left that once he had gone there would be 'dramatic changes'. Nuwar seized on the King's emotional reaction to Dalgleish's departure to persuade him to sack Glubb. Dalgleish feels that Templer's visits were a great mistake. He was tactless with the King, because he came laden with 'goodies' in the shape of the British offer of tanks, guns and planes, and thought Hussein should eat out of his hand. Instead he offended the King, and Glubb could not rectify the situation.

After Glubb's dismissal Ali Abu Nuwar was immediately promoted to general in charge of all Jordan forces. In 1958 Hussein told Dalgleish that he had sacked Glubb 'on impulse', and with hindsight could not understand why he had done it. Dalgleish was like an elder brother to the King, who insisted on a direct telephone line from the Palace to his house and continually visited him. Dalgleish told the author that he was always friendly with Glubb, although there was a 'gap' in age and seniority, but Glubb would not interest himself in the 'palace politics', which were all-important. Glubb continually told Dalgleish he should improve his Arabic, but Dalgleish was more interested in teaching the Jordan Air Force English because all the service manuals were in English.[10]

A few hours after the dismissal notice had been served on Glubb on 1 March, Duke saw a smiling and confident King who told him he wanted to remain friendly with Britain, and that Glubb's sacking would be beneficial in the long run. The King complained of 'grave deficiencies in equipment and stores' and said he had previously warned Glubb of his anxiety and had even spoken of it in London.

Eden's reaction was hysterical. Within forty-eight hours he had sent four telegrams to Amman. His official biographer says: 'These remain sensitive.' This is not my view. They are important historical evidence of Eden's over-reaction. Eden's first instruction to Duke was that he should see the King and impress on him the danger into which he was running his country for no urgent reason, and that Britain as 'Jordan's loyal ally' had the right to be consulted before 'the King embarks on a policy, the consequences and dangers of which internal and external, no one can foresee'. Duke reported that when he delivered this message the King was quite unmoved 'and asked me to assure you that his action did *not* indicate any change in his policy of friendship with HMG or any swing towards any other camp'.

Eden's next message was:

I have just heard from HM Ambassador of the action Your Majesty has taken in relieving General Glubb of his command and ordering him to leave the country immediately. In view of the lifelong and faithful

service rendered to Jordan and your family by this officer, I feel my
duty to tell Your Majesty that the resentment in Britain at this action
will be widespread and deep. I cannot foretell its final consequences
upon the relations between our two countries. Therefore I would
earnestly ask Your Majesty to suspend this order and allow General
Glubb and his fellow officers to continue their loyal service.

Eden also cabled Lloyd, who was in Cairo, that he would have his
'full authority' to go to Amman to protest. Duke intervened, saying:
'The King would not have time to change his mind; moreover a visit
in these circumstances might invite a snub.' This sensible advice
saved Lloyd a useless trip, but Eden then suggested that Lloyd
should visit Amman on his journey home from Karachi. Duke also
sensibly advised against this.

Later, in a cable on 2 March, Duke said:

If we are to retain any credit in Jordan and perhaps throughout the
Middle East HMG must react speedily publicly and effectively
against Glubb's removal. An immediate statement of intention to cut
off the Arab Legion subsidy and other financial aid would be going too
far, although such a possibility should not be entirely ruled out at a
rather later date.

This provocative telegram produced a third message from Eden, to
the effect that the King should be told he would have to make 'a
statement in Parliament almost at once' and

if HMG are to be able to give Jordan their continued support they
must be in a position to produce positive evidence of Jordan's sincere
attachment to British friendship and to our Treaty.
    The minimum which will suffice is that he should at once make a
public statement that as proof of the value he attaches to our
friendship and to the Treaty he confirms the remaining British officers
in their posts.

A few hours later the resident clerk at the Foreign Office was ordered
by 10 Downing Street to send a fourth message, which was dispatched in the early hours of 3 March, reiterating the demand for a
statement about the remaining serving British officers, and pointing
out that 'the King's action is contrary to the spirit of our Treaty.'
Duke was unable to deliver the fourth message until the next day, as
the King had gone to sleep.

Lloyd in Cairo had heard the news of Glubb's dismissal while he
was dining with Nasser. At first he was angry, believing Nasser

responsible. But he soon changed his mind and sent this message to London:

> I tackled Nasser at once about events in Amman and said that I supposed he had heard what had happened. He said he had, and assumed that the removal of General Glubb had taken place with British approval. It would certainly, in his view, improve the position in Jordan and strengthen the régime. I replied that this remained to be seen. But the Egyptian campaign against Glubb had become generally known in the United Kingdom and elsewhere. In consequence events in Amman would rightly or wrongly be attributed to Egypt in large measure. This could not fail to have a bad effect on Anglo–Egyptian relations and I was forced to reflect whether my visit could serve any useful purpose.

At the airport Dr Fawzi said the Egyptian press would 'report' Glubb for one day and then drop the subject.[11]

By 4 March Duke was taking a more cheerful view of Glubb's dismissal and wrote:

> On further reflection I wonder if our regard for General Glubb's great personal qualities and services in Jordan and resentment at the ignoble manner of his dismissal have not led us to take a more tragic view than is justified of the significance of this episode. . . . Hussein had repeatedly stressed that the action taken was directed against Glubb personally and they do not want it to impair in any way the close and friendly relationship between Jordan and Great Britain.[12]

When Glubb got back to London he went to 10 Downing Street, calmed Eden down and persuaded him to accept Duke's fresh briefing. The Cabinet minutes for 5 March record that 'it was not necessary to assume that this action was intended as a blow against British influence in Jordan generally', but the next day Eden became restless again and told the Cabinet that 'our next move should be to urge the Government of Iraq to make a direct approach to the Jordan Government and indicate to the Jordan Government if the reliability of the Arab Legion was undermined Iraq should take over some of the responsibilities which we had hitherto assumed in Jordan.' Any such move would have been disastrous, as it would have infuriated both Hussein and Nasser and Jordan would have been driven into the Egyptian dictator's arms.

Fortunately, wiser counsels prevailed. On the day of Glubb's dismissal Sir Alec Kirkbride, former Ambassador to Jordan, had been in Amman en route to Jerusalem to catalogue coins in the museum. He was a close personal friend of the King and was responsible for Duke's soothing message of 5 March; Hussein asked Kirkbride to see him and convinced him the Glubb dismissal was not intended as an anti-British move. At Hussein's request Kirkbride returned immediately to London and reported to Eden, who asked him to attend the Cabinet meeting on 9 March. Kirkbride told it that Hussein had assured him that he did not wish for any change in the traditional friendship between Jordan and the UK, and that Glubb's dismissal derived from long-standing dissatisfaction with his handling of the Legion. Kirkbride emphasized that it would be a mistake to bring Iraq into the discussions, because the Prime Minister of Iraq was hand-in-glove with Saudi Arabia, a bitter enemy of the Prime Minister of Jordan, and strongly opposed to any closer association between Iraq and Jordan; also that Hussein would resent any efforts to involve Iraq. Kirkbride went on that Jordan was unlikely to look to Egypt or Saudi Arabia instead of Britain for finance; what was required was an immediate assurance that the UK Government was not proposing to withdraw support from Jordan, accompanied by an offer to discuss the terms on which British officers could stay on in the Arab Legion. The Cabinet agreed with Kirkbride, and decided to send a personal message to Hussein; a plan was worked out for a British Military Mission to replace officers serving with the Arab Legion. This is what Hussein wanted. He was dependent on RAF officers for his beloved aeroplanes, and on terms of close friendship with one gunner officer who shared his taste for fast racing cars.[13]

In the Commons debate which followed, Eden's speech was an abject failure. He found it only too true, as he had said in his early cable to Hussein, that there was 'widespread resentment' over Glubb's dismissal. The Suez Group barracked Eden and he recorded that it was one of his worst parliamentary performances. With good judgment Eden had mended his fences with Hussein, but the iron entered his soul over Nasser, whom he blamed for Glubb's dismissal and consequently for his discomfiture in the Commons. From then on he was an opponent of Nasser.

On 21 March Lloyd reported to the Cabinet that from his conversations with Nasser he was satisfied that he was 'unwilling to work with the Western Powers' to secure peace in the Middle East. In India Lloyd had talked to Dulles, who told him that the Aswan Dam project would have to be ditched unless Nasser ceased his anti-Western propaganda, accepted the Johnston Plan for the Jordan

waters, and took some specific steps towards an Arab–Israeli settlement. If Nasser would accept these specific points Dulles thought a
bargain could be struck, with the quid pro quo that there should be
no more Arab members of the Pact. With Eden's rage against Nasser
over the Glubb incident, the auguries for the Aswan Dam were not
good. But all was not yet lost.[14]

The Foreign Office brief for Lloyd's March visit to Cairo said:

> Substantial agreement was reached for the Bank to provide eventually
> loans totalling up to $200 million for the second stage of the High
> Aswan Dam. Formal agreement awaits confirmation by the Board of
> Directors of the Bank and Egyptian Council of Ministers. One
> condition is that there must first be a settlement between Egypt and
> the Sudan on the division of the Nile waters.

> [Separate brief]
> The International Bank is not lending money for the first phase of the
> project, the details of which were settled in the Washington talks last
> December. For this phase the United States and United Kingdom
> Governments have offered to provide contributions of $55 million and
> £5.5 million respectively. For the second phase, the two Governments
> have offered 'to consider sympathetically lending their further sup-
> port, through participation in financing the remaining foreign ex-
> change costs of the project, in the light of conditions then existing and
> of the progress and performance during the first stage of construction,
> and subject to necessary Parliamentary action.' It is clearly under-
> stood between ourselves and the Americans that this meant that we
> should almost certainly contribute and we have been negotiating a
> secret [from the Egyptians] agreement with them as to how we should
> share the costs.[15]

Lloyd's brief went on that Nasser now wanted changes in the
aides-mémoire, but did not seem to be pressing this, 'which raised the
suspicion that he wanted to consider himself free to accept communist tenders; Nasser had been pressed to agree that if the American
and British grants were received he would bind himself only to spend
Egypt's own money on work done by Communist firms. Nasser did
not feel that there could be anything in writing, but there might be an
oral understanding that 'wherever possible' preference would be
given to Western firms, and the Foreign Office brief stated: 'The
Secretary of State may well wish to try to extract a more satisfactory
assurance.' Another minor difficulty was that the Egyptian Government would have liked to award the whole of the main contract to the
Anglo–French–German consortium, but the World Bank and the

US Government insisted on competitive tendering as a condition of their participation. However, on the whole it was not a discouraging scenario.

However, when in February Nasser had asked for the preliminary grants from America and Britain for the first stage immediately, so as to begin certain reclamation work, Eden minuted: 'We could never agree to these greedy demands. They certainly won't get the money at present.' Nasser's argument was that, although he had not agreed and signed the aides-mémoire, he wanted the advance money paid over as a sign of goodwill. A Foreign Office objection was that agreement had not been reached with the Sudan on flooding part of her territory; negotiations over this were coupled with Sudan's demand for a separate currency, over which Nasser was said to be dragging his feet. In fact there was never any doubt about Sudan and Egypt coming to a satisfactory agreement.

Trevelyan tried hard to help Nasser, writing to Lloyd: 'If they [UK and USA] earmarked the money now the goodwill gesture would have a good political effect.' Lloyd replied that it was quite unacceptable to him to pay over the money before the work was started, and added: 'I am becoming suspicious of Egyptian intentions', and once they were sure of UK and US grants they would be free to take Russian help in money, machinery and technicians. Kirkpatrick thought Trevelyan was making 'a preposterous suggestion'. This was also Armstrong's view at the Treasury. However Watson, for the Foreign Office, summed up the British position well by minuting: '. . . real answer is we propose to participate in the Dam project to keep the Communists out of Egypt and thus bringing Egypt more completely under their domination'. There is no doubt that if Trevelyan's suggestion had been accepted it would have made a considerable difference to Nasser's future attitude to the West.

On 31 March Kaissouni said to Trevelyan in a *cri de coeur*, 'If only we had been able to get the High Dam arrangements and the division of the waters settled before the Czech arms deal last September.' Rumours spread that Russian offers were in Nasser's pocket. They were unfounded, but on such a report Eden minuted on 29 April: 'Should not our line be that we cannot agree until Sudan is in line too and East Africa, etc. and then take our time about that?'[16]

The British had now agreed to move from a two-stage system of financing the project to a unified stage, which was what Nasser wanted, but the Americans dissented. With reason Nasser insisted that he must have all the money at his disposal before he started work on such a big project. Eden wanted to keep Nasser dangling on the hook, and on 7 May commented that 'we should not be in a hurry to go back to the Egyptians after reaching agreement with the Americans and the International Bank.' He defined his attitude as 'we must keep Nasser in play for the time being.' This go-slow was the worst possible tactic for keeping Nasser on good terms with the West.[17]

When Nasser recognized Communist China, much against American wishes, Dulles hardened against him. On 30 May Lloyd asked for a paper for the Cabinet on the pros and cons of going ahead with the financing of the dam. The survey revealed that the Board of Trade were trying to devise a less ambitious scheme involving a smaller financial contribution from the British Government and reviving the original ideas of the Anglo–German–French consortium; the Foreign Office view then was that if Nasser could be persuaded to think in these more modest terms 'the whole thing could perhaps become more practicable and manageable. But his megolamania may prevent this.'[18]

Now Kirkpatrick had become hostile to the loan, minuting on 4 July:

> If the Russians build the Dam they will increase their influence in Egypt and will appear to be benefactors. But if, as I suspect, Nasser is already sold to the Russians this advantage will be purely marginal. On the other hand if we finance the Dam we not only incur expenditure which we cannot afford, but we have to suffer the serious disability of seeming to do more for our enemies than we are prepared to do for our friends.

The reference to 'friends' was because Britain's partners in the Baghdad Pact (Pakistan, Turkey, Iran and Iraq) were claiming that as Allies they should have the lion's share of any available Western financial aid, and that Egypt, now hostile, should not have priority over them. This was short-sighted, because nothing would contribute more to a stable Middle East than a prosperous Egypt, but Eden, Lloyd and Macmillan now shared Kirkpatrick's views, and if Nasser was to get his money for the dam the push would have to come from either Dulles or the International Bank. In May in Paris Lloyd and Dulles had agreed to keep the Egyptians 'in play', although 'our ultimate intention is to let the project languish'. This brought the sensible comment from Denis Wright that 'we must give Sir H. Trevelyan something to say soon; we should be the losers were our silence to lead to the downfall of Kaissouni and others who still prefer the West to the Communists.'[19]

The last hopes for the loan hinged on a visit by Black to Cairo in the middle of June. His view was that Nasser was not negotiating with the Russians to finance the dam, and he was critical of the British and American refusal to give Nasser a definite answer. After visiting Cairo Black talked to Makins in Washington, and told him that Hoover and Dulles did not know 'what the hell to do'. They had got into difficulties with Congress because they had dissipated the money originally earmarked for the dam project, and there would have to be further provision in a new Foreign Aid Bill. Provided they got a Foreign Aid Bill through, Black 'guessed' that America would go through with the dam project. Black believed that Nasser still wished to go ahead, but it was

> really essential for the British and American Governments to tell Nasser either that they would go through with it as originally proposed or that they would not go through with it or state the terms on which they would go through with it. This must be done before Nasser went to Moscow in August. He thought that the West would be put in a very bad light if they merely allowed the Russians to trump our tricks.
>
> Mr. Black ended by saying while he would like nothing better than to see the Bank out of the High Aswan Dam operation, he could not help thinking that the offer having been made, the Governments ought to go through with it. The Bank still thought that technically the project was feasible.

This was not what Lloyd and Eden wanted to hear. In Cairo Black had seen Nasser and Kaissouni on 21 June; he got the impression that the Egyptian Government wanted to finance the dam through the World Bank and were waiting to hear from London and Washington about the changes they had proposed in the aides-mémoire. Nasser told Black he had 'no doubts whatever' about reaching a satisfactory agreement with the Sudan on the Nile waters. Thus no blame can be attached to Black for the failure of the project. He was more co-operative with Nasser than he had been on his previous visit to Cairo, but now both Eden and Dulles were determined to humiliate Nasser.[20]

On 17 July Lloyd told the Cabinet that the American Government was 'likely to share our view that the offer of financial aid for the building of the High Dam at Aswan should now be withdrawn', and that 'it would probably be best to indicate to the Egyptians that, in view of their commitments for expenditure on armaments and military installations, the two Governments had been forced to the conclusion that the financing of the Dam, even with the assistance

Nasser's triumphal return to Cairo after he had announced the nationalization of the Canal at Alexandria.

The only meeting between Eden and Nasser took place in February 1955 at the British Embassy in Cairo when Eden was Foreign Secretary.

Israeli infantry attacks the Egyptians, according to the plan agreed with the French and British.

Helicopters carry British troops into action for the first time in history at Port Said, 6 November 1955. 45 Commando Royal Marines.

Eden broadcasts to the nation on 8 August 1955 about the deadly threat of the nationalization of the Suez Canal.

Crowds protest in Trafalgar Square against the bombing of Egypt as the Cabinet decide to send in ground troops, 3 November 1955.

which had been proposed, would be beyond Egypt's resources; this might well lead to a deterioration in our relations with Egypt with possibly serious consequences for our trade'. There was no dissent. Lloyd promised to circulate a memorandum on the best way to tell Nasser that the financial help was off. Yet an Egyptian trade mission had just arrived in London, and Nasser had withdrawn all his objections to the aides-mémoire and other conditions.

On 19 July Dulles abruptly and undiplomatically told the Egyptian Ambassador in Washington that the US offer of help over the dam was withdrawn. Eden stated later that Britain had been informed, but not consulted. It is hard to reconcile this with the Cabinet of 17 July. On 20 July it agreed to an announcement about withdrawing aid for the dam in terms which would give Egypt 'no ground for assuming [the decision] had been taken for political reasons'.

Senior officials at the Board of Trade had drawn up their own plan for the Anglo–French–German consortium to go ahead without World Bank aid, which was referred to in the Foreign Office memorandum in June. Thorneycroft went to Downing Street at once to discuss this with the Prime Minister. He told the author that, to his surprise, this resulted in Eden becoming angry and telling him that it was none of his (Thorneycroft's) business and that the Aswan Dam project was 'dead'. Eden did not allow the Board of Trade project to be reported to the Cabinet, and out-of-hand rejected their sensible and constructive proposals – a grave mistake.[21]

9

The Suez Crisis
August–September 1956

IN RETALIATION FOR his humiliation over the Aswan Dam on 26 July, before a huge crowd in Alexandria Nasser announced the nationalization of the Suez Canal, and stated that its revenues would now be used to pay for building the dam. His speech aroused enormous enthusiasm. Eden was the host at a dinner party at 10 Downing Street when the news burst around the world. His guests included Hugh Gaitskell and Nuri Said, the Iraqi Prime Minister. As soon as the other guests left the Chiefs of Staff, the American Chargé d'Affaires and the French Ambassador, together with the Cabinet Ministers present at the dinner, were called urgently to a meeting.

Eden's immediate reaction was that Egypt must be forced by military action to give up the Canal. This remained his aim throughout the crisis, although for short periods his ardour for war waned and he temporarily looked for a negotiated solution provided it was favourable to Britain.

The Chiefs of Staff were ordered to prepare at speed a paper on the military options. According to William Clark, his press officer, who was present, Eden was 'disgusted' because he was told that, although Britain could deal with an atomic war or the Mau Mau in Kenya, she could not deal immediately with 'a little local episode in the Mediterranean'.[1] The problem was that the commandos and parachutists who had to be the spearhead of any assault on Egypt were currently enforcing internal security in Cyprus. Eden had insisted on sending the best-disciplined troops to Cyprus, because elite paras and commandos were less likely to succumb to the enervating Cyprus climate and the cheap wine than ordinary infantry battalions. Now, after several months of police duties, both commandos and paras needed a short, sharp period of retraining before they would be fit for battle.

Eden was also reminded by the Chiefs of Staff that the Arnhem operation in September 1944 had been a disaster because the follow-up of ground troops had been too slow. This lesson had been learnt for the crossing of the Rhine in March 1945, when, as a result of airborne troops being quickly relieved by ground troops, the drop was a resounding success. If paras and commandos landed in Egypt they would have to be followed up quickly by conventional troops with armour and heavy equipment, and it would take weeks to organize such a force and requisition and load the necessary ships. The only possible early airborne landing would be in the Alexandria zone, because 10th Armoured Division was stationed close by in Cyrenaica, but it was two thousand below strength and it was doubtful if the rulers of Libya would countenance such an operation. The Chiefs of Staff were not going to let the politicians place the flower of the British Army at risk in a hasty, ill-planned operation. Their outline plan, 'Action Against Egypt', ready on 1 August, stated: 'We wish to emphasize that the parachutists and assault forces must not be committed to operations inadequately trained, and time must be allowed in the programme for adequate rehearsal for amphibious and airborne assault forces.' This did not please Eden.[2]

Evidence of RAF unreadiness comes in a minute to the Secretary of State as late as 5 September, which also stated that the RAF had 'been able to lead the other services in preparation for hostilities'. This stated that Valiants had no visual bomb sights, and Canberras were not cleared for high altitude and high-speed dropping of flares (but this was being put right). Worse was that when the Hunter guns were fired damage could be caused to the airframe, which was dangerous, and that a programme of re-engining the existing Hunters was in progress, which would take a long time. Fortunately twenty-eight Mark 5 Hunters in Cyprus were 'surge free', but none of the earlier models was fit for combat; on certain Mark 5s the Hunter firing problems could not be cleared until 1957; for others there would never be unrestricted clearance.

On American ancillary equipment, which was in wide use on all combat aircraft, the Americans had placed 'strings which mean broadly that it is supplied for use in the NATO area'. The Secretary of State was told that the Ministry of Defence's present policy was not to inform the Americans about 'the extent to which this equipment is being used in current operations'. The Americans had not inquired, and 'there is at least a good chance that they will prefer not to be faced with this problem. . . . What is clear is that if the existing restrictions were to be accepted our preparations would be frustrated.'[3]

On 27 July the Army, RAF and Navy HQ in the Middle East were warned: 'At a meeting of Ministers last night approach to other Governments decided upon. Nasser's announcement re taking over Suez Canal may lead to critical situation for which you should be prepared but no overt action may be taken for the present.' Three days later the CIGS ordered the dispatch of five infantry units urgently to Cyprus to replace the Parachute Brigade and the commando units, which were to be withdrawn to Malta for retraining as soon as possible. The War Office also decided to send an infantry brigade to Libya to free 10 Armoured Division for operations in Egypt, and reported that it was essential to call up reservists to get the brigades and divisions up to strength for war. Two light anti-aircraft regiments were sent to Cyprus. Cabinet authority for the call-up of twenty thousand reservists was immediately forthcoming. Fortunately the total number of units being sent to Cyrenaica was not going to exceed the numbers of the garrison allowed under the Treaty, but the Libyan Government would have to be informed of the troop movements.

In fact eighteen hundred reinforcements, including a high proportion of reservists, were airlifted to Cyrenaica between 12 and 16 August and preparations made to concentrate 10 Armoured Division in eastern Cyrenaica, near the Egyptian border, on the pretext of an 'exercise'. A press statement from Downing Street on troop movements included these words: 'precautionary measures of a military nature including movements to Cyprus and Mediterranean and the call up of reservists'.[4]

The day after Nasser's speech, Eden told the Cabinet that nationalization was not a legal issue, but one of 'widest international importance. . . . Colonel Nasser's action had presented us with an opportunity to find a lasting settlement of this problem, and we should not hesitate to take advantage of it.' The Cabinet agreed that 'our essential interests in this area must, if necessary, be safeguarded by military action and that the necessary preparations to this end must be made. . . . Even if we had to act alone, we could not stop short of using force to protect our position if all other means of protecting it proved unavailing.'

Eden also told his Cabinet that 'any failure on the part of the Western Powers to take the necessary steps to regain control over the Canal would have disastrous consequences for the economic life of the Western Powers and for their standing and influence in the Middle East.' Events were to show how wide of the mark he was. Since Nasser was offering to pay compensation to shareholders in the

Suez Canal Company, the Cabinet agreed they were on weak ground over the issue of illegality. At this meeting the Cabinet agreed to set up a smaller War Cabinet to plan military operations; it was known as the Egypt Committee.[5]

Eden's speech in the House of Commons on 2 August was statesmanlike, well argued and well received. His principal point was that the Canal must not stay under the unfettered control of a single power which could exploit its position with devastating consequences for Britain and the West, and also keep the Canal closed to all Israeli ships as Egypt was already doing. For the Opposition Gaitskell denounced Nasser as 'another Hitler' and was congratulated by Conservative MPs. Herbert Morrison referred to the 'pocket dictator in Cairo'. The British press and MPs on both sides condemned Nasser's action in extravagant and warlike terms; with reason Eden considered that the use of force to recover the Canal would not only be tolerated by the nation, but would make him personally popular.

Eden telegraphed to Eisenhower: 'As we see it we are unlikely to attain our objective by economic pressures alone . . . my colleagues and I are convinced that we must be ready in the last resort to use force to bring Nasser to his senses.' Eisenhower did not contradict him, but dispatched a senior diplomat, Robert Murphy, to London. Macmillan asked Murphy to dinner at 11 Downing Street and alarmed the American diplomat by saying that Britain and France must meet the challenge or 'sink into the rank of second class nations'. Murphy was left in no doubt that the British Government believed the Suez Canal must be recovered by force. Murphy's report upset Eisenhower, who was in the midst of his election preparations. The last thing he wanted was a war in the Middle East before the votes were counted, and Dulles quickly followed Murphy to London.

Dulles brought with him a letter from the President to Eden, expressing concern about Eden's letter 'telling me on a most secret basis of your decision to employ force without delay or attempting any intermediate and less dramatic steps'. Eisenhower went on: 'Initial military successes might be easy, but the eventual price might become far too heavy.' Instead of force Eisenhower wanted a conference, and he warned Eden that force, without showing that every peaceful means of resolving the difficulty had previously been exhausted, could produce 'a reaction that could very seriously affect our people's feelings towards our Western Allies . . . that could grow to such an intensity as to have the most far reaching consequences'.

Eden did not accept the letter at its face value, being misled by Dulles, who was more hawklike than Eisenhower. In his memoirs Eden wrote that in this letter Eisenhower did not 'rule out the use of force'. This was a false interpretation.[6]

The Foreign Office and Eden felt that at this stage Dulles dominated American foreign policy. It may have been true of Eisenhower's early days at the White House, but with the elections in November 1956 so close the President was, regardless of Dulles, adamant that America would not countenance a Middle East war except as a last resort. Whether he would have held a different view after his Presidential victory in November is imponderable.

Eden had agreed before Dulles's visit that military operations against Egypt would not be practicable before September. At first both he and the Egypt Committee were reluctant to accept Dulles's proposal for a conference. But when they met, Dulles did not rule out the eventual use of force, and Eden reluctantly agreed to Dulles's scheme for a conference in London of the eight surviving signatories to the 1888 Suez Convention plus the sixteen other countries most concerned. The Dulles Plan was to create an 'International Authority' to operate the waterway, ensure freedom of passage, fix tolls, carry out improvements and negotiate compensation for the Canal shareholders.[7]

On 1 August Lloyd informed the Cabinet that Dulles had told him: 'Egypt must be made to "disgorge" the Suez Canal, and he was prepared to agree that the communiqué to be issued at the end of the talks should contain a strong condemnation of Egypt's action and an affirmation of the need to place the Canal under international control, but that the supervisory machinery should not be an "agency of the United Nations".' Lloyd, however, warned the Cabinet that Dulles had made it clear the United States Government would 'strongly deprecate "any premature use of force" to secure these objectives'. This was the consistent stance of the United States.[8]

The Conference assembled in London on 14 August. Nasser refused to attend – unsurprisingly, because the principle of an International Authority abrogated Egypt's claim to sovereignty over the Canal. Krishna Menon angered both the Americans and the British by emphasizing that Egypt had acted legally in nationalizing the Canal, although he agreed that there was merit in creating an international advisory body to assure the right of passage and fair tolls. He argued for a 'consultative' body of user interests without prejudice to Egyptian ownership and operation. Eisenhower agreed with Menon, but Dulles preferred his own plan for an executive

International Authority, and a resolution to set this up on Dulles's original formula was carried by eighteen out of the twenty-two nations at the Conference. Had the alternative Menon resolution prevailed, Nasser would almost certainly have accepted and the crisis been nipped in the bud. From then on the eighteen-power proposals assumed great importance.

Eden though that Dulles 'was the one, the only man who is capable of handling the matter in Cairo'. But Dulles would not take the proposals to Cairo, telling Eisenhower: 'I think it is preferable that we should become less conspicuous.' Instead a Committee of Five was appointed, with Robert Menzies, Prime Minister of Australia, as chairman; they went to Cairo on a mission doomed in advance to failure – just what Eden and Mollet, the French Prime Minister, wanted. As one distinguished British diplomat put it, Eden knew 'there was not actually a hope in hell'.[9]

Anticipating that Menzies would get nowhere with Nasser, the British and French pushed ahead with military plans, and even before the London Conference began Eden told the Cabinet that 'the military precautions being taken by the United Kingdom Government were now being completed and with a contribution from the French Government there would be ample force to deal with Egypt'; the only military problem was the question of timing, because the forces could not be held ready for any 'protracted period'. Eden insisted that the Committee of Five must bring their negotiations with Nasser to a head urgently, and on 28 August expressed 'horror' to Loy Henderson, a US diplomat and expert on the Middle East who was a member of the Committee of Five, at the delay of one day. However, Eden was delighted when on 27 August Menzies indicated that Australia would give military support.

Back in Washington, according to Makins Dulles agreed that 'the general concept of excluding military action until recourse had been had to the United Nations was a sound one; United States public opinion would consider this a United Nations matter and he believed that this was probably true of a large sector of public opinion in the UK.' Against this Eden wrote: 'Mind his own business.'[10]

On 31 August Nasser told Byroade in Cairo that he presumed the Menzies mission might take two days to give him their view; it would only take him one hour to give his. However, he would invite all the delegations and their Ambassadors to dinner. Ominously for the success of the mission, he went on that when a man fell in love with somebody else's wife 'a compromise was difficult without a divorce'. He had no intention of arranging to divorce the Canal from Egypt.

On Trevelyan's telegram giving the news of this Byroade–Nasser conversation Eden wrote: 'Has FS seen this? Could this not be publicised?'

According to Trevelyan, Nasser's attitude was that, having realized he had underestimated the strength of Western reaction, he was concerned about Western military preparations and his own future, but he estimated the risk of invasion as ten to one; his tactics were to impress visitors on the one hand with his essential reasonableness and readiness to give every possible guarantee to ensure the proper functioning of the Canal and freedom of navigation, and on the other with his determination not to yield on the question of principle . . . 'he takes great risks but he has been known to retreat [e.g. over the Sudan]'.

As the telegrams came in from Cairo about the Menzies mission Eden congratulated the Australian Prime Minister in terms which can only be described as unctuous. Menzies found Nasser courteous, but as hard as nails. They did not get on. In one of their conversations Nasser said that his researchers had discovered that Britain had nationalized the Manchester Ship Canal 'without regard to contracts'. Menzies, not having been briefed, was nonplussed. Nasser might have added that in 1947 the Attlee Government had nationalized coalmines belonging to the French, but his researchers had not discovered this.

On 9 September a seven-page reply from Nasser arrived at 10 Downing Street. It was the answer Eden had hoped for and expected. To save the Prime Minister reading it, de Zulueta attached a handwritten note to the document: 'This is Nasser's reply. There is nothing new in it and it is an unequivocal rejection of international control. Nasser does say (page 4) that he is ready to reaffirm or renew the 1888 Convention, but that is all.'[11]

Nasser's reply stated that 'the proposed system aims at securing for a group of the users of the Canal control by their taking over its operation' and that 'the purpose is to take the Suez Canal out of the hands of Egypt and put it into some other hands. It would be . . . the beginning of trouble.' Nasser added that Egyptian policy 'remains the freedom of passage through the Suez Canal and its secure use without discrimination'. As Israel was already denied passage these words had a false ring, especially for Eden.

On 6 September Menzies reported that he was 'up against a brick wall'. The same day Eden told his Cabinet that Parliament must be recalled within a few days and the Government should seek support for military preparations. In discussion it was agreed that since there was little prospect of the Security Council being able to secure a settlement it was desirable that 'we should be seen to have made the fullest possible use of all available international machinery in our search for a peaceful settlement'. Eden wanted to clear his military adventure with Parliament and the United Nations, so that he could give the Chiefs of Staff the early D-Day which they insisted was vital, because the Expeditionary Force being assembled could not be kept at the 'ready' indefinitely.[12]

During the discussion on 6 September, it was almost certainly Macmillan who warned that military operations against Egypt would probably cause a run on the £, but that this consequence might have to be accepted 'if the alternative was slow economic strangulation as Egypt extended her control over the Arab world and the oil-producing countries. . . . The interruption of oil shipments through the Canal for such a period would involve us in very serious financial and trading losses', and although the USA had undertaken to make good from the western hemisphere deficiencies in oil supplies which resulted from closure of the Canal, 'they had not undertaken to finance the supply and Britain was unable to pay for it herself'.[13]

In response to a verbal complaint by Sandys, Minister of Housing and Local Government, Eden wrote to him on 22 August that, if there was to be a military operation, the Cabinet as a whole would take the final decision. It would not, however, be possible for the Cabinet as a whole to discuss the plans for any military operations that might have to be undertaken, and for security reasons details must be confined within the narrowest possible circle. The next day Sandys wrote to Eden:

> 2. Whilst I appreciate your assurance that, if the necessity to use force should arise, the Cabinet as a whole will be asked to take 'the final decision', I do hope that we shall be consulted as soon as possible about the broad lines of the military plan which is being prepared.
>
> 3. I recognise that, for security reasons, knowledge of the details of the operational plan must be kept within a restricted circle. On the other hand, the extent of the territorial objective of the operation, the manner of initiating it, and, above all, the grounds on which we should justify it to the world, are obviously matters of major political importance.
>
> 4. The choice of the right moment to consult the Cabinet is naturally a matter for your decision; but I hope that you will take us into your confidence before it is too late for any views we may have to be taken into account.

Home, Sandys and Butler must have discussed their unease together, because on the same day Home wrote to Eden:

> My dear Anthony,
>   I sense that Rab is very unhappy. I know your time is full but if you could see him alone it would be well worth while.
>   He is not against the use of force, but he fears that we have got ourselves into a position where we shall press the button before we have a moral basis for action which will carry conviction in this country, the free world and the Conservative party. He feels that there should be more flexibility so as to allow time for the fullest diplomatic action the extent of which cannot be foreseen.
>   I have told him that the pressing of the button is entirely within our control and that an intensive study is being made of the 'casus belli' and the justification for armed intervention.
>   I think his anxiety derives very largely from the fact that he was away for a fortnight and feels that possibly irrevocable decisions have been taken before the full implications of the use of force have been weighed.
>   I may be wrong about this diagnosis but I am certainly right about his state of mind and I think if you can see him you can put everything into perspective and he will feel he has had a chance to tell you what he feels.
>   I am sorry to add this to your preoccupation but I thought you should know.
> Yours, Alec
> Rab, of course, does not know I am telling you of this.[14]

However Butler, contrary to the impression he gives in his own memoirs, did not take a firm stand against war. Home wrote to the author:

> I don't recall whether I met with Rab and Duncan together, but Rab was constantly asking us all what we thought. In the end he always supported the Prime Minister's decisions with the rest of the Cabinet.
>   None of us liked the use of force, but most of the Cabinet had reconciled ourselves to the situation that, after all else had failed, we would probably have to do so.[15]

The meeting of the Egypt Committee on 24 August produced an explosion by Monckton against a war with Egypt, which was not recorded in the printed minutes. The Prime Minister had said in Cabinet that Britain might 'be faced with the choice of slow strangulation of her economy' (if no satisfactory settlement was found), and that he had also emphasized to Dulles the determination of the French to achieve a satisfactory settlement; the French Foreign Minister had stated to him (Eden) that 'with the exception of the Communists the French public were solidly behind the policy of the Government'.

Eden went on that America objected to any reference to the UN at the moment, but in his view Britain and France 'could use force within the Charter'. This must have produced the outburst against force being used from Monckton, a serious matter coming from the Minister of Defence, because as soon as Salisbury got back to his own office after the meeting he wrote to the Prime Minister:

> Walter M's outburst at the end of this morning's meeting was, I thought, as I am sure you agree, both painful and rather disturbing. Not that it came as a great surprise. I think that both you and I knew that he had for some time had doubts against a firm policy over Suez. But I suspect there will be a measure of support for his views when the Cabinet meets on Tuesday.
>
> Rab is clearly not happy, and I gather from what he said to me after the meeting that he has been making enquiries and finds there are quite a number of others, especially among the younger members of the Cabinet, who have not yet made up their minds . . . the case for force will clearly need to be closely and cogently argued by those of us who agree with it. I need not say that I am absolutely at one with you. . . .
>
> Yours ever, Bobbety

On the same day Lennox-Boyd wrote to Eden that Sandys's minute to the Prime Minister might have been inspired by 'an understandable desire to be kept in the picture', but 'if it is in any way due to second thoughts as to a tough policy it is indeed a serious matter'. He went on:

> I was horrified by the doubts expressed by the Minister of Defence. All these difficulties stood out miles when we first embarked on our policy. You call international control of the Canal a matter of life and death for us. This, though true of Suez itself, is still more true if this outrage is as we believe a step in a careful plan to drive us out of the Eastern Mediterranean and the Middle East.
>
> If there really is uncertainty in the Cabinet we can't be surprised if it exists in the country.

Lennox-Boyd also wrote that if Nasser 'wins or even appears to win, we might as well as a Government (and indeed as a country) go out of business'.[16]

Thus at the end of August the Cabinet was tending to divide into hawks and doves, although the hawks were immeasurably stronger; but it was evidence that war would produce a divided Parliament and a divided country.

In the full Cabinet on 28 August Monckton's 'recorded' objections were muted. He agreed

> that if all other methods proved unavailing force would have to be used. On the other hand the Cabinet should weigh the disadvantages of using force . . . our action would be condemned by a substantial body of public opinion in countries overseas including several of the independent countries of the Commonwealth. Within the United Kingdom itself opinion would be divided. . . . Moreover once we had sent military forces into Egypt it would not be easy to extricate them.

Salisbury hoped Britain would go to the United Nations before using force; Kilmuir said that 'while it would be wrong to disregard the U.N., it would be equally wrong to allow the real issue to be eroded by ineffective international debate', and Butler 'that from the Parliamentary point of view it was specially desirable that some reference should be made to the Security Council'. Monckton's outburst may have shocked the Egypt Committee, but in full Cabinet he was only a wishy-washy opponent of war, because in summing up the discussion on 28 August Eden was able to say that the Cabinet was '*united*' in the view that the frustration of Colonel Nasser's policy was a vital British interest which must be secured in the last resort through the use of force.

Monckton comes out of it badly. With his opposition to war he should have resigned then. William Clark has recorded that Monckton told him on 27 August that the Prime Minister was pressing the Cabinet for the immediate use of force, and that he had had to speak up on the 24th because Eden and Macmillan were 'trying to rush things through'. Monckton 'was not prepared to press the button now which made war inevitable', and refused to agree with their 'going in' if Nasser would not accept internationalization. Monckton spent the whole of Sunday with Macmillan 'being toughened up'. Clark also recorded that 'Duncan Sandys was belly-aching because he does not know military plans or the justification.'[17] Eden's authorized biographer states that the other members of the Cabinet 'tacitly accepted that these grave matters should be handled by the Prime Minister's inner team'. The archives do not support this view altogether.

On 26 August Eden sent a secret minute to the members of the Egypt Committee, pointing out the dangers attached to any reference to the United Nations, and suggesting raising the matter at NATO. 'There we are among friends . . . we have after all been urged many times to take Cyprus to NATO. Why not Suez which may be geographically more distant but is even more important to the survival of the majority of its members? Paris is anyway a better atmosphere than New York.'

In reply Salisbury expressed doubts, writing to Eden on 27 August:

> our main difficulties . . . arise from our undertakings as a member of the United Nations under the Charter. By my reading, the Charter says clearly, and again and again, that no member may embark on forceful action until he has referred his problem to the Security Council. I cannot feel that we can get out of that definite understanding . . . I may be wrong, but every time I come up against that snag. Cyprus is not a true analogy. For the issue over self determination did not involve the use of force.[18]

Salisbury was trying to put a brake on the Prime Minister's ardour for war. On 9 August he had written to Eden that if Nasser was

> to snap his fingers at the [London] Conference the nations represented there may be so incensed that it may become very easy for Great Britain and France with the overwhelming support of their peoples to employ force against him. . . . If we are likely unhappily to have to proceed to extremes a debate in Parliament is going to put us in an almost impossible position . . . it will surely be very difficult to maintain the position that Parliament has no right to be consulted at all . . . both in Korea and the two Great Wars we were involved in hostilities because of previous aggression by another nation, and if we proceed to force we must try and carry the bulk of public opinion with us, and at present I should doubt whether we have more than half the country behind us and the official Labour Party are steadily sliding away.[19]

The original Chiefs of Staff plan was for an assault at the northern end of the Canal and a threat to Alexandria, combined with a massive air bombardment to neutralize the Egyptian Air Force and to 'assure' that the landing did not encounter serious opposition. Macmillan was the most warlike member of the Cabinet. On 7 August, in a memorandum for the Egypt Committee, he advocated 'a different plan altogether the purpose of which would be to seek out and

destroy Nasser's armies and overthrow his Government. . . . Can
we not consider whether by pressing forward the Armoured Division
from Libya and by landing somewhere west of Alexandria we cannot
take Alexandria in reverse and seize the harbour facilities?' He also
suggested co-operation with Israel, so that Egypt would have to fight
on two fronts. Co-operation with Israel had been raised at a meeting of Treasury officials with Macmillan at 11 Downing Street on
3 August, when they discussed a paper by Jebb entitled *France and
the Middle East*. Then they agreed with Jebb that

> the primary object should be the early establishment of an acquiescent
> Government in Cairo, until which time military occupation of the
> whole of Egypt would be necessary. . . . The occupation of a limited
> zone in face of opposition from the Government in Cairo was impos-
> sible. It was unlikely that an Egyptian Government could be
> found capable of ruling Egypt which would acquiesce in the per-
> manent abrogation of Egyptian sovereignty in the Canal zone.

Significantly, this meeting recognized that 'it would probably be
difficult, perhaps impossible, to restrain the Israelis who could in any
case be expected to try to extract a price for meeting our wishes'. Jebb
had written in his memorandum that it was:

> important that we and the French (and the Americans) should agree
> to use our influence to keep Israel right out of the dispute. . . . We
> may later have to consider the possibility of the Israelis making
> threatening noises on the Egyptian frontier but we . . . should not
> mention it to the French for the present. . . . But if the general line to
> be adopted is a moderately tough one so far as the Israelis are
> concerned it might be advantageous if there were a leak.[20]

This suggestion was the germ of the plan of collusion with Israel
which had fatal attractions and disastrous consequences. Israeli
military help had more appeal for Macmillan than for Jebb or the
Treasury knights. This support for collusion with Israel finds no
place in the Macmillan memoirs, but his memorandum was considered by the Egypt Committee on 7 August. The 'collusion' plan
did not find favour with Eden, Lloyd or the majority of the Committee, but when Churchill saw Eden at Chequers on 6 August he
argued for inviting Israel to take part in a joint attack on Egypt,
admitting that he had been inspired by Macmillan.[21]

On 3 August Lloyd had told the Crown Prince of Iraq and Nuri
that they ought to spread word in the Middle East that 'Britain meant

business', and asked Nuri to use his influence with King Idris and Ben Halim, Prime Minister of Libya, to prevent them making difficulties. As the French were already encouraging the Israelis to attack Egypt, nothing could be more calculated to whet their appetite for an aggressive strike against Egypt in the Sinai desert than a leak that Britain meant business.[22]

Meanwhile a committee of top civil servants had been set up, known as the Official Committee. On 24 August they were told that the object of the military operations was to 'destroy' the Egyptian Army and bring down the Nasser Government, 'whereupon there were good reasons to believe that . . . a successor Government could be formed' which could produce order with the help of the police, and they were to work on the assumption that the 'successor' Egyptian Government would need political and material support rather than military. They invited the Foreign Office to discuss with the force commanders plans for military action against 'Nasser's agencies' in or near Cairo.

At this first meeting they decided that Civil Affairs 'detachments' would be formed; certain areas were to be allocated to the French, as they would participate in the Civil Government; however, at a second meeting it was decided that the Canal must not be run by the French because this would look like a 'return to the old order'. Instead it would be preferable for it to be run by the Royal Navy, because this would obviously be an 'interim' arrangement. The Foreign Office view expressed at the Committee was that since prospects of establishing an 'effective successor Government were reasonably good', comprehensive plans for full military government were not justified. Nevertheless the Treasury were instructed to compile lists of British people suitable for military government posts in Egypt. The Egyptian civil service had not been long disbanded, and some former members still in the prime of life hoped for a brief period that their interrupted careers in Egypt might be resumed. The minutes of the Official Committee show that they were thinking in terms of military government as in Italy and Germany during the Second World War.[23]

On 10 August the Chiefs of Staff had presented a revised paper to the Egypt Committee; they now took the Macmillan line and strongly recommended a full-scale assault on Alexandria after the destruction of the Egyptian Air Force. However, a warning from the British Ambassador in Tripoli that there would be violent reaction and that British forces would have to be used to restore order in the country 'if Libya was used as a springboard for British military operations against Egypt' ruled out the use of 10 Armoured Division as Macmillan had wanted. The French had offered to supply two divisions and one brigade for an operation to be called Musketeer, and a joint Anglo–French planning staff was set up despite grave misgivings about the risk of the French leaking information.

D-Day was to be 15 September; eighty thousand men would be involved; a pitched battle with the Egyptian Army was expected outside Cairo, and Cairo was to be occupied on D+8. Then the victorious army would depose the Nasser Government and set up a co-operative 'successor' Government. Because Menzies's negotiations were still in progress in Cairo there had been postponements of D-Day which the Chiefs of Staff emphasized posed grave problems for the Combined Air, Navy and Army Planning Staffs.

The plan to land at Alexandria remained in force until 7 September with continual postponements of D-Day. However the Chiefs of Staff had, much to the Prime Minister's displeasure, changed their minds; now they wanted to land at Port Said, mainly because of the risk that the Egyptians would find out about the alternative plan and deploy the bulk of the Egyptian Army around Alexandria to thwart a quick build-up of the landing troops. It was known that the French had been careless in their talk.

Accordingly, on the morning of 7 September the Chiefs of Staff went to Downing Street to discuss with Eden their new plans. They had sent him a memorandum stating that

> if D Day occurs up to 26 September we consider operation Musketeer has every chance of success. After 26 September the chances grow progressively worse, and we should almost certainly need to start the period of preliminary bombardment earlier than D–2. . . . We emphasise that in our view if D Day has to be postponed after 6 October Musketeer is not a sound operation of war.[24]

In favour of the new plan the Chiefs of Staff asserted categorically that it would cause far fewer casualties to the civilian population and less damage to civilian properties than an assault landing and subsequent operations through Egypt. They also said they had become

> increasingly concerned that [Musketeer] must inevitably result in great destruction and loss of life in built up areas particularly Alexandria and Cairo. There is no doubt that the new plan would greatly reduce loss of life and destruction other than to military targets . . . it avoids an initial assault on a heavily populated civilian town, and may allow the reoccupation of the Canal without the occupation of the rest of Egypt.

A new assessment of the implications of the Alexandria landing was produced for the Prime Minister, whose pencilled notes on his copy are evidence of his irritated reaction and reluctance to change course. Against the item that on D–14 a 'warning' must be issued to reduce to a minimum the number of ships in Egyptian ports and passing through the Canal he wrote: '*Mad!* What warning?'; against the reasons why no further postponement of D-Day was possible, he put a question mark and wrote 'When?'; he wrote in three places 'No' against the conclusions which stressed the difficulties of further postponements and that D–18 was the latest day 'upon which a decision to mount or dismount the operation can be made'.

Against a note by Keightley that it was 'of the greatest importance that this invasion of Egypt is launched with our moral case unassailable and the start of the war clearly and definitely Nasser's responsibility' he wrote, 'Yet he won't delay to strengthen it. AE.'; and against the comment that pro-Egypt propaganda 'must be counteracted' he wrote 'How?'; against 'the weather being unpredictable in the Mediterranean at this time of year,' he wrote: 'Not at all'; and against 'Egypt giving us a casus belli' he wrote: 'How?'[25]

Clearly Eden was angry because his military advisers wanted to reject the Alexandria Plan. The discussion at 10 Downing Street on the morning of 7 September between the Prime Minister and the Chiefs of Staff, General Keightley and General Stockwell, was acrimonious. Eden's authorized biographer recorded 'that against all his inclinations and experience and with great reluctant and unhappiness Eden felt he had to accept the military advice'. This is unfavourable to Eden, who was essentially a humane man, and the author is sure the cogent arguments about the lower loss of life likely in the Port Said operation carried great weight with him. Also the generals put it to him that 'the new plan is attractive in that it is flexible in its timing to the extent that the operation could start at fairly short notice and could be held ready without detriment . . . for the time being'. This 'flexibility' must have had attractions for Eden, as it gave more freedom for manoeuvre with the United Nations. The great advantage of the Alexandria operation for Eden was that Cairo would have been captured, so that Nasser could have been easily deposed. This was his first priority; even internationalization of the Canal was subsidiary to toppling Nasser. The Prime Minister also knew that the French would dislike the change of plan because they wanted desperately to occupy Cairo to stop Egyptian aid to the Algerian rebels.[26]

Even Churchill at the height of his authority during the Second

World War would have been reluctant to over-rule his military advisers when they pronounced a plan 'Not a sound operation of war', and on the afternoon of 7 September Eden reluctantly recommended the revised plan to the Egypt Committee, telling them that he had been gravely concerned about two points in the Alexandria Plan. The first was that 'it now seemed apparent that in the assault extensive devastation and loss of life would be inevitable'; the second point was perhaps even more serious. This was the lack of flexibility in the present plan. He stressed that in the new plan air bombardment would eliminate the Egyptian Air Force, destroy the Egyptian oil supplies and so damage the Egyptian Army that when the landings were made there would be little or no opposition to them. His statement to the Egypt Committee reinforces my view that he agreed to the plan primarily to avoid loss of life. After all, Alexandria had a large international community, and widespread destruction there from the preliminary bombardment would have caused dismay and disapproval around the world. The new plan was approved by the Egypt Committee and by the Cabinet, and christened Musketeer Revise.[27] The code name Musketeer was not dropped altogether because the Chiefs of Staff wanted to keep it as a cover for the Port Said operation. They believed that, through the French indiscretion, the Egyptians thought that Musketeer referred to Alexandria.

Shortly before Musketeer Revise was presented to the Egypt Committee Field Marshal Montgomery told Winston Churchill, who was about to see the Prime Minister, that he proposed landing at Mersa Matruh and an advance on and capture of Cairo. He also made disparaging remarks about General Keightley, commander of the force. Anthony Head, Secretary of State for War, wrote to Eden: 'We should avoid entangling ourselves by fighting in and the subsequent occupation of Cairo', and said that he and the Chiefs of Staff had complete confidence in Keightley – Keightley was 'a fine commander'. Perhaps Monty had visions of being recalled to lead the invasion. After all, it was only eleven years since his western European triumphs.[28]

Having achieved Nasser's point blank refusal to accept the proposals of the eighteen nations on 9 September, Eden still had to get the United Nations out of the way before he could ask Parliament to approve the use of force. On 11 September the full Cabinet was told that the Egyptian Government had 'flatly rejected' the eighteen nations' proposals, and that the Prime Minister had been discussing the situation with the Governments of France and the United States.

Eden was anxious to bring the dispute to a head because he was being criticized both by the hawks for not taking rapid military action, and by the doves on account of his preparations for war.

Eden was maddened when Dulles put to Makins on 4 September brand-new proposals for a Suez Canal Users' Association (SCUA), under which the users would employ their own pilots and pay Canal dues to the new Association, out of which Egypt would receive 'a fair share'. Dulles had rightly anticipated the failure of the Menzies mission. After initial hesitation Eden became partially converted to the SCUA plan, and despite his desire to solve the crisis by early military action was attracted temporarily by this possible peaceful solution which might be seen by the world as a climb-down by Nasser.

At the 11 September Cabinet meeting Macmillan, still the leading hawk, pointed out that the establishment of SCUA ought to be only a step towards the ultimate use of force; it should, however, serve to bring the issue to a head. He also gave a dire warning that, if a settlement was long delayed, 'the cost and uncertainty would under-mine our financial position'. He had just been given a report by Bridges containing a top-level Treasury warning that the £ would be in danger if military action was taken against Egypt without US and Commonwealth support. On Bridges's report Macmillan wrote: 'Yes, this is just the trouble. U.S. are being very difficult. H.M.' But it did not diminish his enthusiasm for force, nor cause him to take precautionary measures to defend the £.

At this Cabinet Monckton argued against force even if SCUA failed, but Kilmuir and Salisbury thought that, if Nasser would not accept SCUA, 'force' would not be 'inconsistent' with the United Nations Charter. The Cabinet gave Eden, as he wanted, an over-whelming mandate for a military attack on Egypt if SCUA failed.[29]

10

Diplomatic Solution, UN
October 1956

EDEN LIKED THE suggestion that Canal tolls should be paid to SCUA and not to Nasser, and that SCUA would decide the ratio to be paid to Egypt. This, he felt, would be more of an affront to Nasser's dignity than the eighteen powers' proposals, and with Dulles playing a leading role in this new 'international authority' Eden hoped that, if Nasser refused to co-operate, the Americans would join in fierce economic sanctions against Egypt or even agree to force being used by Britain and France. But the French Government was dismayed: Mollet and Pineau looked on SCUA as a device to postpone the war. Meanwhile Nasser debunked the SCUA proposal, replying to Dulles: 'It is impossible to have two bodies to regulate navigation through the Canal' and compared it to 'a Port of London Users' Association' which would operate the port and 'pay the British whatever it thought was a fair share of the port charges'.[1] Eisenhower had written to Eden: 'I must tell you frankly that American public opinion flatly rejects the thought of using force', and urged him to agree to SCUA. Rather reluctantly Eden decided to sponsor SCUA in the two-day debate in the Commons on 11 and 12 September.

Opening, Eden stated that appeal to the UN would be deferred until SCUA had been explored, but that in the event of interference with SCUA by Egypt 'Her Majesty's Government and others concerned will be free to take such further steps as seem to be required.'

Unfortunately Eisenhower did not see eye to eye with Dulles on SCUA, and at a press conference disassociated the USA from the aspects of the plan which appealed to Eden. Then between the first and second days of the debate Dulles held a press conference and said that, if opposed, 'American ships would not, repeat not, shoot their way through the Canal. No! they would go round the Cape.' The timing of Dulles's press conference enabled Gaitskell on the second day of the debate to force Eden to answer whether 'Britain would shoot their way through the Canal'. Eden replied evasively that if SCUA was rejected he would go to the Security Council. His statement, made off the cuff, was ambiguous, and was severely criticized. Eden was angry with Dulles because he felt Nasser would cock a snook at SCUA now that he was sure America would not use force.[2]

The eighteen nations reassembled at Lancaster House on 19 September, and Dulles came to London again. Most nations had realized that SCUA was either a pretext for using force or a plan for boycotting the Canal, and as none of them wanted to go round the Cape there was no enthusiasm. Three days before, Nasser had stated: 'We shall not allow the Western-proposed Canal Users Association to function. We Egyptians shall run the Canal smoothly and efficiently.' Although the outlook for SCUA was dim, Dulles still did not want the matter referred to the UN. Eden was itching to get the UN out of the way so that he could fix D-Day for his war, and minuted to Lloyd two days after the Conference had started: 'I have been thinking over the question of the UN. I agree strongly with you that it must be called together early next week even if only for a preliminary meeting. Otherwise we shall appear to drift – and in fact be drifting.'

The same day Lloyd spoke to Dulles, who thought ten days should be allowed for the eighteen countries to decide to join SCUA; he was afraid that if action was taken before then some of the eighteen nations would wait to see what happened at the UN before adhering to SCUA. Dullies then became 'evasive' about the UN.

By now Dulles and Eden were on bad terms again, and another misunderstanding arose. Eden, Dulles and Lloyd dined together on Thursday, 20 September, and Dulles later claimed that the Prime Minister had told him that 'he was in no hurry to go to the UN'. Eden denied this. On the Friday at lunch several representatives of the eighteen nations told Eden and Lloyd that to go to the UN would help them to join SCUA. The French also urged the British to go.[3]

The Conference results were disappointing so far, and Eden had become impatient for the Canal to be debated in the Security Council. On 22 September Lloyd sent an urgent message to Dulles, now back in Washington, that the British Government had 'come to the conclusion that she must take urgent action to get the Suez problem inscribed on the Agenda of the Security Council' and that he would attend a UN meeting on 2 October in New York. The reasons given were that the Russians were contemplating a similar move and 'we cannot accept the diplomatic defeat which would be involved if we were taken to the Council as defendants if opinion was disturbed as result of Conference . . . we must dispel appearance of indecisiveness about reference to UN'. Dulles was furious. He felt Eden had gone to the Security Council behind his back and suspected it would be a prelude to invasion. Eden now studiously avoided giving Dulles any assurance that he would not start a war. Makins reported that 'the incident upset Dulles more than we suppose or perhaps than he himself realises'.

Macmillan was in Washington, and on 23 September Eden cabled to him: 'It was impossible to hold our approach to the United Nations any longer. The Security Council will not in any event function effectively on it for another ten days and that can hardly be called precipitate. You will recall that we have prepared the way with the French for this approach . . . and there is no reason for Dulles to be surprised about this.' But Dulles was surprised as well as angry. Macmillan saw Eisenhower early on 25 September and had a friendly talk. Macmillan wrote: 'Ike is really determined somehow or another to bring Nasser down. I explained to him our economic difficulties in playing the hand long, and he seems to understand. I also made it clear that we *must* win . . . or the whole structure of our economy would collapse. He accepted this.' But at that time Eisenhower was 100 per cent opposed to Britain making war on Egypt and Macmillan had grossly misread the President's attitude. Later on the same day Macmillan saw Dulles. He sent an account of their talk to Eden, writing: 'Since it is so private I hope you will keep it to yourself or show it only to Selwyn.' First Dulles made a scene in front of Macmillan and the British Ambassador about Britain going to the Security Council without securing his approval, but once Dulles was alone with Macmillan he became genial. Here is Macmillan's note of their *à deux* conversation marked 'Top Secret'.

> After the general conversation at which the Ambassador was present and Mr. Dulles was surrounded by his advisers, he took me into his small private room which he keeps for special interviews. We were alone.
>
> 1. He began by excusing his outburst of indignation. He thought perhaps he ought not to have said so much in front of the others. But he really felt that he had been very badly treated. If H.M.G. had not decided to go to the United Nations (which he understood was the case when he left last Friday) and if they wanted to reverse their decision, they might at least have waited until he arrived back in Washington. He said that the last thing the Prime Minister had said to him at dinner on Friday [actually Thursday] was that he agreed with

his [Dulles's] view that we had better keep away from the United Nations a bit longer. However, he said that, although he was hurt, he understood the pressure under which we all worked and that he would put the matter out of his mind. It is no good jobbing backwards, he said, and we must now make the best of it and get out of this United Nations trouble the best way we could.

2. He went on to talk about different methods of getting rid of Nasser. He thought that these new plans might prove successful. But of course they would take six months. I said that I did not think we could stand for six months, unless, of course, Nasser was losing face all the time. But our information from the Middle East was that he was not doing so. (I had just read the telegram from Michael Wright in Baghdad to this effect.)

3. Dulles then observed that he quite realised that we might have to act by force. Indeed, in his broadcast on his return he had made that clear. He thought that our threat of force was vital, whether we used it or not, to keep Nasser worried. He also thought that the idea of sending ships round the Cape ought to be kept alive, although he understood how difficult it was for us from an economic point of view. But it might be used to frighten the Arab States, who would see the disappearance of their royalties. He thought even a little well-advertised additional sale from Venezuela might be worth doing purely from this point of view. I said that I thought that might be considered among the various points which our special experts were to discuss with his next week.

4. Dulles said that at present Suez was not playing much part in the election. The Republicans did not understand it, and the Democrats were frightened of it. But if anything happened it might have a disastrous effect. He reminded me of how he and the President had helped us in May 1955 by agreeing to the Four-Power meeting at top level, which had undoubtedly been of great benefit to us in our electoral troubles. Could we not do something in return and try and hold things off until after November 6th?[4]

Surely this should have been the red light for Eden not to attack Egypt until Eisenhower had been safely re-elected. But the Prime Minister ignored it.

Having made their decision to take Suez to the United Nations, Eden and Lloyd went off to Paris on 27 September to talk to Mollet and Pineau about plans for war against Egypt. Eden reported that the discussions were 'very difficult'. Pineau was particularly suspicious, and both he and Mollet 'were anxious to know that our policy was unchanged', which Eden assured them it was. Obviously the French feared that the Eden Government had got cold feet about attacking Egypt. However, Lloyd explained first that some negotiations at the

United Nations were inevitable. The French received this 'with concern' and maintained that the only possible basis of negotiation was the eighteen-power proposals, and the British politicians had difficulty in persuading the French not to vote against the inscription of the British motion on Egypt on the Security Council Agenda. The French stated that 'continuous reinforcements in tanks and aircraft were arriving in Egypt from Russia, and every week that action was delayed made the military situation more dangerous for us'. Eden felt that Mollet would like a settlement on reasonable terms if he could, but that Pineau wanted no settlement at all. Clearly the French were pushing Eden towards war, and he was holding back in the hope that the SCUA negotiations might produce the type of settlement he wanted – one which would do great damage to Nasser's prestige. The French, preoccupied with the running sore of the Algerian rebellion, were desperately anxious to launch an immediate invasion of Egypt, and had already entered into military conversations about a combined attack with the Israelis. The French, Eden remarked, and particularly M. Pineau, 'are in the mood to blame everyone, including us, if military action is not taken before the end of October'. They alleged that the weather would preclude a later attack, which Eden contested.[5]

Eden sent a report from Paris to Butler, who had been left in charge in London. In a handwritten letter Butler welcomed 'Anthony' home and, hoping he would go to Broadchalke for a holiday, said 'I don't think that the French action is altogether unexpected.' Butler, like Eden and Lloyd, was ready for war unless the United Nations could make Nasser capitulate.

Lloyd arrived in New York on Tuesday, 2 October, for the Security Council debate. On the same day Dulles said at a press conference: 'The United States cannot be expected to identify herself 100% either with the colonial powers or the powers uniquely concerned with the problem of getting independence as rapidly and as fully as possible'; of SCUA he said 'there is talk about teeth being pulled out of the plan, but I know of no teeth; there were no teeth in it so far as I am aware'. Selwyn Lloyd admitted in his memoirs that this made him feel 'very bitter'. Makins reported that ' "the fearful gaffe" by Dulles about colonialism was a subconscious reaction to his irritation about the UK going to the UN without his knowledge'.[6]

The British aim, agreed between Eden and Lloyd, was a peaceful settlement provided it came quickly, but they were adamant they would not agree to long drawn-out debates on the setting up of a negotiating committee nor have their hands tied by a Resolution forbidding the use of force. Eden, more than Lloyd, looked on the appeal to the Security Council as an operation to be carried out in order 'to clear the decks for action' (Lloyd's words), which was also, the strongly held French view.

Not much was achieved by the formal UN debates, but, behind the scenes, realistic bargaining took place between Lloyd and Fawzi, the Egyptian Foreign Minister; this was much helped by Hammarskjold, the Secretary General of the UN. In his memoirs Lloyd claims that these negotiations did not come close to success. He had a vested interest in establishing their failure, while Nutting had a vested interest in claiming they were close to success. The archives support Nutting, not Lloyd, and also contain strong evidence that in the first half of October Eden was ready for a negotiated settlement until he suddenly became attracted to a plan for collusion between France, Britain and Israel in a war against Egypt.

On Friday, 5 October, Pineau, Dulles and Lloyd met privately; Dulles reiterated America's objection to the use of force. Lloyd replied frankly that recourse to the UN was a condition precedent to the use of force as far as Britain was concerned. The meeting was friendly, although the next day the press was full of accounts of disagreements between the British and French on one hand, and Dulles on the other.[7]

Eden replied to Lloyd's telegram giving an account of the 5 October meeting: 'We must never forget that Dulles' purpose is different from ours. The Canal is in no sense vital to the United States and his game is to string us along at least until polling day. I am very glad that you and Pineau spoke so strongly to him. You must keep it up.' Polling day was only four and a half weeks away, but this was too far away for Eden, who had become more belligerent again. The next day Eden, now recovered from a knock-out sudden fever, told Lloyd:

There is a report by Slade Baker in the *Sunday Times* of absolute Egyptian confidence that the Suez crisis, in his words, is 'burnt out.' I suspect that he is right that they feel that way and that Nasser won't make any worth while contribution. On the other hand the Egyptians are very clever at dressing up minor concessions to look like reasonable propositions.

This report re-inforces my own belief that in the last resort action will be necessary. It is therefore very important that while appearing reasonable, we should not be inveigled away, in negotiation from the fundamentals to which we have held all along, and that we should not be parted from the French. I am sure you will agree with all this.

The temperature is normal today and I send you best wishes.[8]

The Prime Minister sent another telegram to Lloyd on 8 October:

When I read the record of your conversation with Dulles and Pineau on 5 October it made me fear more than ever that our position is being eroded. I am glad that throughout you have left Dulles in no doubt of the strength of our feelings and our determination, and that this seems to have made some impression. We have been misled so often by Dulles' ideas that we cannot afford to risk another misunderstanding. . . . Time is not on our side in this matter. I am glad you are standing firmly with the French and stiffening Dulles. That is the only way to a solution.

Lloyd took pains not to meet Fawzi without Pineau, and at first Pineau was obstructive. Almost certainly Pineau was under orders from Mollet to make sure there was a 'break' instead of agreement, so that an early Franco–Israeli assault could be made on Egypt regardless of Britain. Egyptian support for the Algerian rebels was a key factor with the French. Lloyd described Pineau's attitude to Eden:

During the Security Council meetings in New York this month, Pineau behaved in a rather extraordinary manner. In the first three days of the private talks he appeared utterly unreasonable. He came late, went early, made difficulties about long meetings and spent considerable time at the beginning of some of the meetings, arguing about some obviously false point. On the last day of the private talks he suddenly changed and said that he thought the talks were most useful and ought to be resumed. This was a *volte face* with a vengeance. I was left however with the impression that it would be extraordinarily difficult to reach agreement with the French upon a solution of the Canal problem.

Dulles was not unco-operative, although he seemed slightly annoyed that we took the lead in suggesting procedures, etc. I tried to keep him informed about the course of the private talks. He was quite affable in private, although I gather that he had become very angry that we had taken the matter to the Security Council without his permission.[9]

It looks as if Pineau became more or less converted to a peaceful solution during the five days of meetings between Pineau, Lloyd, Fawzi and Hammarskjold, which brought the crisis to the brink of solution. Fawzi was reasonable, and there can be little doubt that he had Nasser's authority for all his offers. By now Nasser was alarmed at Franco–British preparations for invasion, and he did not want to be drawn any further into the Russian camp.

Trevelyan reported from Cairo on 18 October that the situation had 'perhaps somewhat improved from our point of view because inter alia of Nasser's realization of financial difficulties ahead, and the deterioration in the Israeli situation which showed up Nasser's inability to take a major share in Arab defence against Israel during his preoccupation with the Canal'. He also reported that the Egyptian press, which was under Nasser's control, was coming out in favour of a negotiated settlement. On this telegram Eden wrote: 'Too little yet. A. E.'[10]

On 9 October, after the Assembly debate, Hammarskjold invited Pineau, Lloyd and Fawzi to his room for a private talk. Lloyd got the impression that Fawzi 'wanted an agreement'. Fawzi said he was prepared for negotiations on the basis of setting aside a proportion of the revenues of the Canal for its development (in other words they would not all go towards the Aswan Dam) and would enter into an agreement about 'tolls for a number of years'; Egypt was prepared to recognize the Users' Association. Lloyd asked on what basis, and said that Britain could not possibly agree to, for example, Albania and the Yemen having equal voting rights with France and Britain. Fawzi replied that Egypt would recognize an association 'formed on the basis of responsibility . . . it would be difficult to prevent Russia and India becoming members, but in principle Egypt did not object to the Users being responsible for the constitution of their own Association.'

Fawzi went on: 'as a compromise between international and national operation they would accept a system of combined meetings of the Egyptian Board and the Users Association to discuss the operation of the Canal. If there was a disagreement he would not object to arbitration.' Over payment of the dues, Fawzi did not think there would be any objection to the dues for the ships of the Users' Association being paid to the Association (in the first instance, with a proportion being passed on to the Egyptian Board). Lloyd stated that no agreement was possible which 'did not clear up' the question of Israel using the Canal. To this key question at the first meeting Fawzi gave no reply.[11] Here was more than the germ of a settlement. Lloyd's report was considered at the meeting of the Egypt Committee on 10 October. Eden said he was surprised that Egypt 'appeared to be prepared to accept that transit dues should be paid to the Users Association'.

In discussion it was suggested that Egypt would expect most, if not all, of the Canal dues collected to be paid over to them, and the Committee thought 'withholding of payments to Egypt could be used as a sanction', and decisions to withhold the payment of dues to

Egypt should be taken by a majority of votes of members of the Association. The Committee decided that Lloyd should be asked 'to seek urgently' Dulles's support for an arrangement on these lines, emphasizing that there must be some sanction against Egyptian discrimination against the ships of any particular country, and that any agreement with Egypt must specifically cover the free use of the Suez Canal by Israeli ships.[12]

Eden, Monckton and Harold Watkinson, Minister of Transport, next day held a Ministers' meeting at which they were even more optimistic about a negotiated settlement. They had before them a further telegram from Lloyd, showing that Fawzi was being amenable as he had agreed that the Users' Association should have complete access to the books of the Users' Board, and the system should be described as 'one of co-operation between the Canal Authority and the Users'. He also promised to give an answer the next day to the question of what percentage of the dues should be paid to the Egyptian authority, and confirmed that Egypt would pay fair compensation to the old Canal Authority. The Prime Minister commented that the main defect in all the proposals put forward so far by the Egyptian Foreign Minister was the absence of any sanction against major infractions, meaning the principle of free navigation and in particular Israeli use of the Canal. The meeting considered that probably 75 per cent of the transit dues would be controlled by the Association (for instance only non-members would pay their dues to the Egyptian authority direct). This discussion makes it clear that at this moment Eden looked forward to a diplomatic solution. He enjoyed diplomacy, and this was a ploy after his own heart which he thought he could turn to Nasser's disadvantage. The record of the meeting states:

> The Meeting then discussed whether an arrangement on the lines now proposed was consistent with the principles originally put forward in the eighteen-power proposals. It was suggested that the present proposals would at least provide a system of international co-operation with a considerable measure of financial control. Moreover, the consortium of the Users' Association and the Egyptian Board to some extent satisfied the requirement for an international authority postulated in the eighteen-power proposals. The financial control that would be exercised by the Users' Association would also be a valuable psychological weapon, since Colonel Nasser could no longer claim that his action had given Egypt unfettered control over the revenues of the Canal.
>
> The major outstanding problem was to devise an effective sanction

for any breach of the principles of free navigation. As previously suggested the most effective sanction would be to provide in the new agreement that any infringement of the basic principles of the Convention was deemed to constitute an act of aggression which justified the injured country in taking action to protect its interests. This provision would be linked to an appropriate Article in the United Nations Charter.

Another indication that Eden felt the closeness of a diplomatic solution is the fact that he gave instructions for a telegram to Lloyd to state that 'provided the present pressure was maintained on the Egyptian representative in these negotiations, he should not feel himself bound to terminate the discussions by the end of this week if at the time it appeared that a satisfactory agreement would shortly be obtained'. In the telegram sent on 11 October Eden also told Lloyd: 'You seem now to have some hope of securing our first sanction, the payment of dues through SCUA. That would be something in the bag. . . . Keep up all possible pressure on Fawzi. If he will not meet us, I agree there is nothing for it but a break.' At this stage the Americans thought that an administrator for SCUA was essential. The Official Committee had in mind Overauer, a Dutchman, who according to the British civil servants would be acceptable to Egypt and ready to take on the task. In London the six countries engaged in the SCUA discussions were ready to agree to Overauer.

Lloyd's next telegram from New York said that the discussion in the afternoon of 11 October was much better than that in the morning. Fawzi said the Egyptians were working on a paper on 'recourse', which meant the procedure in case of disagreement. Fawzi agreed that the Egyptian Government accepted the principle of free transit without discrimination (for instance Israel could use the Canal); they wanted an international content in the Egyptian Board provided by the United Nations, and to insulate the Board from Egyptian politics he had in mind something like the Tennessee Valley Authority; if the members of the Users' Association wanted to pay dues through the Association, that was 'not the business of the Egyptian Government'. Lloyd told Fawzi that he assumed he, Fawzi, had authority from his Government for this answer. At the next day's meeting Pineau said there would be discussion in the French Parliament during the next week, and he thought negotiations should be resumed in two or three weeks' time at some convenient place in Europe. Lloyd then produced a list of six principles:

1. That there should be free and open transit through the Canal without discrimination, overt or covert;
2. That there should be respect for Egyptian sovereignty;
3. That the operation of the Canal should be insulated from the politics of any country;
4. That the level of dues should be fixed by agreement between users and owners;
5. That a fair proportion of the dues should be allotted to development;
6. That affairs between the Suez Canal Company and the Egyptian Government should be settled by arbitration, with suitable terms of reference and suitable provision for the payment of the sums found to be due.

The next morning, 12 October, Fawzi accepted Lloyd's six principles, and at a private session of the Security Council Hammarskjold informed the Council of the progress made by agreement on the six principles. Eisenhower seized on this good news by telling a press conference: 'The progress made in the settlement of the Suez dispute this afternoon at the United Nations is most gratifying. Egypt, France and Britain have met through their Foreign Ministers and agreed on a set of principles on which to negotiate, and it looks like here is a very great crisis that is behind us.'

In the public session of the Council during the evening of 12 October Lloyd submitted new British proposals embodying the six principles; Pineau had said that the six principles were all right, but the three of them had been unable to agree on a coherent system to carry them out. The first part of the British resolution was carried unanimously, but the second part, calling on Egypt to propose a system to carry out the six principles, was vetoed by Russia after 9 votes to 2 had been cast in favour; this second part contended that Egypt 'had not yet formulated sufficiently precise proposals' and wanted Egypt to repair this omission.

On 13 October Lloyd cabled to the Prime Minister:

At this afternoon's session of the Security Council the Secretary General announced the six principles on which agreement had been reached in our private talks. In my speech I warned . . . against exaggerated optimism and said there were wide gaps between Egypt and ourselves. I believe that the six principles are quite good, particularly the third. . . . I think that that can fairly be claimed as a substantial victory for us.

On 14 October the Prime Minister replied to Lloyd: 'The resolution came in during the night. It seems fully to meet the points we wanted to make. Well done. The vote as heard on the wireless also seems excellent.[14]

Here is *prima facie* evidence that, when these telegrams were dispatched, both Lloyd and Eden envisaged a negotiated solution to the dispute with Nasser. Further evidence of the bona fides of the Egyptian concessions came in a cabled report from Lloyd that Fawzi had conferred with Black on two occasions, on 10 and 15 October, about how the World Bank could help to finance the Aswan Dam and the improvements to the Canal which were beyond Egypt's capacity, even with Canal resources.[15]

When the civil servants discussed the progress of the Lloyd talks at the meeting of the Official Committee on 12 October they were favourably impressed, recording that

> what has been discussed in New York falls short of 'International Management' but recognition by Egypt of the Users Association and the right of that Association to collect dues from the shipping of member countries and to make appropriate payments to Egypt linked with the principle of unrestricted passage through the Canal should serve to limit the authority of the Egyptian Board of Management. . . . Furthermore if one could have the sanctions both of withholding payment to Egypt and a provision that any interference with the fundamental rights of passage through the Canal should be regarded as a threat to peace the settlement could be represented as going a good way towards unfettering the control of the Canal by a single Government and as a considerable advance upon anything thought attainable following the ending of Suez Canal's concession in 1968.

One can imagine how shocked these civil servants were when their masters threw away these promising negotiations in favour of war within a week.[16]

Nutting went through in detail with the author the telegrams from the Prime Minister to Lloyd and the Foreign Secretary's replies, together with Eden's scrawled notes on the incoming telegrams. As Minister of State Nutting had drafted some of Eden's replies, and he feels strongly that these telegrams are convincing documentary evidence that between 11 and 13 October, perhaps only for a few hours, Eden had been persuaded that he must accept a diplomatic solution, which was rapidly becoming available as the Egyptians made concessions. In Nutting's view Eden realized that his hopes for a military conclusion were slipping away, and he did not have the *casus belli* which he wanted – namely that he could say to the world: 'The Egyptians are impossible; we cannot get them to enter into

negotiations.' By 11 October Eden, who always enjoyed diplomatic
negotiation, began to be convinced that the possibility of his military
triumph to topple Nasser had receded now that the crisis had got into
the UN and Hammarskjold had got into the act. Nutting felt strongly
that for this brief period Eden felt he could not ignore the Egyptian
concessions.

Nutting is also sure that Lloyd's instincts were for a diplomatic
settlement, although he recalled that Lloyd said to him he was
not sure that it would 'hold'. Nutting said he replied it would 'hold'
because it meant Nasser would get far more money for the Canal dues
than he had got from the Company previously.[17]

A meeting under UN auspices at Geneva was suggested by
Hammarskjold for 29 October, and agreed by Lloyd and Pineau. It
was hoped that this would produce a Treaty by which the six
principles would be implemented. Nutting was the Foreign Office
spokesman in London, and he followed the negotiations closely and
discussed them with Eden. In his book on Suez Nutting wrote:

> Lloyd gladly accepted these major concessions from Fawzi although
> he feared they would come as a most unwelcome development to his
> chief . . . a negotiated settlement was now in sight which conceded
> Egypt's sovereignty over the Canal in return for protection for the
> users' interests . . . the Eighteen-Power proposals, on which we had
> insisted ever since the Menzies mission went to Cairo, had been
> superseded by an arrangement based on Dulles' concept of a Users
> Club.[18]

Eden was angry at Eisenhower's press statement, telling Lloyd 'I
am glad that you spoke to Dulles as you did about the President's
deplorable statement.' But his final telegram to Lloyd, cleared on the
morning of Sunday, 14 October, is further strong evidence that he
expected a successful conclusion to Lloyd's negotiations:

> I think it important that we and the French should decide our joint
> position and next moves without delay. You have got majority vote at
> the Council for the Eighteen-Power proposals or their equivalent.
> Should not we and the French now approach the Egyptians and ask
> them whether they are prepared to meet and discuss in confidence
> with us on the basis of the second half of the resolution which the
> Russians vetoed? If they say yes, then it is for consideration whether
> we and the French meet them somewhere, e.g. Geneva. If they say
> no, then they will be in defiance of the view of nine members of the
> Security Council and a new situation will arise.[19]

Nutting told the author that he drafted this telegram, and Eden only put on the finishing touches. Lloyd's reply, sent immediately after receipt of the Prime Minister's telegram, shows that he was proud of what he had achieved so far:

> . . . negotiations were in the air from the moment we got here. Unless we had quickly demonstrated our intention to have genuine discussions in some form I am sure matters would have gone badly for us . . . we have changed the United Nations atmosphere towards Britain and France. The suspicion that we were treating the United Nations simply as a formality has been dissipated . . . we emerge without any resolution enjoining us against force or to set up a negotiating committee . . . with the changed atmosphere here we can count on a more understanding reaction if we have to take extreme measures.

On the debit side he considered 'We are now committed to further interchanges with the Egyptians without a time limit, and . . . the Egyptians will now feel that the critical phase is past and that they are no longer in danger of armed attack'; he also feared the limited progress would encourage 'over optimism – the extraordinarily naïve statement by President Eisenhower is the clearest example of this'.[20]

By the time Lloyd's reply was received in the Foreign Office in the early hours of Monday, 15 October Eden was no longer interested in negotiation. He had changed course again and plumped for war at the earliest possible moment.

11

Collusion, Indecision and War
October–November 1956

ON SATURDAY, 13 October, Eden spoke to the Conservative Conference at Llandudno. The world press that morning had given great publicity to reports from New York that Fawzi was moving towards the Anglo–French position, and that an agreement was probable. In his speech Eden warned against 'hasty or over optimism'. He included the words that Britain would continue its military measures in the Eastern Mediterranean, and added: 'We have always said that with us force is the last resort, but it cannot be excluded' and that Britain had refused to say that 'in no circumstances would we ever use force'. Eden received tremendous applause, especially for the passages about force. Even the Suez Group were enthusiastic for the Prime Minister. It was a strong speech and hailed as such by the press, which was immensely welcome to Eden because he had been plagued throughout 1956 by press comment about his weakness and indecision. He tended to over-react to press comment and his press secretary, William Clark, wrote: 'Eden's indecisiveness, and equally important his anxiety about being thought indecisive, was a psychological trait.'[1] By-elections had been going badly for the Conservatives. In Hereford in February the Liberals had come near to winning the seat, having done little for years, and in June in the safe seat of Tonbridge the Conservative majority fell from 10,200 to 1200. Eden's speech brought a bitter complaint from Fawzi to the Security Council, which echoed around the world, but the applause of the Conference and the British press was manna to the Prime Minister at a time when his and the Conservative Party's fortunes were low.

From Llandudno Eden went to Chequers for the weekend. On the morning of the 13th Jebb had sent an urgent message to the Foreign Office that Mollet wanted Albert Gazier, acting Foreign Minister in Pineau's absence, and General Maurice Challe, Deputy Chief of the

French Air Force, to see the Prime Minister with a message of great importance. Jebb also informed the Foreign Office that France had delivered seventy-five French Mystère fighter aircraft to Israel, which was a strong indication that France was plotting an attack on Egypt with Israel. Nutting telephoned the news to Eden, who agreed to meet Challe and Gazier with Nutting on Sunday afternoon (14 October) at Chequers.

When the discussion started, Gazier asked Eden what Britain would do if Israel attacked Egypt. Eden replied that Britain had no obligation to stop such an attack. Challe then asked Eden to stop his secretary (Millard) making notes, and outlined a plan of war by which Britain and France should occupy the Suez Canal. The French suggested that Israel should be invited to invade Egypt across the Sinai peninsula, with a promise that if they did so Britain and France would order both Israel and Egypt to withdraw their troops from the Suez Canal; an Anglo–French force would separate the combatants and occupy the Canal on the nominal grounds that they were saving it from the damage which must be caused by fighting.[2]

This plan had great attractions for Eden, because it meant that the British and French would occupy both Canal terminals and could thus operate it regardless of Nasser. The French disclosed, as Eden already knew, that they had had preliminary discussions with the Israelis. In fact Franco–Israeli military talks had been held in Paris from 29 September to 1 October. Nutting recalled that Eden became very excited, and it is clear he made a spontaneous decision to settle the crisis by war, not diplomacy.

Eden promised to consult his colleagues and give the French his reply on Tuesday, 16 October. Nutting objected vigorously, but Eden refused to listen to his arguments. According to Nutting, from then on Eden was determined to topple Nasser and seize the Suez Canal in alliance with the French and the Israelis. Within a few minutes of the French leaving Chequers Eden telephoned Lloyd in New York and ordered him to come back to London immediately. Lloyd demurred. He had engagements in New York which included a particularly important appointment with Hammarskjold to discuss arrangements for the proposed conference with the Egyptians in Geneva on 29 October. However he complied, and arrived in London on Tuesday morning, 16 October.

Nutting told the author that he remembers well the meeting of the Egypt Committee which took place at 10 Downing Street that morning. No record exists in the archives, and Eden must have ordered Brook to expunge the minutes because the files show that

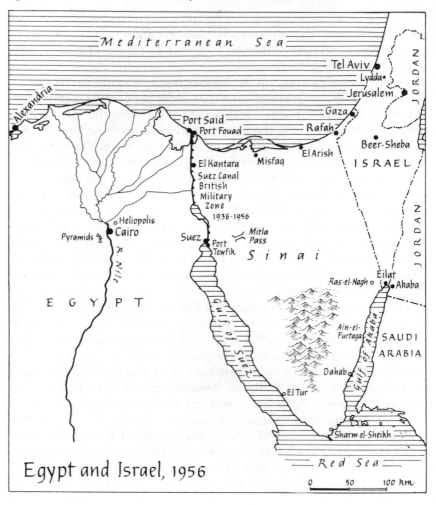

Egypt and Israel, 1956

the thirty-third meeting of the Egypt Committee took place on 10 October and the thirty-fourth on Wednesday, 17 October. (No Cabinet meeting, either, is recorded as taking place between 9 and 18 October.)[3]

According to Nutting, on 16 October Butler was not present as he was conducting the Queen around the Calder Hall power station, but Head, Monckton, Thorneycroft and Kilmuir were there as well as himself. Eden explained the plan for collusion with the French and Israelis which had been discussed at Chequers on the previous Sunday. Nutting says once again he protested vigorously; Monckton also protested, but with less vehemence. The rest of the Committee agreed with the Prime Minister, who said he would now tell the French Government that the plan would go ahead. Earlier in the morning Eden had told Nutting that he was to take the British Government's reply to Paris that afternoon, but after the Egypt Committee was concluded and Lloyd had arrived at the Foreign Office from New York this was altered, because Lloyd told the Prime Minister he would prefer to go on to Paris that afternoon rather than on the next day. Eden then said he would accompany Lloyd to Paris at once; Nutting's services as courier were no longer required. Dixon in New York was told nothing of the Egypt Committee decision, which was communicated to as few people as possible. [4]

Nutting relates that he saw Lloyd as soon as the Foreign Secretary arrived in the Foreign Office on Tuesday morning, recited to him what had occurred at Chequers and 10 Downing Street, and emphasized how opposed he was to collusion with Israel. Nutting writes that Lloyd's reaction was: 'You are right; we must have nothing to do with the French plan.' If this is correct, Lloyd rapidly changed his mind after the Prime Minister had swept him off to Paris and in the plane apparently convinced his Foreign Secretary of the attractions of the French plan.

Eden and Mollet refused to allow the British Ambassador to be present at talks in Paris on 16 October. This was a grave breach of protocol. Jebb complained in a letter to Lloyd:

British Embassy, Paris.
October 17, 1956.

Personal and Confidential.

My dear Secretary of State,

I do not complain, but it is, I believe, a novel arrangement for diplomatic business of the highest importance to be conducted by the Principals without any official being present, even to take a note. I am sure that you feel this is a good method of proceeding, and anyhow it is for you to say. But however great the advantages of the new system, it has one very considerable disadvantage so far as your representative on the spot is concerned. This is that, although he has to live with one of the Principals and has to continue negotiations with him in the absence of his own Principal, he has no means, apart from a few remarks which the latter may let fall, of knowing what actually happened when the Principals met. This being so, the chances of his putting his foot in it or making some unnecessary mistake regarding the real intentions of his own Government are materially increased. There is also the possibility (I should have thought) of real misunderstandings arising if no detailed record (anyhow of the conclusions of conversations of such overriding importance) is made and distributed on both sides to a chosen few.

This letter therefore is to beg you to send me some such document for my information. If you do not want anybody else to see it this can of course be arranged.

> Yours ever,
> Gladwyn Jebb.

Lloyd did not know how to answer Jebb and asked Eden for advice. The Prime Minister replied on the 19th:

On Sir Gladwyn Jebb's letter I fear that you can only say firmly that (a) he knows the position about Iraq–Jordan–Israel because it is all in the telegrams; (b) he knows the position about Suez; (c) beyond this, by arrangement with the French, there is nothing which we can say. We are sorry.

If you like to add that I have seen your note and agree, I should have no objection.

In fact in the war it often happened that we had talks with no officials present, in Washington, London and Moscow.[5]

This was a lame excuse, because Britain was not at war.

On 16 October Lloyd dictated a memorandum about the Paris talks in which he said first that it would be possible to get some form of agreement on the lines of his and Pineau's discussions with Hammarskjold and Fawzi

i.e. on the basis not of international management, but of international control through restrictions on increases in tolls, a fixed percentage of the tolls to be allotted to development, and all differences of opinion with regard to management discrimination, etc. to be referred to an independent body for decision and appropriate means of enforcing decisions.

Mollet and Pineau both said that 'in their view such an agreement would be unsatisfactory'.

Pineau said that with the increasing flow of arms from the Soviet Union to Egypt 'he did not believe that Israel would tolerate the situation', and they would strike before much more Russian war material had been assimilated by the Egyptian forces. Mollet then asked what would happen if Israel attacked Egypt. Eden replied that he felt under no obligation to come to her defence, and 'Public opinion in Britain would be horrified if it was suggested to them that they should fight for Nasser against Israel.' Pineau said that that was very much their position. 'In view of the Egyptian behaviour over North Africa French public opinion would regard any government suggesting such a course as having taken leave of its senses.'

The four then discussed what would happen at the United Nations if Israel attacked Egypt, and they agreed it was unlikely that any action would be taken. Mollet asked Eden whether, if hostilities took place in the vicinity of the Canal, the UK Government would intervene to stop them. The Prime Minister 'thought' the answer was 'Yes'.

Lloyd's memorandum concluded that on the next day, 17 October, Eden's confirmation was sent to Mollet that if it appeared likely that 'hostilities were going to develop in the Canal area we considered that we might have to intervene in some manner to prevent that happening'. Lloyd's memorandum, initialled and dated 18 October, was not copied or circulated to any Cabinet Ministers or civil servants.[6]

At the 18 October Cabinet meeting Lloyd reported on UN proceedings in New York, and emphasized that he had contrived to avoid the appointment of any mediator or negotiating body or the tabling of any amendment which might limit 'our future freedom of action'. The Cabinet asked Lloyd to 'concert with the French Government the terms of a communication to the Egyptian Government inviting them to submit without delay their proposals for putting into effect the principles which had been unanimously approved by the Security Council'. As the Prime Minister was now intent on war and concerting military plans accordingly, this was shadow boxing.

The Prime Minister then reported on the Paris talks, but was far from frank, saying he had 'thought it right to make it known to the Israelis, through the French, that in the event of hostilities between Egypt and Israel the United Kingdom Government would not come to the assistance of Egypt because Egypt was in breach of a Security

Council resolution', and had added that Britain would assist Jordan if the Israelis attacked her. Eden said it would be 'far better from our point of view' that Israel should attack Egypt rather than Jordan, and the Cabinet should be aware that 'while we continued to seek an agreed settlement of the Suez dispute . . . it was possible that the issue might come to a head as a result of military action by Israel against Egypt'.[7]

Immediately he left the Cabinet Room Mountbatten, the First Sea Lord, signalled to the C-in-C Mediterranean, Durnford-Slater:

> As I see it, the real danger time is between now and the date of the American Election on about 6 November. The Jews may well think that now is their last chance to square matters up with the Arabs, and that they will confront everybody with a *fait accompli* before they are geared to do anything effective. Will you therefore unobtrusively bring your 'Cordage' forces to about 72 hours notice.[8]

Cordage was the Admiralty code name for an attack on Egypt.

Lloyd dictated a short report about the 18 October Cabinet. It differs both from the official Cabinet minutes and from his memoirs:

> I reported on the Security Council proceedings and expressed some of my doubts about the possibility of getting the Egyptians to put forward proposals which we would find tolerable. . . . Eden then raised the question of what we should do in those circumstances [an Israeli attack on Egypt], and said that it was his view that we must at all costs prevent fighting over the Canal, and damage to the Canal itself and shipping passing through it. He said that he had discussed this with his some of his senior colleagues and they had agreed to this view. No one in the Cabinet disagreed.[9]

Clearly no hint of 'collusion' was given to the Cabinet, nor of the existence of a definite plan to intervene with Anglo–French forces.

On 18 October Nasser issued a statement in Cairo that he was willing to go to Geneva to meet the Premiers of France and Britain if he thought it would achieve a settlement of the Suez dispute, and that the talks could take place the week after next. Nasser indicated that he would negotiate personally only with the Prime Ministers and not with Lloyd or Pineau, and stated that Egypt was prepared to present certain proposals on Canal tolls at the proposed meeting, but he firmly rejected dealing solely with the Canal Users' Association. He said: 'We are ready to co-operate with all users of the Canal not just those 18 Powers.' Here was a clear indication that Nasser wanted a settlement. It was the last thing the British and French wanted to hear. After a telephone conversation between Neil Cairncross, the Prime Minister's private secretary, and Eden, the Prime Minister ruled that no 'spontaneous statement' should be made in reply, and they would stand by their Paris communiqué of 16 October, which was that they resolved to adhere to the requirements of the Security Council Resolution, and noted with regret that these were already being questioned in certain Egyptian quarters.[10]

At the weekend Lloyd was summoned to Chequers and ordered, after a conference with Eden, Butler, Macmillan and Head, to go to Paris the next day, Monday, 22 October, travelling incognito to meet Ben Gurion and the Israeli leaders for a round table conference with the French to concert plans for a combined attack on Egypt. Lloyd, accompanied by his private secretary, Donald Logan, arrived at a villa in Sèvres at 4 p.m. after being nearly killed in a motor accident. Logan has recalled that they were received by Mollet and the French Minister of Defence, Maurice Bourges-Manoury, David Ben Gurion, General Moshe Dayan, Israeli Chief of Staff, and Shimon Peres, Minister of Defence.

Ben Gurion proposed 'a grand design' for the Middle East. Lloyd was not enthusiastic and stated curtly that all he had come to discuss was the action each of the three Governments might take if Israel attacked Egypt; he reminded the others that little more than a week before he had made progress towards a solution in talks with Fawzi and Hammarskjold, and that important sections of public opinion in Britain and the Commonwealth 'set much store by a peaceful solution'. Dayan thought Lloyd 'antagonistic', with his demeanour expressing distaste. Perhaps Lloyd disliked his task.[11]

However, more to the taste of the Israelis and French, Lloyd added that there might be no solution without the use of force to restore international control, and that British forces, which had been mobilized for this purpose, could not be held in a state of alert much longer. If Israel attacked, British troops as suggested would take the opportunity with the French of seizing the Canal, but the basis of their action must be to intervene to separate the forces and remove the threat of damage to the Canal from the Israeli action. Then Egypt and Israel would be called on to cease hostilities within twenty-four hours, and whatever happened British and French forces would take possession of the Canal.

Ben Gurion did not like this and said Israel was being asked to solve Britain's and France's problems 'by accepting the opprobrium of aggression followed by the ignominy of accepting an ultimatum', and suggested instead that responsibility should be shared equally. Lloyd rejected the idea of making a joint attack on Egypt public news because of the damage it would do to Britain's relations with Arab countries like Jordan and Iraq.

Ben Gurion then told of his fear that the Egyptian Air Force, now equipped with Soviet planes, would bomb Tel Aviv within hours of the attack and before the French and British were in action. Up till now it had been assumed that the RAF would not attack the Egyptian Air Force until forty-eight or seventy-two hours after hostilities had begun, and Lloyd was pressed to reduce this to thirty-six hours. He refused, and the meeting adjourned for dinner. Afterwards Lloyd undertook to report to the Cabinet and reply the next day about the timing of the RAF attack on Egypt.[12]

The next morning Lloyd told Nutting that it did not look as if the French plan would come off because Ben Gurion felt it did not provide sufficient air cover for Israel, and instead wanted to be assured that the RAF would 'take out' the Egyptian Air Force as soon as the attack started, to prevent Tel Aviv being obliterated by Nasser's Russian bombers. According to Nutting, Lloyd said this was impossible because an interval must be allowed to give Egypt time to reject the ultimatum, and also Ben Gurion was unconvinced that Britain would give sufficient support generally, although he had faith in the French.[13]

Eden was 'put out' by the report which Lloyd gave of his encounter with Ben Gurion, and Lloyd told Nutting this. At the Cabinet meeting on 23 October Eden said that, although on the 18th he had thought an Israeli attack on Egypt was likely, it now 'seemed unlikely'. We had a choice between 'an early military operation or a relatively prolonged negotiation'. If we went in for prolonged negotiation 'neither we nor the French could hope to maintain our military preparations in their present state of readiness . . . and our position of negotiating from strength would to some extent be impaired'. The French 'had received "special provocation" from Egypt through the capture of a ship carrying arms from Egypt to the rebel forces in Algeria, and they might regard this as a sufficient ground for military action against Egypt'.

The Cabinet was now informed that the Secretary General of the UN considered that Egypt had put forward proposals which would afford a basis for renewed discussions. Lloyd, obviously despondent about his Sèvres talk with Ben Gurion, said 'he would not exclude the possibility that we might be able to reach, by negotiation with the Egyptians, a settlement that would give us the substance of our

demand for effective international supervision of the Canal.' However, 'he saw no prospect of reaching such a settlement as would
diminish Colonel Nasser's influence throughout the Middle East.'
Eden said enigmatically that 'grave decisions would have to be taken
by the Cabinet in the course of the next few days'. The Prime
Minister was wobbling. However Mountbatten, who was present,
interpreted the mood of the Cabinet in a signal to the C-in-C
Mediterranean: 'Situation has eased substantially. Musketeer can
therefore be regarded as at ten days notice.'[14]

At Eden's request Pineau came to London for talks that evening,
the 23rd; Eden wanted him to press the Israelis to agree to the
Anglo–French plan. Before Eden arrived at their meeting Lloyd put
to Pineau arguments in favour of a diplomatic settlement. According
to Lloyd's written account of the meeting, 'Pineau was unconvinced'.
Eden then joined them. His enthusiasm for the French plan was
'stronger than ever'. The three agreed to think over whether 'in the
event of hostilities developing near the Canal it was thought we might
serve notices on the parties to stop and withdraw a certain distance
from the Canal and threaten them with military intervention by
France and Britain if this was not done'. Lloyd dictated a note about
the talks, but as with the record of the Paris conversations gave
instructions to his private secretary for 'no copies and no circulation'.
Eden reassured Pineau about early RAF intervention, and guaranteed that, if Israel would attack towards the Canal and not just to the
south, Britain would support her fully.[15]

The next day, the 24th, the Cabinet was told that Pineau had
declared that the French were opposed to a resumption of negotiations with the Egyptians but recognized the urgent need to bring
the issue to a head. The Cabinet was told that the military plan
could not be held in readiness after the end of October, and once
reservists were released 'our bargaining position' would be
weakened. In discussion the Cabinet was divided, some fearing
that war would unite the Arab world in support of Egypt. Eden
agreed this was a serious risk, but 'unless early action could be taken
to damage Colonel Nasser's prestige his influence would be extended
throughout the Middle East to a degree which would make it much
more difficult to overthrow him'. Some members favoured bringing
the crisis to a head by diplomatic means but were told (presumably
by the Prime Minister) that the French would object to the early
resumption of negotiations, and that it probably meant abandoning
their objective of reducing Colonel Nasser's influence throughout the
Middle East. Eden must have felt he could not persuade the Cabinet

on this day to give him the go-ahead for war, and it was adjourned for twenty-four hours.[16]

Early the next morning (24 October) Patrick Dean, Assistant Under-Secretary, was summoned to No. 10. Eden briefed him on the plan and said he was to go to Sèvres that day to extract a promise from Ben Gurion that he would attack the Canal and in return the RAF would destroy the Egyptian Air force almost immediately. It was all fresh to Dean; he went to see Kirkpatrick who, although unenthusiastic, told him he must carry out these orders. Logan, who already knew about the negotiations, was ordered to accompany Dean. At Sèvres they met the same French and Israel teams. Dean handed over a letter emphasizing that the British were not asking Israel to take action – an odd move under the circumstances. Dean also produced a written authority which gave him full plenipotentiary powers.[17]

During the discussion Dean and Logan emphasized that, unless the Israelis undertook that their forces would launch a major attack posing a threat to the Canal, Britain would not act. At first Ben Gurion stated that their main objective would be the Egyptian Sharm-el-Sheikh forts dominating the Gulf of Akaba. The British diplomats said this was not satisfactory. Eventually Ben Gurion gave way and guaranteed to attack the Mitla Pass, which led to an area close to the Canal. This was the undertaking Eden wanted, and was good enough for Dean and Logan to tell the Israelis and the French that a deal was struck. The French quickly produced three copies of a typed document: it was the Treaty of Sèvres.[18]

On the afternoon of 29 October 1956 the Israeli forces will launch a large scale attack on the Egyptian forces, with the object of reaching the Canal Zone on the following day.

Having been informed of the event, the governments of Great Britain and France will on 30 October 1956, separately and simultaneously, address appeals formulated in the spirit of the following essential points:

To the Egyptian Government:

– Absolute cease fire.

– Withdrawal of all forces to 15 kilometres from the Canal.

– Acceptance of the occupation by Anglo–French forces of key positions on the Canal, so as to guarantee the free passage of vessels of all nations until the conclusion of a definitive agreement.

To the Israeli Government:

– Absolute cease fire.

– Withdrawal of forces to 15 kilometres from the Canal.

– The Israeli Government to be notified that the French and British Governments have required the Egyptian Government to accept the temporary occupation by Franco–British forces of key positions on the Canal.

Should either government reject the appeal, or not give its consent within twelve hours, the Anglo–French forces would be in a position to take the steps necessary to ensure that their demands were met.

In the event of the Egyptian Government's not accepting the conditions in the appeal it has received, it will not be required of the Israeli Government that it should meet the conditions of the appeal.

If the Egyptian Government does not accept the conditions presented to it within the stipulated period, the Anglo–French forces will launch an attack against the Egyptian forces in the early hours of 31 October 1956.

The Israeli Government will send forces to occupy the west bank of the Gulf of Aqaba, as also the islands of Tiran and Sunagrin, so as to ensure freedom of navigation in that gulf.

Israel will not attack Jordan while the operation against Israel is proceeding. But if Jordan attacks Israel during that period the British Government will not come to Jordan's assistance.[19]

Dean was asked to sign. At first he was reluctant, but Logan reassured him, saying it was an accurate account of the agreement which the Prime Minister had entrusted them to secure. Dean then signed. Champagne was produced, and the two diplomats left for London by air. Logan and Dean arrived at 10 Downing Street at 10.30 and handed the document to the Prime Minister who, although he was pleased with the contents, had not expected anything on paper. Eden blamed Dean and Logan for signing the document without authority.

The next day Logan and Dean were sent back to Paris to try to recover the French copy. They presented the Prime Minister's request to Pineau, who was displeased, and left them for several hours in a locked room without lunch or drink – not what diplomats expect at the Quai d'Orsay. At 4 p.m. Pineau refused to give them the French counterpart of the document on the grounds that the Israelis had taken their copy back to Tel Aviv. The next day Dean was told to send over to Downing Street all copies of the document and the translations that had been made. Without doubt Eden destroyed them there and then. They are not in the Public Record Office.[20]

The Prime Minister's dismay at the document shows that he intended to keep the collusion plan secret indefinitely and set great store on it never being made public. It was an amazing error of judgment for a statesman with Eden's experience to imagine this would be possible. It is hard to avoid the conclusion that his health and the remedies prescribed by his doctors had affected his judgment. According to Sir Richard Powell, Permanent Secretary at the Ministry of Defence, and the surviving diplomats, very few in London were told of the collusion, but it was bound to be leaked by the French and Israelis.[21]

The ultimate paragraph, stating that Israel would not attack Jordan, was a relief to Eden. Throughout the crisis the nightmare for him and the Chiefs of Staff had been that Israel might attack Jordan while Anglo–French troops were bogged down fighting the Egyptians and occupying Egypt.

As recently as 10 October it had been reported to the Chiefs of Staff Committee that Britain had given assurances to the Jordan Foreign Minister and the Iraqi Prime Minister that Britain would provide sea and air support immediately in the event of an attack by Israel on Jordan. At this Committee meeting General Templer said 'we could either go to the aid of Jordan against Israel with sea and air power, or we could launch Musketeer; we could not do both. Once we had launched Musketeer we would not be able at the same time to honour our obligations under the Anglo–Jordan Treaty.' Mountbatten added:

> . . . if during Musketeer Israel attacked Jordan and the United States went to Jordan's aid against Israel then we and the United States would be fighting on opposite sides. We should be the unwilling allies of Israel and our forces in Jordan would be hostages to fortune. If the United States had gone to the aid of Jordan and Egypt before Musketeer was launched, it would not then be practicable for us to launch Musketeer.[22]

Worried Eden might be that the signed document of Sèvres would be used against him in the future as evidence both of collusion and of a dishonest ultimatum to Egypt, but his indecisiveness of 23 October had vanished when the Cabinet assembled on the 25th. He was determined to obtain authority for starting a war against Egypt; his military plans were laid and he wanted to give the commanders the go-ahead at the earliest possible moment.

Eden told his Cabinet he expected Israel to attack Egypt; if they did so the French felt strongly that 'intervention would be justified', and if we declined 'they might take military action alone or in conjunction with Israel'. Eden said if Israel attacked Egypt the British and French should issue an ultimatum to both sides to withdraw. If Nasser complied, his prestige would be 'fatally undermined'. If he did not, there would be 'ample justification for Anglo–French military action against Egypt in order to safeguard the Canal'. Lloyd supported Eden.

The agreed plan of collusion with Egypt and France and the talks at Sèvres were not disclosed to the Cabinet. This was arrant dishonesty. But Eden's hands were tied because by the Sèvres written agreement Britain had promised the French and Israeli Governments that collusion would stay a close secret. It was madness for Eden to enter into the Sèvres agreement at a moment when a diplomatic solution was in sight.

Eden was specifically untruthful in Cabinet over the word 'collusion', saying

We must face the risk that we should be accused of collusion with Israel. But this charge was liable to be brought against us in any event; for it could now be assumed that, if an Anglo–French operation were undertaken against Egypt, we should be unable to prevent the Israelis from launching a parallel attack themselves, and it was preferable that we should be seen to be holding the balance between Israel and Egypt rather than appear to be accepting Israeli co-operation in an attack on Egypt alone.

Some Ministers expressed doubts that

our action would cause offence to the United States Government, and might do lasting damage to Anglo–American relations [and that] in inviting the two sides to withdraw their forces to a distance of ten miles from the Canal, we should not appear to be holding the balance evenly between Israel and Egypt. For we should be asking the Egyptians to withdraw still further within their territory, while leaving the Israel forces on Egyptian soil well in advance of their own frontier;

and in separating the two belligerents 'we should be purporting to undertake an international function without the specific authority of the United Nations'. These arguments did not prevail, and the Cabinet gave Eden the authority he wanted for war without any recorded dissent. It must have been a unanimous vote.[23]

On 25 October the Chiefs of Staff produced a memorandum on the 'military implications' of mounting Musketeer and asked for directions on how to proceed. The Chiefs of Staff assumed that the Government wanted not only to reoccupy the Canal, but also to establish a co-operative successor Government to Nasser's, although their immediate military plans did not extend beyond the occupation of the Canal Zone.

With the approval of the Egypt Committee Eden ordered that D-Day for invasion of Egypt should be 7 November, and that RAF attacks on Egyptian airfield and military installations should start on 30 October. These dates had been agreed with the French and Israeli War Offices. The British sea convoy began its slow journey from Malta to Port Said.

At 5 p.m. on Monday, 29 October, Israeli forces began their assault through the Sinai on Egypt, as agreed with the British and French at Sèvres, and soon posed a threat to the Canal after a successful but hard fought action by parachutists on the Mitla Pass, while other forces pressed south towards the Gulf of Akaba. French planes dropped supplies to the Israeli troops at Mitla in two sorties from Cyprus aerodromes.

On the morning of 30 October the British Cabinet approved draft notes to the Egyptian and Israeli Governments asking that Anglo–French forces should be allowed to move into key positions at Port Said, Ismailia and Suez 'to guarantee freedom of transit through the Canal', and agreed that they should be delivered to the respective Ambassadors in London after approval by Mollet and Pineau, who were on their way there. Late in the afternoon Kirkpatrick himself, with Pineau, delivered the ultimatum to Samy Aboul-Fatouh, the Egyptian Ambassador, and told him that 'it was our intention to exercise our right under the 1888 Treaty to send a warship to Port Said'. Not unnaturally the Ambassador replied that he was 'horrified'. The ultimatum came as no surprise to the Israeli Ambassador; Kirkpatrick went on to the American Embassy and gave a copy to Aldrich, who said that Britain and France had made out 'the best case possible for their action', but added that 'he was afraid there would be hell to pay'.[24]

The military plan had three phases:

1. The elimination of the Egyptian Air Force.
2. An intensive air offensive combined with a psychological campaign.
3. A landing at Port Said followed by the occupation of the Canal Zone.

This necessarily involved considerable destruction of property and heavy Egyptian casualties. The Chiefs of Staff warned the Egypt Committee that, although they would try for 'the minimum loss of life', it would require a certain time to achieve results and therefore they 'presupposed continued public support for the use of force'. They stated that the plan was 'militarily sound', and the French High Command agreed it could be brought into operation at ten days' notice any time after 1 November. The land forces earmarked were 3 Commando Brigade, 16 Parachute Brigade, 6 Royal Tank Regiment, 10 French Airborne Division, 7 French Division Méchanique Rapide, and one battalion of French colonial troops. In addition 3 British Infantry Division and 10 British Armoured Division from Libya would be required after the assault stage was over if there was to be military occupation of Egypt outside the Canal Zone. Keightley was designated Allied Force Commander (AFHQ); 2 Corps HQ was formed to command landings under Stockwell.[25]

The next morning, 31 October, Eden told the Cabinet that Israel had accepted the ultimatum, but Egypt had refused. Eden went on that in these circumstances the approved plan for enforcing compliance would be put into operation, and at dusk that evening air operations designed to cripple the Egyptian Air Force would begin. US citizens were being evacuated from Cairo to Alexandria by a road which ran through the Cairo airfield – one of the RAF targets. The Cabinet agreed that if this operation could not be postponed a special warning should be sent to the US Ambassador in Cairo; the Cabinet invited the Foreign Secretary to issue a public warning advising civilians to keep clear of all Egyptian airfields. There was no dissent.[26]

On 30 October Eden told the Commons of the ultimatum and that Anglo–French forces would intervene 'in whatever strength was necessary'. Labour received the news ill, and after an acrimonious debate there was a division in which the Government had a majority of 52, with 218 votes against them. A divided House of Commons was an inauspicious start for a war. In the Security Council the USA introduced a Resolution demanding an Israeli withdrawal on the grounds that this would remove any reason for the Anglo–French ultimatum. This and a similar Russian Resolution were vetoed by the French and British; this infuriated the Labour Party and passions rose fast in the Commons.

In the Commons on 31 October Gaitskell and other Labour front-benchers made allegations of collusion by the British Government with France and Israel. The Foreign Secretary denied them categorically; he and Eden believed that the details of the Sèvres Treaty could be kept secret permanently. Defending the use of the veto, Eden said that the UN Resolution called on Israel to withdraw to her own frontiers, which was 'a harsh demand'. This was a flimsy argument upon which to base Britain's first use of the veto, and it was also in effect his excuse for going to war. As the extent of the Israeli withdrawal was obviously negotiable it made him appear incredible, and at that moment he lost whatever support he had had from the Opposition benches. A bizarre and not very lucid intervention came from a young pro-Egyptian Conservative MP, William Yates, who told the House that he had learnt in Paris that the Government was engaged in an international conspiracy, and that he might use this information to bring it down. The cat was out of the bag; collusion had been leaked by the French, and from then on rumours, which were extremely damaging to Eden and the Government, snowballed.

The next morning, 1 November, the Egypt Committee was informed by the Chief of Air Staff of Keightley's estimate that the Egyptian Air Force would be 'practically eliminated by the following day'. Head stated that bombing attacks would then switch to Egyptian Army targets and Egyptian oil installations. He asked that further bombing attacks should be directed mainly against Egyptian Army targets, that oil targets should be attacked only if they had a direct bearing on Egyptian resistance to the landing, and that attacks on Egyptian Army targets should avoid those likely to involve civilian casualties. These minutes make it crystal-clear that substantial Egyptian casualties were both expected and accepted.[27] That afternoon, during the debate in the Commons, the news tapes carried accounts of RAF bombing of Egypt. Many Conservative MPs and almost all the Labour MPs (but not the Suez Group) were horrified at Britain bombing another country without a declaration of war. This was what Hitler had done to Poland in September 1939, and there was such shouting that the Speaker had to suspend the session.

The Chiefs of Staff estimate that the Egyptian Air Force would be eliminated proved correct. In Cyprus the RAF were prepared to bomb during the night and early morning of 29–30 October but the raids were postponed to the 30th–31st, to the rage of the Israelis. Their troops were being attacked by Egyptian aircraft, although the much feared raids on Tel Aviv did not materialize. The British excuse was fog; in fact there was none. There was talk of perfidious Albion by the Israeli and French Commanders.[28]

Twenty-four hours later Britain complied with her Treaty obligation to Israel. On the night of 31 October night take-offs were needed for dawn attacks, and the raids went according to plan. No hostile aircraft were encountered, and 1884 thousand-pound bombs were dropped in eighteen attacks on thirteen targets. There were numerous reports of enemy flak. The targets were aerodromes and the Huckstep ammunition and vehicle car park. No instructions were given about populated areas close to the selected targets. The RAF were not satisfied with the accuracy of their bombing, reporting that 'the target marking and bombing were not up to the expected standard but although only a few runways were put out of action . . . the bombing seems to have achieved the required effect of keeping Egyptian Air Force on the ground where its aircraft could be destroyed by ground attack'. Ground attack aircraft were to destroy the Egyptian aircraft after the runways had been put out of action.[29]

The less accurate the bombing, the higher must have been the civilian casualties. The attack on Cairo West airport was postponed for twenty-four hours because of American civilians using the nearby road; the raiders had to be recalled by radio after they had left Malta.[30] The RAF report states that twenty Canberras aimed 98 thousand-pound bombs at Cairo radio station in the early daylight on 2 November 'Most bombs undershot or overshot. One hit reported very close to target. Cairo Radio ceased transmitting.' The British radio station on Cyprus temporarily broadcast on the Cairo wavelength.[31]

Francis Murray, Counsellor at the British Embassy in Cairo, had been recalled to London for the planning of the civilian administration of occupied Egypt, and later was appointed political adviser to Keightley in Cyprus. Murray, who knew how important Eden and Lloyd felt it was to keep collusion secret, became alarmed at the way in which the French were openly giving military support to Israel. His instructions were to report direct to Kirkpatrick and not to any other branch of the Foreign Office, who were all in ignorance of the Sèvres Agreement. On 1 November he sent this telegram from Cyprus exclusive to Kirkpatrick:

1) I am not clear precisely what political risks particularly to Baghdad Pact HMG has accepted in associating themselves with French collaboration with the Israelis, but I trust you are fully aware of the following:

A) The French aircraft operating from Israeli airfields bear joint forces markings.

B) French cruiser *Georges Leygues* shelled Rafah last night in the direct support of Israeli operation there.

C) French asked for destroyer [HMS] *Gazelle* under command of C in C Med to proceed through Channel Enterprise [Gulf of Akaba] to assist Israelis after their alleged capture of Egyptian Ports there; this was stopped as you know by Admiralty and capture of forts [Sharm-el-Sheikh] has been found not to have taken place.

2) As seen from here there is little, if anything, covert about French close and active support of Israel and from attitude of French here I would expect further actions as vigorous and as open as B above.
3) I have shown this to C in C who agrees.

Subsequently Murray signalled that 'two Israeli officers have arrived at this HQ in uniform under French auspices' after the French destroyer had participated in the capture of the Egyptian destroyer *Ibrahim* off Haifa. He went on:

C in C has ordered responsible French officer not to allow Israeli officers here, and is taking it up with Admiral Barjot. I have asked my French colleague [a diplomat] what knowledge he has of lengths to which his Government has authorised French military to go in virtually open support of Israelis. He has no instructions and exercises no influence on Admiral Barjot although he sees the point.

We spoke to Admiral about the *Georges Leygues* bombardment of Rafah, and he has agreed not to issue any communiqué about it. I should be grateful for instructions to what extent you wish me to pursue this issue and in what sense to advise C in C. My French colleague is pointing to a number of obvious problems which will arise when we have troops on the ground east of the Canal and asking for solutions. C in C has seen this telegram and agrees.

Murray's signals caused consternation to Kirkpatrick and Lloyd. 'No copies to be made' was ordered. Anyone reading them could be in no doubt about 'collusion'. If the French interpreted the alliance with Israel realistically and continued in this vein, Kirkpatrick feared it would be impossible to hide from the world the pre-arranged Anglo–French military collusion with Israel. Lloyd asked Eden to send a strongly worded protest to Mollet, and the Prime Minister wrote, after amending the draft in his own handwriting: 'Actions of this sort which cannot possibly remain secret are extremely embarrassing. I hope you will agree that in our common interest they must be discontinued. Nothing could do more harm to our role as peacemakers than to be identified in this way with one of the two parties. I am sure you will share this view.' Mollet replied at once that he would order such operations to cease immediately. They did not.[32]

Although Eden was active in his efforts to stop this overt collusion between France and the attacking Israeli forces, he failed to prevent his own forces doing the same thing during the long drawn-out phase between the bombing and the Port Said landings. The most cold-blooded action was on 4 November, when British carrier-borne aircraft of the Fleet Air Arm attacked four Egyptian E-boats halfway between Cairo and Alexandria, at Brulos. The report said: 'One was blown up, two set on fire and subsequently sunk, and one damaged', and concluded laconically: . . . the damaged E boat was allowed to pick up survivors from the other boats and was seen making its way back to port'. This E-boat incident was spotlighted by the Egyptian press and radio and appeared to the world as piracy on the high seas. Near the Gulf of Akaba on 31 October HMS *Newfoundland* sank the Egyptian frigate *Domyat* after she had failed to respond to a signal; this was claimed to be an accident, but later the *Newfoundland* attacked four Egyptian MTBs.

After the initial bombing attacks the RAF carried out a series of strikes against Egyptian military targets well removed from the proposed Allied landing zones, which must have been of great help to the Israelis. Monckton, while Minister of Defence, had objected that Almaza aerodrome was close to a built-up area and also used by civilian aircraft and he did not want it included in the list of targets. He was over-ruled on operational grounds, and Almaza was bombed regardless of the civilians at 16.15 on 31 October. Head told the Commons that the Almaza hospital was on the edge of the airport but might be used as a barracks and not as a hospital. In fact Almaza was given high priority because of its proximity to Cairo, 'so that the maximum psychological impact on the Egyptian people may be achieved. On 2 November low-level attacks were made on Almaza barracks 'with good results' – so much for Monckton's objections.[33]

Now that it was felt that the Egyptian Air Force had been sufficiently neutralized, French and British planes attacked vehicles, tanks and anti-aircraft sites in Egypt; heavy attacks were made on a concentration of armour in the Pyramids area and on Huckstep, where there were still massed vehicles, while French ground-attack aircraft destroyed fifteen Ilyushins on the tarmac at Cairo airport. Military convoys on the roads heading away from Port Said were attacked; this was overt help for Israel.

There is evidence that the ground-attack aircraft were extremely accurate in their gunfire and bomb drops. From 4 November warnings were given in Arabic on Cyprus radio station, specifying the targets apart from the convoys on the roads. This led to considerable trouble with Egyptian employees at the radio station, and military personnel had to be employed to keep it in action. Three were arrested: one for trying to make an illegal broadcast, the others for sabotage. After the warnings a great number of sorties were flown by the RAF, the French Air Force and carrier-borne aircraft of the

Fleet Air Arm against the Egyptian Army retreating in front of the Israel advance. Eight sorties were flown against Huckstep; all the results were reported as 'satisfactory'.[34] The RAF reported that there was virtually no Egyptian Air Force activity, and no casualties due to enemy action, although ineffective anti-aircraft fire was encountered. Nasser had ordered his Air Force not to engage in battles because of the overwhelming Anglo–French superiority; he preferred to lose his aircraft rather than his pilots.[35]

When the Reverend Arthur Burrell, Provost of the Anglican Cathedral in Cairo, was taking early service during the morning of 1 November he heard the sound of bombs being dropped at regular intervals, which shook the Cathedral. Soon many British subjects who had been living in the residential quarters of Heliopolis and the Pyramids area took refuge in the Cathedral residences because 'their homes had been rendered uninhabitable by blast from the RAF attacks'. In a letter to the author, Burrell wrote that, in face of the unprovoked air attack, the Egyptians behaved to the British 'with laudable courtesy and restraint'.[36]

Eden received great encouragement in letters from his colleagues during this critical stage. On 5 November Home wrote:

> My dear Anthony,
>   The stakes you were playing for yesterday [at the crucial Cabinet and Egypt Committee meetings of 4 November] were the highest – to lose all or to win all.
>   We are not out of the wood, but we have won a decisive round. If our country rediscovers its soul and inspiration your calm courage will have achieved this miracle.
>   With my unstinted admiration,
>   Yours ever,
>   Alec

On the 6th Hailsham wrote:

> My dearest Anthony,
>   At the beginning of this session so fraught with tremendous happenings, I should like to tell you how inspiring I have found your courage and leadership during the past few weeks.
>   May God protect you and give you the wisdom and endurance you need. No answer. Yours ever, Q.H.

Similar letters were received from Henderson Stewart, Under-Secretary Scottish Office; Henry Brooke, Financial Secretary to the

Treasury; Lord John Hope, Minister of State Foreign Office; and John Maclay, Minister of State for Colonial Affairs. In one written reply, on 7 November, Eden said: 'Although we have achieved much of our purpose we are not out of the wood yet.'[37]

Against this, Mountbatten suddenly turned sour and on 2 November made an eleventh-hour appeal to Eden 'to accept' the Resolution of the overwhelming majority of the UN and order the assault convoy to turn back. When Eden refused this 'unprecedented request by a serving officer' Mountbatten wrote to Hailsham (First Lord of the Admiralty) that in his view civilian casualties could not be avoided, and 'I recognise that a serving officer cannot back his protest by resignation at a time like this, so I must ask you to handle this whole matter on behalf of the Navy. Bearing in mind the implications I must ask you after consulting the Prime Minister, to give me an order to stay or to go.' Hailsham ordered him to remain at his post.

Eden had spoken to Mountbatten on the telephone and said he would not turn back the assault convoy, pointing out that 'our operations had been directed only against military targets and that no civilians had been killed'. This was patently untrue as far as civilian casualties were concerned. Mountbatten had earlier voiced doubts at the Chiefs of Staff Committee.[38] On 14 August he said he feared 'that the Egyptian people were now so solidly behind Nasser that it might be impossible to find a [successor] Government'. On 21 August he said that Musketeer 'would cause serious and continuing disorders in the Middle East countries and necessitate long term retention of considerable forces in the area to maintain law and order'. There is no recorded reaction to these remarks from the other members of the Committee. Mountbatten knew the minutes would go to the Cabinet and obviously aimed his remarks in that direction. However, if Mountbatten's dramatic outburst against war on 2 November had been made public it would have endangered the Government, such was his prestige.[39]

Meanwhile Eden was running foul of the United Nations. It was inevitable. The United Nations, like the League of Nations, had been formed specifically to outlaw acts of war such as Britain and France were perpetrating on Egypt. Anger was expressed by most of the civilized nations, with only Australia and New Zealand supporting Britain.

At the United Nations America was, in Lloyd's words, leading a 'ferocious' opposition to Britain. On 2 November the General Assembly adopted a Resolution calling for a ceasefire and the withdrawal of Israeli, French and British forces, and the formation of a United Nations Force 'large enough to keep these borders at peace while a political settlement is being worked out'. Dixon was authorized to state 'if the UN were willing to take over the physical task of maintaining peace no-one would be better pleased than we'. But Eden was determined to humiliate Nasser first and get possession of the Canal terminals; he realized that if he was to occupy the Canal time was running short because a UN expeditionary force would soon be ready to take over the Anglo–French function of keeping the peace. The French were motivated by an over-riding desire to overthrow Nasser in order to prevent Egyptian involvement in Algeria; Eden only wanted to reassert British prestige in the Middle East, and he now abandoned his intention to capture Cairo after the Canal Zone had been occupied. The French Government urged its commanders in Cyprus to speed up the invasion by dropping parachutists in front of the Israeli Army to take the Canal without waiting for the seaborne force, scheduled to arrive on 6 November.[40]

General Ely, French Chief of Staff, sent an urgent telegram to Barjot in Cyprus telling him to examine all possibilities of speeding up the operations and declaring that French troops must be ashore within twenty-four hours. Keightley discussed with the French two plans for airborne operations – Omelette for an airborne drop on Port Said, and Simplex for drops further down the Canal at El Kantara and Ismailia, where the French hoped they could speedily link up with the Israelis. Throughout most of 2 November Barjot argued with Durnford Slater and Keightley for the immediate activation of Omelette or Simplex. French parachutists on Cyprus were alerted, but Keightley rigidly refused to alter his plan for a seaborne landing on 6 November preceded by RAF and French attacks on the 3rd, 4th and 5th. Stockwell, Commander 2 Corps, was also opposed to any airborne landing prior to the scheduled seaborne invasion, although he did not preclude another landing at Alexandria on 7 November. The British said that aerial reconnaissance had revealed a concentration of Egyptian tanks north of the Canal, and therefore the paras would be vulnerable if they landed without support from seaborne convoys. Reluctantly the French stood down their paras, who were ready to go into action at any moment from the Cyprus airfields. However, it was agreed that Stockwell with his 2 Corps HQ should embark on HMS *Tyne* and sail at midnight on 4 November. The French then considered making an airborne landing without the co-operation of the British, but General Beaufre was opposed because of the presence of Egyptian tanks. The French then proposed one Anglo–French drop at Port Said on the 5th, accompanied by another drop at Port Fouad, adjoining Port Said, supported by a small French seaborne landing. They also asked for the rest of Musketeer Revise to be brought forward from the 6th to the 5th.[41]

Keightley complied with the French request for drops on the 5th, but refused to advance the date of the seaborne attack. Eden too wanted to speed things up, and he told the Egypt Committee on 3 November that 'it was politically desirable to establish Anglo–French forces at key points along the Suez Canal at the earliest possible date'. The Committee was told that the Egyptians had 'sizeable armoured forces and were moving reinforcements towards the Suez Canal' but 'the Egyptian forces in Port Said were little more than one brigade'.

Head warned the Committee that 'it would be necessary to eliminate the defensive positions along the sea front in Port Said by preliminary bombardment before the assault forces landed, and that this would cause 'considerable physical damage', and 'civilian casualties might also be heavy'. He spoke of alternative landing places at Haifa, Gaza and El Arish; but there were political objections to the use of Haifa, being in Israeli territory, while neither of the other two had suitable harbours, so that equipment and stores would have to be landed over sandy beaches. To add to the indecision, in discussion members emphasized that from the point of view of world opinion it was important to make every effort to avoid heavy civilian casualties in the assault on Port Said, and that naval guns should not be used – only ground-attack aircraft. Head agreed to fly out to Cyprus to confer with Keightley before final decisions were made. Clearly the Committee were desperately worried at the prospect of an outcry about civilian casualties in Port Said at a moment when world opinion was condemning Britain for the loss of lives and damage already caused by the air raids on Egypt. Meanwhile the conflict of views between Keightley, the French and the Chiefs of Staff was being revealed in a series of telegrams from AFHQ in Cyprus to the War Office.[42]

On the 4th Head arrived in Cyprus at 2 a.m. and left at 5 a.m. He told Keightley and the French commanders that the political situation in Britain had improved and he was anxious not to endanger this by either inflicting a great deal of damage on Port Said or delaying the assault. They decided to drop on 5 November one British parachute regiment on Gamil airfield at Port Said and one French parachute regiment on the southern exits from Port Said; they would occupy Port Said immediately if resistance was slight, but if heavy resistance was met they would wait for the main seaborne assault on the 6th. Head asked that there should be no preliminary naval or air bombardment, and that during the operation naval gunfire would be limited to 'opportunity' and 'on call targets', while air support would consist of ground-attack aircraft only. 2 Corps HQ noted cynically that 'in the interests of creating a more favourable impression on world opinion support for the operation would be severely curtailed'. However both the British and French chiefs agreed they could dispense with the naval bombardment, except that Barjot said he must use naval guns to destroy two Egyptian gun emplacements on the front at Port Said. Head insisted that the operation must be launched as soon as possible, and Keightley told him he could occupy Ismailia in forty-eight hours.

That day the British and French staffs feverishly prepared final plans for the attack; Beaufre's parachute attack on Port Fouad was agreed, and by 10 a.m. final plans were ready, entitled 'Variation Telescope to Operation Musketeer'. Keightley issued the following orders to Stockwell:[43]

> In confirmation of our meeting this morning.
> 1. The object now will be to seize the Canal Zone from Port Said to Suez, ten miles either side of the Canal, and such areas as are necessary in addition for your security.
> 2. The Egyptian Army will only be attacked in the immediate future in order to achieve this object.
> 3. It remains vitally important to avoid to the uttermost civilian casualties and damage to civilian property.
> 4. The assault on Port Said should be made in the hope that damage to civilians and property may be avoided.
> 5. Little movement has been seen over the last 48 hours but this is by no means a certain indication that the enemy has gone.
> 6. He may well have dug his positions and put his tanks and crews under cover ready to move into position immediately the assault starts. The assault must cater for this and HM ships and RAF must have 'their finger on the trigger', and be absolutely prepared and alert to carry out whatever fire support is necessary for the success of the operation.[44]

In London that Sunday there were two meetings of the Egypt Committee and one of the full Cabinet before the Government could decide whether to proceed with or abandon the invasion of Egypt. The records show that Eden must have passed the day in an agony of indecision. The first Egypt Committee was held at 12.30. In discussion there was general agreement that it was essential to occupy the key points on the Canal, if only as an advance guard of a United Nations force to be established as rapidly as possible thereafter, and 'the crucial question was whether we could effect an Anglo–French landing of this kind without causing civilian casualties on a scale which would finally alienate opinion in the United Nations'. Head, just back from Cyprus, said the latest intelligence reports suggested Egypt was withdrawing her forces from Port Said to defend Cairo until a UN force arrived.

> If so, the Allied Force Commanders believed that it would be possible to occupy Port Said by dropping British and French parachutists behind the town. If the opposition proved to be heavier than was now thought likely, it would be necessary to support the parachute drop by enfilade air attack and possibly by a certain amount of naval bombardment. . . . If the Commanders were required to restrain entirely from naval bombardment the landings might be delayed and the risk of casualties amongst the troops would be increased.

He wanted discretion given to the Commander to employ naval guns if the parachute forces were unable to reduce the seaward defences of Port Said, but said that 'it was fully accepted by British and French Commanders alike that such bombardment would be restricted to the absolute minimum'.

Then followed an extraordinary discussion. There was general agreement that operations should proceed 'provided that it proved possible to draft a reply to [Hammarskjold] which would not involve us in either defiance or deception of the United Nations'. The proposed reply was tendentious:

> . . . we were willing to co-operate with any practical plan put forward by the United Nations as soon as it was ready; but that for urgent practical reasons especially *the increasing disorder in the Canal area and the disintegration of authority in the region* [author's italics] it was impossible for us to suspend military operations and we felt ourselves compelled to carry through the initial stages of the police action which was now imperative.[45]

This was a shaming moment in the history of the British people and the Conservative Party. There was no disorder in the Canal Zone; ships were passing normally, Egyptian authority was being exercised as usual and no police action was required because fighting between the Israelis and the Egyptians on the Canal had ceased. The only fighting was at Sharm-el-Sheik, hundreds of miles to the south. The Ministry of Transport were well aware that ships were proceeding normally through the Canal; on 29 October the Minister of Transport, Watkinson, had sent Eden a memorandum to this effect which survives in the Prime Minister's papers.[46]

Doubts must have assailed the Prime Minister, because a further meeting of the Egypt Committee was summoned for 3.30 when, on consideration of what was happening at the United Nations, Eden temporarily lost his resolution for war. The second meeting was told that a letter had been received from Dixon saying that Hammarskjold had called on the UK, France, Israel and Egypt to suspend hostilities immediately, and that at the UN Israel had agreed to a ceasefire provided Egypt also agreed (as she had), and that the British position in Iraq would become untenable unless the United Kingdom condemned Israeli aggression.

The Committee recognized the main issue as being whether further military operations by Anglo–French forces were justified when both Egypt and Israel had agreed to a ceasefire. On the one hand it was suggested that a landing by Anglo–French forces after both Israel and Egypt had agreed to a ceasefire would be difficult to justify, lead to further difficulties in Parliament and not be supported by public opinion; this censure would be particularly severe if the Anglo–French landings were resisted by the Egyptians and there were heavy civilian casualties in Port Said. On the other hand Israel had not agreed to withdraw behind the (1948) armistice lines, so that the full requirements of the UN resolution had not been met, and Israel had rejected the idea of an international buffer force. The Committee felt that a possible course would be to notify the UN that the Anglo–French force was an advance force responsible for policing the Middle East and would hand over to UN troops as soon as possible. If this line was followed, Britain would have to offer to suspend military operations to give the UN an opportunity to reply. The minutes recorded:

> From the military point of view, the shortest practical postponement of the operation planned for the following morning would be twenty-four hours, since the airborne landings would need to take place at first light. It might, however, be possible to go ahead with the present plans for airborne landings but to defer a decision about the main landings at Port Said until it was known whether the Egyptian forces would continue to resist . . . there might be military risks in leaving an airborne force for any length of time in Egyptian territory without the support of seaborne troops and equipment. The United Kingdom and

France would be in a stronger position when effective forces were firmly established in the Suez Canal area.[47]

An alarming telegram had arrived from Pierson Dixon at the UN, warning that further military attacks would alienate the whole world:

> From the conversation that I had with Mr. Lodge between despatch of my telegram under reference and your telephone call, it is quite clear that the President's reception of our response to Assembly resolution is very cool, and that what causes them gravest concern is the uncertainty about our intentions as to further military activities. This concern will be shared by our few friends here and exploited by our many enemies.
>
> It is my considered view, which I urge with greatest possible emphasis that, as things now stand, we have no chance of getting a fair hearing for our ideas unless my French colleague and I are in a position to announce, if possible at the outset of the proceedings, that Anglo–French forces are suspending all further military activities until we know whether the United Nations are prepared to deal with the whole situation effectively. It might lose us a few military tricks but I am sure it would make an incalculable difference politically. I can think of no other way of moving towards our objectives in the Middle East without alienating the whole world.[48]

Dixon, away from London, was in a better position to assess world reaction to what Britain and France had done, but his telegram was not communicated to the members of the Egypt Committee or the Cabinet, apart from Eden and Lloyd.

Eden was wavering and in two minds whether or not to call off the assault. He closed the meeting by saying that it would be necessary to reach agreement with the French, and the issues were so important that final decisions must be taken by the full Cabinet.

If the assault was to be delayed for twenty-four hours it would never take place, because the United Nations Force would soon arrive and the Chiefs of Staff would never agree to the Egypt Committee's rash suggestion at their first meeting that day that parachutists might be left at Port Said unsupported by ground troops; they would not risk a repetition of Arnhem in World War II, and the Egyptians had a sizeable force of tanks which, if deployed in strength, could have annihilated the paratroopers.

Conclusive evidence of Eden's indecision comes in a signal to Keightley sent during the afternoon of 4 November, after the second meeting of the Egypt Committee and during the full Cabinet meeting.

(1) Cabinet now considering with French executive order for your operation

(2) Although we hope otherwise it may be essential to postpone to-morrow's operation by 24 hours

(3) What is the latest time you must receive the decision?

(4) Codeword for this postponement which would be sent en clair would be NOPE, but codeword for instituting the operations to-morrow as planned would be MARCH

Keightley's reply, received while the Cabinet was sitting, was un-equivocal. He was obviously dismayed by the Government's vacil-lation at the eleventh hour when his main forces were already at sea:

We can physically arrange for postponement up to 20.30 hours (GMT) today, 4 November, but consequences would be disastrous. Reasons follow.

(A) Winter weather good now but likely to deteriorate.

(B) Morale and physical state of troops . . . with possibility of no sleep for three days.

(C) Enemy preparations are increasing today and heavier bom-bardment sea and air almost certainly necessary.

(D) Sea convoy must be held in open sea.

(E) French Command horrified.[49]

The fateful Cabinet meeting took place at 6.30. It was a long meeting, although a deadline for the reply to Keightley hung over them. There were two sessions, separated by an interval. The first was held in the belief that Israel had agreed to a ceasefire. The second began after it became known that Israel had reneged on the ceasefire.

The Prime Minister started by informing the Cabinet of the Israeli and Egyptian agreement to the ceasefire, saying that it 'would be difficult to deny that the purpose of our intervention in Egypt had already been achieved', and that a decision had to be made 'whether we should allow the initial phase of our occupation of the Canal area to proceed as planned in the early hours of the following morning, and if so what reply we should send to the UN'.

Three courses of action were discussed:

1. To proceed with the assault, and to inform the UN that this action 'had been made imperative by the need to re-establish auth-ority in the Suez Canal area', while 'we remained willing to transfer the responsibility for policing that area 'to a UN force as soon as such a force could be effectively constituted, and on the spot'.

2. To suspend the parachute landings (as suggested in the tele-

gram to Keightley) for the next twenty-four hours to give time for both Israel and Egypt to agree to accept a UN Force, and for the UN to consider whether an Anglo–French force should effect the landing 'as an advance guard of the ultimate United Nations Force'.

3. To defer military action indefinitely.

It was agreed that there were serious political disadvantages in refusing to suspend military action in defiance of majority opinion in the UN.

The Egyptian Government had already agreed to the cease fire which the General Assembly had demanded; and the latest reports suggested that the Israeli Government had also accepted this demand. If so, it would be difficult to sustain the argument that further military action by ourselves was necessary in order to separate the combatants; and, if the initial phase of the Anglo–French landing encountered opposition and had to be reinforced by air or naval bombardment resulting in heavy civilian casualties, we might well be unable to sustain our position in the face of world opinion. We should run a grave risk that the United Nations would feel compelled to adopt collective measures, including oil sanctions, against the UK and France.

On the other hand the Cabinet felt that if the assault was postponed it would never take place, and they were informed that the outlook for the parachutists was now more favourable than had been expected on the previous day. The Egyptians appeared to be withdrawing from Port Said towards Cairo, probably in order to protect the seat of government until a United Nations Force arrived, and there was now a reasonable chance that 'the parachute forces could be landed at Port Said . . . without . . . heavy bombardment'. It is strange that Head should have volunteered this opinion, which conflicted with some of the views expressed to him by the French and British commanders in Cyprus in the early hours of that morning.

There was a full Cabinet at that session, comprising eighteen members apart from the Prime Minister. Also present were Hailsham, First Lord of the Admiralty; Birch, Secretary of State for Air; and Heath, Government Chief Whip and Parliamentary Secretary to the Treasury. Heath, not an ardent supporter of the proposed war, had as Chief Whip co-operated loyally in easing the strain in the Commons. Hailsham, Birch and Heath had no votes. When the Prime Minister asked for a vote, twelve were for war and six against. Those against were Butler, Kilmuir, Heathcoat Amory, Salisbury, Buchan-Hepburn and Monckton. Amory said he would accept the majority decision, but Monckton dug his heels in and said that, despite the majority being in favour, he could not agree and must reserve his position. The Prime Minister, as chairman, did not vote. It was a divided Cabinet with a two to one majority for going to war. It could not be described as a scratch majority, and the Cabinet minutes record that Eden then said that the overwhelming balance of opinion in the Cabinet was in favour of the military operations as planned.[50]

The Cabinet then adjourned, with a Conservative Government in greater disarray than at any moment since 18 December 1935, when the Baldwin Government disowned their Foreign Secretary, Sir Samuel Hoare, for concluding the Hoare–Laval Pact which had been fully authorized by the same Cabinet a few days before. Then Baldwin said: '. . . he was not rattled, but it was the worst situation in the House of Commons he had ever known'. Eden, a survivor of that meeting, may well have felt he had stepped into Baldwin's shoes. Certainly he was under severe strain.

Accounts of the adjournment vary. Butler wrote: 'The vote seemed to non-plus the Prime Minister. He said he must go upstairs and consider his position. If he could not have united support the situation might arise in which someone else might have to take over from him.' According to the diary kept by Clarissa, Eden's widow, Anthony took Butler, Macmillan and Salisbury aside and told them that 'if they wouldn't go on' then he would have to resign. Rab said if he did resign, no one else could form a Government; Macmillan and Salisbury agreed.[51]

Meanwhile Mollet had telephoned to Ben Gurion and urged him to withdraw Israel's acceptance of a ceasefire at the UN in New York. Ben Gurion agreed and hedged the consent round with such conditions that Hammarskjold declared it 'impudent and an insult to the United Nations . . . it was impossible to do diplomatic business with such people'. But it was accepted at the UN that Israel had now refused the conditions of the ceasefire, and a telegram to this effect reached the Cabinet from Dixon during the interval. Clarissa recorded: 'Everyone laughed and banged the table with relief except Monckton and Birch who looked glum.' The Cabinet formally reassembled and agreed that Israel's refusal to withdraw from the Egyptian territory she had occupied was 'sufficient ground for proceeding with police action'. Unanimously, according to the minutes, the Cabinet decided on war. Monckton did not resign. From 10 Downing Street a message went to Keightley to 'go ahead as planned, and good luck'.[52]

After the capture of Port Said British troops distribute rations to Arab civilians.

British infantry on patrol, with threatening slogans on the front of their vehicle.

Civilians being searched in the streets of Nicosia.

A stone-throwing schoolboy is arrested after British soldiers were murdered in Cyprus, November 1955.

Makarios after a fiery speech at Famagusta, 27 September 1955. 'We seek the unity of the whole Cypriot nation,' declaims the banner.

Clark resigned as press officer, but this was not much of a blow to Eden as they had not been on good terms since de Zulueta had told the Prime Minister that Clark had made fun of Eden at a party attended by journalists – the cause of derogatory remarks by Peter Fleming in his 'Strix' column in the *Spectator*. Paul Gore-Booth, high up in the Foreign Office Middle East Department, sent the following minute to Kirkpatrick:

2. Meantime I believe it to be only right to make you aware of the following. In the course of the week's business I have seen a lot of members of the Office of all ranks, and have been deeply impressed with the dismay caused throughout our ranks by HMG's action. People are doing their duty but with a heavy heart and a feeling that, whatever our motives, we have terribly damaged our reputation.

3. I have not sought this opinion, but it is only honest to add that I myself, with my USA, UN and Asia background have been appalled by what has been done, – even granted the gravity and imminence of the Nasser menace.

4. Against this background, particularly para. 2 above, and with apologies for any officiousness, may I venture to express the hope that some way may be found of responding to the Canadian initiative.[53]

The limited war agreed by the Cabinet of 4 November was a far cry from Eden's original ambition to occupy Egypt militarily, forcibly depose Nasser and replace him with an amenable 'successor' Government. All thoughts of attacking Cairo had been abandoned – although they remained in the long-term military plans – and the sole aim now was the occupation of the Canal terminals, which would improve Britain's negotiating position. In discussions on its future control the Cabinet again ignored the fact that Lloyd had almost secured an acceptable compromise on 'control' of the Canal in New York in October. Perhaps the Cabinet were never given an accurate account of how promising the Lloyd–Fawzi–Pineau talks had been; otherwise it is almost incomprehensible how a responsible Cabinet could throw overboard negotiations in favour of a war which both the Cabinet and the Egypt Committee had recognized carried with it the 'risk of heavy casualties', which would 'finally alienate opinion in the U.N.'. It is a strange quirk of history that Britain went to war on such slender grounds, with Parliament and the nation disunited. There had been a duality in the Cabinet instructions to the Chiefs of Staff since the beginning of the Suez crisis. Their intention had always been both to restore the internationalization of the Canal and to overthrow Nasser. Now both these had disappeared and the *casus belli* was merely to separate the combatants temporarily until the United Nations Force arrived.

The Anglo–French telegram to the UN ran: 'The two Governments remain convinced police action must be carried through urgently to stop the hostilities', but they added that 'they would most willingly stop military action' and give way to a UN peace-keeping force provided it was kept in being 'until satisfactory arrangements have been agreed in regard to the Suez Canal'. Eden announced the contents of the telegram to the Commons on 5 November.

Meanwhile Eden had made a ministerial broadcast on Saturday, 3 November, referring to his record at the League of Nations, and inappropriately, with the intended attack only a few hours off, he described himself as 'a man of peace, a League of Nations man, a United Nations man'. Gaitskell claimed the right of reply; his broadcast made him appear unpatriotic because, just as British troops were sailing into battle, he appealed to Conservatives to find a new Prime Minister who would stop the invasion and order an immediate ceasefire.

A *Daily Express* opinion poll containing a heavily loaded question, taken on 5–6 November, showed slightly over 50 per cent favouring Eden's action, and on 10–11 November a British Institute of Public Opinion (BIPO) poll showed 53 per cent agreeing with the way Eden had handled the Middle East situation. Although there was never a substantial majority in any poll in favour of war, they showed an overwhelming majority of Conservatives strongly behind Eden. The worst poll for Eden had been the BIPO poll on 5–6 September, which showed that 49 per cent would disapprove if Britain gave an ultimatum to Egypt that unless she agreed to 'our' proposals we would send troops to occupy the Canal. On 1–2 November, after the RAF raids on Egypt, in another BIPO poll 37 per cent approved of the action, but 44 per cent disapproved.[54]

Relations between Eden and Eisenhower deteriorated drastically. This should have been a red light for the Cabinet, but it was not shown the exchanges between the two heads of state. On 30 October Eisenhower had written a sinister confidential letter to Eden:

Dear Anthony,

I should like to ask for help in clearing up my understanding as to exactly what is happening between us and our European Allies – especially between us, the French and yourselves.

We have learned that the French had provided Israel with a considerable amount of equipment, including airplanes, in excess of the amounts of which we were officially informed. This action was, as you know, in violation of agreements now existing between our 3 countries. On Sunday . . . we discovered that the volume of communication traffic between Paris and Tel Aviv jumped enormously; alerting us to the probability that France and Israel were concerting detailed plans of some kind. . . .

Last evening our Ambassador to the United Nations met with your Ambassador, Pierson Dixon, to request him to join us in presenting the case to the United Nations . . . we were astonished to find that he [Dixon] was completely unsympathetic stating frankly that his Government would not agree to any action whatsoever to be taken against Israel.

All of this development, with its possible consequences, including the possible involvement of you and the French in a general Arab war, seems to me to leave your Government and ours in a very sad state of confusion, so far as any possibility of unified understanding and action are concerned.[55]

Anthony Nutting told the author that the Americans could read all the French cyphers. These can have left Eisenhower in no doubt as to French–Israeli collusion, and once the State Department knew what the French were up to they would be sure that the British were in it too.[56] Eden was tactless in not informing Eisenhower well in advance of his intention to issue the ultimatum on 30 October. His telegram announcing it arrived at the White House later than anticipated, so that the President first read about it on the Press Association tape and was angry and shocked. His earlier replies to Eden's messages had been sympathetic, although he advocated caution. Now there was no sympathy, only anger. For once, instead of addressing the British Prime Minister as 'My dear Anthony' he began 'Dear Prime Minister' in his second communication to Eden on that fateful day, 30 October:

> I have just learned from the press of the 12 hour ultimatum which you and the French Government have delivered to the Government of Egypt requiring under threat of forceful intervention the temporary occupation by Anglo–French forces of key positions at Port Said, Ismailia and Suez in the Canal Zone.
>
> I feel I must urgently express to you my deep concern at the prospect of this drastic action even at the very time when the matter is under consideration as it is today by the Security Council. It is my sincere belief that peaceful processes can and should prevail to secure a solution which will restore the armistice conditions as between Israel and Egypt, and also justly settle the controversy with Egypt about the Suez Canal.
>
> Sincerely, D.D.E.[57]

Makins had left his post as Ambassador in Washington to become, at Macmillan's request, Permanent Under-Secretary at the Treasury; his successor, Caccia, was at his own request travelling out by sea, so there was no Ambassador to help with this unprecedented crisis in Anglo–American relations. On 31 October Dulles told the Minister in charge of the British Embassy in Washington that what rankled most was what they believed to have been deliberate concealment on the British part. He felt that a peaceful solution had been within their grasp. The attack on Egypt just as the Soviet orbit was crumbling was 'one of the greatest tragedies for our trust in each other'.[58]

After the Cabinet on the evening of 4 November Eden cabled to Eisenhower: 'Now that police action has been started it must be carried through . . . we cannot have a military vacuum while a United Nations force is being constituted.' But he did not disclose the fact that paratroopers would begin the invasion of Egypt in the morning.

> I have always felt, as I made very clear to Mr. Khrushchev, that the Middle East was an issue over which, in the last resort, we would have to fight. . . . If we had allowed things to drift, everything would have gone from bad to worse. Nasser would have become a kind of Moslem Mussolini . . . taking the tricks all around the Middle East. . . . I am sure that this is the moment to curb Nasser's ambitions. . . . By this means, we shall have taken the first step towards re-establishing authority in this area for our generation.

He went on to speak of his grief at having to breach the Anglo–American alliance, and threw himself on Eisenhower's mercy: 'If you cannot approve, I would like you at least to understand the terrible decision that we have had to make.'[59] The day before, Eden had persuaded Churchill to publish a letter to his constituents saying: 'I am confident that our American friends will come to realise that, not for the first time, we have acted independently for the common good.' This was obviously intended for Eisenhower to read.[60]

On 5 November, while Eden was on his feet explaining to the Commons why seaborne landings had been launched on Port Said, he was brought a message that Brigadier Butler had received the surrender of the town from the Egyptian commander. This relieved the tension. The Conservatives cheered and waved their order papers, and Labour criticism was temporarily silenced. Luckily for Eden, a few hours later, when news was received that the ceasefire and surrender were 'off', the House had risen and he was saved from an embarrassing situation. From then on it was all bad news for Eden.

At 8 p.m. a telegram arrived from Dixon reporting that Colonel Ely and Mr Gordon, two UN observers in Cairo, had informed General Burns that the RAF were bombing built-up areas of Cairo and Heliopolis, and that a bomb had fallen near the Cairo central railway station. At the UN the permanent delegates of all countries except France were horrified. Dixon, upset by the fury of other UN delegations, used melodramatic language, unusual for a diplomat, in a telegram received in the Foreign Office at 9 p.m. It may well be that this telegram and a telephone conversation between Ivor Pink and Dixon were potent factors in making Eden decide to stop the war the next day. Dixon's comment that we could not protest against the Russian bombing of Budapest if we were ourselves bombing Cairo must have been particularly galling for the Prime Minister. The telegram was so important that it is reproduced in full.

Early this morning the Secretary-General telephoned to say that, an hour after I had left him, he had received a cable from General Burns (my immediately following telegram) reporting that bombing of the built-up area in Cairo and Heliopolis had begun.

2. He was sending me the report under an informal covering letter in which he would say that 'in view of the reason for continued hostilities implied in your reply to the cease-fire request it will of course attract considerable attention that such actions, which seem to be contrary to declared policy – are confirmed as taking place'. General Burns's report would be circulated at once to the Assembly.

3. He went on to say that in view of this very serious development he was more than ever confirmed in his view that there was no possibility of the United Nations which had shown its strong moral disapproval of our action, appearing in any way to take over from Anglo–French forces in the Middle East. The United Nations could only intervene physically to restore peace in the Middle East on the basis that those who had disturbed the Peace and refused the United Nations demand for cessation of hostilities should have first been declared morally in the wrong.

4. Hammarskjold then told me he was sending me a formal reply to the communication of Her Majesty's Government replying to the request for implementation of the cease-fire. In his letter (which I have since received – see my second immediately following telegram) he had stated that he would in the course of the day be submitting a final plan for a United Nations force to comply with the 48-hour period laid down in the Canadian resolution of November 4 (my telegram No. 1046). In this report on the plan he would have to

express himself on this matter of our bombings of populated areas and this is what he meant by the phrase in the last sentence of his letter.

5. These developments make it absolutely certain in my view that at the inevitable Assembly meeting later today and tonight, delegations will concentrate their attention on our failure to comply with the cease-fire and in particular on the reported bombings of populated areas in apparent contradiction to our declared policy. They will be in a very ugly mood and out for our blood and I would not be surprised if the Arab–Asians and the Soviet bloc did not try to rush through some resolution urging collective measures of some kind against us. Between them they might well cook up an appeal by the Arabs to the Soviet Union to come in and help them.

6. You will recall that two days ago (my telegram No. 1033) I felt constrained to warn you that if there was any bombing of open cities with resulting loss of civilian life it would make our proposals seem completely cynical and entirely undermine our position here. Again in my telegram No. 1035 I urged that, unless we could announce that Anglo–French forces were suspending all further military activities until we knew that the United Nations were prepared to deal with the whole situation effectively, there would be no chance of our being able to move towards our objectives without alienating the whole world.

7. I must again repeat this warning with renewed emphasis.

8. For the purposes of today's proceedings it would be useful if I could have:

(a) A governmental statement on our bombing policy;

(b) Up-to-date figures, if available, of Egyptian casualties so far caused in our operations, in particular of civilian personnel;

(c) Information as to when our limited operation with its limited objectives is going to stop.

9. You will realize that monstrously unjust as it may be in the light of the precautions which General Keightley is taking (and which I realize places him in a grave dilemma in view of his responsibility for British military personnel and for the success of the operation entrusted to him) we are inevitably being placed in the same low category as the Russians in their bombing of Budapest. I do not see how we can carry much conviction in our protests against the Russian bombing of Budapest if we are ourselves bombing Cairo.[61]

Eden was obviously worried about the attitude of the UN during 5 November – the crucial day after the decision had been taken to invade and the actual landings had taken place. He instructed Pink to telephone Dixon, and Pink reported; 'According to Sir Pierson Dixon, it is our bombing in Egypt which is at the moment doing the greatest harm to our interests.' Hammarskjold was very upset by reports from Cairo from General Burns about Ely and Gordon.

Pink continued that Pierson Dixon was

pessimistic about the way this evening's session would go. He considered that there was no prospect that the Assembly would look objectively at our proposals. They would be out for our blood and might well call for collective measures against us and the French. The one thing which might halt them would be an official statement on our bombing policy. The points which . . . he suggested any such statement should include were;

   1) an undertaking not to take air action against targets in populated areas.

   2) an indication of when our bombing would stop.

   3) any casualty figures if helpful.

It seems clear from this that we shall be in for a bad session tonight unless we can give some sort of undertaking that our bombing has stopped or will do shortly.

Eden can have had little sleep that night because at 4.06 a.m. he sent a telegram to Pierson Dixon: 'No air bombing has taken place since my last message. None is taking or will take place.' Perhaps this was technically correct in that heavy bomber attacks on Egypt had ceased, but it was misleading because ground-attack aircraft were strafing Port Said and producing a hideous number of civilian casualties. Still, it is evidence that in the early hours of the morning Eden was considering stopping the assault. But how he could say there was no bombing, with ground attacks going on at Port Said, is extraordinary.[62]

Detailed accounts of the airborne landings on 5 November and the seaborne landings on 6 November have been written by several authors, including Field Marshal Lord Carver. They had no access to the military records, but were able skilfully to reconstruct what happened from survivors, Keightley's published dispatches and other sources. In a political history it is unnecessary to retread the ground, but an accurate and authoritative short account was written at the time at 2 Corps HQ in the lucid language of officers trained at the Staff College at Camberley:

Operation Telescope   5/6 Nov

The Allied transport aircraft took off from Nicosia and Tymdou airfields [Cyprus] and arrived over Port Said at 0515Z. Some inaccurate AA fire was encountered but the drop was made successfully and all aircraft returned safely.

   3 Para Bn Cp of 16 Para Bde, strength approximately 780, dropped

on Gamil Airfield where they were met with considerable fire from tanks, mortars and LAA guns used in a ground role. Initially the enemy resistance was tough but after some 3 hours started to slacken. The airfield was secured by 0900 and was capable of receiving aircraft by 1200. By 1300 3 Para had advanced Eastward and reached the edge of the built up area of Port Said.

The French parachute drop of approximately 500 men from the 2nd Regiment Parachutists Colonial [2 RPC] was made near the Raswa bridges at the same time as 3 Para was landing. They also met with heavy fire from automatic weapons and mortars but no artillery or tanks. The Western bridge was captured intact but the Eastern pontoon bridge was destroyed by the Egyptians. The water works were also secured undamaged and a number of guns captured.

Both British and French parachute forces, who were under the command of Brigadier M. A. H. Butler, Commander of 16 Para Bde, reported that their success was due in large measure to the support of G/A aircraft which consistently knocked out enemy strong points and centres of resistance. During the whole day of constant support from shore based and carrier aircraft only one plane, a French F.84, was lost while the pilot escaped by parachute.

At 1345 a second drop of some 400 French parachutists of 2 RPC was made on the Southern outskirts of Port Fuad.

At 1500 it was reported that the Egyptian Governor and Military Commander had met the C.O. of 2 RPC to discuss surrender terms and request that Allied air attacks should cease. They were referred to Brigadier Butler. At 1920 terms of surrender were reported to have been accepted; within the hour however they were rejected. It appears that the Egyptian authorities in Port Said must have been in contact with Cairo during this time, hence their change of heart. The garrison and populace were encouraged to resist by broadcast vans which announced that Russian help was on the way, that London and Paris had been bombed and that World War III had started. Operations were resumed at 2030.

Allied casualties up to this stage had been comparatively light – British 4 dead, 20 wounded, 15 missing – French 5 dead, 10 wounded. During the same period over 100 Egyptian troops are believed to have been killed.

It was now clear that Port Said could not be captured by the parachute force alone and that the Commandos might have to make an opposed landing next morning. Fortunately, during the night 2 RPC completed the capture of Port Fuad.

The decision to launch a comparatively small airborne force without preliminary naval or air bombardment against a large town, where defences could not be forecast with accuracy, had proved a justifiable risk. The enemy had resisted stubbornly except when engaged by low-level air attack or by fire from destroyers. His tanks and SU 100's

[Russian self-propelled guns] were so well handled as to raise doubts whether they were manned by Egyptians unit [*sic*] or foreign 'volunteers.'

Sporadic fighting continued during the night and at dawn the garrison was still resisting in spite of broadcasts from the Voice of Britain urging them to surrender. [Voice of Britain was the Cyprus Radio Station.]

The Seaborne Assault

. . . the main assault was launched at 0545 on 6 Nov by 40 and 42 R.M. Commandos and a squadron of 6 R. Tanks against Port Said and by 1st Regiment Etranger Parachutistes [1 REP] and three French Navy Commandos (each about 80 strong) against Port Fuad.

The beaches were clear as they landed and indeed the landing was watched by numbers of Egyptian soldiers and civilians as the assault moved towards the town. Shortly afterwards a tank action was reported to be developing on the Golf Course South of the town. The French landing was unopposed as the whole of Port Fuad had been cleared of the enemy by 2 RPC during the previous night.

At 0615 the landing was reported to be going according to plan with only slight opposition. The bathing huts on the foreshore and one of the Raswa fuel storage tanks were on fire. The Egyptians had started the latter fire before the arrival of the Allies. Minesweepers started to sweep in towards the harbour but no mines were detected.

At 0650 45 R.M. Commando took off in helicopters from British aircraft carriers and landed on the beaches without incident. This was the first occasion on which this type of operation had been carried out by British troops.

General Stockwell later reported that, with General Beaufre and the other Task Force Commanders, he was going ashore at 0900 to secure the unconditional surrender of Port Said. This surrender was not achieved, however, for the Egyptian commander did not appear at the rendezvous. Consequently the battle for Port Said continued throughout the day.

At 1017 2 Corps Commander [Stockwell] reported that there was a tough battle taking place in Port Said but the situation was gradually being brought under control. A link-up had been achieved between British and French forces at the water works and he was organising an advance Southwards. Soldiers dressed in civilian clothes and armed civilians, including children of the age of 12 upwards, were proving a considerable nuisance.

From this time onwards it was extremely difficult for AFHQ to discover what was happening in Port Said. One encouraging piece of information stated that at 1000 French reconnaissance units had reached Ras El Ish, 6 Miles South of Port Said. This lack of precise information was equally embarrassing to the British Government on whom the political pressure from UNO to cease fire was rapidly mounting. There was moreover a threat from Russia that she intended to intervene with force in the Middle East.

At this time the first offensive air activity by the enemy took place. Two MIG 15 strafed Gamil Airfield. One of the aircraft was seen to have red markings and was believed to be a replacement flown in during the past few days.

Despite the fact that 2 destroyers and 12 E-boats were seen to be in Alexandria Harbour no attempt was made by the enemy to establish contact with our convoys.

From 1100 onwards the possibility of a general cease-fire and stand-fast on political grounds was the subject of many signals. At the same time orders were given to the Task Force Commanders telling them that they should not cease to exploit their successes until a firm order was received.

In a signal at 1455 the Allied C-in-C [Keightley] warned General Stockwell that a cease-fire was likely to be ordered at any time after 1700; and on receipt of the codeword STOP he was to stop operations and not open fire again unless attacked. . . . The Allied C-in-C was warned that the probable time of the cease-fire was likely to be 2359 hours + and this was later confirmed by signal. . . .

. . . the Egyptians still hoped for outside assistance to wage war against the Allies and were busy repairing runways with the expectation of receiving more Soviet aircraft. A report received during the evening that Russian jet aircraft were flying over Turkey supported this theory. In addition, a Canberra on photographic reconnaissance over Syria was shot down, very probably by a Russian pilot. Because of this the C-in-C ordered certain precautions to be taken, in particular the dispersal of aircraft on airfields and the return to UK of 3 Canberra and 3 Valiant squadrons.

One problem which had been solved for the Allied C-in-C was that the American 6th Fleet, which had been in the Eastern Mediterranean since the beginning of operations, had now withdrawn. The C-in-C Mediterranean Fleet had sent numerous signals asking them to withdraw following the many embarrassing incidents which had occurred and on the night 4/5 Nov they set course away from the paths of our assault convoys.

Twenty-four hours after the landings the weather deteriorated badly and if the operation had been delayed as was suggested by London, it is doubtful if the seaborne assault could have been made. This would have left the comparatively weak parachute force to deal with Port Said on its own – a task which might well have been beyond it unless it received additional help from the air or bombarding ships. The military and political consequences of having to accept a cease-fire with Port Said unsubdued are hard to imagine.

No official surrender of Port Said was made but fighting came to an end during the night, apart from occasional sniping. The cease-fire came into effect at 2359 by which time British and French forces had linked up in the town and advanced elements had reached the area of El Cap, some 23 miles South of Port Said.[63]

It was most unfortunate that the Egyptians issued firearms to all and sundry at Port Said to resist the invasion; this led to a large and unnecessary increase in Egyptian casualties. British and French parachutists were tough troops. When they found they were being fired upon from the balconies and windows of houses, by persons not in uniform, they stifled the resistance by killing many who would otherwise have been taken prisoner or allowed to go home. (Hitler had used the same technique in the closing stages of the Second World War by arming the Hitler Youth and the elderly in the Volkssturm (People's Militia). To save themselves from casualties British infantry shot them wholesale as they advanced into Germany.) In addition the 2 Corps report reveals that, despite the remonstrations of the Cabinet, naval guns were fired at Port Said; these, with their low trajectory, must have added considerably both to the damage to houses and property and to the casualties.

The low figure for British casualties was accurate. The estimate of 100 Egyptian casualties was a wild underestimate, and although the British Government tried to stick to it the Cabinet was forced, by disbelief at home and abroad, to hold an independent inquiry. Even as late as 1 December Head told the Cabinet that total Egyptian casualties at Port Said 'including the French area' were 300. Sir Edwin Herbert, in his capacity as President of the Law Society, was asked by the Minister of Defence to go to Port Said and Cyprus to make an investigation into the number of Egyptians killed and wounded in the action.[64] His estimate was:

Dead	650
Wounded and detained in hospital	900
Slightly wounded	1200
Total	2750

In Port Fouad he estimated there were 100 dead with an equivalent ratio of wounded. These shocking figures in face of the slight British and French military casualties are eloquent evidence of the brutality of the assault; no official explanation of the disparity has ever been given. High civilian casualties were the nightmare the Cabinet had been trying to avoid, and they were relentlessly used as propaganda by Nasser. Herbert's findings were published in December as a White Paper, which recorded that

> The steps taken to protect the interests of civilians jeopardised British lives and increased British casualties. . . . Not one bomb was dropped on Port Said or its environs, all air strikes being low level attacks by rocket, machine gun and cannon of great accuracy and very localised [while] the naval bombardment was both localised to the beaches and reduced in intensity to $\frac{1}{10}$ of the appropriate level.

But even '$\frac{1}{10}$ of the appropriate level' must have had devastating consequences, and the Cabinet's misgivings about the use of naval guns were abundantly justified.

There is evidence in the 2 Corps archives that Herbert may not have found all the records of the Egyptian dead in the British Sector and over Port Fouad he did not have full co-operation from the French. The total figures may well have been considerably higher therefore than his estimate. General Burns's judgment was that 'nearly a thousand Egyptian soldiers, police and civilians had been killed in the fighting at Port Said and Port Fuad'.[65] This is probably correct.

At 9 a.m. on 6 November Keightley signalled to Stockwell:

> Many congratulations your landing and quick advance. London has signalled that Russia announces she may take part in ME with force. Regret these operations losing their select membership. It would be prudent to take normal precautions as if air threat existed. We are dealing with the airfield situation this end. As soon as Port Said is captured your aim will be to occupy Ismailia as quickly as possible with minimum loss of life.

At 11 a.m. the War Office signalled direct to Stockwell: 'It may be essential politically to have an immediate cease fire and stand fast. Could you maintain the force at present ashore indefinitely?' At 14.27 Stockwell was told '. . . probable that cease fire will be ordered in near future', and at 14.50 '. . . essential establish a standing patrol as far south along the road to Kantara as feasible'. At 16.24 Stockwell told his troops in Port Said: 'Cease fire may be ordered any time after 1700. On receipt of Code Word "Stop" you will cease fire and NOT reopen fire unless attacked. NO forward movements from your positions reached on land are to be made after the Cease Fire.' At 18.00 the forward troops, the commandos and paras were told 'Keep cracking until you receive orders from us. The more real estate you occupy the better.'

At 18.00 Keightley told Stockwell that the ceasefire was definitely to be at 23.59 that evening. At 20.25 Beaufre sent a wireless message to Stockwell that he had arranged a break-out aiming at 'reaching El Kantara on evening 7 November' without any parachute drop. At 04.54 on 7 November there was a minor panic because 3 Commando Brigade had not acknowledged the ceasefire message, and might have been racing down the Canal against orders. They were told that this might result 'in severe political consequences'. But at 07.00 calm was restored when the Commando Brigade reported that they had not 'ackd' the ceasefire message because they claimed it was not addressed to them.[66]

It is fair to count 5 and 6 November as belonging to the great days in the history of the British Army: the operations were a complete success. However, thirty years on a telling epitaph on the fighting came from Air Marshal Sir Dermot Boyle (head of the RAF in 1956): 'We were proud of everything in the War; there was much not to be proud of about Suez.'[67]

Soon afterwards, General Stockwell said at a press conference that he could have been in Suez in forty-eight hours. This was ill received by Head, who had been given the hopeless task in the Commons of arguing that it was both right to start and to stop the invasion, and had given as one argument for stopping that it would have taken eight days to get to Suez.

Back in London it was a different story. The Government had a disastrous day. No one can fail to feel deep sympathy for Eden; he must have realized on 6 November that he had staked his political future on a gamble that was failing before his eyes.

Meanwhile on 5 November the Russians, gravely embarrassed by a revolution in Budapest which they were callously crushing, intervened in the Suez dispute with blustering messages to London, Paris and Tel Aviv, asserting that they were 'determined to crush the aggressors and restore peace', combined with threats of rocket attacks. They asked Eisenhower to stop the fighting in conjunction with Soviet armed forces. This Russian move incensed Eisenhower, who said that 'if the Soviet Forces arrived in the Middle East, America would respond with everything in the bucket'. The American Navy was put on full alert, which was made plain to the Russians. Eden too responded firmly to the Russian threat, secure in the knowledge that at that stage Russian rockets could not reach Tel

Aviv, Paris or London. The Russian message helped not only Eden's standing in Britain, but his position vis-à-vis Eisenhower.

The Cabinet met at 9.45 on 6 November. Shortly before the meeting a message had been received from New York that Hammarskjold considered Israel had now given an unconditional acceptance of a ceasefire, and he 'regarded himself as in a position now to ask us to agree that our conditions had been met'. As the Cabinet had only agreed to launch the assault less than forty-eight hours before, believing that Israel had refused this ceasefire, his telegram cut the ground away from under Eden's feet.[68]

Some Cabinet members were alarmed by the Russian message coming on top of American hostility, and feared that fighting in the Middle East might get out of control. Lloyd told the Cabinet they must take into account that it was urgent to regain the initiative in bringing hostilities to an end 'while there was an opportunity to carry with us the more moderate sections of opinion in the General Assembly', and that we must 'shape our policy' in such a way as to enlist the maximum sympathy and support from the US Government, but 'we must not appear to be yielding in face of Soviet threats'. In discussion it was stated that an effective international force might never be established in the Canal area, and then we should appear to have fallen short of that effective occupation of the Canal area which we had publicly declared to be one of our objectives, and if we waited for an international force to be available to remove the obstruction, free transit might not be restored for many months.

However, another potent factor on top of the disturbing news from the United Nations and Russia was a sudden volte-face by Macmillan. Up till 6 November he had been the most enthusiastic advocate of armed intervention. Now he was upset by the possibility of UN oil sanctions and a sudden threat to the £, and according to Butler 'switched almost overnight from being the foremost protagonist of intervention to being the leading influence for disengagement'.[69]

On 5 November, as soon as news of the airborne landings reached them, the Americans started selling sterling viciously around the world; it had to be propped up by the Bank of England at very considerable cost to Britain's inadequate reserves. No hint of this reached the newspapers. The $ rate on convertible sterling in Zurich stayed steady, but the Bank of England and the Treasury were passing to Macmillan the gloomiest reports of this sudden threat to Britain's reserves, which carried with it the danger of a forced devaluation and the collapse of the sterling area.

Macmillan was adamant that the fighting must be stopped because of the danger to sterling, and on 6 November in Cabinet he was supported by Butler and Salisbury. Head and Stuart wanted to go on, but Eden, chastened by his colleagues' irresolution, the UN pressure to stop and the news that Israel had agreed to a ceasefire, decided that he must call the war off.

It was also stated that, although it would be practicable to occupy the whole Canal area, such an action might produce a Soviet invasion of Syria or some other area in the Middle East, and possibly a direct attack on the Anglo–French forces, and that it was probable that other Arab states would come actively to the help of Egypt. In addition the UN might impose oil sanctions 'against the French and ourselves', and 'if we agreed to break off hostilities we could maintain that we had achieved our primary objectives by bringing the Israeli– Egypt fighting in the Canal Zone to an end together with the agreement of the UN to establish an international force.' Eden was downcast, but neither he nor the hawks seem to have pressed the case hard for a continuation of hostilities.[70]

As soon as the Cabinet meeting was over Eden telephoned Paris, where Mollet and Pineau were holding a conference at the Quai d'Orsay with Adenauer, the West German Chancellor. Eden told Monnet of the British Cabinet decision to stop the war, and (according to Pineau) emphasized the threat to sterling. Mollet was angry. The French nation were behind their Government in the attack on Egypt, believing that the downfall of Nasser would result in the defeat of the rebellion in Algeria. Pineau and other members of the Cabinet wanted to go on without Britain, and argued that, if Britain withdrew, Israel would be released from her pledge not to cross the Canal and could occupy the whole Canal Zone in co-operation with the French. Mollet said he must have time to consider the decision and that confirmation must await a Cabinet meeting which could not be concluded before 5 p.m. Adenauer advised Mollet to accept a ceasefire and at 5 p.m., after a stormy Cabinet, Mollet telephoned Eden to say that he agreed.[71] Immediately a telegram was sent to the United Nations from the Foreign Office to the effect that the Prime Minister would make an announcement about the ceasefire in the Commons at 6 p.m. British time, but emphasizing that immediate clearance of the Canal was necessary and that the British salvage fleet was ready to do the job.

Before Eden went into the Chamber he received a telephone call from Eisenhower. The President was affable and told Eden he was delighted at the news, but he did not want any of the Great Powers to be involved in a United Nations peace-keeping force: he was frightened that 'the red boys would demand the lion's share', and he did not 'give a damn about how the election goes,' because they were giving their whole thoughts to Hungary and the Middle East.[72]

When Eden announced the ceasefire in the Commons the House was packed with Members awaiting dramatic news. Eden was heard in pinprick silence as he told them not only of the ceasefire, but about the UN Force, and finished by saying that Anglo–French technicians would clear the Canal at once. Both Labour and Conservative members cheered. Labour thought they had won a political victory. Most of the Tories thought Eden had achieved his aims. Only the Suez Group kept quiet, glum and angry.

Gaitskell attacked the Government, saying that 'there was not a shred of evidence that there was any really serious danger [to the Canal] until we intervened', and that Britain had invoked the law of the jungle as the Russians had done in Hungary. Eden replied that nothing short of the Anglo–French action would have induced the UN to act by sending in a peace force. He refused to answer Gaitskell's taunt that he had abandoned his objective of destroying Nasser's Government, which had been set out in the leaflets dropped over Cairo. Eden was confident, buoyed up by his talk to Eisenhower. The *Manchester Guardian* said that 'he seemed astonishingly fresh and vigorous. He was as self confident as he had been throughout the whole affair.'

When he returned to his room in the Commons the Prime Minister found a written communication sent to him by Eisenhower through the US Embassy in London:

Dear Anthony:

I was delighted at the opportunity to talk with you on the telephone and to hear that the U.K. will order a cease-fire this evening. On thinking over our talk I wish to emphasize my urgent view (A) that the UN resolution on cease-fire and entry of a UN force be accepted without condition so as not to give Egypt with Soviet backing an opportunity to quibble or start negotiations; items such as use of technical troops to clear canal can be handled later; (B) that it is vital no excuse be given for Soviet participation in UN force, therefore all big Five should be excluded from force as UN proposes. Any attack on UN force would meet immediate reaction from all UN; (C) I think immediate consummation UN plan of greatest importance otherwise there might be invitation to developments of greatest gravity.

Sincerely hope you find it possible to agree with these views and can so inform Hammarskjold before tonight's meeting.

Let me say again that I will be delighted to have you call me at any time. The telephone connection seemed very satisfactory.

Warmest regards,

Ike[73]

Eden was highly delighted at this message, believing that his good relationship with Eisenhower had been fully restored, and at 9 p.m. he sent this telegram to Mollet:

The President of the United States telephoned me on his own account. There is no doubt at all that the friendship between us all is retored and even strengthened. I did not therefore think it wise to mention the anxieties which Chancellor Adenauer expressed.

I feel that as a result of all our efforts we have laid bare the reality of Soviet plans in the Middle East and are physically holding a position which can be decisive for the future.

I cannot adequately express to you how grateful I have been for your loyalty and understanding in this difficult period. I am sure history will justify us.

We are all filled with admiration at the gallant conduct of the French troops. Our friendship tested in these days of trial has been strengthened.[74]

The next day Eden telephoned Eisenhower at 9.45 US time. By now the votes in the Presidential Election had been counted, and Eisenhower had an overwhelming majority. The President was warm, telling the British Prime Minister that their disagreement over Egypt was 'no more than a family spat'. Eden asked if he and Mollet could fly over for a conference in Washington the next day. Eisenhower said he would be delighted, and Eden immediately relayed the invitation to Mollet. The following telegram was sent by Lloyd to Washington and repeated for information to Paris at 3.15, and press statements were prepared for release soon after Eden announced the visit in the Commons at 4 p.m.:

Following a conversation with the Prime Minister on the telephone at 1.30 p.m. G.M.T. today, the President has invited the Prime Minister to go to Washington as soon as possible for discussions on the Middle East situation. The French Prime Minister has also been invited and has accepted.

The Prime Minister will be accompanied by myself and a small party. They will arrive in the course of tomorrow, November 8, and it has been agreed with the President that discussions will start on Friday.

The visit will be announced by the Prime Minister in the House of Commons at 4.00 p.m. G.M.T. A simultaneous announcement will be made by the White House and by the French Prime Minister.

After his telephone call to Eden, Eisenhower consulted with Hoover, who was Acting Secretary of State during Dulles's absence in hospital. Hoover objected violently to Eden and Mollet's visit the next day because Ben Gurion had by now refused to accept the UN instructions to withdraw to his previous frontiers, and the State Department felt strongly that if Eden and Mollet, who had broken the peace simultaneously with Ben Gurion, came as honoured guests to Washington at that moment, it would look as if America had approved of the war. Then, they feared, the USA would become unpopular in the Arab world and the mission of the UN peace-keeping force might fail.

Two hours after he had put down the receiver, and a bare half hour before Eden was due to make his statement in the Commons, Eisenhower spoke to him again and said he feared that, since Britain might not go along with the UN plan, the meeting must be post-poned until France and Britain had complied with UN resolutions. The officials in Washington had sensed that Eden would object to the UN Force not having a British contingent, and might not agree to withdraw unconditionally from Port Said.[75]

Eisenhower's refusal was a bitter pill. Eden's house of cards was collapsing. Instead of announcing the visit, he had to tell the Commons that he must have further consultations with the USA, France and the Commonwealth. Gaitskell humiliatingly extracted a promise from him that Britain would not advance from the beach-head or build up forces there for a break-out later. Eden also had to announce a 10 per cent cut in oil supplies, which produced the unkind comment from Labour backbenchers that if petrol coupons were issued they should carry a portrait of Eden. From then on charges that Britain had incited Israel to attack Egypt began to fly both inside and outside the House of Commons.

Immediately the ceasefire was announced, on 6 November, Boyle and Nutting resigned from the Government, having previously notified the Prime Minister of their intention but not wanting to show disunity while British armed forces were in action. These resignations did Eden little harm because at that stage his policy of war was endorsed by an overwhelming majority of the Conservative Party. Boyle managed to make his peace with his constituency association and was afterwards given a Cabinet post in the Macmillan

Government. Not so Nutting! His Leicestershire constituency, in the heart of fox-hunting England, took it ill and he was forced to resign, never to return to Parliament. Thus his glittering political career terminated at the early age of thirty-six, just when it seemed that great things lay in store for him. Eden, with whom he had been on terms of close friendship, and whose protégé he was in some ways, never spoke to him again.

When Nutting prepared his resignation statement for the House of Commons Macmillan sent for him and asked to read it. He told Nutting that it would be 'very dangerous' and 'could easily bring down the Government. You have been proved right and we have been proved wrong. You have also done the right thing by resigning and, if you keep silent now, you will be revered and rewarded. You will lead the Party one day.' So Nutting tore up his draft and kept silent for ten years, but then wrote his book, *No End of a Lesson*, which told the whole sorry story of collusion with Israel. In 1967, when Harold Wilson was Prime Minister, civil servants tried to prevent him from publishing this book as did the lately retired Conservative Prime Minister Harold Macmillan. Strictly speaking Nutting was in breach of the Official Secrets Act and his Privy Councillor's oath of confidentiality, but Churchill and Eden had both done the same thing in their own memoirs, and Nutting went ahead. *The Times* serialized it before publication, amid great publicity. Eden made no reply, but Hailsham wrote in the *Daily Express* that Nutting had emerged 'like a wraith from the past to accuse his friends, colleagues and protectors of what he describes as a sordid conspiracy'. After 1956 no Conservative Prime Minister made any offer of a public post to Nutting.

12

Sterling Crisis and Resignation
November–December 1956

ON 7 NOVEMBER Macmillan held a meeting with his Parliamentary Under-Secretaries and Treasury knights, who now included Sir Roger Makins, at 11 Downing Street. It was disclosed that Britain had lost $85 million propping up the £ on foreign exchanges since the war started, and urgently needed to make a drawing from the International Monetary Fund to replenish the reserves. From soundings made in the USA it was considered likely that the State Department would object to such a drawing, so that the crisis needed to be discussed immediately with the Bank of England and the Washington Embassy. Further gloomy news was that, with the Suez Canal blocked and other Arab countries denying France and Britain oil from their pipelines, 'the prospect was over the next six months that there might be a short fall for Europe and the United Kingdom of 3 to 4 million tons', and to maintain Britain's full supplies from Western Hemisphere sources (North and South America) might involve expenditure of over $800 million.[1]

Macmillan was seriously alarmed by this meeting although, as has been seen, he had written calmly in January to Eden about the likelihood of 'a forced devaluation of sterling in the Autumn', and repeated this on 2 May. Macmillan would not consider other measures to save sterling, such as floating or devaluing the £, or import controls. It must have become plain to him that Eden might not be able to continue as Prime Minister much longer with his poor health and the collapse of the Middle East policy, and it would be detrimental to his own chances of the succession to 10 Downing Street if he should be seen to have failed as Chancellor of the Exchequer by being forced into a crisis devaluation of sterling. Some historians believe this was an important factor in his subsequent behaviour. Of course Britain should have drawn the gold tranche from the International Monetary Fund and claimed the interest waiver on their IMF debt as soon as the threat of war appeared in August. The French sensibly drew their tranche from the IMF in October and the franc was not in trouble when the invasion failed in November.

As has been seen, during the early days of the Suez crisis, on 9 August, Macmillan had raised with his colleagues the fear that a war with Egypt might endanger the £; then Norman Brook, Secretary to the Cabinet, sent a note to Bridges at the Treasury of the conclusions reached together with a memorandum that the Chancellor had mentioned as a precaution that he was thinking of asking Australia 'to sell us some gold and was also considering whether we should not withdraw dollars from the International Monetary Fund'. Brook also recorded that the Chancellor had said that events in the Eastern Mediterranean 'might give us grounds for asking this year for the waiver of interest on the United States loan'. (This waiver could only be claimed if there were exceptional circumstances weakening the £.) Brook added that it was inappropriate to let officials in a number of departments see the record of the meeting at which Macmillan had made these remarks.

In September the Governor of the Bank of England, C. F. Cobbold, played down the threat to the £, and wrote that it would be wrong to give the Chancellor the impression of a situation so serious that steps needed to be taken, but Robert Hall advised: '. . . while prediction is very risky, my own opinion is that sterling could hardly remain a currency in which people would hold substantial balances if we had another devaluation so soon after 1949 . . . [if] forced to move I agree with Bank that we should go on to floating rate'.

Cobbold looked on any change in the exchange rate as a disaster, and was opposed to a drawing from the IMF because he thought it would be self-defeating in that it would demonstrate that Britain had lost confidence in her power to support sterling. Upon Cobbold lies a heavy responsibility for Macmillan's failure to safeguard the £ before embarking on war. Cobbold was a different type from more recent Governors, being a professional City banker without great knowledge of economics.

On reading these papers Macmillan minuted on 12 August: 'It is clear we are pretty well armed for Suez. But I feel more and more convinced that our economy is too weak for us to do without permanent powers.'[2] A note on Exchange Control was prepared by the Treasury on 14 August, saying there were 'full and adequate powers' to block or control the assets in Britain of persons or Governments abroad, whether inside the sterling area or not.

However the wartime power compulsorily to acquire privately owned securities had been allowed to lapse, and there was a potential gap in Kuwait and Gulf territories which would be difficult to block without undermining the rulers' confidence in sterling and in the advantages of the sterling area connection. The paper also noted that 'once confidence in sterling is weakened capital can move out of the country in several ways', one of which was through non-sterling area countries running down their balances.'[3] However, Macmillan took no action prior to the invasion to strengthen the Treasury powers to stop capital moving out of the country, or to draw a tranche from the IMF, or to press the USA to grant the waiver.

There the matter rested until on 7 September Bridges sent the Chancellor a memorandum following a Treasury meeting with the Deputy Governor of the Bank of England and Sir George Bolton to 'discuss the sort of action we might take in the event of war with Egypt'. With foresight they postulated that we might be acting 'in accordance with United Nations wishes and most importantly overt US and Commonwealth support, and support from a good number of other countries'; however, at the other extreme we might be 'acting with the French and perhaps one or two others', but without the overt support of the USA and with a division in the Commonwealth, with India and Ceylon actively disapproving.

In the latter case, Bridges felt 'the strains might be so great that whatever precautionary measures were taken we should be unable to maintain the value of the currency', and this pointed to 'the vital necessity from the point of view of our currency and our economy of ensuring that we do not go it alone, and that we have the maximum US support'. This was prophetic, and should have been a warning to Macmillan to take steps urgently to protect the £. He minuted: 'Yes, this is just the trouble. US are being very difficult.' But he took no action in face of a dire warning from an authoritative source.[4]

On 21 September Rowan reported that there was 'a very dangerous outlook for sterling in the coming months', and 'unless something . . . is done, both soon and successfully, sterling will be in the greatest danger, and our other resources – IMF, dollar securities, etc. will not do much to put off the day.' Here was an even more ominous warning. Again Macmillan ignored it, minuting: 'This is gloomy, but very likely correct.' Thus the Chancellor drifted into the war of which he was a strong protagonist, ignoring the timely warnings from his Treasury advisers. In September and October the USA would have raised no objections to a drawing from the IMF and would probably have agreed to the waiver. By the time Macmillan appealed for American help after the invasion was launched in November, it was too late. By then the USA was not prepared to help Britain.

On Tuesday, 30 October Macmillan, with Makins and Rowan, had seen the Governor of the Bank of England at 5 p.m. at the House of Commons. Macmillan explained to him that within a few hours Britain would almost certainly be involved in hostilities in Egypt, and 'it was quite clear there would be adverse effects on sterling'; he hoped that central banks and currency boards would not seek to take advantage of the position, to the detriment of sterling. The Governor said that sterling had 'already come under pressure', and after a discussion on the long-term aspects it was agreed not to go to the IMF for a standby credit until the general political situation improved. This was a rash decision; the argument was that applying to the IMF would be taken as a sign of trouble over the reserves.

On 31 October Treasury officials held a conference with the Bank of England. The meeting recorded that the drain on the reserves had started and $50 million had been lost in two days, and if the Canal and the pipelines were closed we should be faced with a shortage of oil amounting to 25 per cent of total supplies even if American companies co-operated to the full. If the US administration would not help, the shortage would be greater.

They agreed that the most important question was an IMF drawing; the Bank had previously advised Macmillan that a drawing would be 'bad for confidence in sterling', although France had recently arranged for a standby credit of $260 million. The Bank wanted to wait until there was a definite improvement in the reserve movements and 'we could then draw on the fund without appearing to do so from weakness'.[5]

Even now the Bank thought the time had not come to make a drawing, for they felt that the gold quota and the first credit tranche (amounting to $560 million) could be drawn at comparatively short notice when it was 'clearly necessary'. The Bank pointed out that Britain's right to draw her gold quota ($235 million) would be 'virtually automatic', and access to the first credit tranche 'would normally be given with very few questions asked'; indeed for this reason Britain had not opposed the recent drawing by Egypt of her gold tranche.

Ominously, Sir Dennis Rickett reported to the Chancellor: 'It is conceivable that the United States might oppose a drawing by us, particularly if in the meantime the General Assembly had passed an adverse Resolution', and accordingly advised that a request for the drawing should be delayed 'as long as possible to give tempers time to cool all round'. Macmillan agreed not to apply to the IMF – another mistake. An application on 2 November might have been obstructed by the USA because the RAF were already bombing Egypt, but it must have had some chance of success before the landings of 5 and 6 November. After all, the French had obtained a credit tranche of $239 million from the Fund as late as 17 October.

On 7 November the General Assembly passed a resolution calling for the immediate withdrawal of British, French and Israeli troops. Eden would not comply. He felt it would be ignominious to allow Egyptian troops to take over the British and French positions before the arrival of an effective UN Force to replace them, and although this was being organized it would not be ready in strength for some weeks. Eden and Lloyd were determined, too, that the Canal should be speedily cleared with the help of British salvage ships, and that Britain and France should use their possession of 23 miles of the Canal as a 'gage' to get better terms out of Nasser for the future operation of the Canal, and also as a negotiating counter in a permanent Arab–Israeli settlement.[7]

Lloyd went back to the United Nations in New York on 12 November. There he plugged the argument with the Americans that the Anglo–French occupation of the Canal was the only bargaining counter we had with Nasser. It met a stony reception. When Lloyd saw Hammarskjold he found the Secretary General doubtful if Nasser would allow the UN Force into Egypt. Lloyd said that unless they did we should not remove our troops. Hammarskjold replied that it 'would be unthinkable' for the UN Force to be withdrawn unless there was a firm agreement with Nasser about both the clearance and the future operation of the Canal, although he asked Lloyd if Britain would make a token withdrawal to 'improve the atmosphere'. Lloyd agreed to do so.[8]

Hammarskjold departed for Cairo; Lloyd went to Washington, where Eisenhower refused to see him. Dulles did see Lloyd and Caccia from his sick bed, and made the amazing remark: 'Why did you stop? Why did not you go through with it?' At the State Department Lloyd was told in no uncertain terms that nothing except a completely unconditional withdrawal would satisfy the President and the US Government.[9] When Hammarskjold returned from Cairo he reported that Nasser had refused to negotiate about the future of the Canal until the British and French had withdrawn, although he empowered Hammarskjold to say that he would stand by the undertakings given by Fawzi to Lloyd and Pineau in the October negotiations. This was generous after all that Egypt had suffered from the French and British.

On 23 November the General Assembly met to consider a resolution censuring Britain and France. Lloyd worked hard beforehand, lobbying any delegations likely to show sympathy with Britain. Spaak obligingly put down an amendment calling for the 'expedition' of the troops' withdrawal but omitting the censure. Lloyd made an impassioned speech denying that Britain and France had instigated Israel to attack, that Britain had already made a token withdrawal of one battalion, and offering British salvage ships to help the UN team to clear the Canal. He pleaded in vain. Spaak's amendment was defeated with the USA abstaining, and a vote of censure was passed on 24 November by 63 to 5, with 10 abstentions. Lloyd then told Hammarskjold that Britain would hand over to the UN Force in about four weeks. Hammarskjold replied that this was too long a delay.[10]

On 24 November headlines on the vote of censure were splashed across the front pages of the British national newspapers, to the delight of the Opposition and the anger of the Conservatives. It was a bitter humiliation for Eden. However, he was no longer at the helm. Butler was in charge. The day before, Eden had left for a holiday in Jamaica 'on doctor's orders'. Butler was told by Eden's physician, Sir Horace Evans, that the Prime Minister must not live on stimulants (amphetamines) and 'since he was unlikely to relax in a clinic' he had recommended 'a few weeks in Jamaica for recuperation'. Butler recorded that he was left with 'the odious duty of withdrawing the troops, re-establishing the £, and salving our relations with the US and UN' besides bearing the brunt of the general criticism.[11] It was disastrous for Eden to withdraw to Jamaica at this crucial moment. He could only be reached by messenger over bad roads at Ian Fleming's house, Golden Eye, when official telegrams were sent through to the Governor, Sir Hugh Foot, in the capital.

On 7 November the Egypt Committee had agreed not to insist on a UK contribution to the international force, but they were not prepared to withdraw the Anglo–French force until it could be succeeded by an international force competent to fulfil the purposes which the British Government had in view.[12] At the Egypt Committee on 12 November, Head said that Keightley and Stockwell were concerned at the vulnerability of the Anglo–French force at Port Said, and that if they were attacked they would need larger forces than those used in the original assault. The Chiefs of Staff had submitted a memorandum dated 9 November:

It seems likely that Russia will intervene either covertly (if we remain in occupation of Egyptian territory) in the shape of volunteers or overtly as the agent of the United Nations. . . . Russia is likely to re-constitute the Egyptian Air Force and thereby pose a serious threat to all our forces in the area . . . we should be prepared in the worst case for a Russian sponsored war involving major threats.[13]

Perhaps Mountbatten's hand should be seen in this alarming memorandum, but Eden continued to fight his corner hard, saying at the Egypt Committee on 13 November:

We could not allow ourselves to be put into the insecure position of having to withdraw our troops with no adequate satisfaction regarding the re-opening of the Canal.

. . . we would be prepared to remove our troops, unit by unit, in a phased operation as the United Nations forces came in. We could not, however, accept a condition that our forces should have been totally withdrawn before any agreement for clearing the Canal became operative.[14]

The Committee agreed with him, and a telegram 'in the sense of the Prime Minister's statement' was sent to Hammarskjold. The contest with Nasser was on again, and as long as Eden was still in Downing Street the Government stuck to this defiant attitude despite the implacable hostility shown by Eisenhower. After Eden's departure on 23 November his colleagues capitulated. The reason was the difficulty of defending the £ and satisfying the urgent need for oil supplies with the USA hostile. Had Eden stayed at his post he would have fought much harder, but his alternative must have involved a devaluation of the £ and import controls. Almost certainly it would have led to Macmillan threatening resignation, and by now Eden was not in a strong enough political position to allow this without risking the fall of the Government and a possible dissolution.

The Americans continued to make it crystal clear that they would go on attacking the £ and denying oil unless Britain withdrew unconditionally; but if Britain made a complete surrender they promised full assistance over sterling and oil. Macmillan now became the key figure. He saw the sterling crisis in the starkest terms. Eden's authorized biographer writes: 'Others thought he was making a deliberate move for the leadership' and was determined to force the Cabinet to agree to unconditional evacuation in order to get US support for the £ at the earliest possible moment.[15] His hand was strengthened by a top level Bank and Treasury meeting on 13 November, which reported:

We cannot give any estimate of how long it will be before we may be faced with a run on sterling of a kind which will endanger the rate. It is quite clear, however, that the announcement of our losses for November (published about 3 or 4 December) will give a considerable shock to confidence . . . if sterling collapses and the sterling system with it, then an instrument which finances half the world's trade and payments will be destroyed and *there is no other instrument to replace it* [italics in original].

They recommended that the Chancellor should go for the largest possible drawing from the IMF, and pressed Macmillan to approach the USA urgently. Now Macmillan veered away from Eden's policy, knowing there was no chance of US aid for sterling if Britain stuck to Eden's hard line against unconditional withdrawal.[16]

On 21 November (Eden could not attend because he was ill), Macmillan told the Cabinet that petrol rationing was unavoidable, and this was agreed. Then the Chancellor went on that the Cabinet had to face the grave choice of deciding 'whether to mobilise all our financial resources' to defend the Exchange Rate. These would have had to include compulsory purchase of privately owned foreign stocks, which would have put the City in a near panic, or floating the £. If the £ floated, according to Macmillan it might cease to be an international currency and it would almost certainly lead to the dissolution of the sterling area (omitting to say that such consequences were far from certain and a matter of controversy). Macmillan clinched his argument by stating that to float would be 'a severe blow to the prestige of the United Kingdom and a major victory for the Soviet Union', and 'might entail almost as great a demand on our reserves as the maintenance of a fixed rate'; we could not look for any assistance from the United States until normal political relations with them had been resumed after the situation in the Middle East had been clarified.[17] With hindsight, modern economists would strongly dispute the validity of Macmillan's economic arguments on 21 November, but they were the views of the Bank of England and the Treasury.

Macmillan considered Senator Hubert Humphrey, in charge of the US Treasury, a close personal friend, and he followed up the Cabinet meeting by drafting a long letter to him in excellent prose – an impassioned plea for American help in the hour of need. It lies unread in the archives because the Chancellor was persuaded by his advisers to send a much shorter note, and after much drafting and redrafting and consultation with Caccia in Washington he sent the following message marked 'Top Secret' on 21 November:

1. Your officials receive the weekly figures for our gold and dollar reserves, and they will no doubt have brought to your attention the disturbing trend ever since Nasser seized the Suez Canal at the end of May, which has become much worse since our intervention in Egypt.

2. These losses arise mainly from political and international reasons affecting our position as the major banker for the world; our trading position, and that of the R.S.A., though not so good as we could have wished, has been satisfactory. Recent events, especially the closing of the Canal and the I.P.C. pipeline, must harm our trading position; but if we can stick it out until confidence is restored, the soundness of our basic position must reassert itself.

3. Caccia and I have asked Harcourt to discuss all this with you, as it seems impossible at the moment for me to meet you personally, much as I should like to do so. I hope however that you will be able to come to the N.A.T.O. meeting in Paris in December and that we could have some talk there.

4. I know that there has been a deep division between our two countries in the action which we and the French took in Egypt. We took that action in the belief that it was not only in our own but in the general interest. I can only hope that time will show that we were not wrong. The undermining of sterling would, of course, hurt us, but that would be far from all. It would do irreparable damage not merely to sterling but to the whole fabric of trade and payments in the Free World. This would be a major victory for the Communists. We can surely prevent it – but only if we act speedily.[18]

Humphrey turned a deaf ear to Macmillan's entreaties and was equally unhelpful when Caccia saw him seven days later. Never before can Anglo–American relations have sunk to so low a level, and it was evident that they could only be restored by the ignominious unconditional withdrawal of British forces from the Canal Zone. Caccia's report of his talk to Humphrey is evidence of an unparalleled quarrel between the American and British Governments. He reported that Humphrey had told him 'at the right time' that the United States would be prepared to do everything possible to help sterling, 'but this time had not arrived', they must not appear to be 'openly siding with us', and 'any official meetings or official actions in support of us would be construed as double crossing of the United States friends, many of them newly acquired'. Caccia's report went on:

I said that I concluded from what he had said the United States Government did not consider we had yet given sufficient evidence of our readiness to carry through the United Nations Resolutions. He nodded. I then asked if he could give me some more precise definition of what the United States Government would regard as sufficient action. I told him that I trusted in giving me an answer he would bear in mind the clearing of the Canal. It was the Egyptian Government that was failing to carry out the Resolution of November 2. It surely could not be the attitude of the United States Government that the Egyptians were to be allowed to flout the United Nations while the United Kingdom was to be judged by the most extreme demands of Egypt and the Soviet bloc.

Humphrey said that in the eyes of the world Egypt had been invaded by us and as long as she remained occupied, she would have world sympathy and United States support. If the United Kingdom, by remaining in Port Said, appeared to exert force over negotiations for the clearing of the Canal or the settlement of the future regime for the Canal, the world would never believe that these negotiations were not held at gun-point.

Humphrey more than once used the simile that the United Kingdom was an armed burglar who had climbed in through the window while Nasser was the house-holder in his nightshirt appealing to the world for protection. I told Humphrey more than once that this was an entirely inaccurate simile. It would be more accurate to liken the United Kingdom to the traditional user of a right of way who was being threatened by an obstructionist land-owner holding a shot gun. Humphrey tried to contend that the right of way was one of the things about which there should be negotiation. I had the greatest difficulty in getting him to accept that freedom of navigation was laid down in the 1888 Convention and that the United States Government had never so far suggested that this was one of the things that would have to be re-negotiated with Nasser.

At this point a secretary brought in the President's statement on the maintenance of the Anglo/French/American alliance and the necessity for keeping N.A.T.O. at full strength. This gave me the opportunity to say that if time were allowed to slip and through inaction on the part of the United States, the world's largest banker were forced to put up its shutters, there would no N.A.T.O. for the United States to support. Humphrey's comment was 'there you come back to our difficulty'. . . .[19]

Caccia's bad news must have intensified Macmillan's misgivings. On top, Rowan submitted a memorandum giving gloomy figures about the losses of reserves during November, and a much worse forecast for December, saying: 'It will require a pretty big movement of confidence in our favour to have any real impact on these figures', and by the end of the year our reserves 'could well be within a couple of hundred million dollars of the lowest figures we have reached in the post war years, namely 340 million dollars on September 18th [1949] when we had to devalue; I think the Chancellor ought to be aware of this position before Cabinet meets tomorrow.'

Meanwhile Butler, who at first had shown more resolution than Macmillan in resisting American demands for immediate unconditional withdrawal and no British participation in clearance of the Canal, found his own soundings alarming. On 26 November he spoke on the telephone with Humphrey (with whom he also claimed a 'long standing friendship'). It was a bleak conversation. Humphrey told Butler: 'Once it was possible to talk to Her Majesty's Government again the United States would perhaps be able to negotiate with the Egyptians for a general settlement and put some pressure on Cairo. They would like to get back to the position of being friends with both sides.' When Butler raised the question of clearance, Humphrey said that 'this just showed how difficult it was when there were no contacts between the two Governments'.[20] This conversation must have decided Butler not to try to fight Eden's corner against Macmillan.

At this time Humphrey did not think of himself as a 'close personal friend' of either Butler or Macmillan. This was made clear in a message from Caccia on 23 November:

Evidence is accumulating that Mr Humphrey is the most intransigent member of the Administration about our actions at Suez, and he is most vindictive. This may stem in large part from his belief that we went into Suez without due thought for the economic consequences of our action and that these consequences will almost certainly lead to demands on the United States which will seriously affect his already precariously balanced budget. This as you know is an absolute fetish with him. . . . The feeling within the Administration is infinitely stronger than it is among the general public. Despite the President's warm words the fact is while he will not see the British or Australian Foreign Secretaries his appointment list to-day reads as follows – the Prime Minister of Ceylon, Foreign Minister of Venezuela and Carl Brisson the singer and his wife. . . . This is illustrative of the hostility which now exists and appears recently to have been strengthening within the Administration.[21]

Lloyd, who had gone back to New York to argue the British case at the United Nations, soon became defeatist and on 28 November in a personal telegram to Butler stated that when he had mentioned 'complete withdrawal in 15 days' Hammarskjold had at once become interested in the idea of a package deal, and it completely changed the tone of the conversation. (Previously Hammarskjold had been cold and unco-operative.) Lloyd went on that he had a feeling that Hammarskjold and his associate McCloy, whatever the delay and whatever the cost, meant to use 'our resources to the absolute minimum'. Lloyd thought that (in America)

> the hard core of policy makers, some of whom have been strongly pro-British in the past, are now against us. This will continue until we have made what they would regard as the *amende honorable* by rapid withdrawal. Their feeling is that we have to purge our contempt of the President in some way. Jock McCloy and Lew Douglas are not our friends at the moment for this reason. Bedell Smith and Gruenther [General Gruenther, normally pro-British] . . . also have the feeling about our slight to the President.

Lloyd's telegram concluded:

> 5. If we are going to have difficulty with the [Conservative] party over announcing withdrawal I think we may have to tell certain selected individuals that the Americans have no intention of lifting a finger to help to preserve us from financial disaster until they are certain that we are removing ourselves from Port Said quickly. Although they may help Europe over oil (and possibly us at the same time) on broader economic issues they are just non-negotiable until we have taken this step.
> 6. Much of this American attitude is quite irrational and as they frankly admit contrary to their own long-term interests, but they seem impervious to the consequences of failing to grasp the opportunity which we have created in the Middle East or to the risks of permitting a major Russian success. They are temporarily beyond the bounds of reason and even threats to withdraw ourselves from the United Nations, N.A.T.O., etc. would not bring round those who have to make the decisions to a sense of reality.
> 7. I should like Sir Harold Caccia to comment on this telegram in time for our discussions tomorrow. His assessment may not be the same.

Lloyd was to fly back across the Atlantic that night for a Cabinet meeting on 29 November.

Caccia endorsed Lloyd's view:

> I fully agree with this assessment. We have now passed the point where we are talking to friends. We are negotiating a business deal. The fact that we have been allies in two wars should help very greatly

afterwards with the President and with others in the Administration as well as with a large section of public opinion. But now we are on a hard bargaining basis and we are dealing with an Administration of business executives who rightly or wrongly consider that they are animated by the highest principles.

Dixon telegraphed:

> I agree 100% with Sir H. Caccia that we are on a hard bargaining basis. The past weeks have shown that those directing United States policy are impervious to arguments and appeals to sentimental ties.[22]
>
> If we are to make headway after withdrawal from Egypt I should have thought that we would need to play the hand pretty high. It will not, I believe, be sufficient to try to convince the Americans by argument that they need us, e.g. in N.A.T.O. We may have to bring the point home by bargaining our continued cooperation, e.g. in N.A.T.O. and over American bases in the United Kingdom, in return for their support where we need it.

On his flight home Lloyd decided he must resign, because he had failed to persuade the Americans that it was 'folly to throw away the bargaining counter of possessing twenty-three miles of the Canal'. There is incontrovertible evidence of this in his private papers in the Foreign Office files, and in his book on Suez. His private papers contain a diary entry for May 1958, when he talked to Eden at Broadchalke, recording: 'We would all have been in a much stronger position if I had been allowed to resign at the end of November 1956.' Eden then said he thought 'that was the moment when we all should have resigned', but unfortunately he had been ill, and added

> that he himself had thought that a more appropriate moment for my resignation would have been after Bermuda when we had apparently handed over to the United States authority to settle with the Egyptians on the best terms possible for the reopening of the Canal. I said that that was not altogether a fair description of what had happened but I did not pursue the matter.[23]

The Bermuda Conference between Eisenhower, Macmillan (now Prime Minister) and Lloyd took place on 21 March 1957. Macmillan agreed at that time that Egypt might operate the Canal and receive the dues on much the same terms as Fawzi had offered Lloyd in mid-October. If Lloyd had reason to decide not to resign on 29 November, *a fortiori* he was right to carry on as Foreign Secretary after Bermuda.

Why did Lloyd change his mind about resignation? According to his book, when he mentioned it to his colleagues in Cabinet on 29 November it was the expression on their faces, and because 'one or two doubted his motives'. One can imagine the faces; oh, that Vicky could have drawn a cartoon of them! Perhaps Macmillan and Butler thought Lloyd might be making a bid for the premiership – but this was out of keeping with Lloyd's character. It is more probable that Macmillan talked him out of it. Both he and Butler were very conscious of the immense damage that Lloyd's resignation would do to the credibility of the Cabinet and to the electoral popularity of the Conservative Party. The last thing Macmillan wanted at that moment was a dissolution and a General Election in which the Conservatives would have to defend going to war without a proper *casus belli*, and simultaneously to counter charges of lies and collusion thrown at the Government. Lloyd's resignation would have put the future of the Conservative Government in grave doubt.

On 22 November Makins had minuted to Macmillan:

> The Governor tells me we have had two very bad days on the exchange. . . . London and Continental markets are fairly calm but New York seems to be in a state nearly of panic about sterling and do not trust the situation from hour to hour. He [the Governor] thinks this is due particularly to the fresh uncertainties about the political situation here which has, no doubt, been sensationally reported in the US.

Macmillan wrote on this minute in red pencil: 'Hold on!' On the same day Rowan made a long list of possible measures to save the £, writing that 'the first essential is the re-establishment of relations with the United States'; British policy should be 'to maintain the official parity'; 'action within our own powers' was in his view reduction of foreign commitments, import cuts, rationing, special emergency import tax, increased direct and indirect tax, for example petrol tax and purchase tax, together with an increase in bank rate. On 23 November Makins minuted to Macmillan '. . . another bad day'.

Thus the news about the £ and the US attitude to its plight was uniformly bad, and Macmillan told the Cabinet forcibly on 28 November that it was essential to re-establish satisfactory arrangements with the USA for action to support sterling, and that their goodwill could not be obtained without an immediate and unconditional undertaking to withdraw the Anglo–French force from Port Said. On the 29th Macmillan, armed with devastating Treasury warnings about the danger of a forced devaluation, precipitated the

Cabinet into unconditional withdrawal, to the consternation of some of his colleagues who feared this would split the Conservative Party. On that day, after scaring his colleagues with the possibility of his resignation, Lloyd reinforced Macmillan's argument by saying he had already informed Hammarskjold in New York that withdrawal could be completed within fifteen days. French agreement had to be secured, but by now the French were ready to wash their hands of Suez and to concentrate on the rebels in Algeria. Lloyd was asked to make a holding statement that afternoon to the Commons.

On the 30th the decision to withdraw became absolute and Butler, Macmillan, Kilmuir, Lennox-Boyd and Head set to work to concoct a formula that would appease the Conservative backbench MPs. It was decided that Lloyd, not Butler, should make the statement about unconditional withdrawal in the Commons on 3 December. It was dressed up with words to the effect that the operation had been such a success that the troops could now be withdrawn because we were satisfied about the size of the UN Force. Bevan summarized the Conservatives' humiliation: 'We sympathise with the Right Hon and learned gentleman in having to sound the bugle of advance to cover his retreat.'[24]

After the Cabinet decision Butler telephoned Humphrey to let him know that Britain would capitulate. Almost incredible to relate, so mistrustful was Humphrey that he refused to take Butler's promise at its face value, demanding a firm date for the evacuation. Lloyd telegraphed to Caccia on 3 December that we must 'impress on the administration that we have decided to go without delay, and we intend to go without delay', and 'confidential instructions are being sent to General Keightley to fix his programme with General Burns . . . aiming at complete withdrawal in fourteen days'.[25] Lloyd telegraphed to Dixon: 'It seems to me that your major task is to get it firmly into both Hammarskjold's and Lodge's heads that it is not a stalling operation, and we are anxious to complete the withdrawal as quickly as possible now that we have decided to go.'[26]

Caccia tried without success to see Dulles but obtained an interview with Robert Murphy (Under-Secretary of State) and asked him if sufficient pledges had been given for the USA now to help sterling. Caccia repeated to Lloyd:

After I had gone carefully over the points made in your telegram, I asked whether this would be sufficient pledge on our behalf to enable action on the United States side to follow. Mr. Murphy said that unfortunately it would not satisfy the United States Government so far as action over sterling was concerned. What was needed was a definite date.

I said that I must ask Mr. Murphy to ensure that this was re-considered at the highest level. An Englishman's word was his bond. If the United States Government were now going to act as if they doubted our word, he must know that the results would be most damaging. He knew us. The President knew us, and had more than once expressed his determination to strengthen the alliance. To say the least the present decision of the United States Government would gravely set back that purpose.

Mr. Murphy said that there was no question of the United States Government doubting the word of Her Majesty's Government. What they had in mind was the effect on other people in the Middle Eastern area of our failure to give even a target date.[27]

This is evidence of an extraordinary phase in Anglo–American relations. It almost passes belief that a supposedly pro-British senior American diplomat could have spoken in such terms to the British Ambassador.

With the Foreign Secretary's statement on 3 December in the Commons US doubts were removed, and Caccia was able to report that, although the question of the date was a 'fetish of the boys at [the] State [Department]', Humphrey was off to a meeting with every intention of obtaining US acceptance of our undertaking 'with all guns firing'. Later Humphrey telephoned Caccia and insisted that Macmillan put in his press statement about the IMF drawings: 'This subject has been under discussion between the United Kingdom and United States Treasuries during the past two years' to avoid the impression that there had been collusion between the USA and the UK over the invasion of Egypt. The Americans were still cautious about seeming to be close to the British. However on 11 December, when Macmillan and Humphrey met in Paris, the Chancellor was able to thank Humphrey most sincerely for all the help he had given to the UK, saying: 'The International Monetary Fund application had gone through splendidly.'[28]

Eden in Jamaica had become alarmed at indications that his Cabinet was about to agree to ignominious unconditional withdrawal, to which he objected strongly. He was not kept well informed by Butler. Brook telegraphed after the fateful Cabinet meeting on 30 November to tell him of the decision to evacuate:

From the point of view of our international position they [Cabinet] believe that understandings reached there [New York] afford reasonable basis for withdrawal from Port Said. Main difficulty now foreseen is with Conservative opinion here, partly because these understandings cannot be presented as conditions of our withdrawal. [The 'understandings' were the US terms for support of sterling.][29]

Eden replied to Brook the next day, 1 December:

. . . I do not know what the understandings reached are. Do they meet conditions in my last message to the Foreign Secretary [no withdrawal without assurances about British participation in clearance]. I do not consider we can go back on those.

I am glad of the emphasis on the urgent importance of clearing of the Canal. It is on this issue that Nasser made fresh conditions when Hammarskjold saw him in Cairo after our acceptance of the Armistice. We were all agreed that we could not accept those which included departure of our Troops before the work had been begun on other sections of the Canal.

From what I have read of the present International Force its makeup is not impressive. There is apparently still no Canadian Battalion but only a Yugo-Slav and an Indian one whose sympathies presumably are entirely with Egypt. I set out all this because I can well understand and share Conservative and national feelings on those matters.

As far as I can judge, American opinion is moving our way. I am sure that we should be wrong to depart now from the firm line the Foreign Secretary took at U.N.O.

Butler replied to this telegram at 8 p.m. on the same day that he had consulted with Salisbury, Macmillan, Lloyd and Heath, who 'endorse what follows':

2. All our colleagues are agreed on the form of Monday's statement. It will be a firm declaration which will show that the primary objectives of our intervention in Egypt have been achieved. We have stopped a small war and prevented a larger one. The force which we temporarily interposed between the combatants is now to be relieved by an international force. We have, by our action, unmasked Soviet plots in the Middle East and have done something to awaken the United Nations to the dangers there. Responsibility for securing a settlement of the long-term problems of the area has now been placed squarely on the shoulders of the United Nations. Moreover, we have given a further impetus to the movement in the United States, of which there are now clear signs, towards a recognition of the difficult and dangerous situation in the Middle East and a readiness to play a more constructive part in dealing with it.

3. During the last few days we have made strenuous efforts to

secure greater precision in the assurances given by the Secretary-General on behalf of the United Nations, especially on the clearance of the Canal. As a result we have secured assurances which we believe to be adequate on the following points:–

(a) The United Nations force will be competent, in size and in composition, to discharge the functions assigned to it. It will contain some 700 Canadians.

(b) The Secretary-General has accepted responsibility for organising the clearing of the Canal as expeditiously as possible, and the task has been put in the hands of capable men [McCloy and Lucius Clay].

(c) There will be no discrimination against British and French shipping, after the Canal is clear, on the pretext that a state of war exists.

(d) Negotiations on the future operation of the Canal will be resumed on the basis of the six principles unanimously approved by the Security Council.

4. In these circumstances we and the French are satisfied that we shall now gain nothing further by delaying the withdrawal of our forces from Port Said. We therefore propose to announce that on the basis of the understandings summarised at (a)–(d), we shall continue our withdrawal without delay. . . .

6. For us the two crucial points in this settlement are the timing of the withdrawal and the clearance of the Canal. On the first we do not propose to name a specific date. Instead, we shall say that we are instructing the Commander-in-Chief to seek agreement with the United Nations Commander on a time-table related to military and logistic considerations. On the second the Foreign Secretary hopes to be able to say that clearance of the Canal will begin as soon as it is technically possible. By this means we shall keep withdrawal and clearance separate, as you have wished throughout.

7. You should also know that the November figure for the reserves, which must be announced on Tuesday, is worse than was feared when you left. To prevent confidence from being further shaken and something like a collapse of sterling taking place the Chancellor will need to announce that day the measures which he is taking to strengthen the position. But these depend for their efficacy on our political decision being announced on Monday.

8. Thus we shall have the Foreign Secretary's statement on Monday and the Chancellor's on Tuesday. There will be a Foreign Affairs debate on Wednesday and Thursday. I believe that we shall succeed in holding the Party steady through these four days. The Cabinet is united and firm, and I hope and think that our people in the House can be held.

9. I know how difficult it must be for you to form a judgment without full knowledge of all that has gone on since you left. But we

believe that the policy on which we have decided is consistent with the
course which you set for us. We hope you will feel that we have taken
the right decision.

This telegram alerted Eden to his colleagues' desire for unconditional withdrawal, and immediately on receiving it he cabled to his
Parliamentary Secretary, Robert Allan MP: 'I am better and would
return rather than let the side down or appear in flight.' Allan advised
against return on the grounds that if he was now fully fit 'were you
justified in going to Jamaica'. Eden agreed and cabled Butler again
with his reservations, but unless he returned to take part in the
debate he could do nothing but acquiesce in any Cabinet decisions
taken.

> I feel that you and Foreign Secretary have done everything you can to
> secure greater precision in assurances by the Secretary General.
>   2. Your 3 (b); I suppose that all available means of clearing the
> Canal will be used including our own.
>   3. Your 3 (d); I would have hoped for a reference in our statement
> to 18 power proposals. After all they were only vetoed by Communist
> Powers and Dulles had much to do with them. I have never thought
> the six principles amounted to anything much.
>   4. I will back you and my colleagues to the full in any statement you
> make. You will of course let me know if you want me to return.
>   5. I think Chancellor knows measures I prefer. I suppose I should
> not include it even in this telegram.

Eden's telegram arrived in Whitehall at 10 a.m. on 3 December. Two
Cabinet meetings were held in Downing Street that day. At the
second Butler said he should mention that he had received a cable
from the Prime Minister saying that he would give full support to any
decision reached and 'had indicated that he attached importance to
our being able to make it clear, if possible, that the Anglo–French
salvage resources would be used by the UN in the clearance of the
Suez Canal'.[30]

Butler's reply to Eden, sent after the Cabinet meeting at 4 p.m.
that day, was tendentious. Eden's paragraph 2, as has been seen,
stated that he supposed all available means of clearing the Canal
would be used including 'our own'. The Cabinet already knew that
Nasser would not allow the British salvage fleet to operate. Yet Butler
replied to Eden: 'The answer to your paragraph 2 is "Yes".' Butler
finished his short telegram: '. . . we of course considered very
anxiously whether it was our duty to suggest to you that you should

return. We conclude that you ought not to interrupt your rest. That remains our view. Best love to you both.' Eden's authorized biographer writes correctly that Eden was treated as a retired Prime Minister. Butler and Macmillan did not want him back in London until the statement about unconditional withdrawal had been made and the Commons debate successfully concluded. Eden, they feared, might dig his toes in and refuse to capitulate to the Americans.[31]

On 3 December the Cabinet in effect ignored Eden's reservations. Macmillan told them he had now received assurances that support for the £ would be forthcoming from the USA, and the general feeling was that they must try to make the best of a bad job regardless of Eden. Macmillan wrote in his message to Humphrey that the 3 December decision was taken with the Prime Minister's full approval. Again this was incorrect. Rumours of Eden's resignation now began to circulate, while in the Commons only fifteen Conservative MPs (the Suez Group) went into the division lobby against the Government on 3 December to vote against unconditional surrender. It was inexcusable for Butler to fail to inform the Prime Minister that Macmillan's proposed moves to save the £ and secure oil supplies depended completely on America, and that US assistance would never be forthcoming unless Britain capitulated unconditionally. Despite the bad roads in Jamaica, all messages from Whitehall to Eden arrived and were replied to in a few hours.

Clearance of the Canal was now in the hands of the UN, who refused Anglo–French co-operation when Nasser objected to the presence of the salvage ships. Nasser was triumphant. His propaganda was that his army had defeated the Israeli, French and British forces so that they had been obliged to withdraw ignominiously, and the UN Force and salvage fleet were only present in the Canal Zone because of his goodwill to the rest of the world. His popularity in Egypt and the Arab world soared. Hammarskjold could do nothing without Nasser's consent; the French and British were impotent, even though they occupied 23 miles of the Canal, and the Israelis were forced to withdrew from the Sinai although they kept the forts at Sharm-el-Sheikh so that the Gulf of Akaba was open to their ships and the port of Eilat could be used. This was the one tangible reward.

On 14 December Eden returned to London looking well and hoping that he was cured. He fully intended to continue as Prime Minister. In his absence strange telephone conversations had taken place between Eisenhower, Butler and Macmillan, which on the available evidence show that the President had indicated he would be much more co-operative with Britain if Eden was replaced by one of the other two. These conversations took place before 3 December, when the Cabinet had decided to accede to America's wishes. There is no evidence that Eisenhower still wanted Eden to quit as Prime Minister once Britain had agreed to evacuate the Canal uncon- ditionally; but there is evidence that both Butler and Macmillan were thinking in terms of the future of the Government and the Conserva- tive Party without the encumbrance of Eden, and probably both felt they were the obvious heirs apparent.[32]

When Eden left in November Suez was popular, and had increased Conservative support according to public opinion polls, although the shock news that the Prime Minister was going to Jamaica at a moment when his troops were in peril from Egyptian counter-attacks was adversely commented on and must have been a negative factor. By the time of his return both the Conservative Party and the nation had realized that the Suez operation, mounted at vast expense and costing the lives of British servicemen, was a gigantic failure with no assets to show for it, and instead much ill-will abroad.

In addition, rumours of the collusion with Israel were running riot, although they were not proved absolutely for several years to come. For Eden one of the most alarming features must have been a letter from David Astor, Editor of the *Observer*, to Iain Macleod on 14 November:

> I believe that the 'collusion' charge is going to be proved – that we knew of a French–Israeli military understanding which we either endorsed or connived at, but certainly did not seek to prevent. If the proving of this charge is left entirely to other countries, to the Opposition and to various newspapers (you realise that 'The Econ- omist' and King-Hall are both on to it, and that 'The Times' is said to have ceased to support the Government because they knew of the collusion,) the damage to the Conservative Party will be very great and of long duration.
>
> As I believe that the collusion was arranged by two Ministers and was made known only to a minimum of others, it is in fact unfair that this fate should befall your Party. Certainly the back benchers had no knowledge of it. Presumably most Ministers also did not know.
>
> Whether the whole Tory Party is to be disgraced by this story depends on whether the uncovering of the knowledge and the necess- ary action to clean our national reputation is carried out by a substan- tial element in the Tory Party itself or not. If that does not happen, the Party will be tarnished until it is led by people who are to-day too young to have been in responsible positions. . . .
>
> The reason I approach you is that you have a reputation for honour

and for courage. You are also of an age which makes the future of the Tory Party even more particularly your concern than its present.

Yours sincerely,

David Astor[33]

Macleod brought the letter round to 10 Downing Street but was unable to see Eden. Instead he saw Bishop, Eden's private secretary, and Brook. Bishop's note to the Prime Minister reveals his loyalty to his master:

Prime Minister

Mr. Macleod brought this to me this evening. Sir N. Brook happened to be with me at the time. Mr. Macleod has no intention of replying, but wanted you to see it as soon as possible, as Astor may have made similar approaches to others.

That Astor is using these tactics makes us feel quite sick, but it shows that he, and others, are pressing this point very hard.

We wonder whether this state of affairs affects your plans for a rest. Might it not be wise to ask 3 or 4 of your senior colleagues to meet you on Sat. afternoon, to discuss all this?

(Bobby [Salisbury] is the only other who has seen this)

F.B.

The next day another of the Downing Street private secretaries, Cairncross, minuted to Bishop: 'The PM has seen this and did not think any meeting of Ministers was necessary abt[*sic*]it.'[34] In a letter to the author, Astor wrote:

As far as I can recall, I had a confirmation from William Clark [until 1955 *Observer* Foreign Editor] to my assumption that there had been some kind of collusion. Clark himself was kept completely in the dark, but he noticed that *The Times* had been confidentially briefed – I think by Eden himself – before the Suez operation. It was the custom in those days to treat *The Times* as such a reliable government mouthpiece that they could safely be told of events before they happened. Clark did not know what had been said to *The Times* but, as the briefing took place before the alleged surprise attack by Israel on Egypt, he assumed it must have included an implied admission of collusion.

The Times have never admitted that they were briefed as it was a confidential matter. However, they must have been so impressed, or depressed, by the briefing that they received that they changed overnight at the time of the attack from being backers of the government over the Suez Canal issue to being silent but hostile. The evidence of their hostility was that thereafter they reproduced in their paper every story appearing in an American newspaper which hinted at some kind of collusion. They thus tried to alert their readers without breaking the confidentiality of the briefing they had received.

The hint I received from Clark confirmed what seemed to me a distinct probability. Many others, including Hugh Gaitskell, were also showing a great doubt of the truth of the government version of events.[35]

On 20 November the question of collusion had been raised in Cabinet, almost certainly by Macleod, as a result of Astor's letter. Eden was ill and not present; Lloyd was in New York, and although there was knowledge of Sèvres amongst some present, the conclusion was:

> Attention was drawn to the continuing speculation in certain sections of the press about the extent of the foreknowledge which the United Kingdom and French Governments had had of Israel's intention to attack Egypt. While there could be no question of acceding to requests for an independent enquiry on this point, the Government might well be pressed to make some further statement on it. It was the general view of the Cabinet that the best course would be to repeat the assurances which had been given by the Foreign Secretary in the debate in the House of Commons on 31st October. It was, however, agreed that Ministers should consider, after the Foreign Secretary's return to London, whether anything further should be said on this question.[36]

At this period 'collusion' was accepted neither by civil servants nor by supporters of the Government. Even Nicholls, Ambassador in Tel Aviv, disbelieved it, reporting on 13 December that although in the Arab States and the United States there was widely held suspicion that the Allied intervention was a concerted plan, Israeli senior officers would not admit it, and many of them felt

> the Allied intervention was a sad misfortune since it led the Egyptians to withdraw forces from Sinai instead of reinforcing them, with the result that the Israelis were able to destroy only a third rather than an expected two-thirds of their army, and the Egyptians would not have dared to raid Israeli towns for fears of the chaos that even minor reprisal raids on Cairo might have caused.

Nicholls went on:

> Of the imaginary evidence freely retailed by press and agency correspondents I need only say that one such, when asked by a colleague if he really intended to telegraph as fact such a farrago of unsubstan-

tiated rumours, replied 'Collusion stories are what they want, and collusion stories are what they're going to get.'[37]

In mid-November Reuter reports from America showed that American newspapers were carrying stories of alleged private briefings by Dulles about collusion and his recriminations against Britain and France; these were avidly seized on by Nasser's propagandists.[38] Air Vice Marshal Lees wrote to the RAF Commander in Cyprus in January, from the Air Ministry: 'We are under continual fire here through Parliamentary Questions and the like about the recent operations in Egypt, particularly, of course, on our alleged collusion with Israel.' He wanted 'incontrovertible facts' to repel further assaults and asked for details of French aircraft passing through Cyprus before the attack, but stressed that his inquiry must be kept secret. The information that he received from Cyprus about French aircraft movements must have added to the Air Marshal's doubts about collusion.[39]

Eden was disappointed at the cold reception he received after 14 December – in marked contrast with the public enthusiasm for him before he went to Jamaica. When he reappeared in the Commons only one Conservative backbench MP cheered and waved his order paper, and then was nonplussed by the silence. Lord Bracken wrote to Lord Beaverbrook that, although Eden returned in high spirits, these lasted only a few hours; then a deputation arrived in Downing Street, led by Salisbury and Butler, informing him that unless his health was fully restored by Easter they felt that a new head of government would be necessary. Bracken was a great retailer of political gossip, often false, and it will never be known if this tale is true or whether, if true, the main motivation of the deputation was Eden's health or the desire to find a scapegoat for the unpopularity of the Conservative Party as a result of Suez.[40]

Eden spoke in the Commons on 18 and 20 December. Neither speech aroused any spark. He misjudged the mood of the country and the Commons and of his own backbenchers over the grave disappointment in the unconditional withdrawal. (All British troops were to leave Egypt on 23 December.) On 18 December he also spoke to the 1922 Committee of Conservative backbenchers. Cross-examined about collusion by Nigel Nicolson, an anti-Suez Conservative, he gave an equivocal reply, but on the 20th he was drawn into saying in the House that 'there was not foreknowledge that Israel would attack Egypt'. This was a lie.[41]

Was the lie justified? Lloyd argues that if Eden had told the truth it would have damaged the situation in the Middle East, and quotes as peacetime precedents for misleading the Commons Attlee's refusal to say he had authorized the manufacture of the atomic bomb, and Cripps in 1949 telling the House that he had no intention of devaluing the £. It is not easy to pass a judgment on this plea, but as more and more became known about Sèvres, anti-Eden criticism became harsher.

One diplomat who knew about collusion was Gladwyn Jebb, who had been told of it by Lloyd over a drink on 26 October. On the day after Eden denied collusion in the Commons he wrote to Lloyd that either the Foreign Secretary knew more about it than the Prime Minister, or that the Prime Minister was simply not telling the truth. In a letter to the author Lord Gladwyn wrote: 'To this I received no reply except an invitation to talk about it when next we met.'

A note in Lloyd's private papers in his own handwriting states that he received a letter from Jebb dated 21 December 1956, 'a protest against A. E. in H of C', and another on 27 December 'asking to see the records'. Lloyd also wrote: 'I have the originals'. The letters are not in the archive. On 23 November in Paris Jebb wrote a memorandum, which he entitled 'Collusion with Israel over Suez', anticipating an official inquiry in which he would be required to give important evidence. It has not been published.[42]

On 23 December a telegram arrived from Dixon saying that Egypt was making claims and counter-claims, and was preparing for the UN a draft Resolution that an Investigator should be appointed who was acceptable to France, Egypt and Britain, and who would record and assess claims (without going into the question of liability). Dixon suggested a 'mutual waiver of claims . . . if the value of British property in Egypt is as great as I understand, the balance might be in our favour'. However, Kirkpatrick feared that the UN Assembly might pass a Resolution requiring us 'to pay £300 million'. Eden minuted plaintively: 'Surely we are not going to *pay* the Egyptians on top of all.'[43] It was a low moment for the Prime Minister; everything was recoiling on him about the Suez war. Over Christmas Eden had doubts about the wisdom of continuing as Prime Minister. How far this was due to his health, the state of mind of his colleagues, the impossibility of keeping collusion secret, or the realization of the extent of the failure of his Suez policy, will never be known.

At a meeting of Ministers at Chequers (Butler, Kilmuir, Lennox-Boyd, Salisbury, Lloyd George and Head) the claims for compensation by Egypt were reported, but even more serious was the news that the Egyptian Government, contrary to the understanding reached between Fawzi and Hammarskjold, would not allow British salvage ships required by the United Nations to help clear of the Canal. No British ships would be allowed to work south of Port Said 'under any conditions', and there was a fear that now British troops had departed they might be seized by the Egyptians as 'prize'. Eden and his Ministers agreed that we could not run the risk of losing 'our' salvage fleet to the Egyptians, nor of being compelled to withdraw by force. They decided to order the salvage fleet out. It was one last humiliation for Eden. After the meeting Eden told Kilmuir privately that he was unlikely to carry on as Prime Minister because of his health; after further consultations with his doctors he decided to resign, and went to Sandringham to tell the Queen on 8 January.[44]

Eden went down fighting. After he had made his decision to quit he received a Cabinet memorandum from Macmillan on 4 January: 'The Suez operation has been a tactical defeat. It is our task to ensure that, like the retreats from Mons and Dunkirk, it should prove the prelude to a strategic victory. It *can* [Macmillan's italics] be done. But it can only be done if we nerve ourselves to bold decisions.' The memorandum went on to outline what economic measures were needed in the 1957 Budget. Eden's written reply on 7 January for the Cabinet was resolute and a defiant point-blank contradiction of Macmillan, although it was almost his last act as Prime Minister and he knew he could not be involved officially in any debate over it:

Note by the Prime Minister
I do not think that the events of Suez can be reckoned as a tactical defeat. It is much too early to pronounce on an operation of this kind.
   This much is certain:
   The Soviet Egyptian air force has been destroyed. The Israelis have eliminated one-third of the Egyptian army and its equipment.
   Jordan and Syria have been kept from active alignment with Nasser, whose personal position has not (according to our reports) been strengthened.
   The extent of Soviet penetration into the Middle East has been exposed, with the result that the United States at last seems to be taking the action for which we pleaded in vain throughout 1956. It may be that the United States attitude to us in the Middle East dates from our refusal to give up Buraimi. But even so we would rather have them in the Middle East than the Russians.
   The United Nations has been given a chance to take effective action, if it is capable of it.[45]

On 9 January an official statement was made that the Prime Minister had resigned. Macmillan succeeded him.

Postscript

AFTER MACMILLAN BECAME Prime Minister he instructed Millard to prepare a report for the Cabinet on relations between the UK, the USA and France in the months following nationalization of the Canal. Millard wrote that Suez had severely shaken the basis of Anglo–American relations and exposed 'the limitation of our strength . . . on the face of it Britain and France had nothing to compensate for a political defeat of the first magnitude'.

Lloyd asked Logan to write a detailed account of the diplomatic exchanges. Logan's finding was that when traffic through the Canal was resumed, on 24 April 1957, the Egyptian Declaration 'could be closely compared with the Egyptian position in the first private talk in New York on 9 October'. This was authoritative, as Logan had accompanied Lloyd and taken notes at the Foreign Secretary's meetings with Fawzi and Pineau in mid-October in New York.

The Egyptian Declaration of 24 April 1957 accepted the 1888 Convention, provided that tolls would not be increased by more than 1 per cent per annum, and 25 per cent of all revenue would be put aside for development and capital expenditure. There was no question of Suez Canal profits being used to finance the Aswan Dam. Egypt declared that complaints of violation of the Canal Code, if not resolved by reference to the Canal Authority, should be referred to independent arbitration, and disputes arising out of the 1888 Convention or the present Declaration were to be settled in accordance with the Charter of the United Nations; differences arising between the parties to the Convention were to be referred to the International Court of Justice, whose compulsory jurisdiction the Egyptian Government accepted.

All that was satisfactory. However, Logan commented that the Egyptian Declaration contained no institutional arrangement for co-operation with user bodies and no special provisions by which Egypt might be made to conform to her obligations affirmed by the Declaration. He pointed out it was exactly on these matters that Lloyd, the Secretary of State, had asked for more precision at the meeting in New York on the afternoon of 11 October; 'then and afterwards in conversation with Sir Humphrey Trevelyan, Fawzi had seemed willing to give it.' Although Fawzi then offered to go further, the Declaration by Egypt in April 1957 at the peak of Nasser's negotiating strength is evidence that Fawzi had Nasser's support for the concessions he had offered to Lloyd and Pineau in October in New York.

Eden claims in his memoirs: 'Suez was a short term emergency operation which succeeded and an attempt to halt a long term deterioration . . . some successes were gained.' It would have been better if he had admitted his mistakes and their consequences. For Eden's reputation, his major mistake after resignation was to rush out his memoirs, covering his period as Prime Minister, as early as 1960. They are in three volumes. He sent drafts of the Suez period material to the Foreign Office for vetting and approval in 1959. Their comments were sent to Lloyd, still Foreign Secretary, early in August 1959. He was horrified, as the following letter to Brook, marked 'Personal and Confidential' and dated 8 August, reveals:

I have glanced this weekend through the Office comments on Sir Anthony Eden's book. I have made certain of my own which will be incorporated in anything sent to you. I am sorry that it has taken so long. There has been a good deal of passing to and fro and perhaps a degree of perfectionism. I did, however, tell the Office to err on the side of carefulness, and I should like Sir Anthony Eden to know this. It is not just an attempt to find fault, but I did ask them to bring forward any comment of any sort which they had.

I trust you will extract the book as quickly as you can from the Office so that you can consider your own comments. I think it is a pity that the two books were not dealt with separately. I know that Eden is up against quite a tight programme with his publishers and you may consider whether, in considering your comments, you can get Part II off fairly quickly.

My own principal preoccupations about the book can be summarised as follows:-

(a) He quotes what people still in a position to influence have said in confidence.

(b) There is a strong anti-American bias throughout. I think certain criticisms are legitimate, but the legitimate ones lose force because there is such a strong persistent prejudice running through the book.

(c) His partisanship of the Israelis against the Egyptians is rather crude. His statement that he would have done exactly what Ben Gurion did and his belief that the Israeli–Egyptian explosion was advantageous to the free world will increase the suspicions that he inspired what happened in October 1956.

(d) His attitude to the Arabs will not help our efforts to improve our relations in that part of the world.

The difficulty about all this is that had Sir Anthony's book appeared in 1970 or even in 1965 there could not have been any possible objection to this kind of statement. But 1960 is too soon after the events. His colleagues principally concerned will all still be in active politics whether in government or opposition and many of the persons concerned will still be in positions of authority in other countries. If a statesman chooses to publish his memoirs very soon after the events to which they refer, I think it means he has to accept that they will be more jejune than otherwise.

My principal criticism of the book, however – and only my affection and admiration for Sir Anthony have led me to this criticism – is that I think it will damage his own reputation so much. Many of the things said in it seem rather petty and to indicate personal malice and resentment of criticism. I had hoped for something showing a broad-minded, tolerant, statesmanlike view of what had happened; mistakes we made wittingly or unwittingly; mistakes our allies made wittingly or unwittingly; and a judgment upon the whole episode which would stand the test of history and befit his great reputation. I feel that to publish the book in anything like its present form is a mistake from his personal point of view. I am afraid that he is committed to publishing it. Therefore, the best help that we can give Sir Anthony is to do everything within our power to improve it. I hope he will appreciate that that has been the spirit in which the Foreign Office have sought to comment upon the book and not resent the volume or nature of the criticisms made.

He added a postscript:

P.S. Naturally I would not want anyone other than you, except at your discretion the Prime Minister, to see this letter.

Lloyd left in the Foreign Office an extract from his personal diary about a revealing talk with Eden at his country cottage at Broadchalke on 30 May 1958:

1. *Sir A. Eden's Book*
He said that he had not yet decided when it was to be published. He would rather like to have published it in the right order, which meant Volume I at the earliest next July and Volume II July 1960. An alternative course was to publish Volume II first. There was still a great deal of work to be done on that. He had not yet done any work on the period 1945–1955. If he were to decide to publish Volume II first,

it would mean a lot of hard work but he thought he could do it by July or August of 1959. He said that the Americans in particular were pressing the latter course. 'The Times' was controlling the whole business and he believed they had sold the American rights to Mr. Luce on good terms. There was also the question of serializing. He assumed that the serialized articles would come out about three months before actual publication. He said that he would have to decide on this matter in June or at the latest July and he would like my considered view.

2. *Suez*

He thought that our cause was going by default. People like Lord Scarbrough told him that events were proving us to have been right but he did not think that was being got across. He thought he himself had one outstanding quality and that was his capacity to gauge public opinion. He sensed that public opinion also thought that events were proving us right, but he considered that leading Conservatives should state this fact more frequently. He agreed that I was probably not the right person to do it, but he thought the Prime Minister should. I said I thought it would be helpful if the ex-Ministers like Head and Thorneycroft, instead of criticizing the Government, should point this lesson. Eden said he would speak to Head about that.

3. *The Contents of the Book*

He said he would of course show it to me and Harold Macmillan before it was published. He did not think I would find anything to complain about in it. He said that he had given me full credit for my efforts to prevent him agreeing to the Users' Organisation. I asked whether there was any suggestion in the book that he had at any time been let down by his colleagues. He said 'Of course not'. He had made it absolutely clear that he had approved of every decision and he had not reproached his colleagues at all. I said that papers like 'Daily Express' were still saying that he had been let down. He said that he had spoken to Lord Beaverbrook about that and the latter had promised not to say it any more. If I could find any cases in which a Beaverbrook paper had said it during the last nine months, he would like to know. He was seeing Lord Beaverbrook again in a day or two. . . .

8. *Suez*

Finally he returned to the question of Suez and the public presentation of the rightness of our case. He begged me to impress upon our colleagues that they under-estimated the degree of popular support for our action and the extent to which the public now realised that we had been right. Nasser had been saved by the Americans after Suez. The next thing had been the expropriation by the Indonesians of the Dutch; the Yemen was next on the list, then had come the Lebanon and so it would go on. It all stemmed from condoning the original illegality of the Egyptians in nationalizing the Canal.[1]

There is no means of telling how much Eden toned down his memoirs for 1956 because of advice from Lloyd, Brook and the Foreign Office. However, many of Lloyd's criticisms of *Full Circle*, which covered 1951–5, and appeared in 1960 before the other two volumes, are valid. Eden's authorized biographer has disclosed that he was paid £100,000 for serial rights by *The Times*, apart from royalties. Unfortunately for Eden, at the same time authoritative revelations of collusion were published, which contradicted Eden's account. These caused Eden grave concern and he even considered legal action.

Even more serious for the former Premier was a move led by Michael Foot in the Commons for a full inquiry – like the Dardanelles Commission of 1916 – into the Suez events, but to his credit Harold Wilson, as Prime Minister, had no taste for this sort of history which would be bound to descend into a squalid party squabble. When Wilson decided to reduce the fifty-year rule on the closure of archives in the Public Record Office to thirty years, he considerately asked Heath, then Leader of the Opposition, to ask the living former Conservative Prime Ministers for their agreement. Macmillan and Home gave it, but, as readers of this book might expect, Eden demurred.[2]

The published memoirs of Eden, Macmillan, Butler, Lloyd and Kilmuir put a gloss over Suez. They wrote believing that the documents for Suez would remain hidden until the twenty-first century. The archives revealed in this book tell a different story, which is the truth about a disgraceful episode in the history of British Cabinets.

Chronological Table

1951
18 April	European Coal and Steel Treaty signed.
25 October	Conservatives win General Election. Churchill becomes Prime Minister.

1952
23 July	Neguib seizes power in Egypt.
10 August	European Coal and Steel Community established.

1953
5 March	Death of Stalin.
4 April	Eden's gall bladder operation is unsuccessful.
2 December	Bermuda Conference with France, UK and USA opens.

1954
21 July	Agreement signed at Geneva on Armistice and partition of Vietnam.
30 August	French National Assembly rejects EDC Treaty.
8 September	South-East Asia Collective Treaty signed in Manila.
3 October	Agreement reached on alternative to EDC at London Conference.
19 October	Anglo–British agreement signed on withdrawal of British troops from Suez base.
14 November	Nasser seizes power in Egypt.

1955
4 April	Britain joins Baghdad Pact already agreed by Turkey and Iraq.
5 April	Churchill resigns. Eden becomes Prime Minister.
18 April	Bandung Conference opens.
14 May	Austrian Treaty signed in Vienna.
26 May	Conservatives win General Election.

5 June	The Six meet in Messina.
18–25 July	Summit Conference at Geneva.
27 September	Announcement of Soviet arms deal with Egypt.
7 December	Britain tells the Six in Paris that she will not join the Common Market.
22 December	Macmillan becomes Chancellor of the Exchequer, Selwyn Lloyd Foreign Secretary.

1956

25 January	Eden sails in *Queen Elizabeth* to Washington.
16 February	Macmillan makes Financial Statement in Commons.
9 March	Makarios deported from Cyprus.
25 May	Venice Conference of the Six.
13 June	British occupation of Suez Base ends.
26 June	Six meet in Brussels.
28 June	Silverman Bill to abolish hanging passes Commons Third Reading.
17 July	British Cabinet takes decision not to finance the Aswan Dam.
19 July	Dulles tells Egyptian Ambassador in Washington that the USA will not finance the Aswan Dam.
26 July	Nasser announces nationalization of Suez Canal.
27 July	British reservists called to the colours.
14 August	Eighteen-power Conference on Suez Canal begins in London.
19 September	Suez Canal Users' Conference begins in London.
2 October	Selwyn Lloyd arrives in New York for negotiations in United Nations on Suez Canal.
14 October	Eden speaks to Conservative Conference at Llandudno.
24 October	Sèvres Protocol signed.
29 October	Israel invades Egypt.
30 October	Anglo–French ultimatum to Egypt and Israel.
31 October	RAF bombing of Egypt begins.
5 November	Anglo–French airborne landings at Port Said.
6 November	Seaborne landings by Anglo–French troops at Port Said followed by ceasefire at midnight.
23 November	Eden goes on holiday to Bermuda.
14 December	Eden returns to London apparently in good health.
20 December	Eden tells Commons there was no foreknowledge of Israeli attack on Egypt.

28 December	Chequers Conference decides to withdraw British Salvage Fleet from Port Said. Eden mentions possible resignation to Lord Kilmuir.

1957
9 January   Eden resigns as Prime Minister.

1958
1 January   Rome Treaty comes into force without Britain.

Sources

Initials and numbers refer to papers in the Public Record Office, Kew. Interviews and correspondence took place in 1985, 1986 and 1987.

Chapter 1

1. Colville, *Fringes of Power*.
2. Shuckburgh, *Descent to Suez*.
3. Rhodes James, *Anthony Eden*.
4. Ibid.
5. Colville, *Fringes of Power*. Rhodes James, *Anthony Eden*.
6. Prem 11/864.
7. Ibid.
8. T 171/449.
9. T 171/450.
10. Prem 11/864. 70 per cent convertibility was probably correct. This shows how important convertibility seemed to Eden.
11. Prem 11/883.
12. T 171/450.
14. Samuel Brittan, *Treasury under the Tories*. J. R. C. Dow, *Management of the Economy*.
15. The Times, *House of Commons 1955*.
16. Ibid.
17. Ibid.
18. Cab 128/28. The Times, *House of Commons 1955*. Monopolies Commission Report on Supply and Export of Rubber Tyres, HMSO, 8 December 1955.
19. See *New Statesman*, 14 January 1956.
20. Kilmuir, *Political Adventure*. Butler, *Art of the Possible*. Nutting, interview with author.
21. *New Statesman*.

Chapter 2

1. Prem 11/1029.
2. Prem 11/824.
3. Cab 128/27. Cab 129/72.
4. Ibid.

5. Prem 11/824.
6. Cab 129/73. Cab 128/29.
7. Prem 11/824. Cab 129/75.
8. Ibid.
9. Prem 11/824.
10. Cab 129/77.
11. Cab 129/77.
12. Ibid. Prem 11/824.
13. Interview with author. In a letter to the author Lord Stewart of Fulham, who was in 1955 influential on the Labour front bench in the Commons, wrote that in his view the Labour Party would have opposed very strongly any legislation for secret ballots, and for bans on West Indian immigration, but that, also in his view, opposition to an Immigration Bill would have been muted if it had included controls on immigration from all sources and not just on West Indians.
14. Cab 128/29. Cab 129/77.
15. Avon, *Full Circle*. Cab 129/75. Lab 10/1392.
16. Cab 134/1273. Cab 129/75.
17. Cab 134/1273.
18. Ibid.
19. Prem 11/1402.
20. Prem 11/1029.
21. Ed 136/861.
22. Ibid.
23. Cab 129/75. Ed 136/861. The author is much indebted to A. D. Peterson for his comments on the Eccles memorandum. Peterson feels strongly that 'grammar schools could not have been saved that way'. Peterson is a former Director of the Department of Education at Oxford University, and was headmaster of both a public school and a grammar school.
24. Ed 136/861.
25. Cab 128/30. Cab 129/77.
26. *Journal of Education*, June 1956.
27. Ed 136/870.
28. Cab 129/84.
29. Ed 136/894.
30. J. B. Christoph, *Capital Punishment and British Politics*.
31. Cab 128/30.
32. Cab 129/78. Cab 128/30.
33. Cab 128/30.
34. Cab 129/79. Cab 128/30.
35. Cab 128/30.
36. Ibid.
37. Cab 129/83. Cab 128/30.
38. *Times*. Interview with author.

Chapter 3

1. Dow, *Management of the Economy*.
2. Shonfield, *British Economic Policy Since the War*.
3. Cab 128/77.
4. Macmillan, *Tides of Fortune*. Cab 129/77.
5. Cab 128/29.
6. Ibid.
7. T 171/468.
8. Ibid.
9. T 171/467.
10. T 171/468. Avon, *Full Circle*.
11. Ibid.
12. Ibid.
13. Ibid.
14. Ibid.
15. Ibid.
16. Cab 128/29.
17. T 171/468. Macmillan, *Tides of Fortune*.
18. Shonfield, *British Economic Policy Since the War*. Lord Thorneycroft, conversation with author.
19. Macmillan, *Tides of Fortune*.
20. Dow, *Management of the Economy*.
21. T 273/312.
22. Macmillan, *Tides of Fortune*.
23. Cab 134/1230. Cab 129/79.
24. Macmillan, *Tides of Fortune*.
25. Prem 11/1326.
26. Ibid.
27. Ibid.

Chapter 4

1. *Documents on British Policy Overseas*, Series Two, Volume One, 1950, 1952, HMSO, 1985. Cab 130/60.
2. *DBPO*. Cab 134/224.
3. *DBPO*.
4. Ibid. T 229/749.
5. *DBPO*. FO 953/1207.
6. Ibid. FO 953/1207.
7. *DBPO*. Prem 11/153.
8. Ibid.
9. Cab 129/48.
10. *DBPO*.
11. Prem 11/153.
12. *DBPO*.

13. Cab 129/50. Prem 11/153. Cab 128/24.
14. Prem 11/618. I am indebted to the Marquis de Folin, who was present at Chartwell as Mendès-France's Chef de Cabinet, for his comments and a copy of the Chartwell record from the French archives at the Quai d'Orsay; it differs from the British version.
15. Letter from Bretherton. Charlton, *Price of Victory*.
16. Ibid.
17. Lord Gladwyn and Lord Thorneycroft, interviews with author, 1986. Macmillan, *Tides of Fortune*.
18. Cab 129/76.
19. Cab 128/29.
20. FO 371/115999. Cab 129/76. Cab 128/29.
21. Cab 134/1004.
22. FO 371/116035 b. Cab 134/1044. Cab 134/1029/1030. Cab 134/1226.
23. Cab 134/1028/1029/1030. FO 371/1160354.
24. Ibid.
25. Charlton, *Price of Victory*. FO 371/11599.
26. FO 371/116035 b.
27. Ibid. Charlton, *Price of Victory*.
28. Cab 134/1226. Ministers present on 11 November were, in addition to the Chancellor of the Exchequer: Woolton, Duchy of Lancaster; Lennox-Boyd, Colonies; Thorneycroft, Board of Trade; Eccles, Education; Selkirk, Paymaster General; Home, Commonwealth Relations; Monckton, Labour; Heathcoat Amory, Agriculture; Birch, Minister of Works; Reading, Minister of State for Foreign Affairs; Boyle, Economic Secretary, Treasury; and Salisbury, President of the Council.
29. FO 371/115999. Interview with author.
30. FO 371/116035 b.
31. Ibid.
32. Cab 134/1030. FO 371/116035 b.
33. Ibid. FO 371/116011.
34. FO 371/116035b.
35. Cab 134/1030. FO 371/116035. FO 371/116035 b.
36. FO 371/116035 b.
37. FO 371/115999.
38. FO 371/116049.
39. T 234/182. FO 371/122022.
40. FO 371/122022.
41. FO 371/122023.
42. T 234/182.
43. T 234/183.
44. Ibid.
45. FO 371/122024.
46. FO 371/122023.
47. FO 371/122022. FO 371/122023.

48. Interview with author.
49. Camps, *Britain and the European Community*.
50. BT 11/5402. T 234/183.
51. T 234/183.
52. T 234/184.
53. FO 371/122046.
54. Cab 129/82.
55. Ibid.
56. Ibid.
57. FO 371/122032. Cab 128/30.
58. Macmillan, *Tides of Fortune*.
59. FO 371/122035.
60. Cab 128/30.
61. FO 371/122035. On 16 October Macmillan had sent a personal message to Spaak:

> There will be much discussion whether the Colonial Territories as opposed to Commonwealth Territories should be in or out. I hope that we may be able to discuss the technical problems of this in the O.E.E.C. working party and that no premature decision will be taken by the Six. . . . I know that the French have certain views. . . . I am not pleading for a decision. I am pleading for a little time before final decisions are made.

Macmillan was becoming alarmed at the danger of Britain being excluded if the Six went ahead.
62. Camps, *Britain and the European Community*

Chapter 5

1. Prem 11/645.
2. Ibid. Carlton, *Anthony Eden*.
3. Prem 11/645. Shuckburgh, *Descent to Suez*.
4. Prem 11/645.
5. Ibid.
6. Ibid.
7. Ibid.
8. K. T. Young, *Negotiating with the Chinese Communists*.
9. Prem 11/649. Shuckburgh, *Descent to Suez*.
10. Ibid.
11. Prem 11/666.
12. Moran, *Winston Churchill, Struggle for Survival*.
13. Cab 131/14.
14. Ibid.
15. Prem 11/867.

16. Prem 11/650. Prem 11/636. Prem 11/613.
17. Ibid. Cab 128/28.
18. R. P. Stebbins, *U.S. in World Affairs, 1954*.
19. USFR 1952/54, Vol. XIV, p. 610.
20. Prem 11/867. Avon, *Full Circle*.
21. Ibid.
22. The letters between Eisenhower and Churchill until the end of Churchill's Premiership are on Prem 11/867 and Prem 11/879.
23. Prem 11/867.
24. Prem 11/879.
25. Ibid.
26. Ibid.
27. Ibid.
28. Cab 128/29. Prem 11/879.
29. Ibid.
30. FO 371/114974. FO 371/111504.
31. Prem 11/879.
32. FO 371/114974. FO 371/111504. Prem 11/879.
33. Cab 129/76. Blake, *Decline of Power 1915–64*.
34. Prem 11/879.
35. Ibid.

Chapter 6

1. Prem 11/832. Cab 128/29.
2. Prem 11/832. FO 371/117638.
3. Prem 11/832.
4. Prem 11/834. Cab 128/29.
5. Prem 11/834.
6. Ibid. FO 371/117648.
7. Cab 128/29.
8. *Economist*, 10 September 1955.
9. Prem 11/834.
10. Interview with author. Cab 128/29.
11. Prem 11/834.
12. Ibid.
13. Ibid.
14. Avon, *Full Circle*. Crawshaw, *The Cyprus Revolt*.
15. FO 371/123867.
16. *Times*, 24 January 1956. FO 371/123867.
17. FO 371/123871.
18. Avon, *Full Circle*. Crawshaw, *The Cyprus Revolt*.
19. Cab 129/30. FO 371/123882. FO 371/123876.
20. FO 371/123884. FO 371/123885.
21. FO 371/123888. FO 371/123890. FO 371/123892.
22. FO 371/123894.

23. Cab 128/30. FO 371/123901.
24. FO 371/123909.
25. FO 371/123911. CO 926/552.
26. FO 371/123916. FO 371/123917.
27. FO 371/123918.
28. FO 371/123929. Cab 128/30.
29. FO 371/123929.
30. FO 371/123937.
31. FO 371/123928. Anti-personnel mines were designed to wound feet and legs and can, but seldom, kill. Trip flares merely light a flare so the person setting it off can be seen in a bright light.
32. FO 371/123935.
33. Cab 129/62. Avon, *Full Circle*.
34. Ibid.
35. Prem 11/1432. Cab 128/27. Cab 128/29.
36. Prem 11/1432.
37. FO 371/117998.
38. Prem 11/1432. Cab 128/30.
39. Prem 11/1434.
40. Cab 129/80. Cab 128/30. FO 371/124260.
41. Prem 11/1491.
42. Ibid. Cab 128/30.

Chapter 7

1. Quoted in Wilson, *The Chariot of Israel*.
2. Ibid.
3. Ibid.
4. Prem 11/618. Stebbins, *U.S. in World Affairs, 1954*.
5. Prem 11/702.
6. Ibid.
7. Ibid. Shuckburgh, *Descent to Suez*. *Hansard*, 29 July 1954.
8. Northedge, *British Foreign Policy*.
9. Shuckburgh, *Descent to Suez*. Heikal, *Nasser, The Cairo Documents*. Heikal, *Cutting the Lion's Tail, Suez*. Macmillan, *Tides of Fortune*.
10. Shuckburgh, *Descent to Suez*. Heikal, *Cutting the Lion's Tail, Suez*.
11. Cab 128/. FO 371/119051.
12. Interview with author.
13. Macmillan, *Tides of Fortune*. Shuckburgh, *Descent to Suez*. FO 371/115869.
14. Prem 11/941. FO 371/115965.
15. FO 371/115695.
16. Prem 11/941. A copy of this document is referred to in Cab 128/28, which is the archive for Cabinet memorandum, but this copy is closed until the year 2020; another copy is available to researchers on Prem 11/941.

17. Cab 129/74. Cab 129/75.
18. FO 371/115869.
19. Cab 128/29.
20. Love, *Suez, The Twice Fought War*. Hoopes, *The Devil and John Foster Dulles*.
21. FO 371/115872.
22. FO 371/114974. Prem 11/897.
23. FO 371/115872.
24. Cab 129/76.
25. FO 371/115873.
26. FO 371/115875.
27. FO 371/115874.
28. FO 371/115875. FO 371/115874. Macmillan, *Tides of Fortune*.
29. Letters to author from Lord Sherfield and Sir Andrew Stark.
30. FO 371/115874. FO 371/115875.
31. Prem 11/945. Shuckburgh, *Descent to Suez*.
32. FO 371/115874. Shuckburgh, *Descent to Suez*.
33. FO 371/115879.
34. Cab 128/29.
35. FO 371/115879.
36. Ibid. Letter to author from Sir Evelyn Shuckburgh.
37. Ibid.
38. FO 371/115922. FO 371/115700.
39. Cab 128/29.
40. Cab 129/78.
41. Prem 11/859.
42. Ibid. Shuckburgh, *Descent to Suez*.
43. Cab 128/29.
44. Prem 11/859.
45. Shuckburgh, *Descent to Suez*.
46. FO 371/115880.
47. Ibid.
48. FO 371/115882. Shuckburgh, *Descent to Suez*.
49. FO 371/115884.
50. FO 371/115885.
51. Ibid.
52. FO 371/115886.
53. Ibid.
54. Ibid.
55. Ibid. FO 371/115887.

Chapter 8

1. Shuckburgh, *Descent to Suez*. Love, *Suez, The Twice Fought War*.
2. FO 371/119047. FO 371/119048.
3. FO 371/119046.

4. FO 371/119048.
5. Ibid.
6. FO 371/119049.
7. FO 371/115683.
8. Ibid. Snow, *Hussein*.
9. FO 371/121540.
10. FO 371/115681. Letter and telephone call from author to Dalgleish.
11. FO 471/121540.
12. FO 371/121541.
13. Cab 128/30.
14. Ibid. Shuckburgh, *Descent to Suez*.
15. FO 371/119053.
16. FO 371/110054.
17. Ibid.
18. FO 371/119053.
19. Ibid.
20. FO 371/119055.
21. Lord Thorneycroft, conversation with author.

Chapter 9

1. Clark, *From Three Worlds*.
2. Defe 4/89. Cab 134/126.
3. Air 19/857.
4. WO 216/907.
5. Cab 128/32.
6. Prem 11/1100. Macmillan, *Tides of Fortune*. Avon, *Full Circle*.
7. *Documents on American Foreign Relations*.
8. Cab 128/30.
9. McDermot, *Eden Legacy*. Hoopes, *The Devil and John Foster Dulles*. Love, *Suez, The Twice Fought War*. Rhodes James, *Anthony Eden*.
10. Prem 11/1102.
11. Ibid.
12. Cab 128/30.
13. Ibid. Macmillan is not referred to specifically in the Cabinet record but it is obviously his remark.
14. Prem 11/1152.
15. Letter to author, 1987. In his biography of Butler Anthony Howard gives a rather contrary impression of Butler's attitude.
16. Prem 11/1102.
17. Cab 128/30. Clark, *From Three Worlds*.
18. Prem 11/1100.
19. Ibid.
20. Cab 134/1217.
21. Rhodes James, *Anthony Eden*.
22. Cab 134/1216.

23. Cab 134/1225.
24. Prem 11/1104.
25. Ibid.
26. Ibid. Rhodes James, *Anthony Eden*.
27. Prem 11/1104. Cab 128/30. Cab 134/1217.
28. Prem 11/1104.
29. T 236/4188. Cab 128/30.

Chapter 10

1. Love, *Suez, The Twice Fought War*. Heikal, *Nasser, The Cairo Documents*.
2. Rhodes James, *Anthony Eden*. Love, *Suez, The Twice Fought War*.
3. Prem 11/1102.
4. Ibid.
5. Ibid.
6. Ibid.
7. Lloyd, *Suez 1956*. Prem 11/1102.
8. Ibid.
9. FO 800/725.
10. Prem 11/1103.
11. Prem 11/1102.
12. Cab 134/1216.
13. Cab 128/30. Prem 11/1102. Cab 134/1225.
14. Prem 11/1102.
15. Ibid.
16. Ibid.
17. Interview with author.
18. Nutting, *No End of a Lesson*.
19. Prem 11/1102.
20. Ibid.

Chapter 11

1. Clark, *From Three Worlds*.
2. Nutting, *No End of a Lesson*, and interview with author.
3. Cab 134/1216.
4. Nutting, *No End of a Lesson*, and interview with author.
5. Prem 11/1120.
6. FO 800/725.
7. Cab 128/30. FO 800/728.
8. Adm 205/137.
9. FO 800/728.
10. Prem 11/1103.
11. Logan, *Financial Times*, 8 November 1986. Dayan, *Diary of the Sinai Campaign*.

12. Logan, *Financial Times*, 8 November 1986.
13. Nutting, *No End of a Lesson*.
14. Cab 128/30. Adm 205/137.
15. FO 800/728. Lloyd, *Suez 1956*.
16. Cab 128/30.
17. Logan, *Financial Times*, 8 November 1986.
18. Ibid.
19. Pineau, *1956 Suez*.
20. Logan, *Financial Times*, 8 November 1986.
21. Seminar, Institute of Historical Research.
22. Defe 4/91.
23. Cab 128/30.
24. FO 371/118902. Prem 11/1104.
25. Prem 11/1104.
26. Cab 128/30.
27. Cab 134/1217.
28. Air 20/9628.
29. Ibid.
30. Adm 205/150.
31. Air 20/9628.
32. Prem 11/1212.
33. Air 8/2093. Air 20/9675. Adm 205/150.
34. Air 20/9675.
35. Heikal, *Nasser, The Cairo Documents*.
36. Burrell, *Cathedral on the Nile*. Interview with author.
37. Prem 11/1154.
38. Prem 11/1090.
39. Defe 4/89.
40. Prem 11/1105. Lloyd, *Suez 1956*.
41. Adm 205/150. Beaufre, *L'Expédition de Suez*. Thomas, *Comment Israël fut sauvé*. Azeau, *Le Piège de Suez*. Prem 11/1105. Cab 134/1216.
42. Cab 134/1216.
43. Adm 205/150. Beaufre, *L'Expédition de Suez*. Azeau, *Le Piège de Suez*.
44. WO 288/138.
45. Cab 134/1216.
46. Prem 11/1103.
47. Cab 134/1216.
48. Prem 11/1105.
49. Prem 11/1105. Cab 128/30.
50. Cab 128/30. Rhodes James, *Anthony Eden*, which states that the author has seen another record 'giving details of how the Ministers voted'.
51. Butler, *Art of the Possible*. Rhodes James, *Anthony Eden*.
52. Rhodes James, *Anthony Eden*. Adm 205/150.
53. Gore Booth Papers, Bodleian.

54. Epstein, *British Politics in the Suez Crisis*.
55. Prem 11/1105.
56. Interview with author.
57. Prem 11/1105.
58. FO 800/728.
59. Prem 11/1105.
60. Rhodes James, *Anthony Eden*.
61. Prem 11/1105.
62. Ibid.
63. Adm 205/150.
64. Cab 128/30. Prem 11/1107.
65. WO 32/16709. Prem 11/1107.
66. WO 288/4141.
67. BBC Radio 3, *A Canal Too Far*, 31 January 1987.
68. Love, *Suez, The Twice Fought War*. Cab 128/30. Prem 11/1105.
69. Cab 128/30. Butler, *Art of the Possible*.
70. Cab 128/30.
71. Pineau, *1956 Suez*. Love, *Suez, The Twice Fought War*. Prem 11/1105.
72. Love, *Suez, The Twice Fought War*.
73. Prem 11/1105.
74. Ibid.
75. Prem 11/1105. Love, *Suez, The Twice Fought War*.

Chapter 12

1. T 236/4189.
2. T 236/4188.
3. Ibid.
4. Ibid.
5. Ibid.
6. Ibid.
7. Lloyd, *Suez 1956*. Avon, *Full Circle*.
8. Lloyd, *Suez 1956*.
9. Interview with author.
10. Lloyd, *Suez 1956*.
11. Rhodes James, *Anthony Eden*. Lloyd, *Suez 1956*.
12. Cab 134/1217.
13. Ibid.
14. Cab 132/1216.
15. Rhodes James, *Anthony Eden*.
16. T 236/4189.
17. Cab 128/30.
18. T 236/4189.
19. T 236/4190.
20. FO 800/742. Butler, *Art of the Possible*.
21. T 236/4190.

22. FO 800/742.
23. FO 800/728.
24. Cab 128/30. *Hansard*, House of Commons. T 236/4190.
25. T 436/4190.
26. Prem 11/1107.
27. T 436/4190.
28. Ibid.
29. Prem 11/1107.
30. Ibid. Cab 128/30.
31. Prem 11/1107.
32. Carlton, *Anthony Eden*.
33. Prem 11/1127.
34. Ibid.
35. Letter to author.
36. Cab 128/30.
37. Air 19/857 contains Secretary of State for Air's copy of Nicholls's printed dispatch.
38. *Egyptian Gazette* (Cairo), 15 November 1956.
39. Air 20/9890.
40. Carlton, *Anthony Eden*.
41. Thomas, *The Suez Affair*.
42. FO 371/728. Lord Gladwyn, letter to author.
43. Prem 11/1107. The value of the British military stores in the Canal Base was probably £40 million.
44. Cab 130/122. Kilmuir, *Political Adventure*.
45. Cab 129/84. The Buraimi oasis was disputed between the rulers of Muscat and Abu Dhabi on the one side, and Saudi Arabia on the other. Saudi Arabia occupied it illegally in 1952. The USA pressed the Saudi Arabian case when Eden and Lloyd visited Washington in 1956, but Britain continued to side with Muscat and Abu Dhabi, to the irritation of the Americans.

Postscript

1. FO 800/728.
2. Heath, conversation with author.

Bibliography

Austin, D., *Malta and the End of Empire*, London, 1971.

Azeau, Henri, *Le Piège de Suez*, Paris, 1964.

Beaufre, Général, *L'Expédition de Suez*, Paris, 1967.

Beloff, Norah, *Transit of Britain*, London, 1973.

Ben Gurion, David, *Recollections of David Ben Gurion*, London, 1970.

Blake, Robert, *Decline of Power 1915–64*, London, 1985.

Blouet, Brian, *The Story of Malta*, London, 1967.

Brittan, Samuel, *The Treasury under the Tories*, London, 1964.

Bromberger, M. S., *Les Secrets de l'expédition d'Egypt*, Paris, 1957.

Burrell, A., *Cathedral on the Nile*, Oxford, 1984.

Butler, D. C., *British General Election 1955*, London, 1956.

Butler, Lord, *The Art of the Possible*, London, 1971.

Butler, Sir Michael, *Europe; More than a Continent*, London, 1986.

Cable, James, *The Geneva Conference of 1954 on Indo-China*, London, 1986.

Camps, Miriam, *Britain and the European Community 1955–63*, London, 1964.

Carlton, David, *Anthony Eden*, London, 1981.

Carver, Michael, *Harding of Petherton*, London, 1978.

Calvocoressi, Peter, *Suez Ten Years After*, London, 1967.

Charlton, Michael, *The Price of Victory*, London, 1983.

Christoph, J. B., *Capital Punishment and British Politics*, London, 1962.

Churchill, Randolph, *Rise and Fall of Sir Anthony Eden*, London, 1959.

Clark, William, *From Three Worlds*, London, 1986.

Colville, John, *The Fringes of Power*, London, 1985.

Crawshaw, Nancy, *The Cyprus Revolt*, London, 1978.

Dayan, M., *Diary of the Sinai Campaign 1956*, London, 1967.

Documents on British Policy Overseas, Series 2, Vol. 1, HMSO, ed. R. Bullen and M. E. Pelly, London, 1985.

Dow, J. C. R., *The Management of the British Economy 1945–60*, London, 1964.

Drummond, Roscoe, and Gaston Coblentz, *Duel at the Brink*, London, 1961.

Eban, Abba, *An Autobiography*, London, 1978.

Eden, The Rt. Hon. Sir Anthony (Earl of Avon), *Full Circle*, London, 1960.

Epstein, Leon D., *British Politics in the Suez Crisis*, Illinois, 1964.

Finer, H., *Dulles over Suez*, Chicago, 1964.
Foot, M., and M. Jones, *Guilty Men*, London, 1957.
'Foreign Relations United States', Washington, various dates.
Gladwyn, Lord, *Memoirs 1914–63*, London, 1972.
Gore-Booth, P., *With Great Truth and Respect*, London, 1972.
Heikal, Mohamed, *Nasser, The Cairo Documents*, London, 1972.
Heikal, Mohamed, *Cutting the Lion's Tail, Suez*, London, 1986.
Hoopes, Townshend, *The Devil and John Foster Dulles*, London, 1974.
Howard, Anthony, *Rab, The Life of R. A. Butler*, London, 1987.
Hughes, Emrys, *Sydney Silverman, Rebel in Parliament*, London, 1969.
Ierodiakonou, Leontios, *The Cyprus Question*, Stockholm, 1971.
Kilmuir, David, *Political Adventure*, London, 1964.
Love, Kennett, *Suez, The Twice Fought War*, London, 1970.
Lunt, James, *Glubb Pasha*, London, 1984.
MacDermot, Geoffrey, *The Eden Legacy*, London, 1969.
Macmillan, Harold, *Tides of Fortune*, London, 1969.
Macmillan, Harold, *Riding the Storm 1956–59*, London, 1971.
Massu, Jacques, *Vérité sur Suez 1956*, Paris, 1978.
Monnet, J., *Memoirs*, London, 1978.
Moran, Lord, *Winston Churchill, Struggle for Survival*, London, 1966.
Northedge, F. S., *British Foreign Policy, The Process of Readjustment 1945–61*, London, 1962.
Northedge, F. S., *Descent from Power, British Foreign Policy 1945–72*, London, 1974.
Nutting, Anthony, *No End of a Lesson*, London, 1967.
Panteli, Stavros, *A New History of Cyprus*, London, 1984.
Pinder, John, *Britain and the Common Market*, London, 1963.
Pineau, Christian, *1956 Suez*, Paris, 1976.
Randle, K. F., *Geneva 1954, The Settlement of the Indo-Chinese War*, New Jersey, Princeton, 1969.
Rhodes James, Robert, *Anthony Eden*, London, 1986.
Selwyn-Lloyd, John S. B., *Suez 1956*, London, 1978.
Shonfield, Andrew, *British Economic Policy Since the War*, London, 1958.
Shuckburgh, Evelyn, *Descent to Suez*, London, 1986.
Snow, Peter, *Hussein*, London, 1972.
Spaak, P.-H., *The Continuing Battle*, London, 1971.
Stebbins, R. P., *U.S. in World Affairs, 1954*, Washington, 1955.
Stebbins, R. P., *U.S. in World Affairs, 1955*, Washington, 1956.
Stebbins, R. P., *U.S. in World Affairs, 1956*, Washington, 1957.
Stephens, Robert, *Cyprus. A Place of Arms*, London, 1966.
The Times, *House of Commons 1955*, London, 1955.
Thomas, Abel, *Comment Israël fut sauvé*, Paris, 1970.
Thomas, Hugh, *The Suez Affair*, London, 1966.
Trevelyan, Humphrey, *The Middle East in Revolution*, London, 1970.
Watkinson, Harold, *A Record of Our Times*, Salisbury, 1986.
Williams, Philip M., *Hugh Gaitskell*, Oxford, 1982.

Wilson, Harold, *The Chariot of Israel*, London, 1981.
Young, K. T., *Negotiating with the Chinese Communists, the U.S. Experience 1953–67*, New York, 1968.

Unpublished Works

Proceedings of Joint Seminar of Institute of Historical Research and Institute of Contemporary History on 'Suez – What the Papers Say', London, 18 February 1987.
Wing Commander Jock Dalgleish's 'Recollections of King Hussein'.
John Young, 'The Parting of the Ways, Britain, the Messina Conference and the Spaak Committee, June–December 1955', paper delivered to Kings College Seminar, London, March 1987.

The author is much indebted to Air Marshal Sir Charles Pringle for the following:

Valiant At the time of Suez the Valiant had only recently come into service and had been cleared only for release of conventional and nuclear bombs by radar navigation. It was never intended to use in a visual bombing role and there was no provision for a visual bombsight – then or later.
Canberra Flare dropping was not a priority requirement before Suez, and routine clearance for this role was taking place at the Armament and Aircraft Experimental Establishment at Boscombe Down. Flare dropping can be dangerous to the dropping aircraft and clearance was well in hand but not complete in August 1956.
Hunter The early Hunters had Avon Series 100 engines; the later versions – Mark 6 onwards – had Avon 200 engines. The latter did not have a gun firing problem, but there was a grave problem with the Avon 100 Series. When the gun was fired the engine 'surged' due to the extra turbulence and hot air in the vicinity which upset the smooth flow into the engine intake. 'Surge' in the engine caused a rapid rise in engine turbine entry temperature, and if rapid action was not taken – throttle back or in bad cases shut down the engine – this high temperature was likely to cause severe internal damage to the engine; there was no risk of danger to the airframe. This was one of the early problems of jet engines and not entirely understood.
The *Hunter Mark 6* was the most outstanding fighter of its generation, and if production had been kept in being for a little longer it might have made an export 'killing' throughout the Western World, and it is still in operation by foreign air forces, notably the Chilean.

Index

Abdullah, King of Jordan, 155
Aboul-Fatouh, Samy, 244
Aden, 156
Adenauer, Konrad, 67, 99, 275, 277
Air Ministry, 188
Akaba, Gulf of, 161, 180, 240, 244, 249, 299
Aldrich, Winthrop, 244
Alexandria, 156, 199, 209, 210, 211, 212–14, 245, 252, 270
Algeria, 103, 213, 220, 222, 238, 252, 275, 294
Allan, Robert, 298
Almaza aerodrome, 249
Alpha (plan for Egypt–Israeli settlement), 161–2, 163–72, 178–80
Amery, Julian, 63, 157, 158
Amory, Derek Heathcoat, 37, 55, 92, 259–60
Anderson, Robert, 183
Ankara, 132
Arab League, 159, 163
Arab Legion, 155, 156, 186–8, 191, 192
Armitage, Sir Robert, 130, 131, 132, 134, 135
Armstrong, Sir William, 185, 194
Arthur, G. (Foreign Office), 180
Assheton, Ralph, 157
Astor, David, 300–2
Aswan High Dam, 173, 176, 183–6, 192–7, 198, 227, 306
Athens, 139
Athens Radio, 131–2, 137, 140, 142
atomic weapons, 114–15, 119–20
Attlee, Clement, 59, 66, 204, 304; 1955 election campaign, 9–11; education policy, 31; rejects Schuman Plan, 60; and Cyprus, 129; Palestine problem, 153, 154–5; Suez Canal base negotiations, 158
El Auja, 176–7
Australia, 77, 95, 106–7, 115, 117, 118, 124, 203, 251, 281
Austria, 153
Austrian Peace Treaty (1955), 12

Baghdad Pact, 129, 140, 143, 159–60, 166, 176, 180, 186, 188, 195, 247
Baker, Slade, 221
Baldwin, Stanley, 18, 176, 260
Balfour, Arthur, 152
Balfour Declaration (1917), 152, 153
Bandung Conference (1955), 124–5
Bangkok Conference (1955), 119, 120, 121–2
Bank of England: 1955 sterling crisis, 8, 9, 40–2; and proposed European Free Trade Area, 95;

and the Suez crisis, 274; 1956 sterling crisis, 280–3, 286–7
Bank of International Settlements, 41
Bao Dai, Emperor, 103
Barbados, immigrants, 24
Barjot, Admiral, 248, 252, 254
Basle, 41
BBC, 68, 75
Beamish, Tufton, 63
Beaufre, General, 252, 254, 269, 273
Beaverbrook, Lord, 303, 309
Beaverbrook press, 13
Bedell Smith, Walter, 110, 111, 113, 115, 116, 291
Beersheba, 161, 170
Ben Gurion, David, 155, 178, 179, 182, 183, 237–8, 240, 260, 278, 307
Ben Halim (Libyan Prime Minister), 211
Benelux countries, 60, 61, 67, 68, 70
Bentley, Derek, 35
Bermuda, 103, 146
Bermuda Conference (1953), 114
Bermuda Conference (1956), 292
Bernadotte, Count, 155
Beugel, Ernst van, 75
Bevan, Aneurin, 9–11, 106, 294
Bevin, Ernest, 12, 60, 61, 153, 154, 179
Beyen, Dr Johan Willem, 70–2, 75, 77, 79–85
Bidault, Georges, 103–5, 107, 108, 110
Birch, Nigel, 49, 259, 260
Bishop, Frederick, 301
Black, Eugene, 185–6, 195–6, 227
Blake, Robert, 126
Board of Customs and Excise, 95
Board of Trade, 12, 23, 69, 86, 88, 89, 95, 97, 195, 197
Bolton, Sir George, 282
Boothby, Robert, 63, 64
Bourges-Manoury, Maurice, 237
Bowker, Sir James, 137
Boyd Carpenter, John, 70
Boyle, Air Marshal Sir Dermot, 273
Boyle, Edward, 75–6, 92, 278–9
Bracken, Lord, 303
Bray, Frederick, 32
Bretherton, Russell, 68, 72–3, 75, 79, 81, 86, 94, 101
Bridges, Sir Edward, 6, 8–9, 44, 45, 47–50, 51, 54–5, 215, 281, 282
British Army, 62, 153, 199, 267–73
British Employers' Confederation, 26
British Guiana, 130